Knitting

FOR

DUMMIES®

A Wiley Brand

3rd Edition

by Pam Allen, Shannon Okey, Tracy L. Barr, and Marly Bird

FOR

DUMMIES®

A Wiley Brand

Knitting For Dummies®, 3rd Edition

Published by: **John Wiley & Sons, Inc.,** 111 River Street, Hoboken, NJ 07030-5774, www.wiley.com

Copyright © 2014 by John Wiley & Sons, Inc., Hoboken, New Jersey

Media and software compilation copyright © 2014 by John Wiley & Sons, Inc. All rights reserved.

Published simultaneously in Canada

For general information on our other products and services, please contact our Customer Care Department within the U.S. at 877-762-2974, outside the U.S. at 317-572-3993, or fax 317-572-4002. For technical support, please visit www.wiley.com/techsupport.

Wiley publishes in a variety of print and electronic formats and by print-on-demand. Some material included with standard print versions of this book may not be included in e-books or in print-on-demand. If this book refers to media such as a CD or DVD that is not included in the version you purchased, you may download this material at http://booksupport.wiley.com. For more information about Wiley products, visit www.wiley.com.

Library of Congress Control Number: 2013947511

ISBN 978-1-118-66151-2 (pbk); ISBN 978-1-118-80525-1 (ebk); ISBN 978-1-118-80526-8 (ebk)

Manufactured in the United States of America

10 9 8 7 6 5 4 3 2

Contents at a Glance

Table of Contents

Chapter 7: Oops! Fixing Common Mistakes 107

Chapter 8: Knitting in the Round 121

Chapter 9: Practicing with Simple Projects 131

Introduction

As knitters, we've heard many reasons for why people want to learn to knit: "My grandma used to do it, and I've always wanted to learn"; "I just retired and need something to do with my spare time"; "I have lots of little kids in my family, and I want to be able to knit things for them"; or "It's always looked like fun, so I thought it was time to try it out!" Whatever your reason, one thing is certain: When you're a knitter, you're part of a true community of people who are passionate about what they do. Knitters have a passion for the process of knitting, a passion for the fiber they knit with, and a passion for the final product.

Knitters like to share this excitement with other knitters. Knitting has become the new social gathering activity for people young and old. Groups of knitters get together in cities and small towns to have drinks, watch a ball game, or even cruise to Alaska. You can even partake in World Wide Knit in Public Day! But knitters also share their thrill for knitting with the world. In some cities, you often see the work of local "yarn bombers" who have decorated property fences, lamp posts, and tree trunks with knitted fabric. These random acts of knitting are meant to improve the concrete paradise and share the beauty of this fiber art.

Needless to say, you can hardly go anywhere in the world without encountering someone knitting. It's the thing to do! Now is a great time to learn to knit. With the wonderful communities available online and at local yarn stores, the amazing number of lovely and imaginative yarns from which to choose, and so many stylish and sophisticated patterns to work with, the sky's the limit for your knitting.

About This Book

Beautifully illustrated books and magazine articles that explore and document knitting techniques and designs from all parts of the world are regularly published, and scores of patterns are available online from talented independent designers. You can find knitting activities of all kinds, from workshops, conferences, cruises, and camps to yarn shows, classes, and spa weekends. No matter where you go, plenty of fellow knitters are happy to share their love of knitting with you.

The purpose of *Knitting For Dummies,* 3rd Edition, is to put all the need-to-know information about knitting in an easy-to-read and easy-to-follow book. We've created fantastic online video support that includes step-by-step instructions for many of the techniques from the book, and we've designed great projects. Although you can jump in anywhere you find a topic that interests you, this book progresses from basic to more-advanced skills. To that end, each chapter is divided into sections, and each section contains important skill-building information about knitting, such as the following:

- ✔ How to cast on, knit, purl, and bind off — the four basic skills needed to complete any knitting
- ✔ How to read pattern instructions and charts
- ✔ How to combine knit and purl stitches with increases and decreases for different effects
- ✔ What to do if you drop a stitch or inadvertently add one
- ✔ How to create different kinds of cables, lace, and more

In addition, you'll find lots of fashionable projects that enable you to practice and perfect your skills. For interesting but nonessential tidbits, check out the shaded sidebars and anything marked with a Technical Stuff icon; they aren't required reading, but they're still worthwhile.

Foolish Assumptions

In writing this book, we made a few assumptions about you:

- ✔ You've never, ever knitted before and want to learn how because you've seen other people do it and it looks like fun.
- ✔ You know the basics of knitting and now want to expand your repertoire to include some more-complex stitch patterns.
- ✔ You saw a pattern you liked, but the instructions that accompanied it were too hard to follow. Although you're not ready to give up, you need help making sense of what appears to be an almost indecipherable code.
- ✔ You're looking for a hobby that's relaxing and portable and lets you create things that you can use yourself or give to others.

Icons Used in This Book

Throughout this book, we use icons to catch your attention and highlight important information to ease your knitting journey.

This icon lets you in on some secrets most knitters learn from one another. It also indicates special ways to make your project just a little bit better. You can get by without applying this info, but if you do take our advice, your project will be that much nicer.

This icon alerts you to something that you'll need to remember and apply in the project at hand or in other projects down the road.

If you see this icon, we're pointing out hazards on the knitting path. Pay attention to these warnings if you don't want to find yourself in tangles.

This icon indicates information on the structure of knitting. It's info that you don't absolutely have to have in order to knit but that will facilitate mastery. And you may just find it interesting.

This icon invites you to check out a video demonstration of a knitting technique online.

Beyond the Book

In addition to the material in the book you're reading right now, this product comes with some access-anywhere goodies on the web. Check out the free Cheat Sheet at www.dummies.com/cheatsheet/knitting for easy-reference lists of knitting abbreviations, a glossary of knitting techniques, and formulas for converting pattern measurements. Plus, you can find free articles on maximizing your gauge swatch, knitting on the bias, and more at www.dummies.com/extras/knitting.

But that's not all! This book comes with downloadable content — 16 helpful videos to guide you through a variety of stitches and techniques that you're sure to encounter in your knitting adventures. You can also access two project videos — the Slouchy Hat with Pompom and the Horseshoe Cable Cowl with Buttons — to accompany the patterns in Chapters 10 and 11, respectively. Go to www.dummies.com/go/knittingfd to download all this great companion content.

Where to Go from Here

If you're an absolute beginner knitter, start at the beginning and read and practice your way through Parts I and II — the basics. Those chapters will ground you in the moves you need to know in order to progress to more complicated kinds of knitting. If you already know how to knit and purl, you'll find plenty in Parts III and IV to build your skills and confidence.

Maybe you've had your eye on a pattern for a complicated-looking Aran sweater but you've never worked a cable, or maybe you've seen a shawl with a lace border but have no idea how to read the chart for it. If so, head to the appropriate chapter and jump right in.

Bottom line: You decide where to go. And if you haven't a clue, browse the table of contents or the index for a topic that strikes your fancy.

Part I
Getting Started with Knitting

In this part . . .

✔ Get an idea of the yarns, needles, and other tools of the trade that you can expect to find in online shops as well as in your local knitting store.

✔ Find out about gauge and why it's not a step you can skip (no matter how badly you want to dive into knitting your actual project).

✔ Open yourself to the wider world of knitting projects by understanding the language and graphics in knitting patterns and charts.

Chapter 1

Two Needles, a Ball of Yarn, and a Little Know-how

Knitting is a relatively simple process requiring minimal tools — two needles and a ball of yarn. Its basic structure of interlocking loops couldn't be less complicated. Yet the possibilities for design and pattern innovation are endless. Knitting has more than cozy socks and colorful sweaters to offer; it's also an excellent way to mitigate some of the stresses and frustrations of day-to-day life.

This chapter introduces you to knitting — what it is and what it takes, why it's so darn good for you, and how to best go about picking up knitting from a book. With the info you find in this chapter and the skills you gather in the others, you'll be able to explore with confidence the myriad things you can do with two needles and a ball of yarn.

Why Knit?

Knitting's been around for hundreds of years, and for a large portion of that time, it was a utilitarian endeavor. But chances are you're not taking up knitting because you need to restock your sock drawer or whip up much-needed sweaters and scarves to keep out the winter chill. So why knit?

Knitting up good karma

Ask knitters why they knit, and you'll get a variety of answers. But the one you'll hear from nearly all knitters, regardless of the other reasons they may give, is "It's relaxing."

The repetitive movements of needles and yarn truly knit up the raveled sleeve of care. Have you ever noticed a knitter's face while he or she is working away on the needles? Did you see the expression of relaxed alertness? The rhythmic movements of knitting, together with the mental focus needed for building fabric stitch by stitch, make for a kind of meditation. It's real. Ask anyone who knits.

And if you carry your knitting along wherever you go, you always bring a little well-being with you. In an increasingly global and anonymous world, a knitting project at hand reminds you of the comforts and familiarity of things small, local, and individual.

Inspiring a feeling of accomplishment

A skein of yarn can be anything, but it's nothing — despite how beautiful the color or how soft the feel — until someone gives it shape and purpose. So when you knit, you use your skill, your imagination, your patience, and your perseverance to create something from nothing.

Turning skeins of yarn, stitch by stitch, into hats, afghans, socks, bags, sweaters, cardigans, and more gives you a feeling of competence and accomplishment that few other hobbies can offer. And it's a sense that grows with each row, with each wearing, with each "Oooh, it's so beautiful (or warm, or soft)" comment that you hear.

Keeping your mind and hands occupied

If you knit a little while waiting for your computer to load screens, red lights to turn green, and commercials to end, you'll never have to worry about wasting time again.

Knitting is portable, too, so you can work on your project wherever you find yourself. You can knit in the living room while you're watching TV or in the kitchen while waiting for the pasta to cook. You can knit while waiting to catch a plane or while sitting on a park bench watching your children play. You can take your knitting with you, whether it's a challenging project that requires quiet concentration or something simple that you can tote along and pull out at the odd moment for a quick row or two.

Studies have shown that hobbies like knitting can even be good for your waistline; it's really hard to snack while watching TV if your hands are busy.

Creating a one-of-a-kind piece

Knitting is a process of combining yarn, needles, pattern, and color. Even if all you do is follow a sweater pattern by using the exact yarn and needles it calls for, each stitch is of your own making, and no two sweaters from the same pattern worked by different knitters are ever exactly the same.

After your first project or two, there's a good chance that you'll be venturing with pleasure into the wonderland of new combinations of yarn, pattern stitch, color, and embellishment. You'll be wondering how you'll ever find the time to make all the ideas in your head a reality.

Creativity is less about being born with a friendly muse and more about putting time and effort into developing know-how. Granted, moments of inspiration *can* wake you up at 4:00 in the morning, but rarely do they happen unless you first lay the groundwork. Work all day on finding the right color combination for a project, and the solution will come at an unlikely moment. By learning, practicing, and mastering your art and craft, you become creative.

What Knitters Need

You can go into the craft section of any discount store and get yarn and needles, but of all those available, which is the best for the thing you want to make? Step into a specialty yarn shop, and the selection is even more vast. And what exactly are the minimum skills and knowledge needed to knit? Without this basic info, any knitting pattern you pick up is sure to overwhelm you before you begin.

Before you pack it in, read this section, which serves as a very basic overview of the key knitting necessities. By the end, you'll have discovered that you really, truly don't need much in order to knit. Needles. Yarn. A little know-how. And some time. With those few things, you can knit up all sorts of neat and exciting things.

The tools

In the 1600s, men's waistcoats were knit (by men) in fine silk thread on steel needles no thicker than wire. In the 18th and 19th centuries, the women of the Shetland Isles turned out several sweaters a year, knit on fine needles while they walked and between chores. Today, you can use the same width of needles the knitting forebears used, or you can knit with yarn as thick as rope on needles that measure an inch or more around.

The knitting supplies that you absolutely can't do without are knitting needles and yarn. That's it. The trick is to get the right yarn and the right needles for the project you want to create. Here are the two main things to know:

- ✔ **Yarns come in different weights, textures, and colors.** Although the color may be the first thing to catch your eye, the things you really have to pay attention to are the yarn's weight (essentially its thickness) and its texture. These are the two key factors affecting how the knitted fabric feels.

- ✔ **Needles come in different sizes, are made from different materials, and fall into two main categories: straight and circular.** Although you may think the most important thing about needles is whether they're straight or circular, the other characteristics are more important. Needle size has a huge impact on the look and feel of the knitted piece. The material the needle is made from has a big impact on how the needle feels in your hand. Most knitters have a favorite needle material, and some are better than others for beginners or for different types of knit work.

In addition to yarn and knitting needles, a variety of other knitting tools are indispensable to knitters. Head to Chapter 2 for a rundown of all the knitting supplies you'll need or want.

In order to practice knitting, you need a ball of medium-weight yarn and a pair of size US 8 (5 mm) or 9 (5½ mm) needles. You don't have to buy the best-quality yarn, but if possible, choose wool, the knitter's best friend. Wool is elastic, making it easy to get your needles in and out of the stitches. Cotton doesn't "give" enough to make it a good choice for your first forays into knitting, and 100-percent acrylics can give you sweaty palms. Whatever yarn you choose, pick a light or bright color yarn, which makes it easier to see the stitches.

An understanding of the basics

To perform the most basic knitting, you just need to know how to do the following things, all of which we explain in Part II:

- ✔ **Cast on:** When you *cast on,* you create a series of loops on one needle as a starting row.

- ✔ **Knit:** A *knit* stitch is the most basic stitch in knitting; a *purl* stitch is its very close cousin. With these two stitches you can create a variety of patterns. Knowing only how to knit and purl, you can have a lot of fun knitting up square or rectangular pieces: hot pads, table mats, afghans, bags, and so on. To move beyond pieces with this basic shape, you need to know how to add (increase) or remove (decrease) stitches. Increasing and decreasing in a deliberate way creates pieces with more sophisticated shaping (think garments, socks, gloves, and so on) and lacework.

✔ **Bind off:** When you're done knitting, you have to remove the stitches from the needles in such a way that your hard work doesn't unravel. Sometimes (like when you want to create buttonholes or a neck opening in a sweater) you may bind off in the middle of a row.

✔ **Fix mistakes:** Knitters of all stripes mess up periodically. The most common mistake, for novice and expert alike, is inadvertently dropping or adding stitches.

With a bit of practice casting on, knitting, purling, and binding off, you'll soon be amazed at your nimble fingers and ready to move on to more challenging techniques such as creating stripes, cables, and lacework and working with multiple colors of yarn. You can find those in Part III. And when you're ready to move on to garments, head to Part IV.

There's one more important thing to know as a knitter: how to figure gauge. *Gauge* is the one-word shorthand for "how big this thing will be when it's done." Although you can knit anything without determining gauge, you won't know what size you'll end up with until all is said and done. This uncertainty isn't usually a problem for pieces for which size doesn't matter (such as scarves and bags), but gauge is important when you want to make clothing. Chapter 3 tells you what you need to know about measuring gauge.

An understanding of knitterese

To make it through the instructions in this book and in any knitting pattern you pick up, you need to know what we call "knitterese" — a language full of abbreviations, asterisks, parentheses, and strange ways of spelling out (or rather, *not* spelling out) instructions. To the untrained eye, these abbreviations look like gibberish: inc, k1, ssk, RH, WS, psso, and m1. Believe us — everyone who has knitted from a pattern has spent more time than they want to remember staring in earnest at the page, hoping that the sheer intensity of the gaze will unlock the meaning of the odd "instructions."

Some patterns may convey instructions in chart form, like the one in Figure 1-1, which shows a chart for a Guernsey knit-purl pattern (you can find this pattern in Appendix A). Before you drop this book and clutch your eyes, keep in mind that charts like this one typically simplify what otherwise would be fairly complicated written instructions.

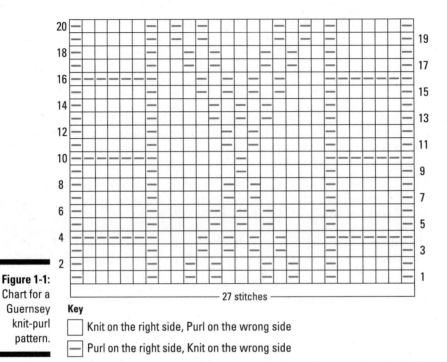

Figure 1-1:
Chart for a
Guernsey
knit-purl
pattern.

27 stitches

Key

☐ Knit on the right side, Purl on the wrong side

⊟ Purl on the right side, Knit on the wrong side

Illustration by Wiley, Composition Services Graphics

Chapter 3 tells you everything you need to know about deciphering either written or charted instructions. Soon you'll be breezing your way through patterns, relishing the pleasure of understanding.

Teaching Yourself to Knit from a Book

Everyone learns a new skill in a different way. If you're not confident that you can teach yourself to knit from a book, you can do the following things to make the process easier and to help ensure success:

✔ Study the illustrations carefully and compare them with what your own hands, needles, and yarn are doing.

✔ Use your right hand (not your left) if a right hand is pictured.

✔ Notice the path of the yarn in the illustration and see whether yours is doing the same thing. For example, does the yarn cross from right to left or over or under the needle?

✔ Keep a pad of sticky notes nearby and use them on the book pages to help you focus on the illustration or text you're trying to understand.

✔ If you get stuck, gather your materials and head to your local knitting shop. Most store personnel are happy to help a new knitter get up and running. While you're there, ask whether the store sponsors a knitting group or knows of any that meet in your area. You can learn loads from other knitters. Or sign up for a knitting list on the web, and you don't have to leave home. Whatever you do, don't give up. The rewards of being a knitter are worth the effort of learning how to be one.

Swatching

Swatching (making a sample of knitted fabric) is to the knitter what scales and exercises are to the pianist and what rough sketches and doodles are to the painter. A *swatch* is a sample of knitting. It can be big (50 stitches and 50 rows) or small (20 stitches and 20 rows). Most of the time, knitters make a swatch to measure gauge (to see how many stitches and rows there are to an inch). But dedicated knitters also work up swatches to learn, to practice, to experiment, and to invent.

Your swatch can tell you

✔ Whether your yarn and needles work up to the necessary gauge

✔ Whether your yarn shows off your stitch pattern or obscures it

✔ Whether your chosen color combination works or needs tweaking

✔ Whether you understand a new technique

As you go through or skip around this book, we urge you to keep your yarn and needles handy to try out the patterns, stitches, and techniques given. In some cases, we even provide specific instructions in the project sections for making a sampler of a particular technique.

The swatches you make will keep you limber, stretch your knowledge, and be your best teacher.

Putting it into practice

Each part provides projects to allow you to practice the skills introduced. Pick a few of these items to knit up. Although swatches are invaluable when you want to practice a particular technique, there's nothing like an actual project to let you practice multiple techniques at one time. By making real things, your knowledge and confidence grow immeasurably — even if what you initially end up with are things that you wouldn't want anyone else to see!

Whatever you do, don't give up. Before you know it, you'll be wearing your knitted pieces out in public or giving them as gifts to family and friends. And when people inquire, "Did you *make* this?" you'll be able to proudly answer "Yes, I did!"

Chapter 2

Tools of the Trade

Truth be told, you can spend quite a few hours happily knitting away with nothing more than some spare yarn and an old pair of knitting needles. If you take to knitting, however, your satisfaction with these basic supplies will soon morph into a desire to experiment with the array of beautiful yarns and designer needles that are available.

With so many choices in stores and online, choosing the yarns and needles that are right for you — or the project you have in mind — can be a bit daunting. This chapter's here to help. It gives you the lowdown on different kinds of yarns and needles and explains how to pick the right tools for your projects.

Yearning for Yarn: The (Quick) Consumer's Guide

A nice yarn shop is a knitter's paradise. Heck, even the yarn section of a discount or craft store can be a little slice of heaven. Why? Because of all the traditional and specialty yarns that are available. With such an abundance of choices, how do you decide what yarn to buy? Knowing a little bit about the different types of yarn and their general characteristics helps. So first things first.

Yarn is made from short fibers that come from animals or plants or are synthetic. The fibers are combed, or *carded,* to align them into a soft untwisted rope (called *roving*). Then they're spun (twisted) into a strand or *ply* of yarn. This single ply is usually combined with other plies to form the final yarn.

The following sections explain the two main factors — fiber and weight — that account for the wide variety of yarns available. Whether you prefer your yarn plain or fancy, some knowledge of yarn basics can ensure that what looks great on the shelf will look great in your finished project, too.

Fixating on fiber fundamentals

All yarn is made from natural or synthetic fibers. Different fibers have different qualities — some good, some not so good. Often, to offset an undesirable characteristic, yarn manufacturers combine different fibers. (A *blend* is a yarn made from fibers of different origins — for example, wool/cotton, wool/silk, or alpaca/cotton.) More than anything else, the combination of fibers in your yarn determines its ultimate look, feel, and wearable comfort.

Yarn consists of one or more plies. *Plied yarns* are made from two, three, or four plies of yarn twisted together. Multi-plied and firmly twisted yarns are usually strong, smooth, and even. Lightly twisted plied and single-ply yarns are closer to their roving (unspun) state and, though sturdy enough when knitted up, can pull apart into strands if they're over-handled. They also can be slightly uneven, have more loft and softness, and be warmer than their twisted sisters.

A fabric's *hand* is how it feels to the touch. Just as pieces of woven fabric from silk or wool differ in *drape* (how they fall) and softness, so do knits from different fibers. But fiber isn't all that accounts for drape and softness. The size of the needle you use with a given yarn affects the feel of your knitted piece. The larger the needle and looser the stitch, the softer and drapier the fabric. The smaller the needle and tighter the stitch, the stiffer the fabric.

Wool and other fleece yarns

Wool (made from the fleece of sheep) is the queen of yarns, and it endures and remains a popular choice for knitters for a number of excellent reasons.

Wool is a good insulator — warm in winter, cool in summer. It can absorb lots of moisture without feeling wet, and it absorbs dye beautifully. It's resilient — the fibers can stretch and bend repeatedly but always return to their original shape. It's soft, relatively lightweight, and beautiful to look at. And, key to beginning knitters, wool is easy to knit with because it has just enough give. It also can be pulled out and reknit easily, a bonus when you're just learning the basic stitches.

Although all wool yarns are wonderful to work with, they vary tremendously depending on the breed of sheep or combination of breeds they come from, how they're spun, whether they're plied or single stranded, and whether they're treated for washability or not. Following are some of your wool yarn options:

✔ **Lamb's wool:** This wool comes from a young lamb's first shearing. It's softer and finer than wool from an older sheep's fleece.

✔ **Merino wool:** Merino wool is considered the finest of the fine breeds. Long, lustrous fibers make a soft and exceptionally lovely knitted fabric.

✔ **Pure new wool/virgin wool:** *Pure new* and *virgin* refer to wool that's made directly from animal fleece and not recycled from existing wool garments.

✔ **Shetland wool:** Real Shetland wool is a traditional 2-ply heathery yarn that's made from the small and hardy native sheep of Scotland's Shetland Islands and used in traditional Fair Isle sweaters. It's usually available in sport or fingering weight (see "A weighty matter: Considering yarn weight" later in the chapter for an explanation of weights). This wool originally came in sheep's colors, including all shades of charcoal and deep brown to white. Shetland wool is now also available in an extraordinary range of beautiful dyed colors.

✔ **Icelandic wool:** This rustic, soft, single-ply, medium-weight to heavy-weight yarn was traditionally available only in natural sheep's colors (black, charcoal, light gray, and white). Today, it's also available dyed in bright jewel and heathered colors as well as in a lighter weight appropriate for thinner "indoor" sweaters.

✔ **Washable or "superwash" wool:** This wool is treated chemically or electronically to destroy the outer fuzzy layer of fibers that would otherwise *felt* or bond with each other and shrink in the washing machine.

Sheep aren't the only animals to provide fibers for yarns. Fuzzy mohair and luxurious cashmere come from Angora and Kashmir goats, respectively. Warm, soft alpaca comes from members of the llama family; *alpacas* are small, South American cousins of the camel. Yarn made from yak down is one of the most luxurious fibers found. Warmer than wool and as soft as cashmere, it's an extremely durable and lightweight fiber that preserves heat in the winter yet breathes for comfort in warmer weather. The delicate underwool of the Arctic muskox is one of the most sought-after fibers in the world because of its rarity, softness, and warmth. Qiviut is softer than cashmere and is light as a feather. It's an insulating fiber and is comfortable to wear in any climate. Lighter than air and fuzziest of all, *angora* comes from the hair of Angora rabbits.

Silk, cotton, linen, and rayon

Silk, cotton, linen, and rayon yarns are the slippery yarns. Unlike rough yarns from the hairy fibers of animals, their smooth and often shiny surfaces cause them to unravel quickly if you drop a stitch. These yarns are inelastic and may stretch lengthwise over time. Often, they're blended with other fibers (natural and synthetic) to counteract their disadvantages. But silk and cotton, even in their pure state, are so lovely to look at and comfortable to wear that they're well worth knitting.

Synthetic yarns

Originally, synthetics (nylon, acrylic, and polyester) were made to mimic the look and feel of natural materials. Just as wool yarn is spun from short lengths of carded fibers from a sheep's fleece, synthetic yarns begin as a long filament made from artificial, usually petroleum-based ingredients cut into short lengths and processed to look like wool yarn.

Knitters give mixed reviews to 100-percent synthetic yarns:

- ✔ **On the plus side:** All-synthetic yarns are inexpensive and hold up well in the washing machine. For people who are allergic to wool, synthetics make for a look-alike substitute (at least from a distance).

- ✔ **On the downside:** All-synthetic yarns don't have the wonderful insulating and moisture-absorbing qualities of natural yarns and therefore can be uncomfortable to wear. For the same reason, they can make your hands clammy when you're knitting. They *pill* (form small fuzz balls) more readily than wool or other fibers, and after they're exposed to heat (a hot iron is deadly), they lose all resilience and become flat.

These complaints and synthetic yarns' dubious reputation have encouraged manufacturers to come up with new and better applications for synthetics. Perhaps the best use for synthetic yarns is in combination with other fibers. Manufacturers now engineer blended yarns for certain qualities. For example, nylon is extremely strong and light. Nylon adds durability when blended in small amounts with more-fragile fibers such as mohair. A little nylon blended with wool makes a superb sock yarn. A little acrylic in cotton makes the yarn lighter and promotes *memory* so that the knitted fabric doesn't stretch out of shape.

Straddling the border between natural and synthetic are soy, bamboo, corn, and other unusual yarns made using plant-based materials. Spun into microfilaments that are extruded by using a process similar to that employed for acrylic and other synthetic yarns, these fibers have become increasingly popular, particularly in yarn blends such as soy/wool, bamboo/silk, and even tree-, corn-, and seaweed-derived fibers.

Novelty yarns

Novelty, or specialty, yarns are easy to recognize because their appearance is so different from traditional yarns. Their bright colors and whimsical textures can be hard to resist. Eyelash yarns, for example, feature tiny spikes of fiber that stick up, resembling eyelashes. Following are some of the more common novelty yarns you may come across:

✔ **Ribbon:** This option is usually a knitted ribbon in rayon or a rayon blend with wonderful drape.

✔ **Boucle:** This highly bumpy, textured yarn is comprised of loops.

✔ **Chenille:** Although chenille is tricky to knit with, the attractive appearance and velvety texture of this yarn make your perseverance worthwhile. It's usually available in rayon (for sheen) or cotton.

✔ **Thick-thin:** Often handspun, these yarns alternate between very thick and thin sections, which lends a charmingly bumpy look to knitted fabric.

✔ **Railroad ribbon:** This ribbon-style yarn has tiny "tracks" of fiber strung between two parallel strands of thread.

✔ **Faux fur:** Fluffy fiber strands on a strong base thread of nylon resemble faux fur when knitted. It's available in many different colors.

✔ **"Traditional" novelty yarns:** Long before shiny synthetic eyelash and faux fur yarns became popular, knitters had other types of yarn at their disposal to create special looks in their knitted items. Tweed, heathered, marled, and variegated yarns all create subtler effects than modern novelty yarns do and can add lovely variety to your knitting basket.

   • **Tweed:** Usually wool, this yarn has a background color flecked with bits of fiber in different colors.

   • **Heather:** This yarn has been blended from a number of different-colored or dyed fleeces and then spun. Heather yarns are muted in color; think of them as the yarn equivalent of watercolors.

   • **Marled (ragg) yarn:** This option is a plied yarn in which the plies are different colors.

   • **Variegated yarn:** This yarn is dyed in several different colors or shades of a single color. Hand-dyed yarn (often called *handpainted*) is very popular and knits up in a series of random color repeats that would be difficult to imitate using even a large number of different-colored yarns.

Some novelty yarns can be tricky to work with. Others — like those with complex textures, no give, or threadlike strands that are easy to lose when you knit from one needle to the other — can be downright difficult. If you're dying to work with a novelty yarn, start with a variegated dyed or painted single-ply yarn. These choices give lots of color variation and interest, but the strand of yarn is itself easy to see. Identifying individual stitches in highly textured yarns is difficult, if not impossible, making it hard to fix mistakes or rip out stitches.

A weighty matter: Considering yarn weight

Yarns come in different *weights,* or thicknesses. The weight of your yarn (among other things) has a huge impact on the look of your final product and certainly the amount of time it takes to knit it up.

The weight of a yarn determines the *gauge,* or how many stitches it takes to knit 1 inch. A medium-weight yarn that knits up 5 stitches and 7 rows to the inch takes 35 stitches to make a square inch of knitted fabric. A bulky yarn at 3 stitches and 5 rows to the inch needs 15 stitches to make a square inch. You can see how weight affects gauge in Figure 2-1.

Figure 2-1:
Different weights create different effects.

Medium-weight yarn   Bulky yarn

Illustration by Wiley, Composition Services Graphics

Although no official categories govern yarn weights, many knitting books and yarn manufacturers use common terms to indicate a yarn's thickness and the size of needle the yarn is usually worked on. Table 2-1 lists these categories for you.

Table 2-1	Common Yarn Weights	
Yarn Weight and Common Uses	*Symbol*	*US Needle Size and Stitches Per Inch*
Lace: Lace knitting	 **0** LACE	US 000–1 8–10 stitches
Super fine, fingering, or baby-weight: Light layettes, socks	 **1** SUPER FINE	US 1–3 7–8 stitches

Yarn Weight and Common Uses	Symbol	US Needle Size and Stitches Per Inch
Fine or sport-weight: Light sweaters, baby things, accessories	**2** FINE	US 3–6 5–6 stitches
Light worsted or DK (double-knitting): Sweaters and other garments, light-weight scarves	**3** LIGHT	US 5–7 5–5½ stitches
Medium- or worsted-weight, afghan, Aran: Sweaters, blankets, outdoor wear (hats, scarves, mittens, and so on)	**4** MEDIUM	US 7–9 4–5 stitches
Bulky or chunky: Rugs, jackets, blankets	**5** BULKY	US 10–11 3–3½ stitches
Super Bulky: Heavy blankets and rugs, (increasingly) sweaters	**6** SUPER BULKY	US 13–15 2–2½ stiches

The thickness of a given yarn is determined by the individual thickness of the plies, *not* by the number of plies. If the plies are thin, a 4-ply yarn can be finer than a heavy single-ply yarn.

Looking at yarn packaging

Yarn is packaged (sometimes called *put up*) in different ways — balls, skeins (rhymes with "canes"), and hanks. Each comes wrapped with a label that you should read carefully. It contains useful information and lets you know whether the yarn is a good candidate for the project you have in mind. If the yarn begs to be purchased before you know what you want to make with it, the information on the label lets you know what kind of project best suits it.

Label talk

A yarn label has tons of vital information (Figure 2-2 shows a typical label). Pay particular attention to the following:

✔ **Gauge and suggested needle size:** This information gives you an idea of what the final knitted fabric will look like. A size US 11 (7½ mm) needle and a gauge of low numbers (3 stitches and 5 rows per 1 inch) yield a heavy, chunky fabric. A size US 5 (3¾ mm) needle and a gauge of 5 stitches and 7 rows per 1 inch yield a finer, more traditional fabric.

The gauge listed on a yarn label is only a suggested gauge and not mandatory.

✔ **Fiber content:** This detail lets you know whether the yarn is wool, cotton, acrylic, a blend, or something else. If you intend to make a washable garment, check to see whether the yarn is machine- or hand-washable or strictly a dry-clean fiber.

✔ **Dye lot number and/or color number:** This information indicates what batch of dye this yarn came from. When you buy multiple skeins of yarn, compare these numbers to ensure that they're the same (that is, that all your yarn comes from the same dye batch). Even if you can't detect a difference in color between two balls of different dye lots, chances are the difference will become apparent when you knit them up one after the other.

To avoid unwanted color variations, buy enough yarn from the same dye lot at one time to complete your project. If you have to buy more later, you may not be able to find yarn from the same dye lot.

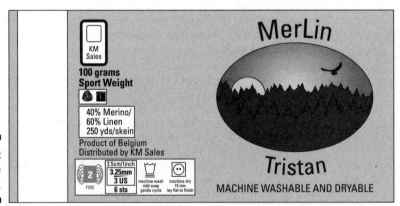

Figure 2-2:
A sample
yarn label.

Illustration by Wiley, Composition Services Graphics

Ball, skein, or hank?

Yarn comes in balls, skeins, and hanks (shown in Figure 2-3). Balls and skeins come ready to knit. After you find the end, you can *cast on* (create the first row of stiches on the needle) and go. Hanks need to be wound into a ball before you can use them. If you try to knit with the yarn in hank form, you'll quickly end up with a tangled mess.

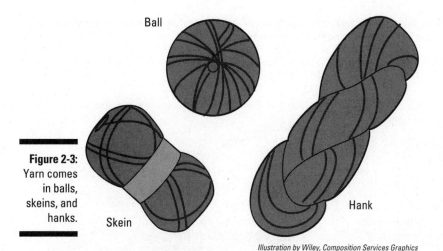

Ball

Skein

Hank

Figure 2-3:
Yarn comes
in balls,
skeins, and
hanks.

To wind a hank, follow these steps:

1. **Carefully unfold the hank (it's formed into a large circle) and drape it over a chair back, a friend's outstretched arms, or your bent knees if you're sitting.**

2. **Locate the ends of the yarn and, if they're tied, cut or unknot them.**

3. **With one end, begin by making a butterfly (see Figure 2-4).**

   Wrap the yarn in a figure eight around the thumb and little finger of your hand. Make about 20 passes if you're winding a medium-weight yarn; make more passes for a finer yarn or fewer for a thick yarn.

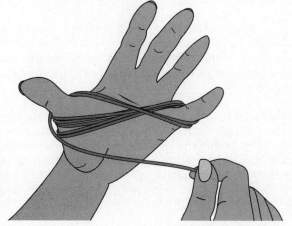

Figure 2-4:
Making a
butterfly.

4. **Take the "wings" off your finger and thumb and fold the butterfly in half, holding it between thumb and fingers.**

5. **Continue wrapping yarn *loosely* around the folded butterfly (and your fingers), as shown in Figure 2-5.**

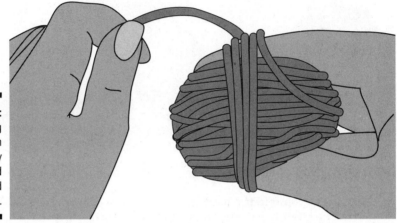

Figure 2-5: Wrapping the yarn loosely around thumb and fingers.

Illustration by Wiley, Composition Services Graphics

6. **When the package gets bulky, slip it off your fingers, turn it, and continue to wrap the yarn into a ball.**

   Neatness isn't important. *Looseness* is. Always wrap the yarn around as many fingers as you can, slipping them out when you change position. The space they take up ensures that the yarn isn't stretched as it waits to be knitted. If you knit with stretched yarn, guess what happens to your knitted piece when the yarn springs back to size?

 Your local yarn store may offer a winding service to convert hanks of yarn to center-pull balls by using a *yarn* (or *ball*) *winder* and a *swift* — two pieces of equipment that allow you to make an easy-to-use "cake" of yarn that sits flat as you knit it. If you find yourself with many hanks to wind, you can even buy your own winder and swift!

 If at all possible, you want to start knitting with the yarn end that comes from the *inside* of the skein or ball. This way, the skein or ball remains in place as you knit and doesn't roll around the floor, attracting the attention of a cat (or other pet) on attack. If you're lucky, the inside end will already be pulled to the outside, ready to go. If not, you have to reach in and pull out a small hunk of yarn in order to find this end and then rewrap the extra — not ideal, but better than trying to retrieve the ball after it has rolled under the couch (for the third time).

Choosing yarn for a project

Yarns, garment shapes, and stitch patterns must work together for your project to be successful. With so many yarn choices available, how do you choose? If you plan to knit a scarf or a blanket — something for which sizing doesn't need to be precise — pick any yarn you take a fancy to and let its characteristics dictate the outcome of your project. If you're making a sweater (or anything else for which sizing is important) from a pattern, purchase the yarn the pattern specifies or one with a similar gauge to be a suitable substitute.

Matching the yarn to the stitch

The yarn you choose can either accentuate the effect you're trying to create or camouflage it. As a general rule, the wilder the yarn, the simpler the sweater shape and pattern stitch should be. The plainer the yarn, the more texture and shaping details will show up. Here are some guidelines:

- **Smooth-plied yarn in a solid color:** Use these yarns for cables and more complex stitch patterns. They give your stitches a crisp look, showcasing your effort. Cables and pattern stitches worked in soft single plies have a slightly softer appearance than when worked in highly twisted yarns. In general, plied and twisted yarns are sophisticated and classic. Single plies are rustic and relaxed. Smooth-plied yarns in contrasting colors are also good for Fair Isle and intarsia patterns because they give you clear and readable patterns.

- **Variegated and novelty yarns:** Don't knock yourself out with tricky stitch work if you're using variegated or highly textured yarns. The stitches won't show up, and all your stitch-making effort will be for naught. Simple stitches, such as stockinette and garter, are best with these yarns. (For details on these stitches, check out Chapter 5.)

- **Cotton, silk, soy, bamboo, and other inelastic yarns:** Look for patterns that don't depend on ribbing for fit. Find patterns that hang straight to highlight the drape of these yarns.

If you shop in a specialty yarn store, chances are that the people who work there have experience with their yarns and with knitting in general. Feel free to ask questions about the yarn you're considering for your project. Here are some good ones to keep in mind:

- Does it pill?
- Is it colorfast?
- Will it stretch?
- Is it easy to knit with?

✔ Does it work with the pattern I've chosen?

✔ What size needle does it work best with?

Remember that your local yarn store (LYS, in online parlance) is an excellent resource for other knitting help, too. Sales associates can help you avoid many of the common pitfalls beginning knitters make in choosing yarn for projects. Many stores also offer drop-in help sessions, if you're struggling with a particular stitch or pattern and need expert help.

Predicting what yarn in a ball — especially novelty yarn — will look like when it's knitted up isn't easy. Check to see whether the yarns you're interested in have been knitted into samples. Many yarn shops knit up sample swatches or entire sweaters in the yarns they carry so that you can see what they look like worked up.

Substituting one yarn for another

Substituting one yarn for another can be tricky. It's not enough to pick a yarn that looks the same or that you like. You have to think of other things as well, including the following:

✔ **Yardage:** Be sure to pay attention to actual yardage listed on the label, not just number of grams or ounces. A 50-gram, 1.75-ounce ball of yarn that's 148 yards isn't the same amount as a 50-gram, 1.75-ounce ball of yarn that's 126 yards.

✔ **Weight:** If you're substituting yarn, be sure the weight is the same. If the pattern you've chosen expects you to get 4 stitches and 6 rows to the inch and you substitute a yarn that gives you a different gauge, your sweater will turn out a different size from the one given in the pattern. (See the earlier section "A weighty matter: Considering yarn weight" for general information on yarn weight and gauge; Chapter 3 explains how to measure gauge.)

✔ **Fiber:** Yarns of different fibers, even if they have the same gauge, have different characteristics. Be sure you know the characteristics of the yarn and are comfortable with the way these differences will affect the finished piece. (The earlier section "Fixating on fiber fundamentals" covers different kinds of yarn fibers and their characteristics.)

If you don't want to use or can't find the yarn specified on a pattern, the safest option — at least until you're experienced enough to take into account all the factors that affect gauge, drape, and so on — is to talk to a sales associate in a specialty yarn shop. Chances are that anyone working in your local yarn shop is a knitter and can give you good advice based on experience. In a chain store, that may or may not be the case.

Just because two yarns have the same gauge doesn't mean that they can substitute for each other successfully in a given pattern. If they have different
characteristics — texture, drape, fiber, and color — the final garment will look
and feel different from the one pictured on your pattern.

Selecting Knitting Needles

Knitting needles come in a stunning assortment of materials, styles, and sizes
to mesh with your knitting style, the particular project you're working on,
your aesthetics, and your budget.

Exploring needles

You can choose from three kinds of knitting needles: straight, circular, and
double-pointed (see Figure 2-6 and the following sections).

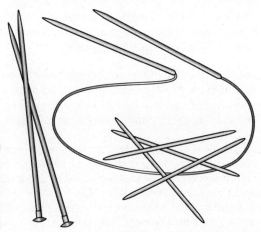

Figure 2-6:
Three kinds
of knitting
needles.

Illustration by Wiley, Composition Services Graphics

Telling it straight

Straight needles are generally used for *flat knitting* — knitting on the right
side and then turning and knitting on the wrong side. Straight needles come
in many standard lengths, ranging from 7-inch "scarf needles" to those that
are 10, 13, and 14 inches. The larger your project, the longer the needle you'll

need. (You also can knit flat with a circular needle for wide projects; see the next section for details about circular needles.) Figure 2-7 shows the various parts of straight needles.

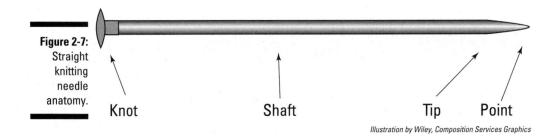

Figure 2-7: Straight knitting needle anatomy.

Knot   Shaft   Tip   Point

Illustration by Wiley, Composition Services Graphics

Going in circles

A *circular needle* is simply a pair of straight knitting needle tips joined by a flexible cable. You can use a circular needle to *knit in the round* — knitting in a continuous, spiral-like fashion without turning your work. This technique creates a seamless tube large enough for a sweater body or small enough for a neckband. You also can use a circular needle as you would straight needles to work back and forth. This approach can be particularly handy for length-wise-knit scarves, blankets, and other very wide pieces.

Circular needles are available in many different lengths, most frequently 16, 24, 29, and 36 inches, although they're also available as long as 60 inches! For smaller circumferences, some knitters find that double-pointed needles, described in the next section, are more comfortable to work with.

 When you buy a circular needle, check to make sure the spot where the needle tip meets the cable (called the *join*) is smooth to prevent stitches from snagging. Several manufacturers now make circular needles with inter-changeable needle tips and various cable lengths. These babies are useful for a wide variety of projects and make it very easy to swap needles when you're attempting to find the right gauge for your chosen yarn.

 The needle size appears on the package (which you can use as a storage case), but it doesn't always appear on the needle itself, which can be a bit of a pain. Our recommendation: Invest in a small metal or plastic needle gauge with graduated holes to help you determine the size of your needle.

Doing rounds with double-pointed needles

Double-pointed needles (abbreviated *dpns*) have a point at each end and are sold in sets of four or five needles. They work the same way as a circular needle — in rounds. You use them to make small tubes when your knitting has too few stitches to stretch around the circumference of a circular needle — for such things as sleeve cuffs, tops of hats, socks, mittens, and so on. They come in 7- and 10-inch lengths and have even shown up in 5-inch lengths — a great boon to those who enjoy making socks and mittens.

Sizing them up

A needle's size is determined by its diameter. The smaller the size, the narrower the needle and the smaller the stitch it makes. Figure 2-8 shows needle sizes and their US and metric equivalents.

Popular Knitting Needle Sizes

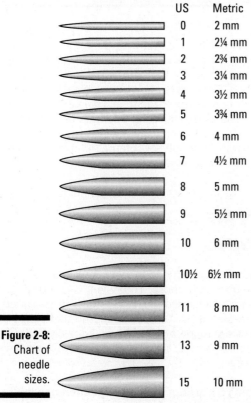

US	Metric
0	2 mm
1	2¼ mm
2	2¾ mm
3	3¼ mm
4	3½ mm
5	3¾ mm
6	4 mm
7	4½ mm
8	5 mm
9	5½ mm
10	6 mm
10½	6½ mm
11	8 mm
13	9 mm
15	10 mm

Figure 2-8:
Chart of needle sizes.

Illustration by Wiley, Composition Services Graphics

Finding the perfect match for your project

Yarn labels *suggest* appropriate needle sizes, but the best needle size for your project is dictated by your yarn, your gauge, and/or the *hand* (the way the knitted fabric feels in your hand) you want your final project to have. In general, medium- or worsted-weight yarn is knit on needles anywhere from size US 6 (4 mm) to size US 9 (5½ mm), depending on how tightly you knit and how you want the final fabric to look and feel.

After knitting a sample with the suggested needle size, you may feel that the fabric is more open than you want (needle too large) or too stiff (needle too small). In that case, try another needle size. Keep in mind that if you're making a garment or project and you want to achieve the finished measurements given in the pattern, you need to meet the gauge and live with the hand of the sample. If you're making a scarf or project where getting the exact number of stitches per inch isn't important, you can experiment to your heart's content with different needle sizes until you produce a fabric you like.

If you aren't sure what needle sizes you'll need in the future, try a circular knitting needle set with interchangeable tips. Even though the needle is designed for circular knitting, you can also use it to knit back and forth. Some sets feature plastic needle tips, some metal. These sets allow you to combine different-sized needle tips with different connector cords to make a very large range of needle sizes on the fly. An interchangeable circular needle is especially handy when you're unsure which needle size to use for a given yarn. If the current size isn't giving you the right gauge, simply switch the tip up or down one size instead of starting over on another needle.

Accounting for needle makeup and tip type

Knitting needles, which were first mass-produced in steel, have been made in ivory, tortoiseshell, silver, whale bone, and more. Today you can find them made in ebony and rosewood, sherbet-colored pearly plastic, Teflon-coated aluminum, and even 14-carat gold-plated (we kid you not). And that's only the beginning. Whatever your needles are made of, the material does contribute more or less to your knitting comfort, speed, and the quality of your stitches. Here are some recommendations:

- ✔ **If you're new to knitting, you're working on double-pointed needles, or you're executing color patterns, good choices include wood (bamboo, walnut, and so on) and plastic.** Wood and some plastics have a very slight grip, giving you more control over your work and discouraging dropped stitches.

> ✔ **If you're knitting in stockinette or a straightforward stitch pattern, a slippery needle makes sense.** The fastest ones are nickel-plated brass and call themselves Turbo. Use these needles and watch your stitches fly by before your eyes. (Also watch for more-easily dropped stitches.)

Although all needles look pretty much alike, you do notice a difference in the feel of various kinds of needles and in their interaction with your knitting style and the yarn you're using. If you find that some feature of their construction or material is annoying you or interfering with the flow of your project, try a different kind of needle. Switching may make the difference between a knitting experience on cruise control and one that stops and starts and sputters along.

Needle tips can be long and tapered or rounder and blunter (see Figure 2-9). If you're working a project with a lot of stitch manipulation (as in lace or cables), or if you're a snug knitter (that is, your stitches are tight rather than loose), you'll have an easier time if you use a needle with a long, tapered tip. If you're knitting with a loosely spun yarn and/or you're a relaxed knitter with looser stitches, you may prefer a blunter point.

Figure 2-9:
Two kinds of
needle tips.

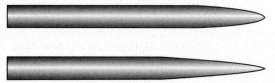

Illustration by Wiley, Composition Services Graphics

Though they don't fall directly into the category of different needle composition or tip type, square needles can be a great choice if you're new to knitting. They're made of metal or wood, and the shape makes them easier for the hands to hold. Stitches don't fall off these square needles as easily as the standard round ones.

Collecting Gizmos and Gadgets

Lots of knitting gadgets are available on the market. Some make life a little easier, and others are out-and-out lifesavers. Some you have to buy, but you can improvise others from what you already have on hand.

Stocking up on the essentials

For the most part, knitting gadgets are small and portable. Keep these essentials in a little zippered bag, and you can carry them anywhere your knitting goes.

Scissors or thread cutters

Small, portable scissors are a must. In a pinch, you can break certain yarns with your hands, but others have to be cut with scissors. Collapsible scissors that fold up and don't leave any sharp points exposed are great. You can find them in most knitting stores. Other small scissors come with a little sheath that covers the tips so that you can carry them in your knitting bag without them poking through.

A *thread cutter* is a small, portable scissor substitute meant only for cutting yarn. It resembles a disc with notched edges and can even be worn as a necklace while you work so that it's always at hand.

 If you're traveling by plane and want to carry on your knitting, be sure to check with the Transportation Security Administration (TSA) for restrictions (www. tsa.gov/traveler-information/prohibited-items). As of this writing, knitting and crochet needles are generally permitted in carry-on luggage, but scissor size is restricted for carry-ons, and thread cutters with blades have to go in your checked baggage. When traveling, consider bringing fingernail clippers or an empty dental floss case to easily snip your yarn while in flight.

Tape measure

A small retractable tape measure marked for inches and centimeters can go anywhere. Use it to measure your gauge swatch and to check your knitted pieces as you go along.

Tapestry needles

Tapestry needles, also called *yarn needles,* are simply large-eye needles with a blunt point that you use to sew knitted pieces together. When joining pieces of knitted fabric, you're working in the spaces around the stitches, not through the yarn strand. A blunt point ensures that you don't split the yarn.

Safety pins

Safety pins are handy for a variety of tasks. Pinned to your piece at strategic points, they can help you keep track of when you've worked an increase or decrease or signal the right side of reversible fabric. They work well as miniature stitch holders for small groups of stitches and for securing dropped stitches. In knitting shops and specialty catalogs, you can find several sizes of pins without coils, which are less likely to catch on your yarn than regular safety pins.

Needle gauge and tension gauge

Needle gauges and tension gauges are indispensable. A *needle gauge* is a small rulerlike gadget with graduated holes in it for measuring the size of your knitting needles (and crochet hooks, but that's a subject for another book — *Crocheting For Dummies* by Susan Brittain, Karen Manthey, and Julie Hoeltz [Wiley], in fact). If you knit a lot on circular needles, which frequently aren't labeled for size, or if you're prone to finding a lost double-pointed needle under the sofa cushions, a needle gauge is essential for size identification. Buy one that shows both metric and US sizes.

A *tension gauge* (also called a *stitch gauge*) often comes as part of a needle gauge. It's a flat piece of metal or plastic with a 2-inch L-shaped window for measuring stitches and rows. You lay the tension gauge over your knitting, lining up the window along a row of stitches horizontally and vertically, and count the rows and stitches exposed. The drawback to using this tool is that 2 inches isn't always a large enough measure for an accurate gauge count. You can see a typical combination needle and tension gauge in Figure 2-10.

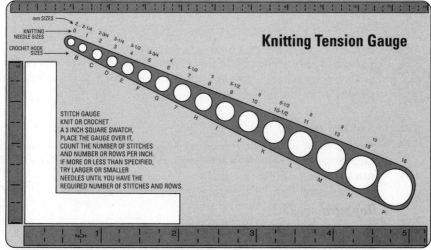

Figure 2-10: A common needle and tension gauge.

Illustration by Wiley, Composition Services Graphics

TIP

You can make a great tension gauge by cutting a very accurate 4-inch window in a piece of sturdy but thin cardboard. Lay this tool over your knitting and clearly count 4 inches worth of stitches and rows.

Cable needles

A *cable needle* is a short needle that's pointed at both ends, has a divot or curve toward the middle, and is used to hold stitches temporarily while you work on their neighbors. There are several versions of the two main types:

U-shaped and straight (see Figure 2-11). Try out a couple of styles to see which you like better.

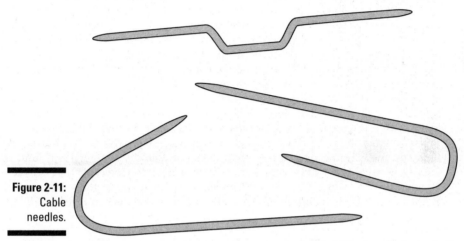

Figure 2-11:
Cable
needles.

Illustration by Wiley, Composition Services Graphics

In a pinch, you can use a double-pointed needle or even a long nail or tooth-pick as a cable needle, but a tool especially designed for this task is best and a small price to pay for its convenience. Obviously, if you don't plan to knit cables, leave this item off your list.

Crochet hooks

Even if you don't plan to crochet edgings on your knits, a crochet hook comes in very handy when picking up dropped stitches. They're sized by number and/or letter. A medium-size one, say, 5 mm or so, is good for your supply bag or basket.

Examining nice-to-have extras

You can get by without buying the gadgets in this section, but you may find some of them worth the small investment. For example, after years of using strands of yarn tied in a circle for yarn markers, we marvel at how much we prefer the little rubber rings and find ourselves using those markers in ways we never thought of before. Figure 2-12 shows some of our favorite knitting gadgets.

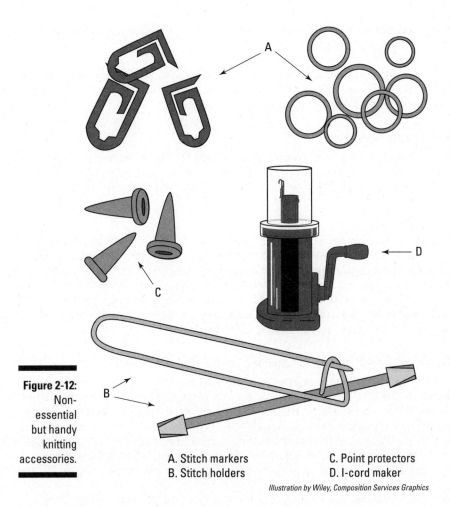

Illustration by Wiley, Composition Services Graphics

Figure 2-12:
Non-
essential
but handy
knitting
accessories.

A. Stitch markers
B. Stitch holders

C. Point protectors
D. I-cord maker

Stitch markers

A *stitch marker* is a small ring that you slip onto your needle between stitches to alert you to places in your knitting that you need to pay attention to: the beginning of a round, the beginning and end of a repeat, the spot to work an increase or a decrease. When you reach a marker, you slip it from the LH needle to the RH needle and carry on.

You can find several styles of markers on the market. Some are wafer thin, and others are small plastic coils that open up and can be placed on the needle in the middle of a row. Some are made from rubber and won't come whizzing off the end of your needle when you get to them. (Of course, if you don't have any bona fide knitting markers, you can always use a contrasting yarn color tied in a loop or a safety pin.)

Choose a stitch marker that has approximately the same circumference as the needle you're using. Failing to do so may result in an unintentional column of stretched stitches where the stitch marker is placed.

Point protectors

Point protectors are small, pointed rubber caps that fit over the tips of your needles to protect them and prevent your stitches from sliding off when you put down your work. They come in different sizes to fit your needles.

Stitch holders

Stitch holders resemble large safety pins but have a blunt point and no coil so as not to split the yarn; you use them to secure stitches that you'll work up or finish off later. They come in a variety of lengths, from 1¾ inches to 8 inches. If you don't have any stitch holders, you can always transfer the stitches to a spare circular or double-pointed needle (put point protectors at each end) or to a contrasting yarn threaded on a tapestry needle. Still, stitch holders are the best tools to hold a lot of stitches.

Magnetic board and strips and magnetic line magnifier

If you plan to knit anything from a chart, a magnetic board with strips is a wonderful item to have. You put your chart on top of the magnetic board and lay the magnetized strip on the row of squares *above* the row you're working on. After you work the row shown on the chart, you move the strip up, exposing the next row to knit. A magnetic line magnifier is a see-through ruler that works like the magnetic board and strips but also magnifies the line you're working on. You put the magnifier on top of the row you're working on.

Of course, you can use sticky notes for marking your row on a chart. The downside is that the notes often are shorter than the width of your chart and more vulnerable to cats skittering across the table or someone looking for paper to use for something (seemingly) more important than keeping your place on the knitting chart. Another alternative is painter's tape, which has very low tack and doesn't stick to the pattern.

Pompom maker

After years of creating wimpy, lopsided pompoms, we bought pompom makers. What a difference they make! Now we can make solid and rainbow pompoms in three sizes. This small and inexpensive gadget is one of those simple but brilliant ideas that turn a tedious job with questionable results into something quick with spectacular results. (It's so much fun to use that you may be tempted to add pompoms to everything.)

Tassel and fringe maker

Everything we say about the pompom maker also applies to the *tassel and fringe maker*. It's a small adjustable plastic frame that allows you to wrap any number of threads around it before cutting the wraps for fringe or tassels. No more hunting around for the book or piece of cardboard just the right size for wrapping.

Graph paper

Graph paper is very useful for diagramming patterns and charting designs and motifs. Figuring on 5 or 8 squares to the inch works fine for sweater plotting and texture patterns. If you plan to design your own color patterns or motifs, look in your local yarn shop for knitter's graph paper, which has flattened-out squares (5 squares across and 7 squares up to the inch) to reflect the grid of knitted fabric — more rows per inch than stitches. You also can find knitter's graph paper online (see Appendix B for suggested websites).

I-cord maker

If you find yourself making lots of I-cords for bag handles or just for decoration, a hand-cranked I-cord maker will more than pay for itself in time saved. Available at many craft and yarn stores, these small machines make quick work of I-cord. For more information on I-cords and how to make them, head to Chapter 9.

Notebook or folder

You'll find many good reasons to keep a notebook or folder among your knitting supplies. It's a good place to keep a knitting diary, recording your projects and saving labels from the yarn you're using. Never throw away the label that comes with your yarn. You may need it to match the color and/or dye lot numbers if you run out of yarn on a project. Labels are also handy records of the yardage used to knit a project (especially a sweater) just in case you love it so much that you want to knit another just like it. You can also write down the needle size you ended up using and the gauge you got on a specific project. In addition, you can jot down ideas, technical questions to ask your knitting mentor, patterns you want to swatch, and so on.

Eyeing Blocking Equipment

Blocking is the process of using steam or water to smooth out and gently uncurl and flatten your knitted pieces so that you can easily join them together. Blocking equipment makes the difference between a tiresome, awkward task and an easy, streamlined one. The basic blocking equipment includes the following:

✔ **Steam iron:** You probably already have a steam iron. The more steam, the better.

✔ **Blocking board:** A *blocking board* is not your ironing board. It's a flat surface made from a material that you can stick a pin into. It should be large enough to hold at least one pinned-out sweater piece. Ideally, it should be marked with a 1-inch grid so that you can pin out your knitted piece to its proper dimensions without using your tape measure. If you have enough space, you can leave the blocking board up all the time for checking your project's measurements as you go along. Ready-made blocking boards or kits for making them are available from sources listed in Appendix B. In a pinch, you can use your bed, but a real blocking board is better.

✔ **Blocking wires:** *Blocking wires* are long, slightly flexible stainless steel wires in various lengths. Threaded through the edges of your knitted piece, blocking wires allow you to pin the piece into shape so that the edges don't become scalloped at the pin sites. They're a wonderful invention and well worth the investment.

✔ **T-pins:** Large T-shaped straight pins help you pin out the edges of your project pieces. T-pins are easy to get a grip on, and because they don't have any plastic parts (like straight pins with colorful plastic heads do), they don't melt under your iron while you're steaming your knitted piece.

Organizing Your Equipment

When you're new to knitting and have only one or two pairs of needles and a few balls of yarn, you can organize your equipment just by finding a place for it on your mantle, in a drawer, or in one of those pretty knitting baskets that sit beside your couch or chair. When you have a bouquet of straight needles, a tangle of circular needles, enough yarn to cover a city block, and lots of itty-bits jangling around the bottom of your "storage" space, you may decide that you need to organize your equipment a little more deliberately. Here's some advice:

✔ **Invest in a needle case.** Spare needles rattling around your knitting bag are prone to getting lost, bent, or even broken. A needle case is the answer. Fabric needle cases have narrow pockets for filing your needles, and you can roll them up and tie them for storage and travel. Cases also are available in more rigid wood or plastic. If you splurge on some especially lovely needles — such as rosewood or ebony — you may want to invest in a case just for them. (Wouldn't you store your pearls in a jewelry box?)

✔ **Get a canvas wall holder, especially for your circular needles.** Of course, you can store your circular needles in the plastic container they come in, but this system keeps them curled up. Before you can comfortably knit with them, you need to unkink them in hot water. A solution is to purchase a canvas wall holder with slots for each size. Stored this way, the circular needles rest in their slots with their point ends hanging down, unkinked and ready to knit. Interchangeable circular needle systems come in their own cases.

✔ **Store your extra yarn out of direct sunlight in a container that can breathe.** If you find yourself collecting more yarn than you can knit up in a given year (or more), store your precious skeins in a bin of some kind that allows air to circulate. If you want to put your yarn in a plastic bin, leave the lid askew or drill a hole or two in the sides so moisture and air can flow in and out. Many yarns fade in direct sunlight, so never store them where they'll be exposed to daily sunshine.

TIP

Add a few mothballs to the container or bin. Some yarns are already mothproofed, but those that aren't are susceptible to moths, and it's a frustrating thing indeed to be knitting along and suddenly find that your yarn strand has ended while a full ball remains in the basket. If you're allergic to mothballs, several herbal equivalents are on the market. And if you do happen to find moths, don't panic: Put your yarn in plastic bags in the freezer to kill the moths and their eggs.

✔ **Get a tote bag especially for your knitting.** The bag should be big enough to stow your project and essential equipment, but not so big that your equipment gets lost in its depths. If your bag has pockets of various sizes, all the better. Kid-sized backpacks, canvas beach bags, and fashion fabric totes from yarn shops are all good choices.

✔ **Use a small, zippered bag for your essential small gadgets.** Look for a clear plastic one you can see through. You may find one in the cosmetics section of your local drugstore or department store.

Chapter 3

Taking the Mystery Out of Patterns and Gauge

In This Chapter

▶ Making sense of knitting pattern lingo

▶ Reading written and chart-style patterns

▶ Taking time to get the right gauge

You can knit — and enjoy it — for years without ever cracking a knitting book or learning about gauge, but unless you have a mentor who can help you increase your repertoire and fine-tune your technique, you'll be limited as to what you can create. Simple scarves and plain afghans can inspire you for only so long. Eventually, you'll want to try new things, and you'll find your inspiration online and in the many knitting books and magazines that are out there.

But to recreate those things — the lacework shawls, the finely shaped garments, the argyle socks, or the cabled jackets — you need to know how to decode instructions and how to control the sizing of a knitted piece. Fortunately, this chapter is devoted entirely to those topics.

Reading Stitch Patterns

Directions for stitch patterns can be in written form or chart form. Written instructions tell you what to do with the stitches in each row as you come to them, whereas a chart shows a picture of each stitch and how it's worked. Some people prefer written instructions, and others like to follow a graphed picture of the pattern. Nowadays, the trickier the pattern, the more likely it is to be charted out. Not true for vintage patterns, however. Being familiar with both ways of describing a pattern enables you to convert a chart into written instructions if you find it easier to work with words and, conversely, to convert a convoluted set of written instructions into graph form by drawing a chart.

Stitch patterns are based on *repeats* — both stitch repeats and row repeats. A given stitch sequence repeats horizontally across a row. A series of rows of given stitch sequences repeats vertically. Together, they make up a stitch pattern that determines what your knitted fabric will look like: smooth, bumpy, cabled, or striped.

Deciphering Knitterese: Common abbreviations and shorthand

To save space, patterns are written with many abbreviations and a lot of shorthand. As you work with patterns, you'll become familiar with the most common abbreviations — for example, RS (right side), WS (wrong side), beg (beginning), and rep (repeat). Pattern instructions explain any unusual abbreviations or ones that may vary from pattern to pattern. Table 3-1 presents some of the most common pattern abbreviations.

Table 3-1	Common Knitting Abbreviations		
Abbreviation	**What It Means**	**Abbreviation**	**What It Means**
beg	beginning	pwise	purlwise (as if to purl)
CC	contrasting color	rem	remain(s) or remaining
ch	chain	rep	repeat
cn	cable needle	RH	right-hand
dec	decrease(s), decreased, or decreasing	RS	right side(s)
dpns	double-pointed needles	rnd(s)	round(s)
foll	follows or following	sc	single crochet
inc	increase(s), increased, or increasing	sl	slip, slipped, or slipping
k	knit	sl st	slip stitch
k2tog	knit 2 stitches together	ssk	slip, slip, knit the slipped stitches together

Abbreviation	What It Means	Abbreviation	What It Means
k-b	knit in stitch below	St st	stockinette stitch
kwise	knitwise (as if to knit)	st(s)	stitch(es)
LH	left-hand	tbl	through the back of the loop
lp(s)	loop(s)	tog	together
MC	main color	WS	wrong side(s)
m1 (or m)	make 1 stitch (increase 1 stitch)	wyib	with yarn in back
p	purl	wyif	with yarn in front
pat(s)	pattern(s)	yb	yarn back
p-b	purl in stitch below	yf	yarn forward
pm	place marker	yo	yarn over
psso	pass slipped stitch over (used for decreasing)		

In addition, knitting patterns use certain phrases that can be confusing until you have some experience with them. Here are some common phrases that you'll come across in knitting patterns and garments:

- **As established:** When your instructions set up a series of steps or patterns to work instead of repeating them row by row, they tell you to continue working *as established*.

  Example: If you're knitting a cardigan with the center front band knitted in, the stitches for the center front band may be worked in a pattern different from the rest of the sweater body. After the pattern tells you how many border stitches to work in the border pattern and how many stitches to work in the sweater body pattern, it tells you to continue to work the patterns in the front piece *as established*.

- **At same time:** This phrase indicates that two things need to happen at the same time. Be on the lookout for this phrase; it's easy to get going on one task and forget to pay attention to the other.

  Example: "dec 1 st every other row 4 times, *at same time,* when piece measures same length as back to shoulder, work shoulder shaping as for back." Translation: The neckline shaping (dec 1 st) continues as the shoulder shaping begins.

- **Back of your work:** The back of your work is the side of your work that faces away from you as you hold your needles. Don't confuse this with the right side (RS) and wrong side (WS) of your work, which refer to how the piece is worn or which side should be presented as the front.

- **Bind off from each neck edge:** When you shape the neckline on a pullover, you work both edges of the neckline at the same time, but you shape the right side (as you wear it) on right-side rows and shape the left side on wrong-side rows. Although this instruction may sound tricky, it's quite obvious and simple when you're doing it. You may see this phrase in a form like this: "bind off from each neck edge 3 sts once, 2 sts twice. . . ."

- **End with a WS row:** Finish the section you're working on by working a wrong-side row last. The next row you work should be a right-side row.

- **Front of your work:** The front of your work is the side of your work that faces you as you hold your needles. It can be the wrong side or the right side.

- **Inc (or dec) every 4 (6, 8, or whatever) rows:** This is how the increases (or decreases) along a sleeve seam are written. Increase or decrease on a (usually) right-side row, and then work 3 (5, 7, or whatever) rows without shaping.

- **Inc (or dec) every other row:** Increase or decrease on the (usually) right-side row, and then work the following row without increasing or decreasing.

- **Pat rep (pattern repeat):** When instructions tell you to repeat a certain stitch pattern, it's written this way. Pattern repeat refers to what's given between an asterisk and a semicolon (* . . . ;) in written patterns and between heavy black lines in a chart.

- **Pick up and knit:** Use a separate strand of yarn to create a row of stitches on a needle by pulling loops through along a knitted edge, usually the front of a cardigan or a neckline. See more on picking up stitches in Chapter 16.

- **Pm (place marker):** A *marker* is a plastic ring or tied loop of yarn that sits between stitches on your needle to indicate the beginning of a round in circular knitting or to mark pattern repeats. When you see the instruction to place a marker, as in "join, pm, and begin round," you simply place a marker at that location. (As you knit, you slip the marker from one needle to the other. But usually your pattern doesn't tell you to do that — your common sense does.)

- **Preparation row:** Some stitch patterns require a set-up row that's worked only at the beginning of the pattern and isn't part of the repeat.

- **Reverse shaping:** When you knit a cardigan, you work two pieces that mirror each other. Most patterns have you work the side that carries the buttons before you work the side that carries the buttonholes. Instead of writing a separate set of instructions for each side, the pattern asks you to work the shaping in the opposite direction on the second piece, as in "work to correspond to front, reversing all shaping." This means that you work bind-offs and neck shaping on the reverse side of the fabric as well. If you work the shaping on the wrong side in one piece, you work it on the right side when you reverse the shaping.

✔ **Right:** When a pattern specifies a right front, it means the front that would be on your right side *as you would wear the finished piece.* When in doubt, hold your knitting up to you (wrong side to your body) to determine whether you're looking at the right or left front.

✔ **When armhole measures . . . :** This phrase signals that your instructions are about to change. Measure the armhole not from the beginning of the piece but from the marker you've (we hope) put near the middle of the row on which the armhole began. The pattern should have told you to place this marker.

✔ **Work as for . . . :** This phrase usually refers to working the front piece the same as the back. It saves writing out the same instructions twice. You may see it in a form like this: "work as for back until piece measures 21½ inches from beg."

✔ **Work even:** Continue in whatever stitch pattern you're using without doing any shaping.

✔ **Work to end:** Work in whatever stitch pattern you're using to the end of the row.

You may run into other phrases that aren't as clear as they could be, but experience will make you familiar with them. Eventually, you'll be surprised at how well you understand this language, and you'll wonder why it ever seemed confusing.

Following written stitch patterns

Written instructions give you row-by-row directions for a single repeat. They follow certain conventions and use lots of abbreviations (see the preceding section). The key to understanding written instructions is paying attention to commas, asterisks, and brackets or parentheses; they mean more than you may think. Here's a punctuation translation:

✔ **Single steps are separated by commas.** The instruction "Sl 1 wyif, k5" tells you to slip a stitch with the yarn on the front side of the work and *then* to knit 5 stitches as normal (meaning you have to move the yarn to the back before knitting, even though the instructions don't tell you to).

✔ **An asterisk (*) indicates that whatever follows gets repeated (rep).** For example, the instruction "K1, * sl 1, k3; rep from * to last st, k1" means that you knit 1 stitch, and then you work the stitches between the asterisks (slip 1 stitch and knit 3 stitches) over and over until you reach the last stitch of the row, which you knit.

✔ **Brackets (or parentheses) function much like asterisks, except you repeat the series of stitches a specified number of times.** For example, the instruction "* K5, (p1, k1) twice, p1; repeat from * to end of row" means that, after you knit 5, you purl 1/knit 1 *two times,* followed by another purl 1, and then you repeat this entire sequence across the entire row.

The following example shows a stitch pattern in written form:

Row 1 (RS): * K2, p2; rep from * to end of row.

Row 2 (WS): * P2, k2; rep from * to end of row.

Translation: On the first row (the right side is facing you on the first row in this pattern), you knit 2 stitches, purl 2 stitches, knit 2 stitches, purl 2 stitches, and so on to the end of the row. (Your row would have to be a multiple of 4 stitches for these instructions to come out evenly.) On the next row (wrong side facing now), you begin by purling 2 stitches, then knitting 2 stitches, purling 2 stitches, knitting 2 stitches, and so on to the end of the row.

As you read patterns, pay attention to row designations. To save space, many written instructions combine rows that repeat the same stitches. For example, this ribbon eyelet pattern combines a couple of rows:

Cast on multiple of 2 sts, plus 2 sts.

Row 1: Knit.

Row 2: Purl.

Rows 3 and 4: Knit.

Row 5: P1, * yo, p2tog; repeat from * to last st, p1.

Row 6: K2, * k1 tbl, k1; repeat from * to end of row.

Row 7: Knit.

Row 8: Purl.

Rep Rows 1–8.

As you can imagine, the more intricate the pattern, the more complicated the instructions. But if you read your instructions carefully, work each step between commas as a complete step, look at your work, and think about what you're doing, you won't have any problems.

Reading charted stitch patterns

Charts use a square to represent each stitch and a symbol inside the square to indicate how to work the stitch. Although there's no universal set of symbols, each pattern that uses a chart also provides a key to reading it. Always begin by finding the key to the chart.

The trick to reading chart patterns without getting confused is to remember that you don't read them from top to bottom and left to right as you would a book. Instead, you read a chart from the bottom up because it shows the knitted piece as it's knitted, and in nearly all knitting, you knit from the bottom up. Whether you read from right to left or left to right depends on the row you're working:

- ✔ **Right-side rows:** You read from right to left.
- ✔ **Wrong-side rows:** You read from left to right.

Charts represent the pattern of the knitted fabric as you're looking at it — the *right* side of the fabric. This means that on wrong-side rows (from left to right) you must purl any stitch that has a knit symbol and knit any stitch that has a purl symbol. This switch isn't difficult once you get the hang of it, and the pattern key will remind you. Of course, if you're knitting in the round, you can follow the chart without worrying about whether you have the wrong side or right side of the fabric facing. See Chapter 8 for more about knitting in the round.

Figure 3-1 shows a very simple chart. In fact, it's the same pattern as the K2, p2 pattern from the preceding section.

Row 2

Row 1

Figure 3-1: Pattern instructions in chart form.

Key

Knit on the right side
Purl on the wrong side

Purl on the right side
Knit on the wrong side

Illustration by Wiley, Composition Services Graphics

Because of the way they can condense complicated stitches and techniques into simple symbols, charts often are used for lacework, cables, and other patterns that incorporate special effects, such as bobbles and scallops, to save space. And they're indispensable for intarsia, Fair Isle, and other multi-color techniques. Figure 3-2 shows what a chart for a repeating color pattern may look like for a sweater pattern.

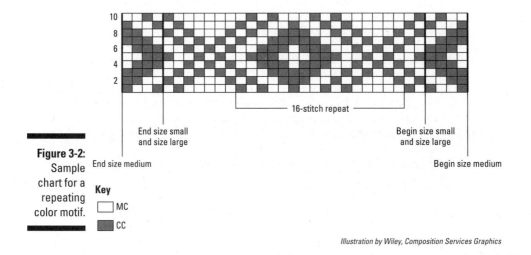

Figure 3-2:
Sample chart for a repeating color motif.

16-stitch repeat

End size small
and size large

Begin size small
and size large

End size medium

Begin size medium

Key

☐ MC

■ CC

Illustration by Wiley, Composition Services Graphics

If the design uses a repeating pattern, as the one in Figure 3-2 does, the chart generally shows a single or double repeat and not the whole garment piece. Unless the number of stitches in the piece you're making is an exact multiple of the repeat, you'll have to begin and end on a part of the repeat. The chart tells you where to begin knitting the repeat.

If you don't have a magnetic board with strips (see Chapter 2 for an explanation of this handy tool), buy the longest self-stick notepads you can find and keep them with your knitting project. Use them to keep track of your place on the chart by sticking them along the row *above* the row you're currently working on. Seeing only the rows on the chart that you've already worked helps you orient yourself.

When reading charts, pay careful attention to the key provided. Various publishers, designers, and charting software programs may chart the exact same stitch or series of stitches using different symbols.

Gauge: Getting the Size Right

Every knitted fabric is made up of stitches and rows. *Gauge* is the number of stitches and rows it takes to make 1 square inch of knitted fabric. Figure 3-3 shows the stitches and rows that make up 1 square inch of a stockinette *swatch* (a sample made specifically to test gauge). Stockinette and most other knitted fabrics have more vertical rows than stitches per inch. Understanding how to measure and work with gauge is what allows you to go from a knitted swatch or sample to a finished project that measures what you want it to.

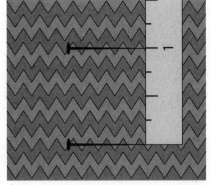

Figure 3-3:
One square inch of stockinette measured.

Illustration by Wiley, Composition Services Graphics

If you've spent some time around knitters, you may already know that mention of the word *gauge* often elicits a groan. Gauge has a bad reputation among many knitters for three reasons. First, it represents an unpleasant "should." Second, it's a tedious task that has to be accomplished before the fun part of the project — the *knitting* — can begin. Finally, it involves math. However, getting comfortable with gauge gives you a leg up in knitting. Without knowing your gauge, you couldn't do the following:

- Knit away, comfortable in the knowledge that after you work the thousands of stitches required to complete your project, it will fit.

- Substitute another yarn for the one given in the pattern.

- Use the size of needle that makes the best fabric for your chosen yarn, even if it means you don't match the pattern's gauge.

- Design your own projects and sweaters.

The first step in any knitting project is to determine the gauge of the knitted fabric you're making. Gauge (sometimes called *tension*) is listed at the beginning of a pattern before the instructions begin. It's given as a number of stitches and rows over 4 inches or 10 centimeters, and it tells you which needle and which stitch pattern were used to determine the gauge. Check your pattern to see how many stitches and rows should make up 4 inches of knitted fabric. You need to measure *your* gauge against that given in the directions.

Gauge isn't always important, such as when you're making a scarf, an afghan, a bag, or anything else for which a precise size isn't essential. But when size *does* matter, the right or wrong gauge can make or break the finished piece.

Knowing what affects gauge

Gauge varies depending on the yarn, the needle size, and the stitch pattern you use:

- ✔ **Yarn:** Yarns of different weights produce different gauges. A bulkier yarn produces a larger stitch, and a finer yarn produces a smaller stitch. Head to Chapter 2 for detailed information on yarn weights and the effect weight can have on the knitted fabric.

- ✔ **Needles and stitch size:** The same yarn knitted on different-sized needles will have different gauges. Because you make a knit stitch by wrapping yarn around a needle, the size (circumference) of the needle determines the size of the stitch.

  Figure 3-4 shows how needle size can affect the way the finished fabric looks. The smaller the needle is, the tighter the stitches and the denser the knitted fabric. The larger the needle is, the looser the stitches and the drapier (and stretchier) the fabric.

Figure 3-4: Smaller needles result in tighter stitches; bigger needles, in looser stitches.

Photograph by Wiley, Composition Services Graphics

- ✔ **Stitch patterns and stitch size:** The same yarn knitted on the same needles but in different stitch patterns will have different gauges. For example, cables and ribs pull in, requiring more stitches to make a square inch; lace and slip stitch or garter stitch patterns spread the fabric out, so they require fewer stitches to make an inch. Figure 3-5 compares the gauges of two different patterns that use the same number of stitches.

Gauge also can vary with the time of day you're knitting, how long you've been knitting at a stretch, and what you're thinking about. The tension you put on the yarn traveling around the needle contributes to stitch size, so being tired or tense can affect the flow of your yarn and stitch size.

Figure 3-5:
Gauge on different stitch patterns.

Photograph by Wiley, Composition Services Graphics

Making a gauge swatch

To find out whether your gauge matches the pattern, you begin by making a gauge swatch. A gauge swatch is a small sample that you work using the same pattern, yarn, and needles you intend to use for your project.

It's important that you use the *same* yarn for your gauge swatch as for your project, not the same brand in a different color. Different dyes can affect how a specific yarn knits up, and believe it or not, a yarn in one color can give you a different gauge from the same yarn in a different color.

To make your swatch, follow these steps:

1. **Cast on the appropriate number of stitches.**

   In general, cast on the number of stitches given in the pattern for 4 inches, plus 6 more stitches. For example, if the gauge is given as 18 stitches and 22 rows over 4 inches, cast on 24 stitches.

   If the stitch pattern needs to be worked in a specific multiple, cast on any multiple that will yield a swatch larger than 4 inches in order to get an accurate gauge measurement. For example, if the pattern is worked on a multiple of 6 stitches plus 1 more, and the gauge given is 4 stitches to an inch, cast on *at least* 25 stitches (a multiple of 6 + 1). At 4 stitches to the inch, your swatch will be more than 4 inches wide, giving you a good area for measuring.

Many patterns give dimensions in centimeters rather than inches or include metric measurements alongside US ones. You can calculate inches from centimeters by dividing the centimeter number by 2.5. For example, 10 centimeters divided by 2.5 equals 4 inches. Or just use a ruler with centimeters.

2. **Work in the stitch pattern specified for the number of rows required to make 4 inches, plus 6 more rows.**

   For the same gauge specifications as in Step 1 (18 stitches and 22 rows over 4 inches), you work in the given pattern for 28 rows.

   These extra stitches and rows will give you a border around the area you're measuring. Edge stitches are frequently distorted and shouldn't be included in what you measure for gauge unless your swatch is a good 6 inches square.

3. **Bind off loosely and cut the strand of yarn, leaving an 8-inch tail, and draw it through the loops of the last row.**

4. **Block the swatch in the same manner you plan to use for your finished project.**

   Your stitches may shrink a bit when they're steamed. *Now* you're ready to measure it. For blocking instructions, head to Chapter 16.

Measuring your gauge

To measure your swatch, smooth it out on a flat surface; a blocking or ironing board is good for this task. Pin the edges down if they're curling in — be careful not to stretch your swatch — and follow these steps:

1. **Lay a ruler along a row of stitches and mark the beginning and end of 4 inches with pins.**

   If your second pin lands at half a stitch, don't be tempted to stretch or slightly squish your knitting to make the 4 inches end on a whole stitch.

2. **Note the number of stitches in 4 inches, fractions and all.**

3. **Lay your ruler along a vertical line of stitches, aligning the bottom of the ruler with the bottom of a stitch (the bottom of a V), and put a pin in to show where the first stitch begins. Place another pin 4 inches up.**

4. **Count the stitches between the pins and note the number of rows.**

These steps give you gauge over a 4-inch (10-centimeter) square. Check whether your 4-inch gauge matches the one in the pattern. If it does, thank your lucky stars. If it doesn't, head to the next section.

Measuring gauge on highly textured yarns

With fuzzy or highly textured yarns, it can be difficult to see your stitches clearly enough to take an accurate measurement by counting stitches. In this case, use the following steps to measure your gauge:

1. **Make a swatch larger than 4 inches and write down the total number of stitches and rows in your swatch.**

2. **Measure the entire swatch side to side and top to bottom.**

3. **Use a calculator to plug your numbers into the formulas that follow:**

To find *stitch gauge* (number of horizontal stitches per inch): Divide the number of stitches in the swatch by the width of the swatch in inches. This gives you the number of stitches per inch.

To find *row gauge* (number of vertical stitches per inch): Divide the number of rows by the overall length of the swatch in inches. This gives you the number of rows per inch.

To find your gauge over 4 inches, multiply stitches per inch or rows per inch by 4. For information on measuring gauge over cable patterns, turn to Chapter 11.

Matching your pattern's gauge

If your gauge swatch doesn't match the one specified in the pattern and you want your project to come out the same size as the pattern measures, change your needle size and make another swatch. If your first swatch is smaller than specified, use larger needles. If your swatch is larger than specified, use smaller needles.

Keep adjusting your needle size and remaking your swatch until you get the number of stitches and rows in a 4-inch square that your pattern requires. If you can't get both stitch and row gauge to match the pattern's gauge, work with the needle that gives you the right *stitch* gauge.

The cumulative effect of knitting at a gauge as small as half a stitch less than the pattern calls for can be disastrous. For example, if your project piece is supposed to measure 20 inches and calls for a gauge of 5 stitches per inch, your finished piece will measure 22 inches if you're knitting at 4 stitches per inch. And if you're off by 2 inches on both the front and back of a sweater, the total difference between the pattern and your sweater will be 4 inches overall. That's why gauge gets so much attention in knitting books and why taking the time to measure it is so important.

Designing with gauge in mind

As you begin to knit projects, you may find yourself imagining sweaters and hats you'd like to make but can't find a pattern for. Making your own pattern for a project isn't all that difficult. No matter how fancy the pattern stitch or shaping, how large or small the project, it all comes down to stitches and inches. Figure out your gauge on the yarn and needles you want to use, and then determine the dimensions of the finished project.

To determine the number of stitches to cast on for a project you're imagining, work the formula for determining gauge in reverse: Decide how wide you want your piece to be, and then multiply that number by your gauge. For example, if you're imagining a scarf in one of the patterns in Chapter 5 or Appendix A, make a gauge swatch. If your gauge is 5 stitches to the inch and you want your scarf to be 7 inches wide, cast on 35 stitches and start knitting.

Part II
Knitting Primer

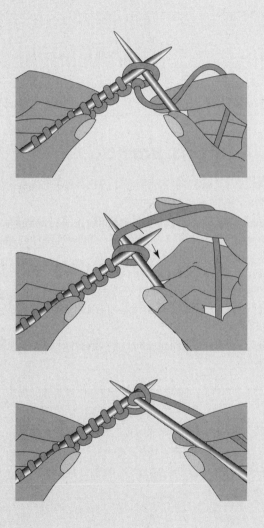

In this part . . .

- Familiarize yourself with the basics of knitting: casting on, knitting, purling, and binding off.

- Advance your knitting skills by learning how to increase and decrease stitches. Use these two techniques to shape a project and create design.

- Lower your chances of knitting disasters by knowing how to detect a mistake and fix it as soon as it happens.

- Discover how to use circular needles and knit in the round to create just about any knitted project.

- Practice the skills and techniques in this part with a variety of projects.

Chapter 4

The Fundamentals: Casting On, Knitting, Purling, and Binding Off

In This Chapter

▶ Casting stitches on and off your needles

▶ Getting the hang of basic knitting techniques

▶ Changing things up with basic purling techniques

▶ Giving Continental style a whirl

*H*ere you are, a ball of yarn in one hand and two knitting needles in the other. To be a successful knitter, the first things you need to do are figure out how to get the one (yarn) onto the other (the needles) and, after achieving that, how to make the thing grow. The answers? Casting on and knitting and purling. Knit and purl stitches are the two stitches upon which all other knitting techniques are based. When you're comfortable with these stitches, you can create any number of amazing things.

Knitting is hugely relaxing — after you know the basics. As you pick up the techniques and practice them, keep these things in mind:

✔ Learning to knit can be a little stressful. Your fingers have to work in ways they're not accustomed to, and the illustrations that are decluttered for clarity make actual yarn-on-needles resemble a tangled mess — even if nothing's wrong. When you feel yourself getting tense or frustrated, set your knitting aside and do something else for a while, or head to Chapter 21 for suggested exercises to unkink yourself.

✔ Throughout this chapter and the rest of the book, the abbreviation *LH* refers to the left hand, and *RH* refers to the right hand. We use these abbreviations when talking about the needles. You can find a list of other common abbreviations in Chapter 3.

Casting On

Creating the first row of stitches is called *casting on.* You can cast on in various ways, and different knitters have their favorites. The following sections outline three common cast-on methods. Whichever you use, be sure to cast on your stitches evenly. They make up the bottom edge of your knitting, and neatness counts.

Here are a couple of tips about casting on:

✔ **Don't cast on too tightly.** Doing so makes the first row hard to work because you have to force your needle tip through each loop. If you find yourself doing this, you may want to start over and cast on with a needle one size larger to counteract the tension. Then switch to the requested size for the actual knitting.

✔ **When you're casting on a lot of stitches, place a stitch marker at particular intervals — like every 50 stitches.** That way, if you get interrupted or distracted as you're counting (and you will, sometimes multiple times), you don't have to begin counting again at the first stitch. As you work the first row, just drop the markers off the needle.

No matter which method you use, before you cast-on for a project, use some scrap yarn and needles to practice casting on. Cast on some stitches, and then take them off your needles and do it again. Our experience is that casting on is the first thing we learn as knitters and the first thing we forget.

Two-strand (or long-tail) cast-on

The two-strand method (sometimes called the *long-tail* method) is a great all-around cast-on for your starting repertoire. It's elastic, attractive, and easy to knit from. For this cast-on method, you need only one needle: the RH needle.

Visit www.dummies.com/go/knittingfd to watch a video demonstration of the two-strand cast-on method. Then try it yourself by following these steps:

1. **Measure off enough yarn for the bottom part of your piece and make a slip knot on your needle.**

   To figure how long the tail should be, you need approximately 1 inch for every stitch you cast on plus a little extra. Alternatively, you can measure the bottom of the knitted piece and multiply this total by 4.

To make the slip knot, make a pretzel-shaped loop and place your needle into the loop, as in Figure 4-1a. Then gently pull on both ends of yarn until the stitch is firmly on the needle but still slides easily back and forth, as in Figure 4-1b.

Figure 4-1:
Get the slip knot (the first stitch) on your needle.

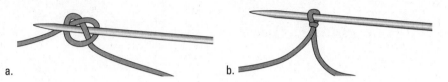
a.   b.

Illustration by Wiley, Composition Service Graphics

2. **Hold the needle in your right hand with the tip pointing away from your hand. Insert your left hand's thumb and forefinger into the "tent" formed by the two yarn ends falling from the slip knot on your needle.**

3. **With your left hand's ring and pinkie fingers, catch the yarn ends and hold them to your palm so they don't flap around underneath (see Figure 4-2a).**

4. **With your right hand, pull the needle between your left thumb and forefinger so that the "tent" sides aren't droopy.**

   This setup resembles a sling shot.

5. **With the RH needle tip, go around the yarn on your thumb from the left (see Figure 4-2b) and then around the yarn on your forefinger from the right (see Figure 4-2c) and pull the new loop through (see Figure 4-2d).**

   Figure 4-2e shows the finished stitch.

6. **Tighten this new loop (your first cast-on stitch) onto the needle — but not too tight!**

   You'll quickly find that if you don't let go of the yarn after creating the stitch, you can use your thumb to tighten the stitch onto your needle. Finishing and tightening each stitch gets easier with practice.

   Although this is the first cast-on stitch, it's the second stitch on the RH needle because you also have the initial slip knot.

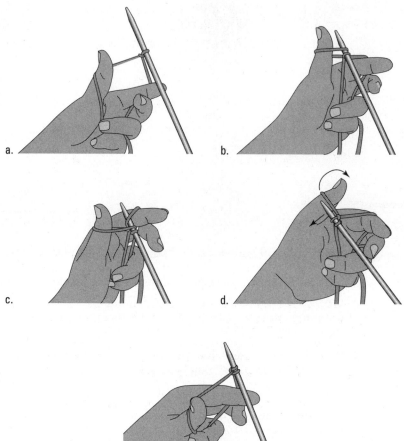

a.

b.

c.

d.

e.

Illustration by Wiley, Composition Service Graphics

Figure 4-2:
Catch a loop
from your
left hand.

7. Repeat Steps 5 and 6 until you have the number of stitches you need (see Figure 4-3).

If you need to put your work down or if you lose your place, you may have to pull the stitches off the needle and start from Step 2 instead.

Although casting on may feel awkward at first and you have to pay attention to each movement, with time and practice you'll no longer have to think about what your hands are doing. You'll be surprised at how quickly you'll learn the movements and make them smoothly and effortlessly while you think about something entirely unknitterish.

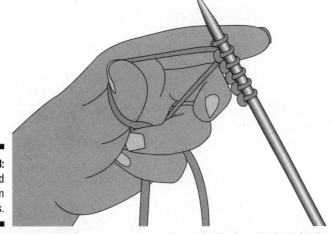

Illustration by Wiley, Composition Service Graphics

Figure 4-3:
Finished
cast-on
stitches.

Cable cast-on (cable co)

The cable cast-on, or *knitting on,* is less elastic than the two-strand cast-on. Use it when you need a sturdy, not-too-stretchy edge or when you need to cast on over buttonholes (see Chapter 18). If you're making a brand-new cast-on row, start with Step 1. If you're adding on at the beginning of an existing row or making new stitches over a buttonhole, start from Step 2.

1. **Make a slip knot on your needle, leaving a 6-inch tail.**

   Refer to the preceding section for help making a slip knot.

2. **Knit into the first stitch (see Figure 4-4a), but instead of slipping the old loop off the LH needle, bring the new loop to the right (see Figure 4-4b) and slip it onto the LH needle (see Figure 4-4c).**

   If you don't know how to make this first stitch, see the later section "Knitting know-how" for instructions.

3. **Insert the RH needle *between* the 2 stitches on the LH needle (see Figure 4-4d and 4-4e).**

4. **Wrap the yarn around the RH needle, as you do when you knit, and then bring a new loop through to the front (see Figure 4-4f).**

5. **Bring this loop around to the right and place it on the LH needle (see Figure 4-4g).**

6. **Repeat Steps 3 through 5 until you have the number of cast-on stitches you need.**

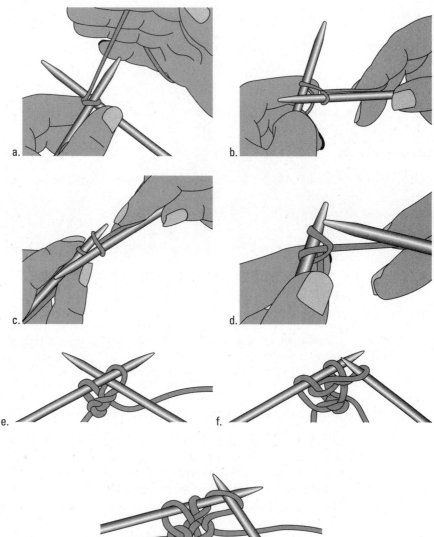

Figure 4-4:
Work a
cable
cast-on.

Thumb (or e-loop) cast-on

The thumb cast-on is quick and easy, but it doesn't look as nice as the cable cast-on, and it isn't easy to knit into. Two-strand and cable cast-ons should be your first choice for beginning a project. Still, the thumb cast-on (sometimes called *e-loop*) has its uses (such as for replacing cast-off stitches in a buttonhole or for a quick and easy increase stitch in the middle of a row), so knowing how to do it is worthwhile. If you're using this cast-on method at the beginning or in the middle of an existing row, skip Step 1.

1. **Make a slip knot on your needle, leaving a short tail.**

   Refer to the earlier section "Two-strand (or long-tail) cast-on" for help making a slip knot.

2. **Wrap the yarn around your left thumb, as in Figure 4-5a, and hold the needle in the right hand.**

3. **Insert the needle through the loop around your thumb (see Figure 4-5b), slide your thumb out, and pull gently on the yarn strand to tighten the stitch (see Figure 4-5c).**

The thumb cast-on is very similar to the long-tail cast-on. The difference between the two is that the thumb cast-on uses only the yarn on the thumb, whereas the long-tail uses the yarn on the thumb and the forefinger. So if you can do this cast-on, you're only one step away from the preferred long-tail method.

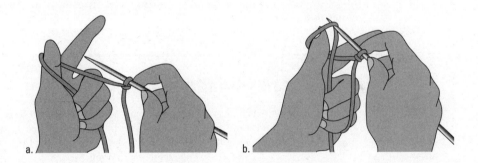

a.   b.

Figure 4-5:
Working a
thumb
cast-on.

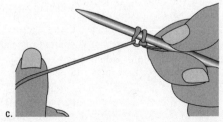

c.

Illustration by Wiley, Composition Service Graphics

Now You're Knitting and Purling

Knitted and purled stitches are made by using a continuous strand of yarn and two needles to pull new loops through old loops. That's it. The following sections explain how to create both stitches.

TIP

Here are a couple of pointers to keep in mind as you pick up knitting:

✔ Finish working an entire row before putting down your knitting. It's too easy to stop midway and pick up your knitting later to find you can't tell the LH from the RH needle. Here's an easy way to tell: The yarn is always hanging down from the last stitch you made, which is generally on the RH needle, no matter what kind of stitch it is. So if you've finished the entire row as we recommend, when you pick up your needles again, the needle with stitches will be in your left hand.

✔ Practice until the movements feel comfortable and relaxed. When you feel like you're getting the hang of it, try an experiment. Close your eyes or look at the ceiling while you knit — let your fingers feel their way. Can you knit without looking yet? Eventually you'll be able to. If you make this your goal, you can get lots of knitting done during your favorite TV shows and movies!

For left-handed knitters

Knitting is a two-handed endeavor. Whether you use your right hand or your left hand to write or stir your coffee, you use them both to knit.

For better or worse, knitting patterns are written for right-handed knitters (those who work from the LH needle to the RH needle). If you can master either of the knitting methods presented in this chapter (that is, English or Continental), you won't have to reinterpret patterns in order to work them in reverse. Chances are, like most right-handed knitters, sooner or later you'll work out a series of movements that feel natural and easy, and your stitches will be smooth and even.

If you find that the initial awkward feeling isn't going away, try to work in reverse — moving the stitches from the RH needle to the LH one. Follow the instructions for either the English or Continental style, substituting the word "right" for "left" and vice versa. To make the illustrations work for you, hold a mirror up to the side of the relevant illustration and mimic the hand and yarn positions visible in the mirror image.

If you find that working in reverse is the most comfortable method, be aware that some directions in knitting patterns, such as decreases, look different when worked in the opposite direction. This quirk will be most problematic for lace patterns, but it's a small price to pay for comfortable knitting.

Knitting know-how

To knit, hold the needle with the cast-on stitches in your left hand, pointing to the right, and hold the yarn in your right hand. Make sure that the first stitch is no more than 1 inch from the tip of the needle.

Visit www.dummies.com/go/knittingfd to watch a video demonstration of the knit stitch, and then try it yourself by following these steps:

1. **Insert the tip of the empty (RH) needle into the first stitch on the LH needle from left to right and front to back, forming a T with the tips of the needles.**

   The RH needle will be behind the LH needle (see Figure 4-6).

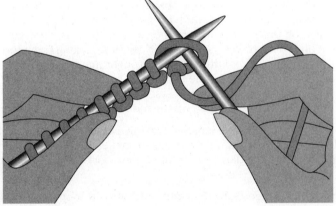

Figure 4-6:
Insert the RH needle into the first stitch on the LH needle.

Illustration by Wiley, Composition Service Graphics

2. **With your right hand, bring the yarn to the front from the *left side* of the RH needle, and then bring it over the RH needle to the right and down between the needles.**

   You can try to maneuver the yarn with your right forefinger, as Figure 4-7a shows, or just hold it between your thumb and forefinger for now.

3. **Keeping a slight tension on the wrapped yarn, bring the tip of the RH needle with its wrap of yarn through the loop on the LH needle to the front.**

   The RH needle is now in front of the LH needle (see Figure 4-7b). Keep the tip of the left forefinger on the point of the RH needle to help guide the needle through the old stitch and prevent losing the wrap of yarn.

Figure 4-7:
Complete a
knit stitch.

a.

b.

Illustration by Wiley, Composition Service Graphics

Don't hold the needles near the knob like a sword; keep your fingers in the action. Control the stitches on your needles by keeping your fingers close to the tip of the needle and use them to secure the stitches and keep them from falling off too early.

When you bring the new loop through the old, bring the RH needle up far enough that the new stitch forms on the large part of the needle, not just on the tip. If you work too close to the tips, your new stitches form on the narrowest part of your needles, making them too tight to knit with ease. Tight stitches have brought many a new knitter to a frustrated halt. By the same token, don't knit too far from the tips. Keep the stitches on the LH needle close enough to the tip so that you don't struggle and stretch to pull off the old stitch.

Note that when you've finished making a knit stitch, the yarn is coming out the *back* on the side of the needle facing away from you. Be sure that the yarn hasn't ended up in front of your work or over the needle before you start your next stitch.

4. **Slide the RH needle to the right until the old loop on the LH needle drops off.**

   You now have a new stitch/loop on the RH needle — the old stitch hangs below it (see Figure 4-8). Congratulations! You've just made your first knitted stitch!

5. **Repeat Steps 1 through 4 until you've knitted all the stitches from your LH needle.**

   Your LH needle is now empty, and your RH needle is full of beautiful new stitches.

Some beginners worry about the tension of their knitting and make the mistake of trying to tighten up the stitches by pulling the two needles apart. This move is a no-no. Doing so only results in a lot of slack between the stitches and doesn't make a pretty fabric. You want the needles to be close to one another as you knit (or purl). Notice in Figure 4-8 how far apart the needles are; that's about the same amount of distance you want between your own needles.

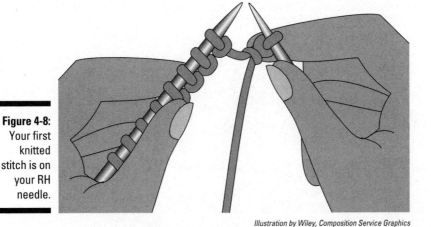

Figure 4-8:
Your first knitted stitch is on your RH needle.

Illustration by Wiley, Composition Service Graphics

In the meantime, don't worry about the tension of your knitting. As you practice more and more, you'll figure out how to control the tension of your stitches by keeping control of the working yarn as you knit. The more snug you keep the working yarn, the more snug your stitches will be.

6. **Turn your work (that is, switch hands so that the needle with stitches is in your left hand) and knit the new row.**

   When you turn your work, the yarn strand coming out of the first stitch to knit is hanging down in the front (see Figure 4-9). Also notice that the stitch just below the first stitch (labeled "Big loop" in Figure 4-9) on your LH needle is larger than the rest and can obscure your view of where your needle should go.

   You may be tempted to pull the yarn strand over the needle to the back to tighten up the stitch. If you do so, it will look like you have 2 stitches on your needle rather than 1. Keep the strand in front and gently pull down on it, and the big loop if necessary, to better see the opening of the first stitch. Be sure to insert the point of the RH needle in the loop on the LH needle and not into the stitch below.

7. **Repeat these steps for several more rows (or all afternoon) until you're comfortable with the movements.**

   Aim to make these steps one continuous movement, to make even stitches, and to stay relaxed! After you've knitted a few rows, take a look at what you've created: It's the *garter stitch,* and it's one of the most common — and easiest — stitch patterns. You can find it and other common stitch patterns in Chapter 5.

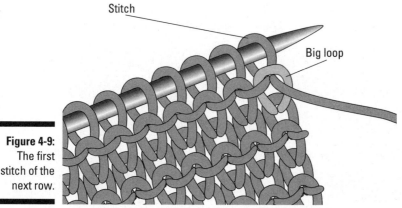

Stitch

Big loop

Figure 4-9:
The first
stitch of the
next row.

Illustration by Wiley, Composition Service Graphics

If you're having trouble getting into the flow, change the way you carry the yarn in your hand. Or prop the knob of your RH needle under your armpit or on your hipbone to keep it stationary while you use the left hand to initiate the movements. Study how other knitters do things and be willing to try different ways until you find your knitting home. When you understand how the yarn travels around your needle to make new loops, you'll sort out the best way to hold your yarn and needles for comfort, speed, and even stitches.

Perfect purling

Purling is working a knit stitch backwards: Instead of going into the stitch from front to back, you enter it from back to front. Combining knit stitches with purl stitches enables you to make a wide variety of textured stitch patterns; we include many of the most common in Chapter 5.

If you're a visual learner, head to www.dummies.com/go/knittingfd to watch a video demonstration of the purl stitch. To purl, follow these steps, holding the needle with the cast-on or existing stitches in your left hand and pointing to the right:

1. **Insert the tip of the RH needle into the first loop on the LH needle from right to left and back to front, forming a T with the needle tips.**

   The RH needle is in front of the LH needle, and the working yarn is in front of your needles (see Figure 4-10a). This setup is the reverse of what you do when you form a knit stitch.

2. **With your right hand, wrap the yarn around the back of the RH needle from right to left and down (see Figure 4-10b).**

Figure 4-10:
Insert the
RH needle
and wrap
the yarn
to purl.

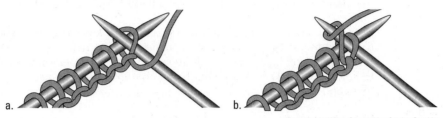

a.   b.

3. **Keeping a slight tension on the wrap of yarn, bring the tip of the RH needle with its wrap of yarn down and through the loop on the LH needle to the *back* side of the LH needle (see Figure 4-11a).**

4. **Slide the old loop off the tip of the LH needle.**

   A new stitch is made on the RH needle. You can see how it should look in Figure 4-11b.

Figure 4-11:
Finish your
purl stitch.

a.   b.

5. **Repeat Steps 1 through 4 until you're comfortable with the movements.**

When you purl, the yarn strand comes out of the new stitches on the side of the knitting facing you. When you knit, the yarn comes out of the new stitches on the side facing away from you.

A purled swatch looks just like a knitted swatch. Why? Because purling is simply the reverse of knitting. Whether you knit all the rows or purl all the rows, you're working a garter stitch (see Chapter 5 for more on the garter stitch).

Knitting and purling, Continental-style

How a knitter goes about holding the yarn and needles while working stitches varies. Some knitters hold the yarn in the right hand and wrap it around the

RH needle as they create stitches. This style, called *wrapping* or *English,* is the one the majority of knitters in the United States learn, and it's the method we explain in the preceding sections. Other knitters hold the yarn in the left hand and pick the stitches through each loop. This style is called *Continental.*

How do you decide which method to use? If you know a knitter who's willing to be your knitting mentor (and we've never met a fellow knitter who didn't love to show off his or her techniques), do what that person does. If you plan to knit color patterns, know that being able to knit with one color in the right hand and the other color in the left hand makes things quicker and easier.

Both methods, Continental and English, give you the same result — loops pulled through loops to make knitted fabric. The most important things are that knitting feels comfortable to you and your stitches look even.

Holding the yarn and needles

When you knit Continental, you hold both the yarn *and* the needle with the stitches in your left hand. The trick is keeping the yarn slightly taut by winding it around your left pinkie and over your left forefinger, as in Figure 4-12.

Figure 4-12:
Carry the yarn in your left hand for Continental style.

Illustration by Wiley, Composition Service Graphics

Your left forefinger should be close to the tip of the LH needle, and the yarn between the needle and your forefinger should be a bit taut. The yarn strand is *behind* your LH needle, as in Figure 4-13.

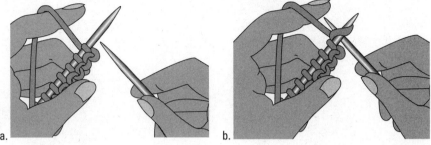

Illustration by Wiley, Composition Service Graphics

Figure 4-13:
Start a
Continental
knit stitch.

a.

b.

Swiveling to catch the yarn

When you knit or purl Continental, you don't wrap the yarn as you do in English knitting (refer to the earlier section "Knitting know-how"). Instead, you have to pick up the yarn and pull it through the old stitch. To do that, you execute a little swivel movement with your RH needle. Envision the needle as a chopstick with a cup on the end that you scoop into the stitch in order to pull up the yarn. (If you're a crocheter, this motion should be familiar to you from working with your hook.)

Knitting the Continental way

To knit in Continental style, follow these steps:

1. **Insert the RH needle through the stitch on the LH needle from left to right and front to back (see Figures 4-14a).**

2. **Swivel the tip of the RH needle to the right and under the yarn strand, scooping up the yarn from your left forefinger (see Figure 4-14b).**

3. **Pull the yarn through the loop (see Figure 4-14c), slide the old loop off the LH needle, and let it drop (see Figure 4-14d) to complete the stitch (Figure 4-14e shows a completed stitch).**

To make Continental knitting a little easier, try the following:

✔ Put the tip of your right forefinger on each new stitch made on the RH needle to secure it while you insert the RH needle into the next stitch on the LH needle.

✔ After you've inserted the RH needle into the next stitch to be knitted, slightly stretch the loop on the LH needle to the right, opening it up somewhat, before you scoop the strand of yarn.

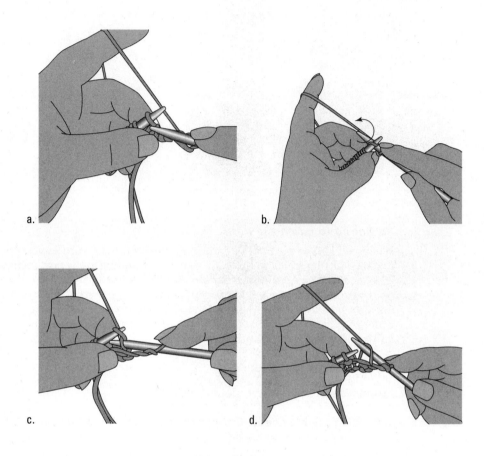

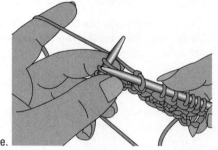

Figure 4-14:
Complete a
Continental
knit stitch.

Illustration by Wiley, Composition Service Graphics

Purling the Continental way

To purl in Continental style, follow these steps:

1. **Make sure the yarn between your LH needle and forefinger is in front of the needle.**

2. **Insert the tip of the RH needle into the first loop on the LH needle from right to left and back to front (see Figure 4-15a).**

3. **Slightly swivel the RH needle tip to the right while the pad of your left forefinger brings the yarn between the needles from right to left and down between the needles (see Figure 4-15b).**

Figure 4-15:
Set up for a
Continental
purl stitch.

 a.  b.

Illustration by Wiley, Composition Service Graphics

4. **Bring the tip of the RH needle with its wrap of yarn through the stitch on the LH needle to the back, away from you (see Figure 4-16a).**

5. **Slip the old stitch off the LH needle, tightening it on the RH needle with the left forefinger (see Figure 4-16b).**

Figure 4-16:
Complete a
Continental
purl stitch.

 a.  b.

Illustration by Wiley, Composition Service Graphics

Joining yarn

Balls of yarn are finite. When you're knitting away and you least expect it, you'll run out of yarn. Time to start the next ball of yarn in a process called *joining yarn*. When possible, start a new ball of yarn on an edge that will be enclosed in a seam, but try *not* to start a new ball of yarn on an edge that will be exposed.

To join yarn at an edge, knit the first stitch of the next row with both ends held together, drop the old strand, and carry on. Or knit the first few stitches with the new yarn only, stop, and tie the two ends together temporarily in a bow to secure them. Either way, leave the ends at least 4 or 5 inches long so that you can weave them in later (see Chapter 17 for finishing instructions).

If you run out of yarn in the middle of a row, your options are the same: Tie a temporary knot with both yarns, leaving 4- or 5-inch ends; or knit the next stitch with both strands, drop the old one, and continue knitting from the new ball.

Binding (or Casting) Off

To finish your knitted piece, you have to *bind off*, which is securing the stitches in the last row worked so that they don't unravel. Like casting on, you can bind off in a variety of ways, each resulting in a different look. Knowing a couple of the available methods can help you choose the right one for your project.

Standard bind-off

The standard bind-off is the most traditional option. It's easy to do if you follow these basic steps:

1. **Knit the first 2 stitches from the LH needle.**

   These become the first 2 stitches on your RH needle (see Figure 4-17a).

2. **With your LH needle in front of your RH needle, insert the LH needle into the first stitch worked on the RH needle (the one on the right, as shown in Figure 4-17b).**

3. **Bring this loop over the second stitch and off the tip of the RH needle, as shown in Figure 4-17c — sort of like leapfrogging over the stitch.**

   At this point, you have 1 stitch bound off and 1 stitch remaining on your RH needle.

4. **Knit the next stitch on the LH needle so that you again have 2 stitches on your RH needle.**

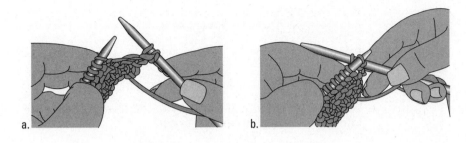

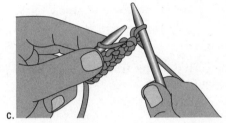

Figure 4-17:
Bind off a
stitch.

Illustration by Wiley, Composition Service Graphics

5. **Repeat Steps 2 through 4 until you have 1 stitch remaining on your RH needle.**

6. **Cut the yarn 6 inches from the needle and pull the tail through the last stitch to lock it.**

   If the piece you've just bound off will be sewn to another piece, leave a tail that's 12 inches or longer for a built-in strand to sew up a seam.

You can watch a video demonstration of the standard bind-off online at `www.dummies.com/go/knittingfd`.

Yarn-over bind-off

The yarn-over bind-off is more elastic than the standard bind-off (see the preceding section) and is a bit more decorative. Use the yarn-over version when you need some stretch to the edge of your project, such as for the cuff of a toe-up sock. It's also useful for the edge of a lace shawl or for ruffles. For details on how to do a yarn over, refer to Chapter 6.

Here's how the yarn-over bind-off works:

1. **Knit 1 stitch, yarn over the RH needle, and then knit 1 more stitch.**

   You now have a stitch, a yarn-over, and a stitch on your RH needle.

2. **With your LH needle in front of your RH needle, insert the LH needle into the yarn over on the RH needle.**

3. **Bring this loop over the second stitch (the last stitch knit) and off the tip of the RH needle.**

   You now have 2 stitches on your RH needle.

4. **With your LH needle in front of your RH needle, insert the LH needle into the first stitch on the RH needle.**

5. **Bring this loop over the second stitch on the needle, leaving 1 stitch on the RH needle.**

6. **Yarn over the RH needle and knit 1.**

7. **Repeat Steps 2 through 6 until you have 1 stitch remaining on your RH needle.**

8. **Cut the yarn 6 inches from the needle and pull the tail through the last stitch to lock it.**

Helpful hints for binding off

Just as casting on evenly gives the bottom edge of your piece a neat appearance, binding off evenly ensures a neat top edge. Here are some suggestions for getting an attractive edge regardless of which bind-off method you use:

✔ The loop below the last bind-off stitch is often (for some mysterious reason) big and baggy. To tighten it up, when you come to the last stitch (1 stitch on the RH needle and 1 stitch on the LH needle), slip the last stitch on the RH needle back to the LH needle. Insert the tip of the RH needle into the left stitch on the LH needle and bring it over the right stitch and off the needle — binding off in the reverse direction. Cut the yarn and draw the tail through the remaining loop.

✔ Unless told otherwise, always bind off according to the stitch pattern given. If you'd normally be working a purl row, purl the stitches as you bind off instead of knitting them. This approach is often referred to as *binding off in pattern.*

✔ Don't bind off too tightly (which, unfortunately, is easy to do). Knitting should be elastic, especially around neck edges if you want to be able to get a sweater on and off comfortably (and who doesn't want that?). To avoid a tight and inelastic bound edge, try working the bind-off row on a needle one or more sizes larger than what you've been using.

Chapter 5

Basic Stitches You'll Use Again and Again

· ·

In This Chapter

▶ Practicing common stitch patterns

▶ Using popular rib stitches to add interest and stretch

· ·

When you know how to knit and purl (refer to Chapter 4), you can combine these stitches in a seemingly endless variety of textured stitch patterns. The stitch patterns in this chapter make a good starting point. You can find more stitch patterns in Appendix A.

The best way to understand how knit-and-purl patterns work is to knit them up yourself. Using a medium-weight, solid-color yarn in a light shade, cast on a multiple of the stitches required for the pattern (but no less than 24) and knit up about 4 inches in the pattern. You can save your swatches in a knitting notebook for later reference, or you can sew them together to create a patchwork scarf (see Chapter 20 for swatch project ideas).

Go-To Stitches: Garter, Stockinette, and Seed Stitches

Knitting and purling, which we cover in Chapter 4, open the door to all sorts of patterns that just involve alternating between knit and purl stitches. But as a beginning knitter, you really only need to know two patterns: *garter stitch,* which you create by knitting (or purling) every row, and *stockinette stitch,* which you create by alternating a knit row with a purl row. Another stitch all knitters should have in their repertoire is *seed stitch.* Although a little more complicated than garter and stockinette stitches, it creates an interesting texture and appears in many patterns.

Knits and purls have a quirky but predictable relationship to each other. When lined up horizontally, the purled rows stand out from the knitted rows. Arranged in vertical patterns, like ribbing, the purl stitches recede and the knit stitches come forward, creating an elastic fabric. When worked in a balanced manner (meaning the same number of knits and purls appear on each side of the fabric), as in seed stitch and its variations, the fabric is stable — it lies flat and doesn't have the tendency to roll in on the edges. These qualities make seed and moss stitches, as well as garter stitch, good choices for borders that need to lie flat and not pull in as ribbed borders do.

Garter stitch

Garter stitch is the most basic of all knitted fabrics. It's made by knitting every row. (You can create garter stitch by purling every row, too. Neat, huh?) You can recognize garter stitch by the horizontal ridges formed by the tops of the knitted loops on every other row (see Figure 5-1).

For a demonstration of garter stitch, check out the video at www.dummies.com/go/knittingfd.

Figure 5-1:
Garter
stitch.

Photograph by Wiley, Composition Services Graphics

Garter stitch has a lot going for it in addition to being easy to create. It's reversible, lies flat, and has a pleasant rustic look. Unlike most knitted fabrics, garter stitch has a square gauge, meaning that there are usually twice as many rows as stitches in 1 inch. To count rows in garter stitch, count the ridges and multiply by 2, or count the ridges by 2s.

Garter stitch has a hanging gauge that stretches more *vertically*. Therefore, gravity and the weight of the garter stitch piece will pull on the fabric and actually make it longer. This is important to keep in mind when you're making a garment that you want to fit properly and not grow two times larger after an hour of wearing it. Refer to Chapter 3 for info on checking gauge.

Stockinette stitch

When you alternate a knit row with a purl row (knit the first row, purl the second, knit the third, purl the fourth, and so on), you create *stockinette stitch;* see Figure 5-2. You see stockinette stitch everywhere: in scarves, socks, sweaters, blankets, hats — you name it. In fact, most beginning and intermediate designs incorporate stockinette stitch.

Figure 5-2:
Stockinette
stitch
showing the
knit side.

Photograph by Wiley, Composition Services Graphics

In written knitting instructions, stockinette stitch (abbreviated St st) appears like this (if you're unfamiliar with the abbreviations, refer to Chapter 3):

> **Row 1 (RS):** Knit.
>
> **Row 2 (WS):** Purl.
>
> Rep Rows 1 and 2 for desired length.

Visit www.dummies.com/go/knittingfd for a video demonstration of stockinette stitch.

Stockinette fabric looks and behaves in a particular way. To successfully incorporate this stitch into your knitting repertoire, pay attention to the following:

✔ **Stockinette stitch has a right side and a wrong side (though, of course, either side may be the "right" side, depending on the intended design).** The right side is typically the smooth side, called *stockinette* or *knit.* On this side, the stitches look like small V's (see Figure 5-3). The bumpy side of stockinette stitch fabric, shown in Figure 5-4, is called *reverse stockinette* or *purl.* The highlighted stitches in Figure 5-4 are the back of the highlighted knit stitches in Figure 5-3.

If you're working in stockinette stitch and you lose track of whether you knit the last row or purled it, not to worry. You can tell what to do next by looking at your knitting. Hold your needles in the ready-to-knit position (with the LH needle holding the stitches to be worked) and look at what's facing you. If you're looking at the knit (smooth) side, you knit. If you're looking at the purl (bumpy) side, you purl. A good mantra to say to yourself is *knit the knits and purl the purls.*

✔ **Stockinette fabric curls on the edges.** The top and bottom (horizontal) edges curl toward the front or smooth side. The side (vertical) edges roll toward the bumpy side. Sweater designers frequently use this rolling feature deliberately to create rolled hems or cuffs, and you can create easy cords or straps simply by knitting a very narrow band in stockinette stitch (say, 4 or 6 stitches across).

But when you want the piece to lie flat, you need to counteract this tendency by working the 3 or 4 stitches on the edge in some stitch that lies flat (like garter stitch, discussed in the preceding section, or seed stitch, discussed in the next section).

To figure out the gauge of a swatch knitted in stockinette stitch, count the V's on the smooth side or right side. They're easier to see and distinguish than the bumps on the wrong side. Of course, if you find the bumps easier to count, it's okay to do so.

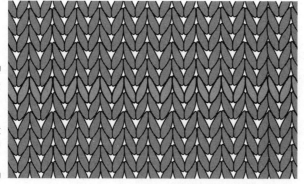

Figure 5-3:
Stockinette stitch showing the knit (or smooth) side.

Illustration by Wiley, Composition Services Graphics

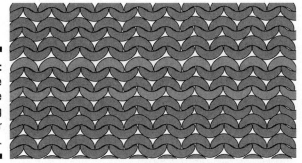

Illustration by Wiley, Composition Services Graphics

The names *garter stitch* and *stockinette stitch* date from the 1500s, when hand-knit stockings were a major industry in England. Garter stitch was used at the top of the stocking, where it needed to expand for the thigh, and stockinette (or *stocking stitch*) was used for the fitted leg portion.

Seed stitch

Seed stitch, shown in Figure 5-5, consists of single knits and purls alternating horizontally and vertically. Its name refers to the way the knitted fabric looks: The little purl bumps look like scattered seeds. Like garter stitch, seed stitch lies flat, making it a good edging for a sweater border and cuffs. It also looks the same from both sides, making it a nice choice for scarves and other pieces of which both sides are visible.

Seed stitch *stitch gauge* tends to be wider than a stockinette stitch stitch gauge. This is important to note if you plan to mix stitch patterns but want to maintain the same measurements in both patterns.

When knitting a stitch, the loose tail of yarn is in *back* of your work. When purling a stitch, the yarn is in *front* of your work. As you switch back and forth within a row, as in seed stitch, you need to move your yarn to the front or to the back as appropriate between the needles. If you forget to do so, you create an unintentional yarn over (refer to Chapter 6), resulting in an extra stitch on the next row and a hole in the work. Unfortunately for novice knitters, who often forget to move the yarn accordingly, instructions don't explicitly tell you to bring your yarn to the front or back of your work. They assume that you know where the yarn should be when you're about to knit or purl a stitch. As you practice the patterns that combine both knit and purl stitches, make sure your yarn is in the proper position for each stitch before you start it, and refer to Chapter 4 for a quick review if necessary.

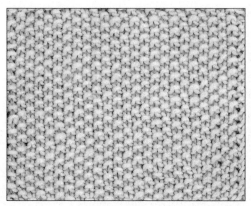

Figure 5-5:
Seed stitch.

Photograph by Wiley, Composition Services Graphics

To create seed stitch:

Cast on an even number of sts.

Row 1: * K1, p1; rep from * to end of row.

Row 2: * P1, k1; rep from * to end of row.

Rep Rows 1 and 2 for pattern.

When working seed stitch, you alternate between knit and purl stitches in each row. The trick to creating the little "seeds" is to knit in the purl stitches of the previous row and purl in the knit stitches of the previous row. For variations on seed stitch, see Appendix A.

For a video demonstration of seed stitch, check out www.dummies.com/go/knittingfd.

If you're working in seed stitch and you lose track of whether you knit the last stitch or purled it, don't worry. You can tell what to do next by looking at your knitting. Hold your needles in the ready-to-knit position (with the LH needle holding the stitches to be worked or the ones you're working on) and look at what's facing you. On the LH needle, if you're looking at a knit stitch, you purl. If you're looking at a purl (bumpy) stitch, you knit. A good mantra to say to yourself is *knit the purls and purl the knits*.

Adding Stretch with Ribbed Stitches

Knit ribs are textured vertical stripes. Ribbing is made by alternating columns of knit stitches with columns of purl stitches. Instead of alternating knit rows with purl rows, as you do in stockinette stitch, when you make a ribbed pattern, you change from knit stitches to purl stitches *within* a row, similar to seed stitch. However, unlike seed stitch, a ribbed pattern has a knit made into a knit of the previous row and a purl made into a purl of the previous row, thus making the columns of stitches.

Ribbing is the edging par excellence on most sweaters because of its elasticity; it stretches to let you in and out of cuffs and neckbands and then springs back into place to hug you. It's also used for the body of many pieces, like sweaters, scarves, and hats.

Measuring gauge of a ribbed fabric is a bit subjective in that knowing how much to stretch a ribbed fabric before measuring for stitch and row gauge is entirely up to the knitter. Some patterns state whether the ribbed fabric should not be stretched, be slightly stretched, or be stretched to fit comfortably when taking gauge; you have to decide what each one of those means for you. A good way to start is to see how stretched the finished ribbing is in the pattern picture and to measure the gauge swatch with about the same stretch. In the end, it doesn't hurt to know all of these measurements, so take the time to measure each on your gauge swatch.

A pattern may have only a stockinette stitch gauge listed, even though it's a ribbed pattern stitch. In those cases, a ribbed gauge swatch isn't necessary for measuring purposes, but you should still make a ribbed pattern swatch to see whether the needle and yarn choices create a finished fabric that's desirable.

The most common ribbing combinations are those that are even (that is, the rib uses the same number of knitted versus purl columns). Examples include 1 x 1 ribbing, in which single knit stitches alternate with single purl stitches, creating very narrow columns; and 2 x 2 ribbing, which alternates 2 knit stitches with 2 purl stitches. Although even columns are among the most common ribbed patterns, the columns don't have to be even. Many attractive and functional ribs have wider knit columns than purl columns.

The elasticity of the final ribbed fabric is affected by the following:

- **Column width:** The narrower the column of stitches, the more elastic the ribbing.
- **Needle size:** Bigger needles result in less elasticity. Also, because ribbed edgings are intended to hug the body, you generally work them on needles one or two sizes smaller than the ones used for the body of the project.

The following sections explain how to create the most common ribbing patterns. Head to Appendix A for more elaborate ribbings.

As you switch back and forth within a row, you need to move your yarn to the front or to the back as appropriate between the needles.

1 x 1 ribbing

The 1 x 1 rib pattern alternates single knit stitches with single purl stitches to create narrow ribs. Figure 5-6 shows this ribbing stretched out a bit so you can see the purl rows (the horizontal lines in the background). When the knitting isn't stretched out, the knit columns contract, hiding the purl columns.

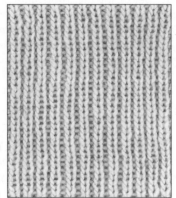

Figure 5-6:
1 x 1 ribbing.

Photograph by Wiley, Composition Services Graphics

To create 1 x 1 ribbing:

Cast on an even number of sts.

Work every row: * K1, p1; rep from * to end of row.

Rep this row for the length of your piece.

You can go to www.dummies.com/go/knittingfd for a video demonstration of ribbing stitches.

After the first row, you can look at your knitting to tell whether you should be making a knit stitch or a purl stitch. If the next stitch on your LH needle is a purl (bump) stitch, purl it. If it's a knit stitch, knit it.

2 x 2 ribbing

As you can see in Figure 5-7, 2 x 2 ribbing alternates 2 knit stitches with 2 purl stitches. It pulls in slightly less than 1 x 1 ribbing.

Figure 5-7:
2 x 2 ribbing.

Photograph by Wiley, Composition Services Graphics

To create 2 x 2 ribbing:

Cast on a multiple of 4 sts.

Work every row: * K2, p2; rep from * to end of row.

Rep this row for the length of your piece.

Note: If you want your piece to begin and end on 2 knit stitches, add 2 to the multiple that you cast on at the beginning.

4 x 2 and 2 x 4 ribbing

There's no reason to keep knit ribs and purl ribs the same number of stitches. You can work ribs in uneven combinations, such as 4 x 2, 2 x 4, and so on. Figure 5-8 shows a 4 x 2 ribbing.

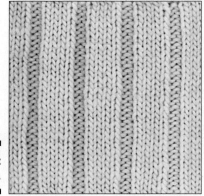

Figure 5-8:
4 x 2 ribbing.

Photograph by Wiley, Composition Services Graphics

To create 4 x 2 ribbing:

> Cast on a multiple of 6 sts, plus 4 sts. (You can work this pattern over a multiple of 6 stitches, but it won't be symmetrical.)
>
> **Row 1:** * K4, p2; rep from * to last 4 sts, k4.
>
> **Row 2:** * P4, k2; rep from * to last 4 sts, p4.
>
> Rep Rows 1 and 2 for pattern.

If you turn this swatch over, you'll have a very different looking pattern — thin vertical stripes instead of thick ones.

4 x 4 ribbing

The 4 x 4 rib shown in Figure 5-9 gives you a vertical stripe pattern that pulls in very little. It's symmetrical in that it's a simple alternation of 4 knit stitches with 4 purl stitches.

Figure 5-9:
4 x 4 ribbing.

Photograph by Wiley, Composition Services Graphics

To create 4 x 4 ribbing:

> Cast on a multiple of 4 sts, plus 4 sts.
>
> **Row 1:** * K4, p4; rep from * to last 4 sts, k4.
>
> **Row 2:** * P4, k4; rep from * to last 4 sts, end p4.
>
> Rep Rows 1 and 2 for pattern.

Chapter 6

Techniques Every Knitter Should Know

In This Chapter

▶ Manipulating stitches: Slipping, doing yarn overs, and twisting

▶ Making increases and decreases

*P*laying around with knit and purl patterns introduced in Chapter 5 can keep you busy for a long time, but you can do a lot more with knitted stitches. Cables, lace, and color work all lie ahead — literally (they're covered in Part III) and figuratively. As you begin to explore stitch patterns and follow patterns for projects and garments, you'll want to familiarize yourself with the different stitch maneuvers that crop up in instructions for more demanding knitted fabrics.

For projects that give you the opportunity to practice the maneuvers that we cover in this chapter, head to Chapter 9.

Slipping Stitches

If your directions tell you to *slip a stitch* (abbreviated sl st), they mean for you to move a stitch from the left-hand (LH) needle to the right-hand (RH) needle without knitting or purling it *and* without changing its orientation (that is, without twisting it).

To slip a stitch, insert the RH needle *purlwise* (as if you were going to purl) into the first stitch on the LH needle and slip it off the LH needle onto the RH needle. Unless your instructions specifically tell you to slip a stitch *knitwise,* always slip a stitch as if you were going to purl it. Figure 6-1 shows stitches being slipped both purlwise and knitwise.

Visit www.dummies.com/go/knittingfd for a video demonstration of slipping stitches purlwise.

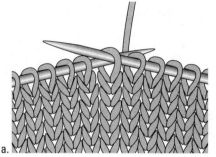
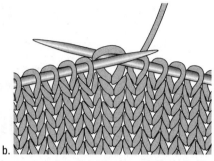

Figure 6-1:
Slipping
stitches purl-
wise (a) and
knitwise (b).

Slipped stitches are used in different ways. You frequently run across them in methods for decreasing stitches — when you want to reduce the number of stitches you have on your needle. They also form the basis of a family of stitch patterns. Like garter stitch, slip-stitch patterns are stable and lie flat — and they're a breeze to knit.

Making a Yarn Over

A *yarn over* (abbreviated yo) is a way of making an extra stitch on your needle and creating a deliberate little hole in your fabric. Yarn overs are an indispensable part of lace knitting (see Chapter 12 for more about using yarn overs in lace). They have a multitude of other applications as well, such as decorative increases, buttonholes, and novelty stitch patterns.

To make a yarn over, you simply bring the knitting yarn (the "over" strand) over the needle between 2 existing stitches on one row and then work that strand as a stitch when you work your way back to it in the next row. You can watch an online video demonstration of a yarn over at www.dummies.com/go/knittingfd.

At some point in your knitting experience, you may have accidentally created a yarn over when you forgot to bring the yarn between the needles from the back to the front when purling or from the front to the back when knitting. If you can do it accidentally, surely you can make a yarn over on purpose. However, until you get used to them, yarn overs can be a little confusing. Here are the things to remember in all cases:

✔ **The working yarn starts in front of the needle.** Sometimes it's already there (if you've been purling); sometimes you have to put it there deliberately (if you've been knitting).

✔ **You wrap the yarn around the needle from front to back and work the next stitch as normal.** Sometimes the pattern instructions ask you to wrap the yarn twice — or more times — around the needle to make a bigger hole. A double yarn over is usually written *yo twice*.

✔ **As you work the row following the yarn over row, you'll recognize the yarn over by the big hole that suddenly appears on your needle where a stitch should be.** Above the hole is the strand of yarn that you've crossed over the needle. Think of the strand as a stitch and knit or purl it as you normally would.

✔ **You will have 1 extra stitch for every yarn over you do.** For example, if you start with 4 stitches and then knit 2, yarn over, knit 2, on the next row, you'll have 5 stitches rather than 4.

To help you keep yarn overs straight, the following sections break down how to make a yarn over when it goes between 2 knit stitches, between a knit stitch and a purl stitch, between 2 purl stitches, and between a purl stitch and a knit stitch.

Between 2 knit stitches

To make a yarn over between 2 knit stitches (which you'd encounter in a pattern as k1, yo, k1), follow these steps:

1. **Knit the first stitch.**

2. **Bring the yarn forward between the needles into purl position.**

3. **Knit the next stitch on the needle.**

   When you knit the next stitch, the yarn automatically crosses the RH needle, forming a yarn over (see Figure 6-2).

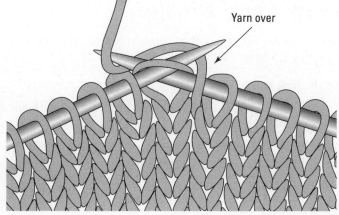

Yarn over

Figure 6-2: Making a yarn over between 2 knit stitches.

Illustration by Wiley, Composition Service Graphics

Between a knit and a purl stitch

Here's how to make a yarn over that follows a knit stitch and precedes a purl stitch (which you'd encounter in a pattern as k1, yo, p1):

1. **Knit the first stitch.**

2. **Bring the yarn to the front into the purl position, wrap it back over the top of the RH needle, and return it to the front into purl position again.**

   Basically you're just wrapping the yarn once around the RH needle from the front.

3. **Purl the next stitch (see Figure 6-3).**

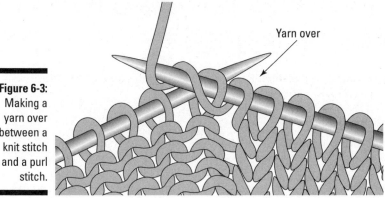

Figure 6-3:
Making a
yarn over
between a
knit stitch
and a purl
stitch.

Yarn over

Illustration by Wiley, Composition Service Graphics

Between 2 purl stitches

To make a yarn over between 2 purl stitches (which you'd encounter in a pattern as p1, yo, p1), just do the following:

1. **Purl the first stitch.**

2. **Wrap the yarn around the RH needle front to back to front so that it ends up in purl position again.**

3. **Purl the next stitch (see Figure 6-4.)**

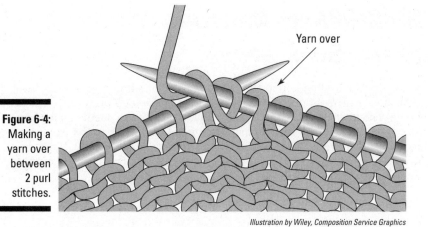

Figure 6-4:
Making a yarn over between 2 purl stitches.

Illustration by Wiley, Composition Service Graphics

Between a purl stitch and a knit stitch

To make a yarn over that follows a purl stitch and precedes a knit stitch (which you'd encounter in a pattern as p1, yo, k1), follow these steps:

1. **Purl the first stitch and leave the yarn in the front of your work.**

2. **Knit the next stitch.**

   The yarn automatically crosses the RH needle when you knit this next stitch (see Figure 6-5).

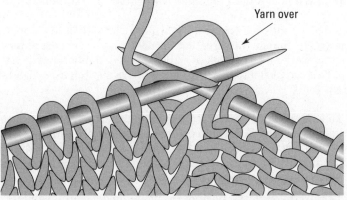

Figure 6-5:
Making a yarn over between a purl stitch and a knit stitch.

Illustration by Wiley, Composition Service Graphics

Twisting Stitches: Knitting through the Back Loop

When stitches are lined up in the ready-to-work position, they have a front and a back. The front of the stitch is the part of the loop on *your* side of the needle. The back of the stitch is, well, on the side of the needle facing away from you. When you knit in the usual fashion, you work into the front of the loop; you insert your RH needle into the stitch from left to right, lifting and spreading the front of the loop — the side of the loop on your side of the needle — when you insert your needle (see Figure 6-6a).

Figure 6-6:
You can knit into the front (a) or the back (b) of stitches.

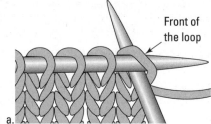 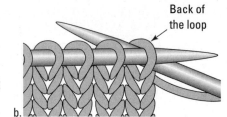

Front of the loop

Back of the loop

a.   b.

Illustration by Wiley, Composition Service Graphics

By *knitting through back of the loop* (abbreviated ktbl), you twist the stitch and create a different effect. Stitch patterns that use twisted stitches have an etched, linear quality. On a background of reverse stockinette stitch, a vertical or wavy line of twisted stitches stands out in sharp definition. Frequently, you find twisted stitches combined with cables in traditional Aran patterns.

If your instructions tell you to knit through the back of the loop, they're asking you to change the direction from which your needle enters the stitch. When you work into the back of a stitch, you're deliberately twisting the stitch. You can purl into the front and back of a stitch as well, as shown in Figure 6-7.

- ✔ **To knit through the back of the loop:** Insert your needle from right to left, with the RH needle *behind* the LH needle, lifting and spreading the back of the loop — the side of the loop on the opposite side of the needle (see Figure 6-6b). Then wrap the yarn around the RH needle and pull a new loop through.

- ✔ **To purl through the back of the loop:** Insert your needle through the back of the loop from right to left (see Figure 6-7b) and purl as normal.

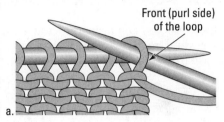

Front (purl side) of the loop

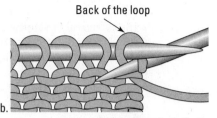

Back of the loop

Figure 6-7: Purling into the front (a) and the back (b) of stitches.

a.

b.

Illustration by Wiley, Composition Service Graphics

If you find you're twisting stitches without even trying (or intending) to, check your yarn position. Wrapping the yarn around the RH needle in the opposite direction when working a stitch results in a twisted stitch on the next row. Just correct the wrapping direction, and you'll be on your way to perfect stitches.

Abbreviations can vary from pattern to pattern. Some patterns use ktbl to mean "knit through back of loop"; others use k-b to mean the same thing. What can be even more confusing is that many patterns use k-b to mean "knit in the stitch below" (a technique discussed in the later section "Knitting into the stitch below"). Before you start, check your pattern to see what its abbreviations stand for.

Working Increases

Not all knitted pieces are square. Being able to increase (abbreviated inc) or decrease (abbreviated dec) stitches along the edge or within the body of a knitted piece enables you to create knitted pieces with edges that taper and expand. When you increase stitches, you add them to your needle. When you decrease stitches, you get rid of stitches on your needle.

As with everything else in knitting, you find several ways to increase and decrease stitches. Some methods are almost invisible, and others are decorative and meant to be seen. And because increases and decreases are often worked as pairs (picture adding stitches at either end of your needle when you're shaping a sleeve), if one slants to the right on the right side of your work, the other slants to the left on the wrong side.

The following sections outline the ways to work increases into your work. Keep in mind that each method has a different appearance. So how do you know which one to use? If the increase is part of a fabric stitch pattern, the pattern will almost always tell you how to make the increase. Other times, you have to decide for yourself. Having a few techniques up your sleeve gives you the flex-ibility to decide which increase will look best in your current project.

Various knitting patterns require that you knit a single increase, work a double increase, or distribute several increases along a given row. Try some of the fundamental techniques in this section to get a firm handle on your choices.

Bar increase, or knit in front and back

So-called because it leaves a telltale horizontal bar under the increased stitch, the *bar increase* is best for increases worked at the edge of your knitting, where it will be enclosed in a seam. Knitting directions for the bar increase read, "Knit 1 into the front and back of the stitch" or "k1f&b."

Check out a video demonstration of knitting a bar increase at www.dummies.com/go/knittingfd.

Here's how you make a bar increase, or k1f&b, when you're working on the knit side:

1. **Knit 1 stitch as you normally would, but don't slide the old stitch off the LH needle.**

2. **Bring the tip of the RH needle behind the LH needle and enter the back of the same stitch from right to left.**

   Refer to the earlier section "Twisting Stitches: Knitting through the Back Loop" for information about the front and back of a stitch.

3. **Knit the stitch as normal and slide it off the LH needle.**

   You've worked 2 stitches from a single stitch.

To make a bar increase, or p1f&b, when you're working on the purl side, follow these steps:

1. **Purl 1 stitch as you normally would, but don't slide the old stitch off the LH needle.**

2. **Keeping the RH needle behind the LH one, insert the tip of the RH needle through the back of the loop of the same stitch, entering it from left to right.**

3. **Purl that stitch again and slide it off the LH needle.**

   You've worked 2 stitches from a single stitch.

If you're using this bar increase several stitches in from the edge as part of a paired increase, adjust the position of the stitch in which you make the increase so that the bar shows up in the same place on each side.

Working a make 1

To work the *make 1* increase (abbreviated m1), you create a new, separate stitch between 2 stitches that are already on the needle. When you get to the point where you want to make an increase, pull the LH and RH needle slightly apart. You'll notice a horizontal strand of yarn, called the *running thread,* connecting the first stitch on each needle. You use the running thread to make the new stitch. The increased stitch will be a twisted stitch that crosses to the right or to the left and leaves no little hole. (Refer to the earlier section "Twisting Stitches: Knitting through the Back Loop" for details on how twisted stitches work.)

The make 1 increase pulls the stitches on either side of the running thread tight and therefore isn't ideal for increasing multiple times within the same row.

After you make the increase, check to make sure that it's twisted in the direction you intended. If it isn't, undo your new stitch — it will only unravel as far as the running thread — and try it again.

Twisting to the right

When you're working on the knit side and want your make 1 increase to twist to the right, work to the point between 2 stitches where you want to increase. Then follow these steps:

1. **Bring the tip of the LH needle under the running thread from back to front.**

   The running thread will be draped over the LH needle as if it were a stitch (see Figure 6-8a).

2. **Insert the RH needle through the draped strand from left to right (see Figure 6-8b) and knit as normal.**

Figure 6-8:
Knitting
a make 1
increase
that twists
to the right.

a.   b.

Illustration by Wiley, Composition Service Graphics

If you want to work a right-twisting make 1 increase on the purl side, follow the preceding steps, except change Step 2 by purling the strand by going into the front loop (the part that's closest to you) from right to left and purling as normal (see Figure 6-9).

Figure 6-9:
Purling a make 1 increase that twists to the right.

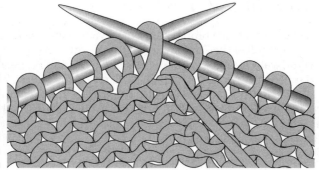

Illustration by Wiley, Composition Service Graphics

You can turn a make 1 into a decorative eyelet (a little hole) increase by knitting or purling into the running thread without twisting it.

Twisting to the left

If you're working on the knit side and want your make 1 increase to twist to the left, work to the point between 2 stitches where you want to increase. Then do the following:

1. **Insert the tip of the LH needle under the running thread from front to back (see Figure 6-10a).**

2. **With the RH needle, knit the strand through the back (see Figure 6-10b).**

Figure 6-10:
Knitting a make 1 increase that twists to the left.

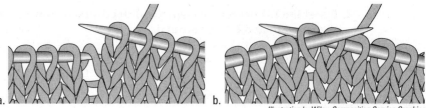

a. b.

Illustration by Wiley, Composition Service Graphics

Follow the same steps when you want your make 1 increase to twist to the left from the purl side, except change Step 2 by inserting the RH needle through the back loop from left to right and purling as normal.

Knitting into the stitch below

Knitting into the stitch below is a technique often used for increasing stitches. If your instructions tell you to "knit (or purl) into the stitch below," often abbreviated k1b or k-b (or p1b or p-b for purling), follow these steps (adjust them to purl into the stitch below):

1. **Insert your needle into the stitch directly below the next stitch on the LH needle (see Figure 6-11); then wrap and knit as you normally would.**

   This step is the increase stitch.

2. **Knit the stitch on the LH needle.**

   You now have 2 stitches where 1 used to be. If you look at the purl side of your work, you'll see 2 purl bumps for the stitch you've made.

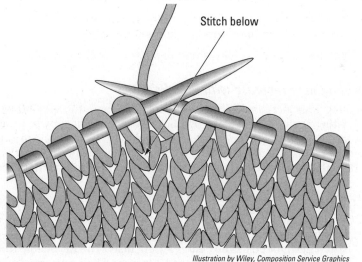

Stitch below

Figure 6-11: The stitch you knit in when you knit into the stitch below.

Illustration by Wiley, Composition Service Graphics

Making a double increase

Some occasions in knitting — in certain stitch patterns or when working a raglan sweater from the neck down — require you to increase 2 stitches in the same place. This task is called *working a double increase,* and it often uses an existing stitch as the increase point.

Doubling your increase with a yarn over

Doubling your increase with a yarn over results in 3 stitches being made from 1 stitch. To use this technique, work to the stitch in which you plan to make the increase and then follow these steps:

1. **Insert your RH needle as if to knit.**

2. **Wrap the yarn around the needle and bring the new loop through to the front, but don't slide the old stitch off the LH needle.**

3. **Bring the yarn between the needles to the front.**

4. **With the yarn in front and down, insert the RH needle as if to knit into the same stitch again.**

5. **Bring the yarn over the RH needle to the back.**

6. **Wrap the yarn around the tip of the RH needle as you normally would, pull the loop through, and slide the old loop off.**

   You'll see 3 stitches clustered together on your RH needle.

Doubling your increase with a make 1

Doubling your increase with a make 1 makes a new stitch on either side of an existing center stitch. Make the increase symmetrical by twisting the m1 increase before the center stitch to the right and twisting the m1 increase after the center stitch to the left. To create a double increase with a make 1, work to the stitch marked for the increase and then follow these steps:

1. **Work a m1 that twists to the right.**

   As in the m1 increase presented earlier in this chapter, insert your LH needle under the running thread between the stitch just made and the stitch designated as the center stitch. Insert the RH needle from left to right through the lifted strand stitch, and knit as normal (refer to Figure 6-8).

2. **Knit the next (center) stitch as normal.**

3. **Work a m1 that twists to the left.**

   With your LH needle, pick up the running thread between the knitted center stitch and the stitch that follows it; then knit the lifted strand through the back (refer to Figure 6-9).

For more ways to work a double increase, check out *Knitting from the Top* by Barbara Walker (Schoolhouse Press). She gives a whopping ten ways to make a double increase.

Increasing at several points in a single row

Patterns sometimes ask you to increase several stitches evenly across a row. It's up to you to figure out the best spacing. Here's how:

1. **Take the number of stitches to be added and add 1.**

   This step gives you the number of spaces between increases.

2. **Divide the total number of stitches on your needle by the number of spaces between the increases.**

   For example, if you have 40 stitches and you need to increase 4 stitches, you'll have five 8-stitch sections between the increases. If your pattern calls for you to work bar increases into existing stitches, make your increases in every 8th stitch across the row. When you're counting the stitches between increases, don't include the increased stitches.

If your numbers don't come out evenly and you have a remainder of several stitches, you can

- ✔ Divvy up the extra stitches and knit them before the first increase and after the last increase.

- ✔ Alternate, working an extra stitch into every other section of stitches between increases until you've used up the extras.

Graph paper is great to have on hand for charting out increases — and for all other manner of knitting math.

Full-fashioning

You can work increases and decreases on the edge or several stitches in from the edge. If a series of increases or decreases is worked 2 or more stitches from the edge, it creates a visible line, and the shaping is described as "full-fashion." This shaping technique is peculiar to knits and sometimes distinguishes a sweater that's cut and sewn from knitted fabric from one that has been knitted to shape. Working increases or decreases several stitches from the edge is both attractive and makes it easier to sew knitted pieces together because you have two untampered stitches at the edges to seam between.

Doing Decreases

A decrease is a method for getting rid of a stitch on your needle. You use decreases for shaping at the edges and/or in the middle of a knitted piece. They're also used in conjunction with increases in various stitch patterns, most notably in lace.

A decreased stitch looks like 1 stitch overlapping another. Depending on the design you're working with, you can make your decreases slant to the left or right. When a stitch overlaps to the right, the decrease slants to the right. When a stitch overlaps to the left, the decrease slants to the left.

Knitting 2 stitches together

When you knit 2 stitches together (abbreviated k2tog), they become 1 stitch. The stitch on the left overlaps the one on the right, and the decrease slants to the right. If you're working decreases in pairs (on either side of a neckline you're shaping, for example), use the k2tog on one side and the ssk decrease (see the later section "Slip, slip, knit") on the other side.

You can find a video demonstration of knitting 2 stitches together at www.dummies.com/go/knittingfd.

Here's how to knit 2 stitches together on the right (knit) side of your knitted fabric:

1. **Insert the RH needle knitwise into the first 2 stitches on the LH needle at the same time.**

2. **Knit them together as if they were 1 stitch (see Figure 6-12).**

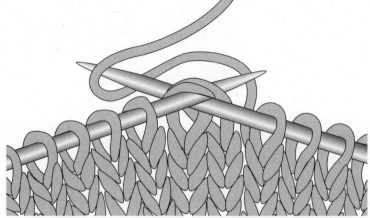

Figure 6-12:
Knitting 2
stitches
together
(k2tog).

Illustration by Wiley, Composition Service Graphics

Purling 2 stitches together

Although most knitting patterns have you decrease on right-side rows only, sometimes you may be asked to work a decrease from the purl side. When you do, you can purl 2 stitches together (abbreviated p2tog) instead of knitting them together. When you look at a p2tog decrease from the knit side, the stitches slant to the right, just as they do with a k2tog decrease.

When you need to work a single p2tog decrease on the wrong (purl) side of your knitting, follow these steps:

1. **Insert the RH needle purlwise into the next 2 stitches on the LH needle (see Figure 6-13a).**

2. **Purl the 2 stitches together as if they were 1 stitch (see Figures 6-13b and 6-13c).**

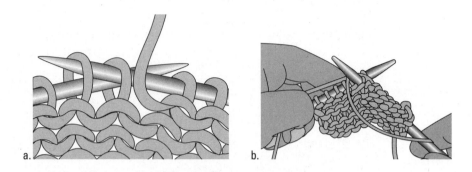

Figure 6-13:
Purling 2
stitches
together
(p2tog).

Illustration by Wiley, Composition Service Graphics

Slip, slip, knit

Slip, slip, knit (abbreviated ssk) results in a left-slanting decrease. The ssk decrease is the mirror image of k2tog: It slants to the left. Use it when you want to work symmetrical decreases.

To work a ssk on the knit side, follow these steps:

1. **Slip the first stitch on the LH needle (as if to knit) to the RH needle without actually knitting it.**

2. **Do the same with the next stitch.**

   The 2 slipped stitches should look like the stitches in Figure 6-14a.

3. **Insert the LH needle into the front loops of these stitches (left to right), as in Figure 6-14b.**

4. **Wrap the yarn in the usual way around the RH needle and knit the 2 slipped stitches together.**

Figure 6-14:
Working a slip, slip, knit (ssk) decrease.

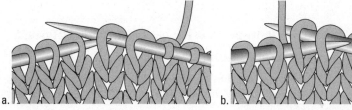

Illustration by Wiley, Composition Service Graphics

To complete this same decrease on the purl side — called a *slip, slip, purl* (ssp) — follow these steps:

1. **Slip the first stitch on the LH needle (as if to knit) to the RH needle.**

2. **Do the same to the next stitch.**

3. **Keeping the 2 slipped stitches facing in this direction, transfer them back to the LH needle.**

4. **Purl the 2 stitches together through the back loops (see Figure 6-15).**

Figure 6-15:
Purling 2 slipped stitches through the back of the loops.

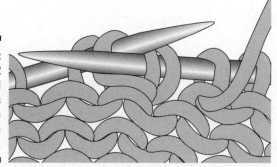

Illustration by Wiley, Composition Service Graphics

Pass slipped stitch over

Psso refers to *pass slipped stitch over*, a less attractive version of the left-slanting ssk decrease but one that's still used in certain stitch patterns and in double decreases (decreasing 2 stitches at once). Essentially, psso makes a bound-off stitch in the middle of a row. You can work it from the knit or purl side of your work.

Here's how to work a psso on the knit side:

1. **Slip 1 stitch knitwise from the LH needle to the RH needle.**

2. **Knit the next stitch on the LH needle.**

3. **Insert the tip of the LH needle into the slipped stitch and bring it over the knitted stitch and off the needle as if you were binding off.**

To work a psso on the purl side, do the following:

1. **Purl 1 stitch.**

2. **Slip the next stitch knitwise to the RH needle and return it in this changed direction to the LH needle.**

3. **Transfer the purled stitch (from Step 1) from the RH needle to the LH needle.**

4. **Insert the RH needle into the slipped stitch and bring it over the purled stitch and off the needle.**

"Pass a stitch over" means to bind it off.

Making double decreases

Sometimes you need to decrease 2 stitches at the same time. Certain stitch patterns depend on this *double decrease* for its effect, and sometimes it's necessary in garment shaping. Like single decreases, the double decrease can slant to the left or right. Or it can create a single vertical line at the decrease point.

Right-slanting double decrease

To work a right-slanting double decrease on the knit side, follow these steps:

1. **Work a ssk.**

   Slip 2 stitches knitwise one at a time to the RH needle, insert the LH needle into the front of the loops, and knit them together. (Flip to the earlier section "Slip, slip, knit" for instructions on making a ssk decrease.)

2. **Slip the stitch you just worked back to the LH needle.**

3. **Bring the second stitch on the LH needle over the decreased stitch and off the needle.**

4. **Return the decreased stitch to the RH needle.**

To work a right-slanting double decrease on the purl side, do the following:

1. **Slip the next stitch from the LH needle to the RH needle.**

2. **Purl the next 2 stitches together.**

   Refer to the earlier section "Purling 2 stitches together" to find out how to do so.

3. **Pass the slipped stitch over the decreased stitch.**

Left-slanting double decrease

To work a left-slanting double decrease on the knit side, follow these steps:

1. **Slip the next stitch on the LH needle as if to knit.**

2. **Knit the next 2 stitches together.**

   Refer to the earlier section "Knitting 2 stitches together" to find the instructions for doing so.

3. **Bring the slipped stitch over the decrease stitch as if you were binding off.**

To work a left-slanting double decrease on the purl side, do the following:

1. **Purl 2 stitches together.**

   Flip back to the section "Purling 2 stitches together" to find out how to do so.

2. **Slip this decreased stitch back to the LH needle.**

3. **With the RH needle, bring the second stitch on the LH needle over the decreased stitch and off the needle.**

4. **Return the decreased stitch to the RH needle.**

Vertical double decrease

This double decrease creates a vertical line rather than a line that slants to the left or right. To make a vertical double decrease, follow these steps:

1. **Slip the first 2 stitches on the LH needle to the RH needle (as if to knit).**

2. **Knit the next stitch on the LH needle.**

3. **With the LH needle, bring both slipped stitches together over the knitted stitch and off the RH needle, as in Figure 6-16.**

Figure 6-16:
Bringing the 2 slipped stitches over in a vertical double decrease.

Illustration by Wiley, Composition Service Graphics

Chapter 7

Oops! Fixing Common Mistakes

*A*s a beginning knitter, you may not notice the mistakes in your project, and that's understandable. After all, you're trying to figure out what to do with your hands, the needles, and the yarn, which is quite enough to worry about, thank you very much! After you have the hang of knitting, however, you'll start to notice things — such as unusual bumps, unraveling stitches, and strange twists — that don't look quite right.

Take heart — all knitters at all skill levels make mistakes. The trick is to do what you can to reduce the number of mistakes you make, recognize them quickly when you do err, and fix them as soon as you recognize them. This chapter explains how to do all those things.

Stopping Mistakes or Catching Them Early

Some mistakes are minor, such as a dropped or added stitch that you can easily fix (or easily hide). Others are the whoppers of the knitting set — obvious errors that can ruin a project. Because you can't avoid mistakes entirely, your goal should be to make as few mistakes as possible and, when you do flub up, to catch 'em early. Following are suggestions for achieving this goal:

✔ **Read the instructions completely and make sure you understand them.** As you read through the pattern instructions row by row, try picturing what's happening. If you're reading a chart, talk yourself through the stitches: "I cast on 98, knit 1, purl 1 for the first 4 rows. Then in the fifth row, I work in stockinette stitch until. . . ." Running through the project in your head before your hands get involved is especially important when you're working complicated patterns or garments that include shaping instructions.

✔ **Practice any stitches, stitch patterns, or techniques you think may trip you up.** Sometimes you can figure out what's going on simply by visualizing the steps. But when you can't picture what's going on — no matter how many times you read the instructions — take a little time to practice with real needles and yarn.

Checking gauge (which we cover in Chapter 3) automatically gives you the opportunity to run through the stitch pattern. If you're one who throws caution to the wind and doesn't check gauge, practice by working up a little swatch with the stitches.

✔ **Look at your work.** We know this sounds obvious. But too many knitters get so into the rhythm of actually knitting that they forget to look at their work. Looking helps you recognize how a particular combination of stitches creates the pattern growing before your eyes. When you recognize that, you're much more aware and able to keep track of the stitches as you work them. Checking your work also helps you identify mistakes early. If something is going wrong with the pattern — perhaps the rib is offset or you don't have as many stitches at the end of the row as the pattern says you should — you can address the problem before it gets worse.

✔ **Beginners: Count your stitches after each row.** One stitch more or less than you cast on frequently indicates a mistake in the last row you worked. Don't panic! You don't have to count your stitches forever. Soon your fingers will alert you to a missed move, and you'll be catching mistakes before they become a nuisance to correct.

Dealing with Dropped Stitches

Dropped stitches are stitches that, for one reason or another, fall off the needle and don't get worked. Dropping stitches is pretty common for both beginning and experienced knitters. Sometimes you're lucky enough to recognize the dropped stitch right away; other times you don't notice it until much later. Either way, you need to fix the error because dropped stitches don't look good, and they unravel when the piece is pulled or stretched, leaving an unsightly ladder of yarn up your work. Think of a run in pantyhose — that's exactly what a dropped stitch resembles.

At www.dummies.com/go/knittingfd, you can find a video demonstration of how to spot and fix dropped stitches in your knitting.

Some yarns, especially *plied* (multistrand) ones, are prone to splitting. When you're fixing mistakes (or just knitting in general), take care not to let your needle separate the plies. You want to go in and out of the *holes* in the stitches, leaving the yarn strand intact.

Finding and securing a dropped stitch

When you suspect that you've dropped a stitch, the first thing to do is find it and secure it so that it doesn't unravel any more than it already has. Contrary to knitting lore, a dropped stitch doesn't immediately unravel itself into oblivion — thank goodness! — but you do need to deal with it immediately.

To find a dropped stitch, carefully spread out your stitches along the needle and slowly scan the row(s) below. The telltale sign of a dropped stitch is a horizontal strand of yarn that isn't pulled through a loop. Here's how it may look:

✔ **If the dropped stitch hasn't unraveled far, or if you just recently dropped it:** It should look like the one in Figure 7-1. Note the horizontal yarn that didn't get pulled through.

Figure 7-1:
A dropped stitch viewed from the knit side.

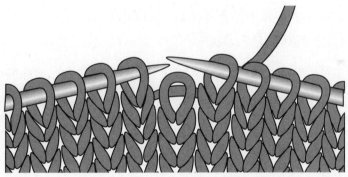

Illustration by Wiley, Composition Services Graphics

✔ **If the dropped stitch has worked itself down several rows, or if you didn't notice its absence immediately:** It should appear as a wayward stitch at the bottom of a ladder of unworked strands (see Figure 7-2). Each strand represents a row.

When you find the dropped stitch, you need to secure it so that it doesn't unravel any more. To do so, carefully work a small needle tip, the blunt point of a tapestry needle, a toothpick, a nail, a bobby pin, or anything into it to secure it and stretch it out a bit. Then use a safety pin (you should have some with your knitting supplies) to secure the stitch.

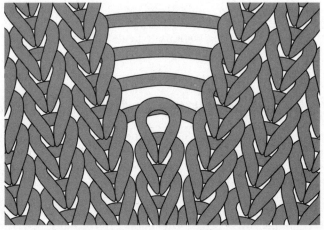

Figure 7-2:
A dropped
knit stitch
and ladder.

Now take a deep breath and follow the instructions in the following sections for getting that dropped stitch back on the needle.

Rescuing a dropped stitch in the row below

After you pin the dropped stitch to secure it (refer to the preceding section), continue working the row above until you reach the pinned stitch directly below. Fortunately, recovering a stitch dropped in the row below is a simple matter. Basically, you just need to pick up the unworked horizontal strand of yarn behind the stitch and pull it through the dropped stitch. How you go about that depends on whether you want to make a knit stitch or a purl stitch.

To make a knit stitch

If the knit side of your work is facing, rescue the stitch as follows:

1. **Insert your RH needle into the *front* of the dropped stitch.**

   Look behind the stitch. You'll see the horizontal strand of yarn that didn't get pulled through. The strand is behind the stitch just like the yarn when you knit a stitch.

2. **With the RH needle, go under the lowest unworked strand from the front (see Figure 7-3). Both the strand and the stitch are on the RH needle.**

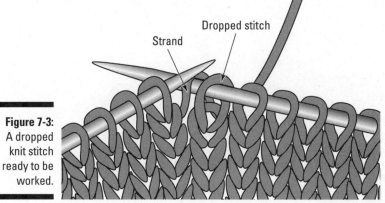

Illustration by Wiley, Composition Services Graphics

Figure 7-3:
A dropped knit stitch ready to be worked.

3. **Insert the LH needle into the stitch from the back (see Figure 7-4) and pull it over the strand.**

   You've just "worked" the stitch that was dropped in the last row. Now you need to knit the stitch in the current row, as the next step describes.

   If a stitch has dropped more than 1 row, repeat Steps 2 and 3 until all horizontal strands have been picked up and knit.

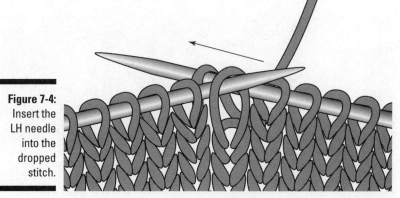

Illustration by Wiley, Composition Services Graphics

Figure 7-4:
Insert the LH needle into the dropped stitch.

4. **Put the new stitch on the LH needle in the ready-to-knit position (see Figure 7-5) and knit as normal.**

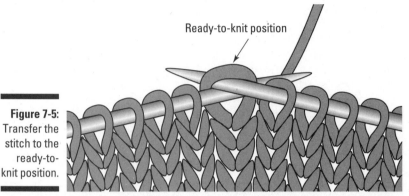

Figure 7-5:
Transfer the stitch to the ready-to-knit position.

Ready-to-knit position

Illustration by Wiley, Composition Services Graphics

Check to see that you've made a smooth knitted V stitch.

To make a purl stitch

If the purl side is facing, or if you're working in garter stitch, rescue the dropped stitch as follows:

1. **Insert the RH needle into the dropped stitch *and* the yarn strand from the back, as in Figure 7-6.**

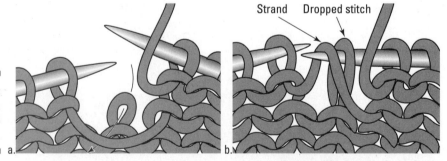

Strand   Dropped stitch

Figure 7-6:
Pick up a dropped purl stitch.

a.   b.

Illustration by Wiley, Composition Services Graphics

If you can't readily pick up a dropped stitch from the back or front, pick it up any way you can and put it on the RH needle.

2. **Using the LH needle, pull the stitch over the strand and off the needle, forming a new stitch on the RH needle (see Figure 7-7).**

Figure 7-7:
Pull the
dropped
stitch over.

Illustration by Wiley, Composition Services Graphics

3. **Place the new stitch on the LH needle in the ready-to-work position (see Figure 7-8) and purl (or knit, for a garter stitch) as normal.**

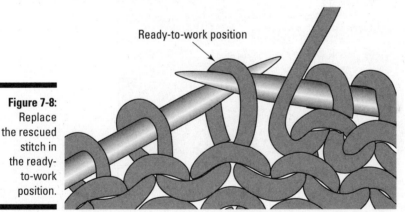

Ready-to-work position

Figure 7-8:
Replace
the rescued
stitch in
the ready-
to-work
position.

Illustration by Wiley, Composition Services Graphics

Check to see that you have a bump below the stitch.

Saving a dropped stitch with a crochet hook

A crochet hook is more than just a tool for crocheters. Knitters find it handy for fixing dropped stitches as well. A crochet hook makes recovering a dropped stitch pretty easy. You just need to know whether to draw the unworked strand through the dropped stitch from the front or the back — and that depends on whether you're working with a stockinette stitch or a garter stitch.

In stockinette stitch

To rescue a dropped stitch from the knit side of stockinette stitch (if the purl side is facing, turn it around), reach through the dropped stitch with a crochet hook and pick up the bottommost strand in the ladder (see Figure 7-9). Then pull the strand through the stitch toward you to form a new stitch. Repeat this maneuver to pull each successive strand in the ladder through the loop until the last strand has been worked.

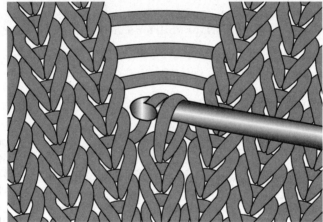

Figure 7-9: Pull through the first strand.

Illustration by Wiley, Composition Services Graphics

Aim to make your rescued stitches the same size as their neighbors. After you work the dropped stitch in and get back to working your current row, give a little tug on your work in each direction to blend the stitches.

In garter stitch

To pick up several rows of dropped stitches in garter stitch, you have to alternate the direction from which you pull the ladder strands through the dropped stitch. Pull through the front of the stitch to create a knit stitch, and pull through the back of the stitch for a purl.

To determine whether you pull through the front or back of the stitch, follow the bottom strand to the side (either way) to see what the stitch connected to it looks like. A stitch that looks like a V is a knit stitch; one that looks like a bump is a purl stitch. (Pull gently on the strand to locate the neighboring stitches if you need to.) You can see the connected stitches in Figure 7-10.

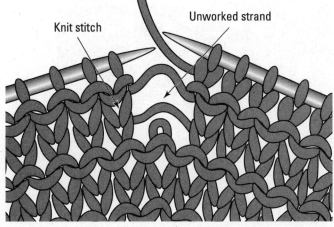

Knit stitch

Unworked strand

Figure 7-10: Knit stitches connected to the strand.

Illustration by Wiley, Composition Services Graphics

When you know whether the first stitch to be rescued is a knit or purl stitch, the fix is a cinch.

1. **Fix the first stitch.**

   If it's a knit stitch (it looks like a V), pick up the dropped stitch from the front. Refer to the preceding section and Figure 7-9 for detailed instructions. If it's a purl stitch, pick it up from the back, as shown in Figure 7-11.

2. **Alternate pulling stitches from each direction until you've pulled through the last strand.**

   If you fixed the first stitch by pulling the strand through the front, fix the next stitch by pulling the strand through the back, and so on.

3. **Put the last loop onto the LH needle in the ready-to-work position and work it as normal.**

If you pull a loop through from a strand in the wrong row, you'll have a major — and unsightly — glitch in your work. So pick up the strands of yarn in the proper order, and check to make sure that the stitch you've made matches the ones next to it.

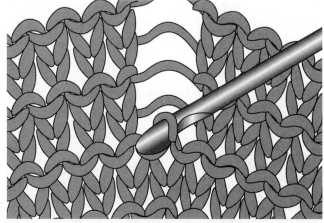

Figure 7-11:
Pick up a
dropped
purl stitch
from the
back.

Illustration by Wiley, Composition Services Graphics

Ripping (Your Heart) Out

All sorts of mistakes require that you rip out your knitting. What are they? Inadvertently adding stitches and any other mistake that requires reknitting to fix. How far you have to go depends on the mistake, though. Adding a stitch in the row you're knitting is a relatively painless fix; finding out that you've been knitting the right side stitches on the wrong side of the piece is a bit more cringe-inducing.

If ripping out your work sounds too stressful or like too much work, you have some alternatives for when perfection doesn't matter, when no one will know that a mistake has been made (1 added stitch in a large afghan, for example), or when you don't want to take the time to redo work you've already completed. Here are your options:

- ✔ **Don't do anything.** If you can happily live with imperfections and the mistake doesn't bother you, let it go and keep on knitting.

- ✔ **When the mistake is a simple added stitch (or two), decrease the same number of stitches in the row you're currently working.** Use one of the decreasing techniques in Chapter 6. This approach is a good alternative when having the extra stitch messes up the pattern and working around it in each row is a hassle.

If the thought of ripping out your knitting is making you a little sick to your stomach, take a minute to laugh at knitting shorthand that online knitters use to refer to ripping out their work: "frog" or "frogging" and "tink." *Tink* is "knit" spelled backwards, indicating you're doing the reverse. Why *frogging*? Because you need to rip it, rip it.

Ripping out stitch by stitch

If you're lucky enough to catch your mistake before the end of the row in which you made it, you can rip back to your mistake one stitch at a time. Basically, you undo what you've just done until you get to the problem spot. Here's how:

1. **With the knit or purl side facing, insert the LH needle from *front to back* (away from you) into the stitch below the one on the RH needle.**

   Figure 7-12 shows how this step looks when you undo a knit stitch or a purl stitch.

Figure 7-12: Unforming a knit stitch (a) and a purl stitch (b).

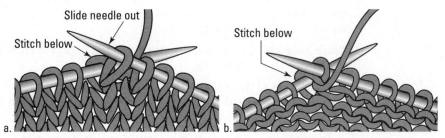

Illustration by Wiley, Composition Services Graphics

2. **Slide the RH needle out of the stitch and gently pull on the yarn to free it.**

   Your work won't unravel because your LH needle has secured the stitch below.

3. **Repeat Steps 1 and 2, stitch by stitch, to the point of your mistake.**

Ripping out row by row

What's the worst-case scenario? You notice a mistake several rows down in your work — a bump or glitch that you can't easily rescue by backing up a few stitches. In such a situation, ripping back one stitch at a time may take longer than simply taking the piece off the needles, undoing your work as far back as necessary, and then starting over. It's a pain. It's no fun. And you'll mourn the time (and possibly inches of finished work) you lose, but sometimes ripping everything out is necessary. When it is, take a deep breath, do an unkinking exercise or two (see Chapter 21), and follow these steps:

1. **Locate the row your mistake is on and mark it with a safety pin.**

   You don't want to rip back any farther than absolutely necessary. If you're working with an exceptionally thin yarn, you may want to thread a so-called *safety line* of yarn through the stitches on the last good row of knitting (the last row without a mistake). Using a tapestry needle and a different, smooth yarn, thread the yarn through the center of each stitch. When you pull out the stitches above, the safety line will keep you from going too far.

2. **Slide your needle out of the stitches.**

   This point is where you probably want to take a few deep, steadying breaths.

3. **Pull gently on the working yarn, undoing the stitches; when you reach the row above the mistake (which you've marked with a safety pin), slowly rip to the end of the row.**

4. **Place your knitting so that the working yarn is on the right (flip the fabric over if you have to).**

5. **Insert the tip of the needle into the first stitch on the row below (from back to front, toward you; see Figure 7-13), and gently pull to free the yarn from the stitch.**

   You should have 1 stitch solidly planted on the RH needle.

   Using a needle several sizes smaller to pick up the last row of your ripped-out knitting makes it easier to snag the stitches. Then, when it's time to begin knitting again, work the next row with your regular needle.

Insert needle here,
back to front

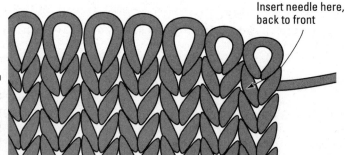

Figure 7-13:
Insert the
needle into
the stitch
below.

Illustration by Wiley, Composition Services Graphics

6. **Repeat Step 5 until you reach your mistake.**

   Figure 7-14 shows what it looks like as you work across the row to your mistake.

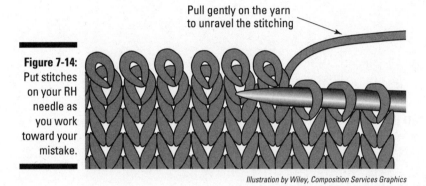

Pull gently on the yarn
to unravel the stitching

Figure 7-14:
Put stitches
on your RH
needle as
you work
toward your
mistake.

Illustration by Wiley, Composition Services Graphics

7. **Rip out your mistake, turn your work, and start knitting again!**

Chapter 8

Knitting in the Round

K *nitting in the round,* in which you knit around and around on a circular needle to create a seamless tube, is deceptively simple, and many knitters of all skill levels prefer it to flat knitting. Why? The two most common reasons for beginners are that knitting proceeds faster because you don't have to turn your work and that you can create stockinette stitch — a common stitch in many beginner and intermediate patterns — without having to purl. More-advanced knitters, especially those who make garments (sweaters, socks, gloves, and so on), like knitting in the round because it cuts down on garment assembly. For these (and a variety of other) reasons, circular knitting is growing in popularity, and many books for beginning knitters include knit-in-the-round patterns.

This chapter explains everything you need to know to successfully knit in the round. For projects that use this technique, head to Chapters 9 and 19.

Why Going in Circles Can Be a Good Thing

When you knit in the round (often called *circular knitting*), you work on a circular needle or double-pointed needles (dpns) to knit a seamless tube. Years ago, circular knitting was a technique associated with more-experienced knitters. These days, many popular patterns for beginners are written in the round. Many knitters — beginner and advanced — prefer knitting in the round because of its benefits, which include the following:

✔ **The right side always faces you.** If you're averse to purling for some reason, knitting in the round allows you to skip it entirely — as long as you stick to stockinette stitch. Having the right side face you also makes working repeating color patterns easier because your pattern is always front and center; you're never looking at the back and having to flip to the front to double-check what color the next stitch should be.

✔ **Although circular knitting is great for sweater bodies, sleeves, hats, socks, and mittens, you're not limited to creating tubes.** By using something called a *steek* — a means of opening the tube of knitted fabric with a line of crocheted or machine-sewn stitches — you also can create a flat piece after the fact. And that's good for such things as cardigans. (We cover steek techniques later in the chapter.)

✔ **You can reduce the amount of sewing required for garments.** When you knit back and forth, you make flat pieces that have to be sewn together. Circular knitting eliminates many of these seams. In fact, some patterns let you make an entire sweater from bottom to top (or top to bottom) without having a single seam to sew up when the last stitch has been bound off.

Choosing Needles for Circular Knitting

Circular and double-pointed needles are designed for knitting in the round and, as Chapter 2 explains, come in the same sizes as regular knitting needles. When you select circular or double-pointed needles for your projects, keep these things in mind:

✔ **Circular needle:** The needle length you choose for your project must be a smaller circumference than the tube you plan to knit; otherwise, you won't be able to comfortably stretch your stitches around the needle. For example, to knit a hat that measures 21 inches around, you need a 16-inch needle because 21 inches worth of stitches won't stretch around 24 inches of needle (which is the next size up from a 16-inch needle).

We know it sounds counterintuitive to need a needle smaller in circumference than the knitted project, but the problem is that because there's no break — no first stitch or last stitch (after all, you're knitting a tube) — you can stretch the fabric only as far as you can stretch any two stitches. A 21-inch circular project won't knit comfortably on a 24-inch circular needle because you can't easily stretch 2 stitches 3 inches apart.

When you first take a circular needle from its package, it will be tightly coiled. Run the coil under hot water or immerse it in a sink of hot water for a few moments to relax the kinks. You can even hang it around the back of your neck while you get your yarn ready; your body heat will help unkink the needle.

✔ **Double-pointed needles:** Lengths vary from 5 to 10 inches. The shorter ones are great for socks and mittens, and the longer ones work well for hats and sleeves. Aim for 1 inch or so of empty needle at each end. If you leave more than 1 inch, you'll spend too much time sliding stitches down to the tip so that you can knit them; if you leave less than 1 inch, you'll lose stitches off the ends.

TIP

If you've never used double-pointed needles before, choose square, wooden, or bamboo ones. Their slight grip on the stitches will keep the ones on the waiting needles from sliding off into oblivion when you're not looking. Note that with square needles especially, gauge is important because you may end up knitting bigger on square needles versus rounded ones.

Casting On for Circular Knitting

To knit on a circular needle, cast your stitches directly onto the needle as you would on a straight needle. (For a refresher on how to cast on, see Chapter 4.) Here's the important bit: Before you start to knit, make sure that the cast-on edge isn't twisted around the needle; if you have stitches that spiral around the needle, you'll feel like a cat chasing its tail when it comes time to find the bottom edge. The yarn end should be coming from the RH needle tip, as shown in Figure 8-1.

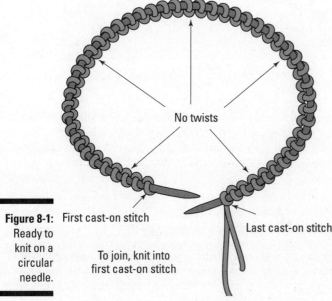

Figure 8-1:
Ready to knit on a circular needle.

No twists

First cast-on stitch

Last cast-on stitch

To join, knit into first cast-on stitch

Illustration by Wiley, Composition Services Graphics

Casting on and getting started on a set of double-pointed needles can be a little trickier than using single-pointed needles. Instead of trying to cast all your stitches onto one small needle (which increases the likelihood that some will slip off the other end) or several separate needles (which leaves needles dangling and extra yarn at each needle change), cast the total number of stitches needed onto a single-pointed straight needle of the correct size. Then work the first round of the pattern onto your double-pointed needles, distributing them in equal or close-to-equal amounts and making sure that the stitches aren't twisted around any of the needles. Leave one of the needles free to start knitting.

If you're using a set of four double-pointed needles, use three needles for your stitches: Form them into a triangle (see Figure 8-2a) with the yarn end at the bottom point. Save the fourth (empty) needle for knitting. If you're using a set of five needles, put your stitches on four needles, as in Figure 8-2b, and knit with the fifth (empty) needle.

Figure 8-2:
Dividing
stitches
among three
(a) and four
(b) double-
pointed
needles.

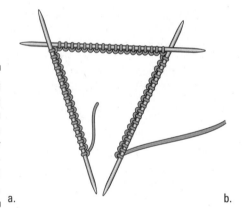

a.

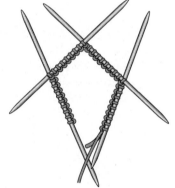

b.

Illustration by Wiley, Composition Services Graphics

Trying to focus on one of your double-pointed needles while the others are flopping around is pretty frustrating. If you lay your work on a table while transferring your cast-on stitches and arranging your needles, you can keep things steady *and* pay attention to what you're doing at the same time.

Joining the Round

After you cast on your in-the-round knitting, pattern instructions tell you to join and begin knitting. *Joining* simply means that when you work the first stitch, you bring the first and last cast-on stitches together, joining the circle of stitches.

The following sections walk you through joining on both circular and double-pointed needles and provide tips on creating a cleaner join. You can also visit www.dummies.com/go/knittingfd to watch a video demonstration of knitting in the round with common stitches.

Joining on a circular needle

To work the first stitch of the round on a circular needle, follow these steps:

1. **Place a marker on the RH needle before making the first stitch if you want to keep track of the beginning of the round.**

   Many in-the-round patterns tell you to place a marker to indicate the beginning of a round. When you're doing color work or any sort of repeating pattern, knowing where one round ends and another begins is vital. And if you have to place other markers later (common with pieces that require shaping), do something to differentiate your "beginning" marker from the others. Make it a different color from the other markers you use or attach a piece of yarn or a safety pin to it.

2. **Insert the tip of the RH needle into the first stitch on the LH needle (the first cast-on stitch) and knit or purl as usual.**

   Figure 8-3 shows the first stitch being made with a marker in place.

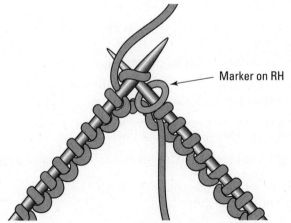

Marker on RH

Figure 8-3:
The first stitch in a round.

Illustration by Wiley, Composition Services Graphics

Joining on double-pointed needles

For double-pointed needles, use the empty needle to begin working the first round. If the first stitch is a knit stitch, make sure that the yarn is in back of your work. If the first stitch is a purl stitch, bring the yarn to the front between the needles; bring the empty needle *under* the yarn and insert it to purl into the first stitch on the LH needle. After the first couple of stitches, arrange the back ends of the two working needles on top of the other needles. (Do you feel like you have a spider by one leg?) The first round or two may feel awkward, but as your piece begins to grow, the weight of your knitting will keep the needles nicely in place and you'll cruise along.

When you knit on double-pointed needles, the stitches worked where the needles meet may be looser than the rest. To keep them neat, give an extra tug on the yarn as you work the first stitch on each needle and remember to tug again after you insert the needle into the second stitch. Or when you come to the end of a needle, knit the first stitch or two from the next one before switching to the empty needle.

Tidying up the first and last stitches

Whether you're working on a circular needle or double-pointed needles, the first and last cast-on stitches rarely make a neat join. To tighten up the connection, you can do one of the following:

- Cast on an extra stitch at the end, transfer it to the LH needle, and make your first stitch a k2tog, working the increased stitch with the first stitch on the LH needle ("k2tog" stands for "knit 2 stitches together," a decrease technique you can read about in Chapter 6).

- Before working the first stitch, wrap the yarn around the first and last cast-on stitches as follows:

    1. Transfer the first stitch on the LH needle to the RH needle.

    2. Take the ball yarn from front to back between the needles and transfer the first 2 stitches on the RH needle to the LH needle.

    3. Bring the yarn forward between the needles and transfer the first stitch on the LH needle back to the RH needle.

    4. Take the yarn to the back between the stitches and give a little tug on the yarn.

You're ready to knit the first stitch.

Working Common Stitches in the Round

As we mention earlier in the chapter, when knitting in the round, the right side is always facing you — which is a good thing as long as you understand how it affects the stitches you make. For example, in flat knitting, you create a garter stitch by knitting every row, but knitting every round in circular knitting produces stockinette stitch. So here's a quick guide to getting the stitches you want:

> ✔ **For garter stitch:** Alternate a knit round with a purl round.
>
> ✔ **For stockinette stitch:** Knit all rounds.
>
> ✔ **For rib stitches:** In round 1, alternate knit and purl stitches in whatever configuration you choose (1 x 1, 2 x 2, and so on). In subsequent rounds, knit over the knit stitches and purl over the purl stitches.

The trick is simply knowing how the stitch is created in flat knitting and then remembering the principle. For example, in seed stitch, you knit in the purl stitches and purl in the knit stitches. Well, you do the same in circular knitting. (Chapter 5 has details on these flat knitting stitches.)

Rounds (rnds) are what you work in circular knitting. *Rows* are what you work in flat (back-and-forth) knitting.

Using Steeks for a Clean Break

Steeks are an excellent way to open up a knitted tube. Traditionally, Nordic-style ski sweaters were knit in the round and then steeked to open the cardigan front and sleeve openings. You can use steeks for this type of project or anywhere else you want to cut open a line of knit stitches.

You can steek with a sewing machine or a crochet hook, depending on your comfort level with either and on whether you have access to a machine. Crocheted steeks are generally simpler to work with for beginners because they're easy to tear out if you make a mistake.

Sewing in a steek

To make a steek with a sewing machine, sew two vertical lines of stitches an inch or so apart (or for added security, sew four lines, as shown in Figure 8-4). Be sure to keep the line of machine stitching between the same two columns of knit stitches all the way down. Use a sturdy cotton/poly blend thread and a stitch length appropriate to the knitted stitches (shorter for finer-gauge knits, slightly longer for chunkier knits).

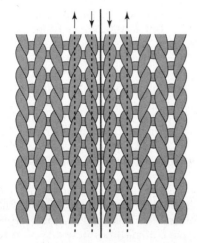

Figure 8-4:
Sew two to
four vertical
lines.

Illustration by Wiley, Composition Services Graphics

Crocheting a steek

To make a steek with yarn, crochet two vertical columns of stitches an inch or more apart by using a slip stitch (see Figure 8-5). Fold the sweater at the line you plan to stitch so the vertical column of stitches looks like the top of a crochet chain; then insert your hook into the first V, yarn over the hook, pull the new loop through the V, and move to the next stitch on your left, repeating as you go. (You can read about yarn overs in Chapter 6.) Be sure to work all your crocheted stitches on the same column of knit stitches; if you veer to the left or right, your steek will be crooked.

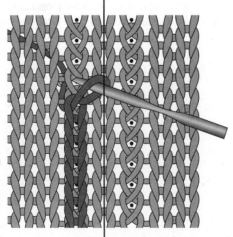

Figure 8-5:
Crocheting
a steek in
place.

Illustration by Wiley, Composition Services Graphics

Cutting your fabric after you steek

After you've sewn or crocheted the steek in place, you can safely cut your knitted fabric between the two lines of stitching, as shown in Figure 8-6. Then you can continue with your pattern as directed.

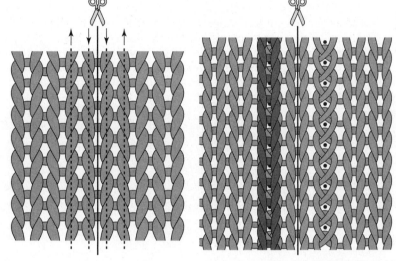

Figure 8-6:
Cut between the two lines to open the fabric.

Illustration by Wiley, Composition Services Graphics

Measuring Gauge in the Round

Knitting stockinette stitch in the round can give you a different gauge than if you were knitting the same stitch flat (back and forth on straight needles). Here's why: A purl stitch is very slightly larger than a knit stitch. When you work stockinette stitch on straight needles, every other row is a purl row, and the difference in the sizes of your knits and purls averages out. However, when working stockinette stitch in the round, you always make knit stitches, which can result in a slightly smaller piece even though you're knitting the same pattern over the same number of stitches. (See Chapter 3 for more on gauge.)

When the gauge for a project worked on a circular needle must be exact, make your gauge swatch by working all the rows from the right side as follows:

1. **Using the same needle you plan to use in your project, cast on 24 stitches or so and work 1 row.**

   Don't turn the work.

2. **Cut the yarn and slide your knitting, with the right side facing, back to the knitting end of the needle.**

3. **Knit another row and cut the yarn.**

4. **Repeat Steps 2 and 3 until you've completed your swatch and then measure your gauge.**

An easier and less time-consuming way to measure gauge in circular patterns is to do it while you knit the piece. Knit at least 1½ inches in the round on the needles you plan to use, stop, and measure the stitch gauge and 1-inch of row gauge. If your gauge is too big, switch to smaller needles on the next round; if your gauge is too small, switch to bigger needles. If your gauge is off by more than a stitch, tear out the stitches you just made and start again. This method is generally accurate enough for any kind of small project you're likely to encounter at the beginning or intermediate level.

Chapter 9

Practicing with Simple Projects

Knitting swatches is fun for a while, but the point of knitting is to make things that you can use — or that you can give as gifts to the people you care about. The projects in this chapter let you practice working the basic knit stitches, reading and understanding patterns for knitted garments, and, if you decide to give them your own dimensions, working with gauge. *And* you end up with a scarf, a bag, or a hat (and multiple variations thereof) that you can wear yourself or give to friends and family.

You can use the yarn we specify for each project, another yarn with a similar stitch gauge, or a yarn with the generic yarn gauge or weight given. Check the label on the yarn you want to use to see whether the stitch gauge matches the pattern, or ask a yarn store sales associate to suggest something. Because this knitting is just practice, you needn't be overly concerned about matching gauge. (See Chapter 3 for detailed information about gauge.) It's not a catastrophe if these projects turn out an inch bigger or smaller. Just knit until the piece you're working on measures the length given in the pattern.

Before you start knitting a project, whether it's a simple one or more advanced, make a photocopy of the pattern to work from. You can keep notes on the working pattern without marking up the original.

Everywhere Bag in Garter Stitch

This basic bag is handy for carrying your wallet, keys, and some lip balm. Make it larger and throw in your glasses case and a notebook. Make it even bigger, add a pocket, and use it to hold your knitting. You can find several ways to vary this project at the end of this section. So cast on and get started!

Materials and vital statistics

- ✔ **Measurements:** 8 inches x 9 inches, with a 4-inch flap
- ✔ **Yarn:** Wisdom Yarns "Poems Chunky" (100% wool roving; CYC #5, 110 yards, 3.5 ounces [100 grams]): Blue Mist, 3 balls
- ✔ **Needles:** One pair of size US 8 (5 mm) needles or size needed to obtain gauge
- ✔ **Other materials:** One button, any size
- ✔ **Gauge:** 18 stitches per 4 inches in garter stitch

Directions

All you need to do to make this versatile bag is knit a rectangle, sew up the sides, make and attach a cord for the strap, make a button loop, and attach a button. Voilà!

Knitting the bag

Cast on 38 sts.

Work in garter stitch until the piece measures 22 inches in length. (**Remember:** In garter stitch, you knit every row.)

Bind off and steam lightly. (See Chapter 17 for instructions on steam blocking.)

Sewing the side seams

Measure down 9 inches from one edge and fold your piece with wrong sides together.

Even though garter stitch is reversible, your cast-on edge looks different from each side. Choose the side you like better and make that side the right side.

Sew the sides closed. You should have 4 inches left over for the flap. It doesn't really matter how you sew the sides closed, but to make a neat seam, use a tapestry needle and a strand of the same yarn. We recommend that you use the basic mattress stitch for this seaming task; you can find instructions for it and other seaming techniques in Chapter 17.

Making and attaching the cord strap

You can make cords in a variety of ways. Following is a good method to get you started. (You can find other ways to make a cord later in this chapter.)

Cast on 189 sts (about 42 inches of stitches).

Work in garter stitch for 3 rows.

Bind off.

Using the same yarn you used for the bag, sew the ends of the strap to either side of the top of the bag.

Elizabeth Zimmerman and her idiot cord (I-cord)

Elizabeth Zimmerman, author of *Knitting Without Tears* (Simon & Schuster), was the first person to bring her simple method for working a cord to knitters' attention and give it the name *idiot cord* (or *I-cord*). Her books are an indispensable part of any knitter's library. Zimmerman's "unvented" techniques and her novel way of thinking about knitting and designing have converted many halfhearted knitters into knitting enthusiasts.

Follow these steps to make your very own I-cord:

1. **Using double-pointed needles the same size as or one size smaller than the needles you used for your project, cast on 4 stitches.**

2. **Knit the 4 stitches.**

3. **Instead of turning your work, slide the stitches you just worked to the opposite end of the needle, right side still facing.**

4. **With the yarn end at the *left* end of your work, knit another row, pulling slightly on the yarn after you make the first stitch.**

5. **Continue knitting a row and then sliding the stitches to the opposite end of the needle in order to knit them again until your cord is as long as you want it.**

When you're done, you'll have created a cord that curls in on itself. The illustrations show what the cord looks like as you're working (a) and what it looks like if you pull the stitches off your needle (b).

Warning: Be careful not to let your stitches slide off the end of your needle. Trying to get them back on in the proper order is a real bear; if you don't get them right, you end up with twisted stitches and a sloppy-looking cord. Many a knitter has ended up ripping out the entire cord and starting over just to avoid the headache.

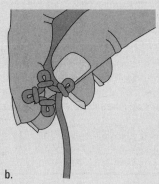

a.

b.

Illustration by Wiley, Composition Services Graphics

Forming the button loop and attaching the button

You can make a small button loop just as you'd make the cord strap — just make it shorter.

Cast on 8 sts.

Knit 1 row.

Bind off.

To attach the button loop to the bag, center the loop on the bag flap with the ends 1 inch or so apart, and attach it with yarn. Using embroidery floss, sew your button on the bag, making sure it's opposite the loop on the flap.

If you work the bag in a plied yarn, you can separate a single ply and use that to sew on your button. Then the "thread" matches your bag exactly!

Variations

You can alter this basic bag in a number of ways. By changing the details, adding a pocket, using more than one color, or using a color-changing yarn that gives the illusion of multiple yarn colors, you can create entirely different bags. You can even alter this pattern a bit to make a pillow — just leave off the strap and stuff it!

Use a different stitch pattern

You don't have to knit this bag in garter stitch. Instead, try stockinette stitch, a combination of garter stitch and stockinette stitch, or any of the stitch patterns presented in Chapter 5 (see the nearby sidebar "Substituting one stitch pattern for another" for tips).

Substituting one stitch pattern for another

If you decide to substitute a different knit/purl pattern for garter or stockinette stitch in any of the projects in this chapter, don't start knitting until you've mapped out how the pattern will be centered on your project piece. You want to be sure that your pattern will come out symmetrically. Use graph paper and plot your pattern by using knit and purl symbols to see that it begins and ends symmetrically. Remember, to be symmetrical, a pattern with a single center stitch needs to go on an uneven number of stitches, and a pattern with 2 center stitches needs to go on an even number of stitches. And as always, a gauge swatch with the new stitch is important.

Make a gauge swatch for the new stitch pattern before you begin the project. Also, remember that textured pattern stitches show up better in a smooth-plied yarn. Consider knitting your project in one stitch pattern and then knitting a pocket for it in a different stitch pattern.

Try a different cord

To make a tubelike cord, cast on 4 stitches, knit Row 1 (RS), and purl Row 2. Repeat these rows until the cord measures 44 inches (or as long as you want it to be). Because stockinette fabric rolls to the wrong side, the strip will form a tube and you won't need to seam it.

If you want to save yourself a little sewing, you can avoid knitting a separate strap that you have to sew onto the bag later. Instead, pick up 4 stitches at the edge of your bag and start knitting on those to create a tube strap. At the end of your cord, you can graft the stitches to the other side of the bag opening. Chapter 17 tells you how to pick up and graft stitches.

For a closed tube cord, you can work a cord in the round on two double-pointed needles. Cast on 4 stitches and follow the instructions for making I-cords in the sidebar "Elizabeth Zimmerman and her idiot cord (I-cord)." Use a needle the same size as or one size smaller than the one you used in your bag.

Make a different closure

For the tubelike button loop, cast on 2 or 3 stitches, work in stockinette stitch for 2 inches, and then bind off. Center the loop on the bag flap with the ends 1 inch or so apart, and sew on with yarn.

Embellish your bag

Work embroidery on your bag before stitching it up. Add beads, fringe, or tassels.

Felt the bag

Felting knitted fabric makes it much more dense, so you face less risk that your lip gloss or keys will poke through the stitches if you have a tendency to fill up your purse! You *felt* (or *full*) knitted fabric by deliberately shrinking it in the washing machine, so don't put any good sweaters in the same load (see Chapter 14).

Felted knits lose more length than width when they shrink. To keep a felted bag the same dimensions as its knit-only counterpart, you need to knit about one-third more rows . . . sometimes even more, depending on the yarn. So if you're supposed to knit the bag piece 22 inches long, you should knit about 28 to 29 inches instead. It should only shrink a little bit widthwise, but to be safe, add an extra 5 stitches to the cast-on width.

If you seam the sides with yarn before you felt the bag, the sides will be stronger than if you sew them together afterward. And if you want a felted strap, don't attach it before felting the rest of the bag — put it in to shrink unattached. Straps can get caught on the center agitator of your washing machine and pull out of shape very easily.

Bias Knit Scarf

This scarf is a straightforward garter stitch pattern that has an increase at the beginning of a row and a decrease at the end of a row to create bias fabric. A bias knit simply means that you knit diagonally rather than up and down or side to side. By using a long color-changing yarn, you make the scarf look like you used a variety of colored yarns when you actually used only one yarn and one color.

Materials and vital statistics

- **Measurements:** 5 inches x 72 inches
- **Yarn:** Red Heart Boutique "Unforgettable" (100% acrylic; CYC #4, 279 yards, 3.5 ounces [100 grams]): Dragonfly, 2 skeins
- **Needles:** One pair of size US 8 (5 mm) needles or size needed to obtain gauge
- **Gauge:** 24 stitches and 34 rows per 4 inches in bias garter stitch pattern

Directions

Cast on 30 sts.

Row 1 (RS): Knit front and back into first stitch, k to last 2 sts, k2tog.

Row 2 (WS): Knit.

Rep Rows 1 and 2 until piece measures approximately 72 inches, ending with a RS row.

Next row (WS): Bind off all stitches.

Finishing: Weave in any loose ends. Block scarf gently.

Variations

You can modify this scarf by using two different colors of long color-changing yarn and then changing colors every 2 rows. This combination will make the scarf look like a multi-striped piece with very little effort. When doing this variation, be sure to use two distinctly different colors to maximize the effect.

A wonderful way to use some of those fun novelty yarns in your knitting is to mix and match them with this pattern. Changing yarns every 3 inches will give this scarf a completely different look.

Always join a new yarn on a RS row in order to keep the tails on the same side. Leave a long tail to make weaving in easier.

Don't like weaving in ends? Not a problem; just tie a knot in the tails of the old and new yarn at the change and leave the tails loose to create fringe along the length of the scarf. Bingo-bango — you've just added your very own design feature.

Scalloped Scarf

This pattern uses stacked increases and decreases to create graceful scalloped edges. You create the wavy texture of this scarf by working increases and decreases in vertical columns. The stitches dip down at the decrease column and curve back up at the increases. To make the ends match, you work the scarf in two pieces from bottom up. You work the center portion of the scarf in a 2 x 2 rib that hugs your neck.

Materials and vital statistics

- **Measurements:** 54 inches x 8 inches

- **Yarn:** Bijou Basin Ranch "Bijou Bliss" (50% yak down/50% cormo; CYC #3, 150 yards, 1.98 ounces [56 grams]): Teal, 3 skeins

- **Needles:** One pair each of size US 6 (4 mm) and US 7 (4½ mm) needles or sizes needed to obtain gauge

- **Gauge:** Instead of trying to match gauge, work up a swatch in stockinette stitch on size US 7 needles. If you like the way it looks, start the pattern. If it feels tight and doesn't have enough drape, go up a needle size. If your swatch appears too loose, go down a needle size.

Directions

Using the larger needles, cast on 41 sts.

Rows 1–6: Knit.

Rows 7, 9, 11, and 13: K2, * k in front and back of next st (kfb), k3, ssk, k1, k2tog, k2, kfb; rep from * to last 3 sts, k3.

Rows 8, 10, and 12: Purl.

Note: It may seem from the instructions that the pattern isn't symmetrical because there are 3 stitches on one side of the decrease and 2 on the other side. But because the increase creates a bar to the *left* of the increase stitch, the knitted fabric is the same on both sides of its center. You'll be able to see this symmetry after you work a few rows.

Rep Rows 2–13 nine more times. Then work Rows 2–6 once more. The piece should measure approximately 20 inches in length.

Change to the smaller needles and begin k2, p2 rib as follows. You decrease 1 stitch in the first row in order for the rib pattern to come out evenly.

Next row: K3, p2tog, p1, * k2, p2; rep from * to last 3 sts, k3 (40 sts).

Next row: P3, * k2, p2; rep from * to last 3 sts, p3.

Continue in rib for 7 inches. Bind off or transfer the stitches to a holder, depending on whether you want to seam the pieces or graft the ends together. (Turn to Chapter 17 for finishing tips.)

Work the second scarf piece as above. Block the pieces gently and seam or graft the center back ends of the scarf together.

Variations

You can modify this scarf in a number of interesting ways. Here are a few possibilities:

- ✔ Turn the scarf into a shawl by making it wider (cast on another 12 stitches, or a multiple of 12). This variation will require more yarn.
- ✔ Work the pattern in colored stripes (see Chapter 10) or in a lightweight mohair yarn on large needles.

✔ Use the chevron pattern (you can find it in Appendix A) and make the scarf pointy rather than scalloped. Cast on a multiple of the chevron pattern plus 4 extra stitches to work a 2-stitch garter edge.

Button Pillow

Pillows are semi-quick knits with a lot of variations. They look great on your favorite chair or couch, and they make welcome gifts, too. This pattern gives you some great ideas and tips for making a knitted pillow.

Materials and vital statistics

✔ **Measurements:** Vary depending on yarn weight and needle size

✔ **Yarn:** Approximately 400 yards of yarn for a standard 14-x-14-inch pillow form (see directions on the pillow form for information on making covers in different sizes)

✔ **Needles:** One pair in a size appropriate for the yarn selected (check its ball band if you're not sure); yarn needle for seaming

✔ **Other materials:** One 14-x-14-inch pillow form; one to three large decorative buttons

✔ **Gauge:** Varies depending on yarn weight and needle size

Directions

Cast on your gauge per inch times 14 (the pillow form's width), plus 4 extra stitches to allow for easy seaming on either side. For example, if your yarn is 4 stitches to the inch and you're making a 14-inch-wide pillow, cast on 60 stitches ([4 × 14] + 4).

Knit until the piece measures 2 times your pillow's height, plus 4 inches.

Bind off and block.

Finishing: Fold the bottom of the piece up until you have a 14-x-14-inch square, and seam the sides. Create your loop closures. As in the Everywhere Bag pattern, you can knit a wide variety of loop closures. Fold the 4-inch flap over the top and stitch your chosen buttons into place evenly below the bottom edge of the flap. Knit loop closures long enough to reach around each button, and sew them into place. Insert your pillow form, and you're done!

Variations

Want to try out buttonholes? Now's your chance! When you're 1 or 2 inches away from the final bind-off edge, space your chosen number of buttonholes across a row (see Chapter 18 for buttonhole directions). Then, after seaming the sides, simply sew your buttons in the appropriate places to match the holes.

Don't like buttons? How about ties? Knit six 4-inch pieces of I-cord and sew three of them evenly across the bottom of the fold-over flap. Sew the other three in corresponding positions on the body of the bag and tie it up.

To make a nice, flat fold line at the bottom and top edges of the pillow, when your piece measures 14 inches long (or a perfect square for your chosen pillow form size), purl 1 RS row of stitches if you're knitting in stockinette or 3 rows of stockinette if you're knitting in garter stitch. Repeat after you knit another 14 inches or the height of your pillow.

Mistake Rib Scarf and Fingerless Mitts

Need that perfect project for a man in your life? This project uses a masculine pattern stitch and some great yarn to make a men's scarf as well as a little matching accessory for you. Ribbing is a quintessential knitting pattern stitch, but if you add just one fewer stitch in a k2, p2 ribbing pattern, you get a *mistake rib* pattern that has great texture and looks fantastic (see Appendix A for more on mistake rib).

Materials and vital statistics

- ✓ **Measurements for scarf:** 6 inches x 72 inches slightly stretched

- ✓ **Measurements for fingerless mitts:** 4½ inches x 8 inches

- ✓ **Yarn:** Deborah Norville "Serenity Chunky" (100% acrylic; CYC #5, 280 yards, 3.5 ounces [100 grams]): Smoke Heather, 3 skeins for set

- ✓ **Needles:** One pair each of size US 9 (5½ mm) and US 11 (8 mm) needles or sizes needed to obtain gauge

- ✓ **Gauge:** 15 stitches and 16 rows per 4 inches in mistake rib pattern on larger needle; 18 stitches and 18 rows for 4 inches in mistake rib pattern on smaller needle.

Scarf directions

With size US 11 needles, cast on 23 sts.

Row 1: * K2, p2; rep from * to last 3 sts, k2, p1.

Rep until piece measures approximately 72 inches.

Next row: Bind off all stitches.

Finishing: Weave in any loose ends.

Fingerless mitts directions

Make two.

With size US 9 needles, cast on 23 sts.

Row 1: * K2, p2; rep from * to last 3 sts, k2, p1.

Rep until piece measures approximately 8 inches.

Next row: Bind off all stitches in pattern.

Finishing: Weave in any loose ends. Fold square in half widthwise. Using mattress stitch (see Chapter 17), sew up the side seam, leaving a 2½ inch opening for the thumb approximately 2 inches from the top of the mitten.

Variation

To make a scarf and fingerless mitts that are similar to the original set but not identical, reduce the number of stitches cast on by 1 and change the pattern stitch to a basic k2, p2 pattern.

Projects Knitted In the Round

When you think of in-the-round projects, you may think of socks and mittens — things that obviously use tube shapes — but in-the-round knitting has broadened beyond the basics. This section includes simple in-the-round projects for beginners: a variety of hats and a textured trendy cowl that keeps you warm and looks great. (Of course, the quintessential in-the-round projects are sweaters. You can find those in Chapter 19.)

Simple Textured Cowl

As a first-time in-the-round project, this cowl is perfect for any knitter. Knitting in fashionable yarn with subtle color changes makes the texture of the simple seed stitch really pop.

Materials and vital statistics

- **Measurements:** 24 inches in circumference x 7½ inches

- **Yarn:** Deborah Norville "Fashion Jeweltones" (57% acrylic/40% wool/3% payette; CYC #2, 99 yards, 1.76 ounces [50 grams]): Blue Sky Jasper, 3 skeins

- **Needles:** One 16-inch size US 8 (5 mm) circular needle or size needed to obtain gauge

- **Other materials:** Stitch marker, tapestry needle

- **Gauge:** 20 stitches and 24 rows per 4 inches in seed stitch pattern

Directions

Cast on 120 sts. Join round, being careful not to twist the stitches, and place marker to denote beginning of round.

Round 1: * K1, p1; rep from * to marker.

Round 2: * P1, k1; rep from * to marker.

Rep Rounds 1 and 2 until cowl measures approximately 7½ inches.

Bind off.

Variations

You can change up this cowl in a number of interesting ways. Here are a couple of possibilities:

- Turn the cowl into a tubular scarf just by making the body of the piece 60 inches or longer. Remember, this change will require more yarn.

- Use a thicker yarn and fewer stitches (the gauge will be fewer stitches per inch) along with larger needles to get a great instant-gratification project with a dramatic flair.

Two-way Hat

Both of the hats in this section are based on the same basic principle: Adult human heads are about the same size (give or take a little), and the hats — knitted in the round with some decreases at the top — will fit no matter what yarn you use. A simple way to make sure a hat will fit you is to try it on after you knit 1 or 2 inches; rip out the existing stitches and move up or down a needle size if it's a little too small or big.

Plain Hat with Rolled Brim

This most basic of hats is nicely shaped for just about every head size. Add any stitch pattern you like after knitting the first 5 rounds. If you stop the stitch pattern just before the decreases, you don't have to worry about adjusting the decreases to the pattern.

Materials and vital statistics

- ✔ **Measurements:** 21 inches in circumference x 7½ inches

- ✔ **Yarn:** Universal Yarn "Deluxe Worsted" (100% wool; CYC #4, 220 yards, 3.5 ounces [100 grams]): Gold Spice, 1 skein

- ✔ **Needles:** One 16-inch size US 7 (4½ mm) and one size US 8 (5 mm) circular needle; four or five size US 8 (5 mm) dpns or size needed to obtain gauge

- ✔ **Other materials:** Stitch marker, tapestry needle

- ✔ **Gauge:** 20 stitches and 24 rows per 4 inches in stockinette stitch pattern

Directions

Using a size US 7 circular needle, cast on 100 sts. Place marker to denote beginning of round, then join round, being careful not to twist the stitches.

Knit 5 rounds.

Switch to size US 8 circular needles, and knit 5 inches.

Begin decreases:

Round 1: * K8, k2tog; rep from * to end of round.

Round 2 and all even rounds: Knit without decreasing.

Round 3: * K7, k2tog; rep from * to end of round.

Round 5: * K6, k2tog; rep from * to end of round.

Round 7: * K5, k2tog; rep from * to end of round.

Note: At this point, you may want to switch to size 8 dpns because the circumference of the round is much smaller than the circular needle's length. Simply distribute the remaining stitches evenly over three or four dpns and knit with the remaining needle (the fourth or fifth, depending on how many you're using).

Round 9: * K4, k2tog; rep from * to end of round.

Round 11: * K3, k2tog; rep from * to end of round.

Round 13: * K2, k2tog; rep from * to end of round.

Round 15 and odd rounds to end: Continue knitting (* k2, k2tog *) until fewer than 10 stitches remain.

Cut yarn, leaving at least a 12-inch tail.

Finishing

Thread tail onto yarn needle and then slip remaining stitches onto yarn needle. Pull opening closed, push yarn tail to reverse side of fabric, and weave in ends.

Ribbed Watchman's Cap

This classically masculine hat looks great on women, too — just choose a bright color or trim it with a knitted flower (see Chapter 20). Patterned yarn such as a handpainted, multishade colorway will be broken up by the 3-stitch rib, which is an interesting visual effect.

Materials and other vital statistics

- ✔ **Measurements:** 21 inches in circumference x 7½ inches (stretched)

- ✔ **Yarn:** Universal Yarn "Deluxe Worsted" (100% wool; CYC #4, 220 yards, 3.5 ounces [100 grams]): Flintstone, 1 skein

- ✔ **Needles:** One 16-inch size US 9 (5½ mm) circular needle; four or five size US 9 dpns or size needed to obtain gauge

- ✔ **Other materials:** Stitch marker, tapestry needle

- ✔ **Gauge:** 18 stitches and 22 rows per 4 inches in ribbed stitch pattern for hat slightly stretched

Directions

Using a size US 9 circular needle, cast on 84 sts. Place marker to denote beginning of round, then join round, being careful not to twist the stitches.

* K3, p3; rep from * until piece measures 6 inches.

Begin decreases:

Round 1: * P1, p2tog, k3; rep from * to end of round (70 sts).

Round 2: * P2, k3; rep from * to end of round.

Round 3: * P2, k1, k2tog; rep from * to end of round (56 sts).

Round 4: * P2, k2; rep from * to end of round.

Round 5: * P2tog, k2; rep from * to end of round (42 sts).

Round 6: * P1, k2; rep from * to end of round.

Round 7: * P1, k2tog; rep from * to end of round (28 sts). Switch to the dpns, dividing stitches evenly.

Round 8: * P1, k1; rep from * to end of round.

Round 9: * K2tog; rep from * to end of round (14 sts).

Round 10: * K2tog; rep from * to end of round (7 sts).

Cut yarn, leaving at least a 12-inch tail.

Finishing

Thread tail onto yarn needle, and then slip remaining stitches onto yarn needle. Pull opening closed, push yarn tail to reverse side of fabric, and weave in ends.

Part III
Techniques for the More Experienced Knitter

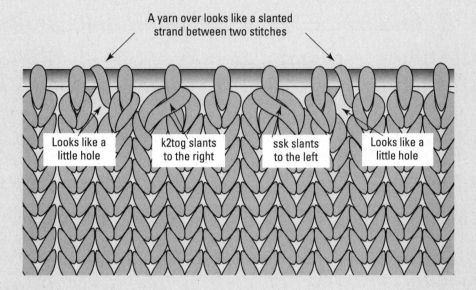

A yarn over looks like a slanted strand between two stitches

Looks like a little hole

k2tog slants to the right

ssk slants to the left

Looks like a little hole

web extras

After you master straight back-and-forth knitting, you can move into shaped territory, exploring knitting curves and diagonals. One technique to play around with is knitting on the bias. By knitting an increase and decrease at precise points in a project, you begin to shape the fabric diagonally. Access free instructions for bias knitting at www.dummies.com/extras/knitting.

In this part . . .

- ✔ Bright, mellow, or traditional — add personality to your knitting with colorful stripes.

- ✔ Make your knitting really pop by mixing in basic and not-so-basic cable stitches.

- ✔ Master stitch increases and decreases and then take your knowledge to the next level by combining the two to create lacework.

- ✔ Get familiar with Fair Isle patterns and simple intarsia motifs, which involve working in more than one color in one row.

- ✔ Practice, practice, practice with projects that let you try out advanced knitting techniques.

Chapter 10

Adding Interest with Stripes

· ·

· ·

*I*f you can knit and purl (see Chapter 4 for how-to info), you already have the skills to knit stripes. If your mind goes straight to prison uniforms or kiddie rompers, take heart: Stripes can be as subtle and elegant or as loud and crazy as you want them to be. The key is knowing how to create the desired effect, and that's exactly the kind of information you find in this chapter. Here you discover how to create textured stripes and stripes of many (or a few) different colors. And because knowing a couple of easy tricks can make stripe patterns easier, we share them, too.

Now is the time to get out that collection of odd balls of yarn culled from the sale bin of your favorite yarn shop and the bits and pieces of leftovers you've saved. Color patterns in general and stripe patterns in particular are great ways to incorporate your precious collection into an original project.

This chapter explains how to knit horizontal stripes. If you want vertical stripes, a ribbed stitch pattern is just the thing. See Chapter 5 for common ribbed patterns and Appendix A for some more-complex selections.

Seeking the Story on Stripes

Never think that stripes are boring. Far from being a single thing, stripes are many-splendored. They offer great variety in scale, balance, sequence, color, and texture. Here are a few ideas of the ways you can arrange stripes:

✔ **Balanced stripes:** One of the most common types of stripe is alternating stripes of equal width.

✔ **Wide stripes:** If you want a stripe pattern that's easy to read (that is, to recognize), use a wide stripe. There'll be no mistaking your intentions, and then you can make the look bolder or more subtle with the colors you choose.

- ✔ **Narrow stripes:** Narrow stripes can be bold or subtle, depending on the colors you choose; combining colors in the same shade, for example, creates a blurred effect, and contrasting colors make the stripes more crisp.

The eye tends to blend very narrow bands of colors together, so before you settle on a particular combination, knit a swatch and view it from a distance to make sure you like the effect.

- ✔ **Alternating stripes:** For added visual effect (and to avoid the prison uniform effect that stripes of equal width tend to create), deliberately vary the width of your stripes.

- ✔ **One stripe:** A single stripe draws the eye and creates an effect all its own. A wide stripe across the bust or chest creates a sporty look, and a narrow stripe beneath the bust creates the impression of a flattering empire waist.

- ✔ **Wild stripes:** These stripes break the rules. Make yours zigzag or start and stop them randomly. Incorporate outlandish colors or textures by using novelty yarn or multicolored yarns. Vary the width of every stripe in the piece.

If you find a striped pattern you like, you can simply follow the instructions to get the look you want. For those times when you're happy with the pattern but not so happy with the colors it uses, substitute colors you like better. Occasionally, you may want to design your own stripe pattern. To discover the myriad options you have, start a collection of stripe ideas by tearing pages from catalogs and magazines when you see interesting striped patterns or color combinations. You also can use a mathematical sequence, such as the Fibonacci sequence, to determine how many rows of each stripe color to knit. (The *Fibonacci sequence* is 1, 1, 2, 3, 5, 8, 13, 21, and so on, with each number the sum of the two before it; Fibonacci-inspired scarves are particularly charming.) Or ask a mathematician for other ideas!

Textured Stripes, or How to Stand Out in a Crowd

When you think of stripes, you may automatically think of alternating bands of different colors. That's fine, but you also can create stripes simply through texture. Here are some options:

✔ **Vary your stitches:** As Chapter 5 explains, you create stockinette stitch —
a stitch with a smooth face — by alternating a row of knit stitches with a
row of purl stitches. By varying the sequence of knit rows and purl rows,
you can create horizontal stripes (sometimes called by their ancient
name, *welts*). The two patterns in this section illustrate how you can
create stripes through texture. In the section "Reverse stockinette stitch
stripes," you create the stripes with rows of reverse stockinette stitch
on a plain stockinette stitch background. In "Garter stitch stripes," you
make the stripes with garter stitch ridges.

✔ **Vary the weight and texture of the yarns you use:** You can mix and
match smooth and fuzzy yarns, shiny and pebbly yarns, and others to
create stripes. If your stripes are narrow, you can even work with yarns
of different weights as long as the difference isn't too extreme.

To balance the different weights, knit the heavier yarns on a smaller
needle and the lighter ones on a larger needle; head to Chapter 2 to read
more about yarn weights and Chapter 3 to find out about gauge. This situation is one time when a circular needle set with interchangeable tips
comes in handy because you can swap the tips as you switch between
yarn weights.

Using same-color yarns to create textured stripes has a subtle effect. For a
bolder stripe, make your textured stripes different colors, too.

Reverse stockinette stitch stripes

Reverse stockinette stitch (rev St st) is just one way to make textured stripes
(see Figure 10-1). This stitch pattern uses rows of reverse stockinette on a
plain stockinette background.

Try the following pattern for a basic reverse stockinette stitch stripe:

Cast on any number of stitches.

Rows 1, 3, and 6: Knit.

Rows 2, 4, and 5: Purl.

Rep Rows 1–6.

Here's what's happening: As you work Rows 1, 2, 3, and 4, you create your
stockinette stitch (the smooth background). Then at Row 5, because you purl
again rather than alternate back to a knit row, you begin the reverse stockinette stitch, which creates the bumped-out stripe, and you continue it with
Row 6, which alternates with Row 5. When you return to Row 1, you return to
the stockinette stitch and the whole pattern starts over again.

Photograph by Wiley, Composition Services Graphics

Figure 10-1:
Reverse
stockinette
stripes.

To vary the width of your stripes or the space between them, simply increase the number of alternating rows in either the stockinette portion or the reverse stockinette portion.

Garter stitch stripes

Garter stitch stripes have a different texture from the stripes made in reverse stockinette stitch. Whereas reverse stockinette stitch stripes create a rolled bump, garter stitch stripes create a flat ridge (see Figure 10-2).

Follow this pattern to create the garter stitch stripes shown in Figure 10-2:

> Cast on any number of stitches.
>
> **Rows 1, 3, 5–11, 13, 15, and 16 (RS):** Knit.
>
> **Rows 2, 4, 12, and 14:** Purl.
>
> Rep Rows 1–16.

By alternating knit and purl rows, you create stockinette stitch. When you work knit rows in succession, you create the garter stitch stripe. To change the width of the background, simply work more or fewer rows in the stockinette pattern; to vary the width of the stripes, simply knit more or fewer rows in succession.

Photograph by Wiley, Composition Services Graphics

Knitting Colorful Stripes

Gorgeous yarn colors are the primary appeal for many knitters. When scanning the jewel-colored skeins in a yarn shop, who can resist gathering together a palette to take home and knit up? Who can walk by the odd topaz- or hyacinth-colored ball in the sale bin? Who can give away the remaining bit of rose and the tail end of periwinkle from the last project? Not us. But what do you do with a basket of single skeins? You knit in color, that's what!

Knitting colored stripes is a quick and easy way to get started in color work. Unlike color techniques that require you to go back and forth between colors in a single row (see Chapter 13), colored stripes allow you to use as many colors as you please while working with only one color at a time.

Maybe you're a little timid about changing colors on a project but still want to have that look. No problem; just pick up some self-striping yarn from your local yarn store. With self-striping yarn, you get an impressive, deceptively complex look while the yarn does all the work. No need to tell anybody that you didn't change yarn colors to create the beautiful pattern; let folks praise your skill and talent with needles and yarn.

Although knitting different colored stripes can be a lot of fun and an opportunity to let your creative juices flow, you need to be able to do a few things before you jump in. The following sections get you ready.

Picking colors for your project

You can knit stripes in two colors, three colors, or as many colors as you like. Use color at random, or plan for a particular mood in your color combination. Stripes in clean, bright colors with a balance of light and dark are pert and lively; stripes in a few close shades of a single color or colors close to each other on the color wheel (such as blue, purple, magenta, and red) are subtle and sophisticated.

You can look for a striped project pattern and follow the sequence, colors, and spacing given in the design; or you can use the stripe pattern as a template and plug in your own colors and yarns. If you're in a spontaneous mood, gather your yarns together and start knitting, changing yarns as you feel like it. If you're in the mood to plot and plan, get out your graph paper, sharpen your colored pencils, and hop to Chapter 13 for advice on how to use and combine colors.

Patterns with multiple colors use a standard set of abbreviations:

> **MC:** Main color (for patterns that use two colors)
>
> **CC:** Contrasting color (for patterns that use two colors)
>
> **A, B, C, and so on:** For patterns that use more than two colors

If, before diving in, you want to get an idea of what a stripe pattern may look like knitted in a specific group of yarns, try wrapping samples of the yarns in the proposed pattern around a stiff piece of cardboard or a cardboard toilet paper roll for a sneak preview.

Counting rows

When you knit stripes, you count rows (or if you're knitting in the round, you count rounds). Why? Because it's an easy way to keep track of the stripe's width. For example, knowing that a stripe spans 7 rows and counting as you go is easier and more accurate than getting out the tape measure. Here's the thing you need to know about counting rows, especially if you're using only two colors: Odd and even rows affect where the yarn ends up — whether it's right there where you want it or at the opposite end of your knitting. Fortunately, a few easy fixes get you out of this dilemma:

✔ **Work on a circular needle.** It doesn't matter where the yarn ends up. If it's not on the end where you need it, simply slide your knitting to the other needle and — voila! — problem solved. Just pick up the yarn and carry on.

✔ **Cut the yarn, leaving the ends to weave in later, and begin anew at the next row.** Weaving in ends isn't hard, but it's a bit tedious, especially if you have many loose ends. Head to the later section "Dealing with old colors and loose ends" for instructions.

✔ **Use three or more colors.** If you use three or more colors, you can organize odd- and even-row stripes so that the yarn for the next stripe will be in the right place. If you use this strategy, you have to start some colors on wrong-side rows and carry the yarn colors up both the left and right edges of your work. ("Carrying the yarn up the side as you go" later in this chapter shows you how to do just that.) Changing colors on both sides rather than just one is a good idea anyway if you're using lots of colors because it keeps the side edges from being too bulky.

Joining colors

When you're ready to change colors in a stripe pattern, you need to join the new color. Unless you're creating random stripes that start and stop anywhere, you usually join colors at the edge. For garments and other pieces that get sewn along the seam, you use one technique. For pieces whose edges remain open, you need to use a technique that lets you hide the join. We cover both techniques in the following sections.

When the edge is hidden in a seam

When you're ready to add a new color in a stripe pattern, secure the new yarn by working the first stitch in the row with the old and new colors held together. To do so, follow these steps:

1. **Insert the RH needle into the first stitch.**

2. **Drape the end of the new yarn behind your work.**

3. **Grab the old and new yarn strands together and work the first stitch.**

4. **Drop the old color and continue on in the new color until it's time to change again.**

When you work back to the edge stitch made with two strands, remember to knit the strands *together*. Otherwise, you inadvertently increase a stitch on the edge. After you work a few more rows, pull on the strand of the old yarn to tighten up the edge stitch.

You don't need to cut the end of the old color if you'll be using it again in the next few inches. When it's time to change back, simply drop the new (now old) color, pick up the old (now new) color, and carry on. Be careful not to pull the color from below too tight, or the side seam will pucker.

When the edge isn't hidden

When you're adding a new color somewhere in the middle of a row or another location where you can't hide your ends at the edge, you need to weave in ends. Follow these steps to make the color switch:

1. **Insert the RH needle into the next stitch on your needle.**

2. **Drape the end of the new yarn over your needle, as if to knit, leaving a 4- to 5-inch tail.**

3. **Work the next stitch with your new yarn.**

4. **Cut the old color, leaving a 4- to 5-inch tail, tie the new and old tails together in a bow, and continue in the new color until it's time to change again.**

5. **When you finish knitting your piece, weave in the ends (see the next section).**

   Make sure you weave the yarns over the small hole created by adding in the new yarn in opposite directions (with the WS-facing old yarn to the right, new yarn to the left).

Dealing with old colors and loose ends

When you're joining all these colors to make stripes, what do you do with all the ends you create every time you start and stop a color? You can either carry them up or cut and weave them in. Which option is better? It depends. If you don't use a color for several inches, it's better to cut the yarn and weave in the end. If you use it again soon, you can carry the yarn along the edge as you go.

Weaving in ends

When you're obliged to cut the yarn, you can weave the end in vertically along the edge of your knitting or horizontally along the edge of a stripe.

When you look at your work from the wrong side, you should see the usual purl bumps. Look below them to see the running threads that connect the stitches. To weave ends horizontally along a stripe, grab a tapestry needle and weave your loose end through four or five of these running threads. Turn to Chapter 17 for more on tying up loose ends. (In stripe work, don't weave ends vertically, because you'll invariably end up in a stripe of the wrong color.)

Carrying the yarn up the side as you go

To avoid cutting and weaving, you can carry the yarn not in use up the side, tucking it around the working yarn and keeping it close to the edge as you go until you need it again.

1. **When you finish working with Color A, work a few rows with Color B, following the instructions for joining in the earlier section "When the edge is hidden in a seam."**

2. **When you're back at the edge where Color A is waiting and about to start the next row with Color B, insert the RH needle into the first stitch.**

3. **With the working strand (A) on the left, bring Color B up the side.**

4. **Pick up Color A from under Color B and make the first stitch.**

   The working strand catches the carried strand (see Figure 10-3). This technique works the same on the purl side as it does on the knit side.

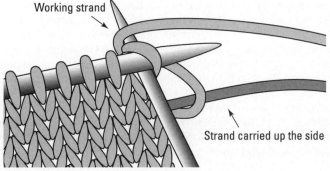

Working strand

Figure 10-3: Carry yarn up the side and tuck it in as you go.

Strand carried up the side

Illustration by Wiley, Composition Services Graphics

You can carry yarn up the side of your piece every time you're at the beginning of the row if you're making a scarf and want a very tidy edge. If the edge will be enclosed in a seam, you need to catch it only every 4 to 6 rows to maintain even tension on the edge stitches and keep the strand along the side from getting out of hand.

Be conscious of the tension on the strand you carry up the side of your work: If it's too loose, you get sloppy edge stitches, and if it's too taut, your sides pull in and have no give. Take a stitch or two in the new stripe color, and then check the strand carried up the side to make sure that it isn't gaping or pulling.

For a scarf or shawlette that changes colors every 2 rows, try a simple detail to carry the yarn up the side of a piece and keep a clean edge. On the row where you're changing colors, bring the old color to the front, slip the first stitch as if to purl, and bring the yarn to the back. Then continue in the established pattern with the new color. This strategy will keep the slipped first stitch in the color opposite to the rest of the row but will otherwise keep the edge nice and tidy. You can see this technique in the Two-row Striped Shawlette pattern later in this chapter.

Untwist your yarns periodically for sanity's sake when you're working them around each other up the side edges. And give a gentle tug on the carried strand now and then to make it neat — but don't pull hard enough to draw up the edge.

Knitting Stripes in the Round

Knitting in the round is a wonderful way to make any object, but it's important to remember that the nature of circular knitting causes stripes to *jog*, or not line up (see Figure 10-4). When you knit in the round, you're actually knitting a large spiral. If you don't take extra steps to make sure the color changes line up, you end up with an obvious jog in the fabric. Have no fear — these extra steps to prevent the jog aren't time-consuming, so the speed you gain by knitting stockinette stitch in the round isn't sacrificed.

When knitting stripes in the round, you may want the beginning and the end of the stripe pattern to align with each other. This technique produces a *jogless stripe* because the stripe doesn't shift out of alignment. To do this, you have to add a step when you change colors:

1. **When you finish working with Color A, work the next round with Color B.**

2. **When you're back at the beginning of the round, slip the first stitch as if to purl from the LH needle (Color B) and then work the rest of the stitches in the established pattern.**

3. **Continue in the pattern for the number of rounds necessary.**

4. **When making more stripes, repeat Steps 1 and 2.**

   To see this technique in action, take a look at the jogless stripe in Figure 10-4.

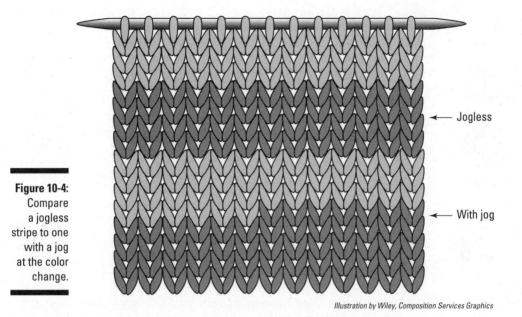

←— Jogless

←— With jog

Figure 10-4:
Compare
a jogless
stripe to one
with a jog
at the color
change.

Illustration by Wiley, Composition Services Graphics

Stirring Up Stripes: Combining Texture and Color

You can work stripes in flat stockinette stitch, or you can make them more interesting by adding texture. Knit an entire project in a stitch pattern with colored stripes running through it or add different textures to different stripes.

If the simplicity and creative pleasure of knitting stripes appeal to you but standard stripes don't inspire you (or you'd rather not wear horizontal stripes), don't give up quite yet. The sections that follow introduce some unconventional ways to work stripes into your knitting.

Varying your stitch pattern

Stitch patterns can affect the way your stripe pattern (or color change) looks. In stockinette stitch, if you knit a row in one color and the next row in another color, from the right side the line where the rows meet is sharp and clean. From the wrong side, the line is broken into dots of color by the purl bumps — different effects, different design possibilities. In ribbing or other stitch patterns where purl bumps show on the right side of the fabric, striped patterns show the dots of color unless both the row of the old and the row of the new show the knit side of the stockinette on the right side.

Knit refers to both how you make a certain kind of stitch *and* how a stitch looks from the right side of a fabric. A knit stitch is a smooth V on the right side, even if you make it by purling on a wrong-side row.

If you want a sharp no-dot line between your colors and you're working a pattern on which the right side shows the purl bumps, simply work knit stitches for the first row of the new color. For example, if you're knitting a ribbed pattern, work the last row of the old color in the knit/purl pattern you've established. If the next row is a wrong-side row, purl; if it's a right-side row, knit. Then continue on in your pattern stitch in the new color. Hard as it may be to believe, as long as your stripes are several rows deep, the knit row is almost undetectable in your pattern stitch, and you have a distinct transition between stripes.

Making waves

To make wavy stripes, knit a chevron stitch pattern at the same time you work your stripe pattern (see Appendix A for a chevron stitch pattern).

If you've found a good basic sweater pattern and want to add a wavy striped border to the bottom and sleeves, sample the chevron stitch on different needles until you match the gauge given in your sweater pattern. Then work the border on the body and sleeves as deep as you like before switching to stockinette stitch for the sweater body.

Striping any which way

You can also break up the strong horizontal feel of stripes by knitting randomly striped strips and sewing them together. Or you can work mismatched stripes in vertical panels by using the intarsia method of color knitting. (We cover intarsia in Chapter 13.) Breaking up stripes prevents them from traveling across the width of the entire piece. Finally, you can make patches of stripes (lots of gauge swatches!) and sew them together at 90-degree angles for a patchwork effect.

Practice Striped Projects

If you have doubts about your creative abilities, or if you feel like you wouldn't know where to begin to invent a color pattern, try knitting the projects in this section. Earlier in this chapter, we tell you all you need to know to tackle the striped elements in these projects: how to change colors and how to carry yarn up the side edge of your knitting. Now, all you need is to relax and indulge in a little color spontaneity. You'll be amazed at the great-looking pieces you can turn out from such simple techniques. (For a refresher on any of the basic techniques used in these projects, check out the chapters in Part II.)

Bold and Bright Scarf

A striped scarf is the classic knitted item par excellence. And the scarf is the classic garment on which to practice stripes! This scarf pattern varies in texture as well as colors. You can follow the pattern given here by using the specific yarns we suggest, or you can substitute yarns from your own collection.

Materials and vital statistics

✔ **Measurements:** 7 inches x 54 inches

✔ **Yarn:** Red Heart "With Wool" (80% acrylic/20% wool; CYC #4, 146 yards, 3.5 ounces [100 grams]):

- **Color A:** Tangerine; 1 skein

- **Color B:** Dahlia; 1 skein

- **Color C:** Pixie; 1 skein

- **Color D:** Gumball; 1 skein

- **Color E:** Tropical; 1 skein

✔ **Needles:** One pair of size US 10 (6 mm) needles or size needed to obtain gauge

✔ **Gauge:** 20 stitches and 20 to 24 rows per 4 inches in the various patterns of the scarf

Directions

Note: Most of the color changes for this scarf occur when the RS is facing. Be on the alert, however, because some of the changes begin with the WS facing.

Using Color A, cast on 30 sts and work 6 rows in garter stitch (knit every row).

Begin stripe pattern as follows:

> With Color A, work 8 rows in St st (knit on RS rows, purl on WS rows).
>
> With Color B, work 2 rows in St st.
>
> With Color C, work 2 rows in St st.
>
> With Color D, work 6 rows in St st.
>
> With Color E, work 4 rows in St st.

With Color A, work 7 rows in St st and 4 rows in garter stitch.

With Color D, work 13 rows in St st.

With Color C, work 4 rows in St st and 6 rows in garter stitch.

With Color B, work 2 rows in St st.

With Color A, work 6 rows in St st.

With Color E, work 4 rows in St st.

With Color D, work 6 rows in St st.

With Color C, work 2 rows in St st.

With Color B, work 2 rows in St st.

With Color A, work 6 rows in St st.

Repeat the stripe pattern 2 more times for a total of three repeats.

End the scarf by working 6 rows in garter stitch in Color A.

Bind off.

Weave in the ends horizontally along color change lines.

Finishing: Block the scarf (see Chapter 17 for blocking instructions).

Variations

Striped projects are easy to improvise. The following variations are just a few ideas to get you going:

- ✔ Use yarns in different fibers and textures. They needn't be labeled for the same gauge, but it helps if their gauges are within half a stitch of each other.
- ✔ Use different stitch patterns in the different stripes. Try seed stitch (see Chapter 5) or one of its variations.
- ✔ Keep the color change sequence but work the entire scarf in a rib or another single-pattern stitch.
- ✔ Play around with scale by doubling or halving the number of rows in each stripe.

Slouchy Hat with Pompom

This trendy hat is quick to knit up and cozy when finished — and you don't have to worry about sewing any seams! Make it in a soft yarn in colors of your choice, and you'll end up with a striped hat that is as bold and bright as the scarf in the preceding section. Visit www.dummies.com/go/knittingfd for a video showing how to knit up this fantastic slouchy hat.

Materials and vital statistics

- ✔ **Measurements:** 24 inches in circumference x 11 inches
- ✔ **Yarn:** Red Heart "With Wool" (80% acrylic/20% wool; CYC #4, 146 yards, 3.5 ounces [100 grams]):
  - • **Color A:** Tropical; 1 skein
  - • **Color B:** Dahlia; 1 skein
  - • **Color C:** Pixie; 1 skein
  - • **Color D:** Lapis; 1 skein
  - • **Color E:** Tangerine; 1 skein
- ✔ **Needles:** One 16-inch size US 8 (5 mm) circular needle; four or five size US 8 (5 mm) dpns or size needed to obtain gauge
- ✔ **Gauge:** 20 stitches and 24 rows per 4 inches in the various patterns of the scarf

Directions

With the 16-inch circular needle and Color A, cast on 80 sts, place marker to denote beginning of round, and join round, being careful not to twist the stitches.

Work in k2, p2 ribbing pattern until brim measures 1½ inches from cast-on edge.

Increase round: Change to Color B, * k1, kfb; rep from * to end of round — 120 stitches.

Work each color change as a jogless join (refer to the earlier section "Knitting Stripes in the Round") in the following stripe pattern:

> With Color B, work 3 rounds in St st.
>
> With Color C, work 4 rounds in St st.
>
> With Color D, work 4 rounds in St st.
>
> With Color E, work 4 rounds in St st.
>
> With Color A, work 4 rounds in St st.
>
> With Color D, work 4 rounds in St st.
>
> With Color C, work 4 rounds in St st.
>
> With Color B, work 4 rounds in St st.
>
> With Color A, work 4 rounds in St st.
>
> With Color E, work 4 rounds in St st.

With Color D, work 4 rounds in St st.

With Color C, work 4 rounds in St st.

With Color B, work 4 rounds in St st.

With Color A, work 4 rounds in St st.

With Color D, work 4 rounds in St st.

Begin decreases:

Round 1: * K8, k2tog; rep from * to end of round — 108 sts.

Round 2 and all even rounds: Knit without decreasing.

Round 3: * K7, k2tog; rep from * to end of round — 96 sts.

Round 5: * K6, k2tog; rep from * to end of round — 84 sts.

Round 7: * K5, k2tog; rep from * to end of round — 72 sts.

Note: At this point, you may want to switch to dpns because the circumference of the round is much smaller than the circular needle's length. Simply distribute the remaining stitches evenly over three or four dpns and knit with the remaining needle (the fourth or fifth, depending on how many you're using).

Round 9: * K4, k2tog; rep from * to end of round — 60 sts.

Round 11: * K3, k2tog; rep from * to end of round — 48 sts.

Round 13: * K2, k2tog; rep from * to end of round — 36 sts.

Rounds 15 and 17: Continue knitting (* k2, k2tog *) until 12 stitches remain.

Cut yarn, leaving at least a 12-inch tail.

Finishing: Thread tail onto yarn needle and then slip remaining stitches onto yarn needle (check out Chapter 6 for a refresher on how to slip stitches). Pull opening closed, push yarn tail to reverse side of fabric, and weave in ends.

Using a pompom maker and all colors of yarn, create a pompom for the top of the hat. Tie a 12-inch piece of yarn to the center of the pompom. Thread the yarn tail through a tapestry needle, and pull the yarn through the center of the top of the hat so that the pompom sits in the right place. Secure the yarn tail to the inside of the hat to keep the pompom in place.

Variations

You can express your creativity — and practice new skills at the same time — by altering the basic stockinette stitch with a texture stitch instead.

Let the color changes show differently on the RS by alternating a stockinette stitch stripe with a reverse stockinette stitch stripe (covered earlier in this chapter). To get reverse stockinette when knitting in the round, you purl every round.

Get a random look by making the number of rounds for each stripe different. If random is difficult for you, try tossing a die and using the number that shows up as the number of rounds you stripe. That's guaranteed to be random.

Two-row Striped Shawlette

A two-row color change can transform a simple garter stitch pattern into something you can't stop knitting. This simple but fun shawlette looks amazing in monochromatic or high-contrast colors. Because you knit this project from end to end and shape it with increases and decreases at one end, you can easily make it larger or smaller.

This delightful accessory is one you'll want to have in every color you wear. It's that perfect little something to wrap around your neck in any season.

Materials and vital statistics

- **Measurements:** 50 inches wingspan x 41 inches depth
- **Yarn:** Drew Emborsky "Inappropriate" (90% extra fine super wash merino/10% nylon; CYC #2, 220 yards, 2 ounces [56 grams]):
  - **Main color (MC):** Grunge, 2 skeins
  - **Contrast color (CC):** Psych, 2 skeins
- **Needles:** One pair of size US 6 (4 mm) needles or size needed to obtain gauge
- **Notions:** Yarn or tapestry needle for weaving in ends
- **Gauge:** 22 stitches and 44 rows per 4 inches in garter stitch pattern

Directions

With MC cast on 3 sts.

Work the increase pattern as follows, alternating between MC and CC every 2 rows. When changing colors, carry the color up the side. On the color-change row, bring the old color to the front, slip the first stitch as if to purl, and bring the yarn to the back. Then continue in the established pattern with the new color.

Rows 1 and 2: Slip 1, k2.

Row 3: Slip 1, k1, yo, k1.

Row 4: Slip 1, p1, k2.

Row 5: Slip 1, k1, yo, knit to end.

Row 6: Slip 1, knit to last 3 stitches, p1, k2.

Rep Rows 5 and 6 until there are 90 sts.

Work the decrease pattern as follows, maintaining the alternating 2-row color sequence.

Row 1: Slip 1, k1, yo, k2tog, knit to end. Notice that this row has an increase coupled with a decrease. Because you're working these 2 stitches in the same row, they cancel each other out; the stitch count will be the same at the end of the row. This pattern maintains the yarn-over lace detail created by the increase stitches on the other side of the shawlette.

Row 2: Slip 1, knit to last 5 stitches, k2tog, p1, k2. This row has the decrease stitches that actually create the decreases on this side of the piece.

Repeat Rows 1 and 2 until 5 stitches remain.

Work the following finishing rows to get back to 3 stitches:

Row 1: Slip 1, k1, yo, k3tog.

Row 2: Slip 1, p1, k2.

Row 3: Slip 1, k1, k2tog.

Row 4: Slip 1, k2.

Bind off.

Finishing: Weave in ends. Block to measurements.

Variations

Spice up this shawlette with a lace border along the yarn-over eyelet edge. It's as easy as choosing a lace pattern you want to use, calculating how many stitches you need to pick up along the edge of the piece, and then picking up that many stitches and working the lace pattern along the edge. For details on lace borders, take a look at Chapter 12.

Make the shawlette really unique by using different colors for the new border or a multiple of different stitches.

Chapter 11

Cable Musings and Interesting Twists

- -

- -

Cables, like knit and purl patterns, offer endless design possibilities. If you're familiar with the creamy cabled sweaters of the Aran Isles, which feature intertwining cable motifs in vertical panels arranged symmetrically across a sweater front, then you're already aware of the wealth of traditional cable designs.

The simple technique of *cabling* — crossing one group of stitches over another by knitting them out of order — lends itself to many interpretations. After you master the basic technique (and it's very easy to do), you can make all kinds of interesting and imaginative cable patterns. All it takes is a little patience and practice.

And that's just the beginning. This chapter presents cable basics that beginners can follow as well as some more intricate cables for when you want to stretch your cabling skills.

Cable Basics

You can make any kind of cable by suspending (or holding) a number of stitches on a cable needle (abbreviated cn) while you knit a specified number of stitches from the LH needle. Then you knit the suspended stitches either by returning them to the LH needle and knitting them or by knitting them straight from the cable needle. (See Chapter 2 for more on cable needles.) This process of knitting stitches out of order enables you to cross stitches to create cables. Whether you're making simple or intricate cables, all you're doing is crossing stitches. Easy, right? Right!

Twisting to the right or left

A cable can twist to the right or left, depending on where you hold the suspended stitches.

- ✔ **Left:** To make a cable that twists to the left, hold the suspended stitches in *front* of your work while you knit from the LH needle.
- ✔ **Right:** To make a cable that twists to the right, hold the suspended stitches in *back* of your work.

Cable instructions typically tell you whether you hold the stitches in front or back. Consider these instructions, which create a 6-stitch left-twisting cable:

Sl next 3 sts to cn and hold in *front,* k3, k3 from cn.

Instructions for the same cable, but twisting to the right, read like this:

Sl next 3 sts to cn and hold in *back,* k3, k3 from cn.

You may also see abbreviations like C3F and C3B. The C before the number tells you that these stitches are cable stitches. The number tells you how many stitches are involved with this particular maneuver. The F or B indicates whether to suspend the stitches to the front or the back of your work. So C3F means that you slip 3 stitches to the cable needle and hold it in front. ***Note:*** Some patterns may list the same cable pattern as C6F and C6B, referring to 6 stitches rather than 3 because you suspend 3 and then knit 3 stitches from the LH needle (3 + 3 = 6). Read the pattern abbreviations for every pattern to make sure you are in fact doing the stitch that the designer intended you to do.

Finding the right cable needle

Various styles of cable needles are available. We prefer to work with a needle shaped like a U with a short leg, because it seems to stay out of our way better than the other kinds and the stitches on hold don't slide off. The other versions have different advantages. For example, the straight-needle type makes it easier to knit cable stitches being held directly from the cable needle, but we sometimes lose stitches with this version and never have been able to figure out what to do with the LH needle while knitting stitches from the cable needle. Try the different types as you practice cables to see which best suits your knitting style. Refer to Chapter 2 for info on the types of cable needles.

Reading cable charts

Most knitting patterns give cable instructions in chart form. These charts show the cable stitches, cable rows, and often some background stitches. Depending on how complicated the cable pattern is, the chart may show you one repeat of the cable or an entire piece.

Although chart symbols aren't standardized, every pattern has a key to the symbols used. Figure 11-1 shows a chart for a 6-stitch left-twisting cable.

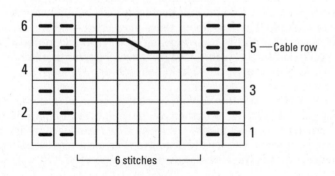

6 stitches

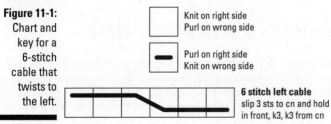

Figure 11-1: Chart and key for a 6-stitch cable that twists to the left.

☐ Knit on right side
Purl on wrong side

▬ Purl on right side
Knit on wrong side

6 stitch left cable
slip 3 sts to cn and hold in front, k3, k3 from cn

Illustration by Wiley, Composition Services Graphics

The chart represents the front side of your knitting. Each square in the chart represents a stitch. Here's a breakdown of this chart according to its legend:

- ✔ **A horizontal line** in the square indicates a stitch that you purl on the right side and knit on the wrong side.

- ✔ **The empty squares** represent the cable stitches, which you knit on the right side and purl on the wrong side. In Figure 11-1, the six empty squares tell you that the cable is 6 stitches wide.

- ✔ **The cable symbol in the cable row** indicates (via the key) whether to hold the stitches in the front or the back. Usually, the symbols mean the following, but be sure to check your pattern's chart key before you begin knitting:

    - When the cable symbol begins at the bottom of the square and jogs to the top (as it does in Figure 11-1, reading Row 5 from right to left), you hold the yarn in front.

    - When the cable symbol begins at the top of the square and jogs to the bottom, you hold the yarn in back.

When you knit cables, you don't have to cross stitches on every row (thank goodness!). You cross the stitches only on the cable row. After the cable row, you work several plain rows, and then you work another cable row.

When following cable charts, you may find it helpful to color in the cable rows. Sometimes we like to color each cable stitch a different color so that they're easily identified by the color. This system is very helpful when working a pattern with multiple types of cables. Use a magnetic board and strip to mark your place on the chart to help you stay on track. Sticky notes work well, too. If you're knitting a pattern that has several panels of different cables, use stitch markers on the needle to help delineate the separate panels.

Remember to pay attention to your knitted piece as well as your chart or instructions. Check to see whether you're cabling in the right direction and have worked the correct number of rows. When you learn to read what's happening in your work, you hardly need the chart or the markers after you knit a couple of repeats of the entire pattern.

Checking gauge in a cable pattern

If you're making a project in a repeating cable pattern, be sure to work a large enough swatch to be able to measure gauge accurately. The swatch should include at least two repeats of the cable pattern horizontally and vertically. If you're working several different cables, you have to check your gauge over each one.

Adding cables to a basic pattern

The combination of knit panels with purl panels (think ribs) and crossing stitches over stitches causes cable patterns to pull in widthwise. A sweater worked in a cable pattern is significantly narrower than one worked using the same number of stitches in stockinette stitch. You need more yarn and more stitches for a cable sweater than for one of the same dimensions in a knit/purl pattern.

If you decide to add a cable (or several) to a plain sweater, be sure to increase enough stitches after you knit your border in order to maintain the overall width. Your gauge swatch is very important here. Use it to play around with the number of stitches you need to add a cable stitch to a plain sweater. Although there are no hard and fast rules, you'll be safe if you add 1 to 2 extra stitches for every 4 stitches in your cable. If you have a ribbed border, you can add the stitches evenly on the last ribbed row. Chapter 6 has instructions on making increases.

Feel like you're wasting time making swatches to check gauge? Make two gauge swatches and sew them together for a cabled pillow or bag.

A Cornucopia of Cables

The patterns in this section are designed to give you an idea of the many ways you can use a simple crossing technique to create a rich variety of cables. Although standard or rope cables are the most basic cables, you aren't limited to those. You can also create

- ✔ A double cable that looks like a horseshoe
- ✔ *Open* cables, where the cable strands separate
- ✔ A braid cable that uses three rather than two cable strands
- ✔ Allover cable patterns, like honeycomb cable

Practice the cable patterns in the following sections in order to improve your cabling technique. Each cable panel includes 3 set-up stitches on both sides of the cable. These set-up stitches make a crisp transition between the background fabric and the cable itself.

Standard (rope) cable

Standard, or rope, cables have the same number of plain rows between cable rows as there are stitches in the cable. If the cable is 6 stitches wide, for example, you work the cable row every 6 rows. These cable patterns generally cross stitches predictably up a single column of stitches. You can make a rope cable over almost any even number of stitches.

Here's the pattern for a 6-stitch left-twisting cable, where the first and last 4 stitches make up the background and the 6 central stitches form your cable (you can see the cable row in Figure 11-2):

> Cast on 14 sts.
>
> **Rows 1 and 3 (RS):** P4, k6, p4.
>
> **Rows 2, 4, and 6:** K4, p6, k4.
>
> **Row 5, the cable row:** P4, sl next 3 sts to cn and hold in front, k3 from LH needle, k3 from cn, p4.
>
> Rep Rows 1–6 and watch your stockinette stitches become a cabled rope.

When you suspend stitches on the cable needle, let the cable needle dangle down in front of your work, giving the yarn a slight tug to keep it taut (you don't need to close the gap).

Stitches from cable needle

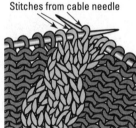

Figure 11-2: Work the cable row.

a. Slip the cable stitches to the cable needle and hold in front.

b. Knit 3 from the LH needle.

c. Knit the stitches from the cable needle.

Illustration by Wiley, Composition Services Graphics

Instead of knitting stitches directly from the cable needle, you may prefer to return the suspended stitches to the LH needle before you knit them. Try both ways and use the technique that's more comfortable for you.

When you work cables, you go back and forth from purl stitches to knit stitches. To switch from a knit to a purl stitch, bring your yarn to the front before you make the next stitch. From a purl to a knit stitch, bring your yarn to the back before you make the next stitch.

Counting cable rows

Get used to counting the rows between cable crossings, and you won't have to rely on your memory. (It's always good to have an alternative to memory.) Look carefully at the cable row: If the cable crosses to the right, you should see a small hole created by the pull of the stitches just to the left of the cable crossing. (You may have to stretch the knitting vertically a bit to see it.) If the cable crosses to the left, the hole is on the right. Just below the hole is a horizontal running thread stretching between the last crossed stitch and the background. The following figure shows you what to look for.

Starting with the running thread *above* the hole, count up running threads to determine the number of rows worked since the last cable row. Alternatively, you can follow the thread to the stitch it connects to — the knit stitch in the cable or the purled stitch in the background. Starting with the stitch *above* the connected stitch, count up to and include the stitch on the needle for the number of rows worked. If you're working a 6-stitch cable and you count 6 running threads or stitches, you're ready for a cable row.

Small hole

Illustration by Wiley, Composition Services Graphics

Open cable

Not all cables are worked on the same stitches over and over. Using basic cabling techniques, you can cross stitches over the background as well to make open cables (sometimes called *traveling cables*). Picture the strands of a basic rope cable separating and moving away from each other and then returning and twisting around each other again, as in Figure 11-3.

Photograph by Wiley, Composition Services Graphics

Figure 11-3:
Open cable.

To work an open cable, you simply cross stitches as in a basic cable, but instead of crossing stockinette stitches over stockinette stitches, you cross stockinette stitches over one or more background (usually purl) stitches. You can open a cable and have the strands move away from each other by using the same crossing technique used for the 6-stitch rope cable in the preceding section.

The open cable pattern in Figure 11-3 consists of a panel of 11 stitches. The point at which they cross is simply a 4-stitch cable row. To knit this open cable, you need two new techniques:

- **Back cross:** Sl next p stitch to cn and hold in back, k2, p the stitch from the cn.
- **Front cross:** Sl next 2 sts to cn and hold in front, p1, k2 from cn.

Knit the open cable pattern as follows:

Cast on 11 sts.

Rows 1 and 3 (WS): K3, p2, k1, p2, k3.

Row 2: P3, sl next 3 sts to cn (2 k sts and 1 p st) and hold in back, k2, sl next p st back to LH needle and p it, k2 from cn, p3.

Row 4: P2, back cross, p1, front cross, p2.

Row 5: K2, p2, k3, p2, k2.

Row 6: P1, back cross, p3, front cross, p1.

Rows 7 and 9: K1, p2, k5, p2, k1.

Row 8: P1, k2, p5, k2, p1.

Row 10: P1, front cross, p3, back cross, p1.

Row 11: K2, p2, k3, p2, k2.

Row 12: P2, front cross, p1, back cross, p2.

Rep Rows 1–12.

Double cable

Also known as a *horseshoe cable,* a *double cable* (see Figure 11-4) consists of a panel of 18 stitches (the cable is 12 stitches wide with 3 set-up stitches on either side of it). Visit www.dummies.com/go/knittingfd for a video demonstration of how this double cable comes together.

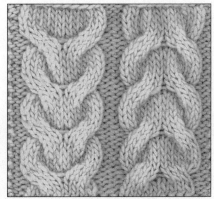

Figure 11-4: Double cable.

Photograph by Wiley, Composition Services Graphics

Follow these instructions to work this double cable pattern:

Cast on 18 sts.

Rows 1 and 3 (RS): P3, k12, p3.

Rows 2, 4, and 6: K3, p12, k3.

Row 5: P3, sl next 3 sts to cn and hold in back, k3, k3 from cn, sl next 3 sts to cn and hold in front, k3, k3 from cn, p3.

Rep Rows 1–6.

Did you notice that this is nothing more than a right cable next to a left cable? You can turn the cable upside down by working a left cable first and then a right one.

Wave cable

A *wave cable* (see Figure 11-5) consists of a panel of 12 stitches (the cable itself is 6 stitches wide). This cable gets its appearance from crossing inconsistently — to the right on one cable row and to the left on the next cable row.

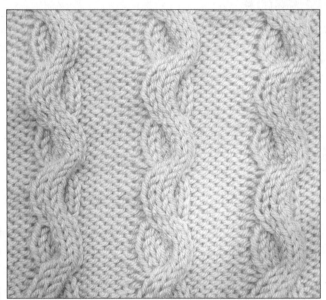

Figure 11-5:
Wave
cables.

Photograph by Wiley, Composition Services Graphics

Work the wave cable as follows:

Cast on 12 sts.

Rows 1, 3, 7, and 9 (RS): P3, k6, p3.

Rows 2, 4, 6, 8, 10, and 12: K3, p6, k3.

Row 5: P3, sl next 3 sts to cn and hold in back, k3, k3 from cn, p3.

Row 11: P3, sl next 3 to cn and hold in front, k3, k3 from cn, p3.

Rep Rows 1–12.

Chain cable

A chain panel (shown in Figure 11-6) consists of 14 stitches; the cable itself is 8 stitches wide.

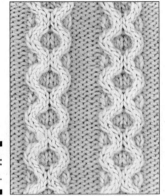

Photograph by Wiley,
Composition Services Graphics

Figure 11-6:
Chain cable.

Work this cable as follows:

> Cast on 14 sts.
>
> **Rows 1 and 5 (RS):** P3, k8, p3.
>
> **Rows 2, 4, 6, and 8:** K3, p8, k3.
>
> **Row 3:** P3, sl next 2 sts to cn and hold in back, k2, k2 from cn, sl next 2 sts to cn and hold in front, k2, k2 from cn, p3.
>
> **Row 7:** P3, sl next 2 sts to cn and hold in front, k2, k2 from cn, sl next 2 sts to cn and hold in back, k2, k2 from cn, p3.
>
> Rep Rows 1–8.

Did you notice that a chain cable is just two wave cables waving in opposite directions and lined up side by side?

Honeycomb cable

A *honeycomb cable* (see Figure 11-7) is made of a multiple of 8 stitches. Because this cable pattern is an allover pattern (that is, it makes up the whole knitted fabric), it's set up as a multiple of stitches rather than as a panel.

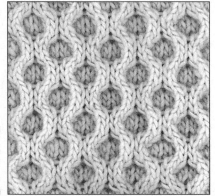

Figure 11-7:
Honeycomb
cable.

Photograph by Wiley, Composition Services Graphics

Knit this pattern as follows:

Cast on a multiple of 8 sts.

Rows 1 and 5 (RS): Knit.

Row 2, 4, 6, and 8: Purl.

Row 3: * Sl next 2 sts to cn and hold in back, k2, k2 from cn, sl next 2 sts to cn and hold in front, k2, k2 from cn; rep from * to end of row.

Row 7: * Sl next 2 sts to cn and hold in front, k2, k2 from cn, sl next 2 sts to cn and hold in back, k2, k2 from cn; rep from * to end of row.

Rep Rows 1–8.

Braid cable

A *braid cable* (shown in Figure 11-8) consists of a panel of 15 stitches; the cable itself is 9 stitches wide.

Knit this pattern as follows:

Cast on 15 sts.

Rows 1 and 5 (RS): P3, k9, p3.

Rows 2, 4, 6, and 8: K3, p9, k3.

Row 3: P3, sl next 3 sts to cn and hold in front, k3, k3 from cn, k3, p3.

Row 7: P3, k3, sl next 3 sts to cn and hold in back, k3, k3 from cn, p3.

Rep Rows 1–8.

This charming baby set features a cozy kimono-style wrap top cardigan with an adorable matching hat, great for a beginner to venture into garment knitting (Chapter 19).

Get comfortable with knits and purls by making a seed stitch cowl from Chapter 9. Use a fashion yarn that has some sparkle, and this cowl will quickly become your favorite accessory.

Sock yarn is for more than just socks! This simple reversible shawlette (Chapter 10) is knit from side to side, alternating two different colors of sock yarn in garter stitch to create a unique look. Wear it over your shoulders or around your neck like a cowl.

You just can't have enough scarves! This fulled scarf in horseshoe lace (Chapter 14) features the unlikely yet stunning pairing of fulling and lace in one project.

This simple rolled-brim hat is an easy way to get started knitting in the round (Chapter 9).

Making slight variations can increase the complexity of a single pattern. This ribbed watchman's cap takes the pattern for a simple rolled-brim hat and kicks it up a notch (Chapter 9).

Reduce, reuse, and recycle with this highly functional lace market bag from Chapter 12. It stretches to hold as much as or more than a standard plastic grocery bag, and it's a wonderful way to show off your knitting skills.

Knit in a bulky weight yarn, you'll be amazed at how quickly this vest flies off your needles. This project, with the option of either a hood or a collar, is great for the beginner knitter ready to venture into garments (Chapter 19).

Crank up the interest on a regular striped scarf by knitting garter stitch on the bias with a self-striping yarn. This scarf is not only fun to knit but also fun to wear (Chapter 9).

Scarves are, by far, the most popular items to knit. Looking at this scalloped scarf, it's easy to see why. Head to Chapter 9 to find out how to knit up this simple yet stunning scarf.

Bulky yarn, seed stitch, and cables — oh my! Practice knitting cables and seed stitch as you make this modern cowl with matching fingerless mitts from Chapter 11.

Just because it's simple doesn't mean it has to be boring! This flattering pullover from Chapter 19 is knit from the top down with raglan shaping, 3/4-length sleeves, and a simple garter stitch border that adds texture. Sew on contrasting buttons for interest.

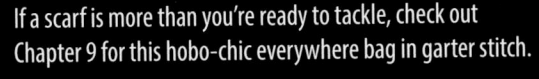

If a scarf is more than you're ready to tackle, check out Chapter 9 for this hobo-chic everywhere bag in garter stitch.

A fun and funky way to show off cables, this cable hat with pompoms from Chapter 11 is a wonderful project to try out this knitting technique.

Make losing that first tooth even more special with this cute tooth fairy intarsia pillow from Chapter 13. Play around with different colors to make it perfect for the little girl or boy in your life.

Pillows are the quickest and easiest way to brighten up your home; add a few embellishments — like the buttons here — and you change the whole look of an otherwise simple pillow. Head to Chapter 9 for instructions.

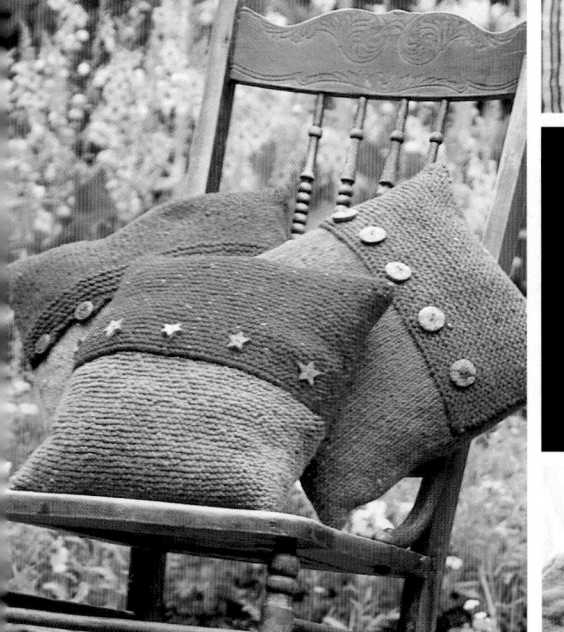

ery knitter needs a fulled bag to carry his or her knitting on the go. This fashionable bag is certain to catch the attention of all your friends — you're sure to be asked to make hem one too! Instructions are in Chapter 14.

Deceptively simple, this scarf with faggot lace (Chapter 12) will cure any lace-phobia you have.

Leg warmers are the latest 80's fashion to make a comeback. Couple the Fair Isle legwarmers from Chapter 13 with a cute pair of boots and a jean and denim skirt for a look that's fun at any age.

Show off your Fair Isle skills from Chapter 13 with this Fair Isle headband, and hit the slopes in style.

You can't go wrong with the knit slouchy hat made in the round (Chapter 10). Stripes in bold colors and a big pompom make this hat really pop! Coordinate it with the bold and bright scarf, or experiment with your own color combinations.

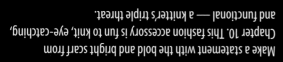

Make a statement with the bold and bright scarf from Chapter 10. This fashion accessory is fun to knit, eye-catching, and functional — a knitter's triple threat.

A twist on an old favorite, this broken rib scarf is reversible and a great way to practice knits and purls (Chapter 9).

Figure 11-8:
Braid cable.

Photograph by Wiley, Composition Services Graphics

You can make a petite version of the braid cable simply by reducing the number of cable stitches (the stitches between the set-up stitches on the edge) to 6. Cross 2 stitches over 2 for this variation.

Varying a cable

Even the simplest cable lends itself to variation. Here are some ideas to try when you're in an experimental mood (keep some graph paper nearby):

- ✔ Change the width of the cable strands.

- ✔ Play around with the number of rows between cable rows.

- ✔ Change the background stitch. Instead of stockinette stitch, work the cable on garter stitch, seed stitch, moss stitch, or something else.

- ✔ Work one cable strand in a different color (see Chapter 13 for info on intarsia knitting).

- ✔ Work one cable strand in a different pattern stitch.

- ✔ Work a twist (essentially a mini cable) in one of the strands; see the next section for a how-to.

- ✔ If you work an open cable with strands that travel out and in, consider the opening a little frame and put something in it — a different pattern stitch, a bobble (see Appendix A), or some embroidery, for example.

The stubborn stitch on the left edge

Often, the left-end knit stitch on a rib or in a cable is noticeably larger than the other knit stitches. When you move from a knit to a purl stitch, the yarn travels a tiny bit farther than it does between 2 knit or 2 purl stitches, resulting in this looser stitch. You can remedy this problem by working the first *2* purl stitches after the cable tighter than normal. After you knit the last stitch, insert your needle into the neighboring purl stitch and give a good tug on the yarn before wrapping and making the stitch. Do so again for the next stitch. This technique helps tighten up the last cable stitch, but *don't* let it tighten up the rest of your stitches.

If you find that you still have a sloppy knit stitch on the left edge of your cable, try this trick: On the right side, work the last knit stitch of the cable. Bring the yarn to the front, slip the next (purl) stitch, and continue on. When you come to the slipped stitch on the next wrong-side row, go into it as if to knit and, at the same time, go under the unworked strand on the right side. With the tip of the LH needle, bring the slipped stitch over the strand, transfer the newly formed stitch to the LH needle in the ready-to-work position, and knit it.

Making Twists

Twists are diminutive cousins of the cable. A twist consists of 2 stitches — 1 stitch crossing over its neighbor. You can twist in either direction: left over right or right over left. To make a 2-stitch twist, you can use a cable needle to take 1 stitch to the front or back while you knit the other stitch. But another method lets you accomplish the crossing, doesn't require a cable needle, saves time, and is easier to do. We show you how to do it in each direction in the following sections.

Twisting to the right

To work a twist to the right, follow these steps:

1. **Slip the 2 designated twist stitches one at a time from the LH needle to the RH needle.**

   Always slip a stitch as if to purl unless your instructions tell you to do otherwise.

2. **Move the tip of the LH needle behind the RH needle, pass up the first slipped stitch, and enter the second slipped stitch from left to right as shown in Figure 11-9.**

   Leave the tip of the LH needle in the slipped stitch.

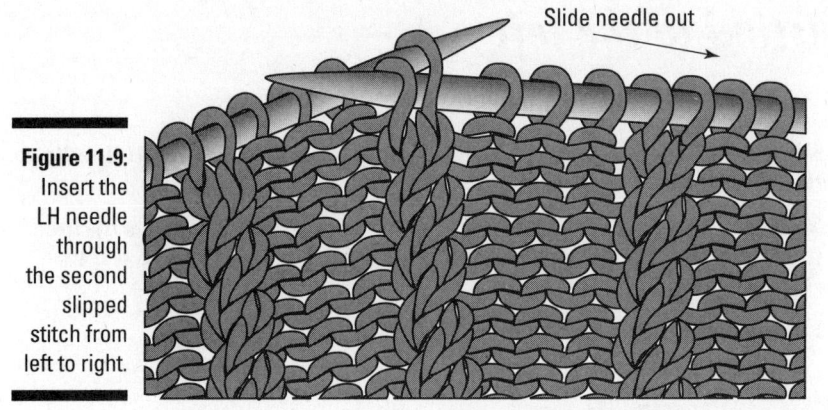

Slide needle out

Figure 11-9:
Insert the LH needle through the second slipped stitch from left to right.

Illustration by Wiley, Composition Services Graphics

3. **Gently slide the RH needle out of both stitches, leaving the second stitch on the LH needle hanging.**

4. **Bring the tip of the RH needle around to the *front* and insert it into the hanging stitch (see Figure 11-10).**

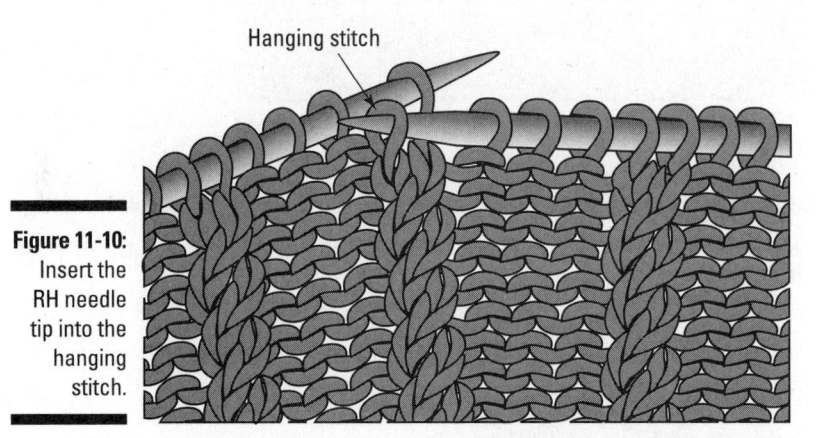

Hanging stitch

Figure 11-10:
Insert the RH needle tip into the hanging stitch.

Illustration by Wiley, Composition Services Graphics

5. **Transfer this stitch to the LH needle.**

   Both stitches are back on the LH needle, with the second one overlapping the first to the right.

6. **Knit both stitches in the usual way.**

Twisting to the left

Here's how to work a twist to the left:

1. **Slip the 2 designated twist stitches one at a time from the LH needle to the RH needle.**

2. **Move the tip of the LH needle in front of the RH needle, pass up the first slipped stitch, and enter the second slipped stitch from left to right (see Figure 11-11).**

   Leave the tip of the LH needle in the slipped stitch.

Figure 11-11:
Insert the
LH needle
from left
to right.

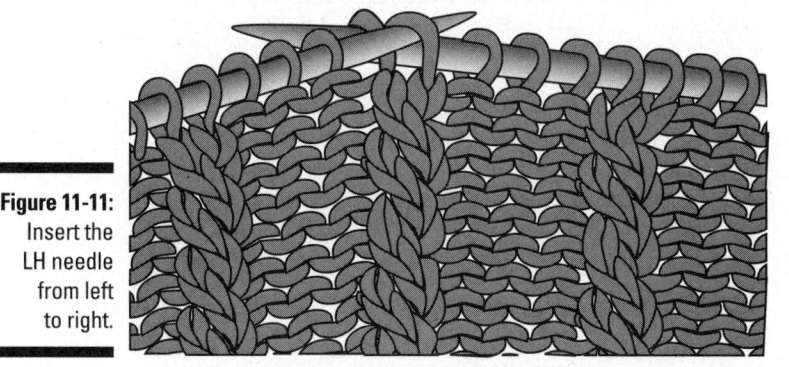

Illustration by Wiley, Composition Services Graphics

3. **Gently slide the RH needle out of both stitches, leaving 1 stitch hanging.**

4. **Keeping the RH needle in *back* of the LH needle, insert the tip of your RH needle into the hanging stitch (see Figure 11-12).**

Pick up hanging stitch

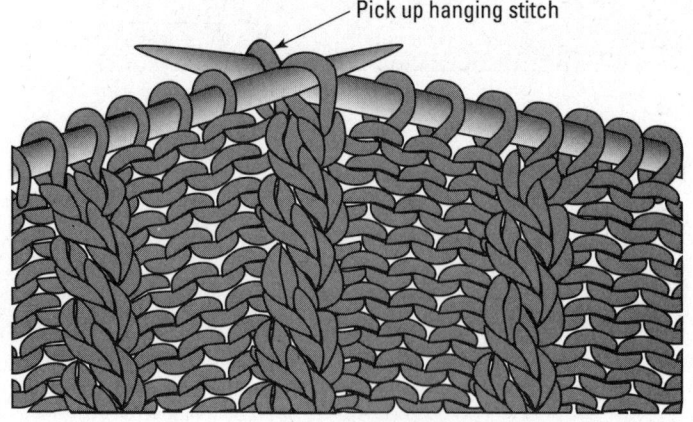

Figure 11-12:
Pick up the
hanging
stitch.

Illustration by Wiley, Composition Services Graphics

5. **Transfer this stitch to the LH needle.**

   Both stitches are back on the LH needle, with the first one overlapping the second to the left.

6. **Knit both stitches in the usual way.**

Practice Cable Projects

Cables lend themselves to almost anything you can knit: hats, pillows, scarves, and sweaters. Even the most basic cables look intriguing, whether alone or in multiples. Follow the patterns for the projects in this section as they are, or use them as guidelines and plug in different types of cables or substitute a column of bobbles (see Appendix A) for one of the cables.

Cable Hat with Pompoms

This Cable Hat with Pompoms is a straightforward hat pattern that uses only one kind of cable: a 6-stitch cable twisting to the right. You make the front and back as separate pieces and seam them along the top and sides.

Materials and vital statistics

- ✔ **Measurements:** 21 inches in circumference (each piece measures 10½ inches wide) x 8 inches

- ✔ **Yarn:** Classic Elite Yarns "Montera" (50% llama/50% wool; CYC #4, 127 yards, 3.5 ounces [100 grams]): Color #3827, 2 hanks

- ✔ **Needles:** One pair each of size US 7 (4½ mm) and US 9 (5½ mm) needles or sizes needed to obtain gauge, cable needle

- ✔ **Other materials:** Pompom maker

- ✔ **Gauge:** 22 stitches and 22 to 24 rows per 4 inches over cable pattern

Directions

With size US 7 needles, cast on 50 sts.

Rows 1–4: * K1, p1; rep from * to end of row.

Change to size US 9 needles.

Row 5 (RS): P2, inc 1, * k2, inc 1, k3, p3; rep from * to end of row (57 sts).

Row 6: * K3, p6; rep from * to last 3 sts, k3.

Work the cable chart (see Figure 11-13), being sure to begin and end each RS row with k3 and to begin and end each WS row with p3:

Row 7 (WS): * P3, work Row 1 of 6-st cable chart; rep from * to last 3 sts, p3.

Row 8 (RS): * K3, work Row 2 of cable chart; rep from * to last 3 sts, k3.

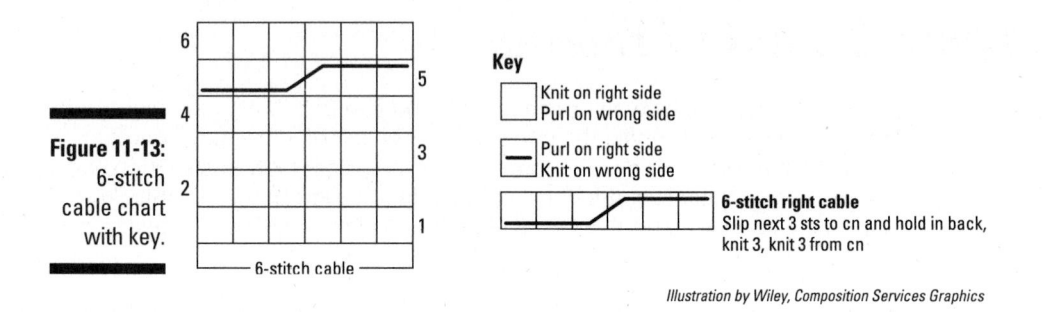

Figure 11-13:
6-stitch
cable chart
with key.

Key
Knit on right side
Purl on wrong side

Purl on right side
Knit on wrong side

6-stitch right cable
Slip next 3 sts to cn and hold in back,
knit 3, knit 3 from cn

6-stitch cable

Illustration by Wiley, Composition Services Graphics

Continue working the chart as established.

Rep the cable chart pattern until the piece measures approximately 8 inches in length, ending with Row 4 (WS) of the pattern.

Note: When working with cables, try to begin and end on a flat part of the cable, between cable rows.

Next row (RS): * P3, k2, k2tog, k2; rep from * to last 3 sts, p3 (51 sts).

Decreasing 1 st in each cable on the final row brings the fabric back to normal width.

Bind off, or if you want to seam your pieces together using the three-needle bind-off (see Chapter 17), run a piece of scrap yarn through the stitches to secure them.

Make a second piece to match the first.

Finishing: After knitting the pieces of your hat, follow these steps to finish it like a pro:

Gently block the squares. Cables are best blocked by using the wet-blocking method (refer to Chapter 17), which allows you to shape and mold the cable pattern.

Seam the top of the hat. Use backstitch or the three-needle bind-off covered in Chapter 17 and then steam the seam.

Sew up the side seams by using mattress stitch and steam the seam.

Add the pompoms. Follow the instructions for using your pompom maker to make pompoms. You can make as many or as few as you like, in the same or different sizes. Leave enough of a tail on the pompoms to braid or twist into a cord. Using a tapestry needle, thread the cords to the inside of the hat and secure them in a seam.

Variations

- ✔ Substitute a column of bobbles for one of the cables. (See Appendix A for bobble-making instructions.)

- ✔ Use a different kind of 6-stitch cable — for example, the wave cable presented earlier in this chapter.

- ✔ Make the hat longer.

- ✔ Use any combination of cable patterns that appeals to you.

Horseshoe Cable Hand Warmers

These stylish Horseshoe Cable Hand Warmers are super-simple to knit. Earlier in the chapter, we introduce a 6-stitch horseshoe cable. For this pattern, we use a 4-stitch horseshoe cable because we're using a heavier weight yarn.

Materials and vital statistics

- ✔ **Measurements:** Approximately 8 inches in circumference x 6 inches; can be shortened or lengthened as desired

- ✔ **Yarn:** Schachenmayr SMC "Big Bravo" (100% acrylic; CYC #6, 131 yards, 7 ounces [200 grams]): Tan, 1 skein

- ✔ **Needles:** One pair of US size 13 (9 mm) needles or size needed to obtain gauge, cable needle

- ✔ **Gauge:** The horseshoe cable is 3 inches wide, and the seed stitch gauge is approximately 8 stitches and 10 rows per 4 inches with the yarn listed here

Directions

It's necessary to have two sets of instructions — one for the left hand and one for the right — in order for the cable to end up on the top of the hand as intended.

Left hand

Cast on 18 sts.

Setup row (RS): P1, k1, place marker, k8, place marker, (k1, p1) four times.

Row 1, 3 (WS): (P1, k1) four times, slip marker, p8, slip marker, k1, p1.

You've now begun the seed stitch outside the markers and stockinette stitch inside the markers. This division remains the same throughout the pattern on every row except the cable row.

Row 2 cable row (RS): Maintain the seed stitch pattern to marker, slip marker, sl next 2 sts to cn and hold in back, k2 from LH needle, k2 from cn, sl next 2 sts to cn and hold in front, k2 from LH needle, k2 from cn, slip marker, work established seed stitch pattern to end.

Row 4: Maintain the seed stitch pattern to marker, slip marker, k8, slip marker, work established seed stitch pattern to end.

Rep Rows 1–4 until hand warmers are long enough to cover the space between the base of your thumb and 1 to 2 inches past your wrist bone. You can make them even longer if you want. Bind off.

Finishing: Seam the right and left sides of the piece together and try it on.

Right hand

Cast on 18 sts.

Setup row (RS): (P1, k1) four times, place marker, k8, place marker, k1, p1.

Row 1, 3 (WS): P1, k1, slip marker, p8, slip marker, (k1, p1) four times.

You have now begun the seed stitch outside the markers and stockinette stitch inside the markers. This division remains the same throughout the pattern on every row except the cable row.

Row 2 cable row (RS): Maintain the seed stitch pattern to marker, slip marker, sl next 2 sts to cn and hold in back, k2 from LH needle, k2 from cn, sl next 2 sts to cn and hold in front, k2 from LH needle, k2 from cn, slip marker, work established seed stitch pattern to end.

Row 4: Maintain the seed stitch pattern to marker, slip marker, k8, slip marker, work established seed stitch pattern to end.

Rep Rows 1–4 until hand warmers are long enough to cover the space between the base of your thumb and 1 to 2 inches past your wrist bone. You can make them even longer if you want. Bind off.

Finishing: Seam the right and left sides of the piece together and try it on.

Horseshoe Cable Cowl with Buttons

This cowl, knit widthwise, is an excellent way to practice cable twists. The best part? Because you knit it widthwise, you can stop knitting whenever you feel you've had enough practice — or when the cowl is as long as you want it to be!

This cowl is knit with chunky yarn for a dramatic look; pair it with the Horseshoe Hand Warmers for a fashionable set this winter. (Access a free video demonstration of this cowl online at www.dummies.com/go/knittingfd.)

Materials and vital statistics

- **Dimensions:** 7 inches x 24 inches, but you can change the dimensions as you work

- **Yarn:** Schachenmayr SMC "Big Bravo" (100% acrylic; CYC #6, 131 yards, 7 ounces [200 grams]): Tan, 1 skein

- **Needles:** One pair of US size 13 (9 mm) needles or size needed to obtain gauge, cable needle

- **Other materials:** 4 buttons

- **Gauge:** The horseshoe cable is 3 inches wide, and the seed stitch gauge is approximately 8 stitches and 10 rows per 4 inches with yarn listed here

Directions

Cowl

Using cable cast-on, cast on 50 sts.

Setup row (RS): P1, (k1, p1) twice, place marker, k8, place marker, (k1, p1) to end.

Row 1, 3 (WS): (P1, k1) to marker, slip marker, p8, slip marker, (p1, k1) twice, p1.

You have now begun seed stitch outside the markers and stockinette stitch inside the markers. This division remains the same throughout the pattern on every row except the cable row.

Row 2 cable row (RS): Maintain the seed stitch pattern to marker, slip maker, sl next 2 sts to cn and hold in back, k2 from LH needle, k2 from cn, sl next 2 sts to cn and hold in front, k2 from LH needle, k2 from cn, slip marker, work established seed stitch pattern to end.

Row 4: Maintain the seed stitch pattern to marker, slip marker, k8, slip marker, work established seed stitch pattern to end.

Rep Rows 1–4 until cowl is approximately 7 inches, ending with a Row 3.

Bind off all the stitches in pattern on the next row.

Button band

Working along the side of the cowl without the cable, with RS facing, pick up and knit 14 sts along the edge.

Rows 1 and 3 (WS): Purl

Row 2 (RS): K2, (yo, k2tog, k1) four times.

Row 4 (RS): Bind off as if to purl.

Make sure that one yarn over makes a large enough hole for your button to go through. If you need a larger buttonhole, yarn over the needle twice in Row 2 to create a double yarn over pair. Then, on Row 3, drop one of the yarn overs in the double yarn over pair and purl the remaining yarn over. This approach keeps the stitch count the same on your row but allows the buttonhole to be larger.

Finishing

Weave in all the ends. Sew the buttons to the opposite side of the cowl adjacent to the buttonhole.

Variations

- ✔ Substitute a different cable stitch for the horseshoe cable. Just adjust the number of stitches between the markers to work with the new number of cable stitches you need and voilà; you have a new cowl!

- ✔ Make it a scarf rather than a cowl. Adjust the cast-on number to have the cable pattern centered between two even numbers of seed stitches on either side. Then work the pattern lengthwise rather than widthwise until it's as long as you want.

- ✔ Instead of seed stitch, try garter stitch or a ribbing for a completely different look.

Chapter 12

Let the Sun Shine In: Knitting Lace

....

....

Knitted lace is versatile. It can be the fabric of an entire garment, the edging on a sleeve, a panel down the front of a sweater, or a single motif in a yoke, to name a few ideas. In a fine yarn on a small needle, it can be intricate and delicate. Worked randomly in a heavy, rustic yarn, it can be minimalist and modern. It can be a small eyelet motif sparsely arranged over an otherwise solid fabric, or it can be light, airy, and full of holes.

And believe it or not, even beginning knitters can make lace. If you can knit and purl, knit 2 stitches together (which we sometimes do inadvertently!), and work a yarn over (explained in Chapter 6), you can make lace. The hardest thing is to keep track of where you are in the pattern (which isn't really a knitting skill . . .).

To familiarize yourself with knitted lace, sample the patterns in this chapter and look closely at your work while you do so. When you can identify a yarn over on your needle and see the difference between an ssk and a k2tog decrease in your knitting (both are explained in detail in Chapter 6), you're on your way to becoming a lace expert.

Reading Lace Charts

Knitted lace makes use of two simple knitting moves — a *yarn over* (an increase that makes a small hole) and a decrease — to create myriad stitch patterns. Every opening in a lace fabric is made from a yarn-over increase, and every yarn over is paired with a decrease to compensate for the increase.

When you understand the basis of lace's increase/decrease structure, even the most complicated lace patterns become intelligible. Of course, you can follow the instructions for a lace stitch without understanding the underlying structure, but being able to recognize how the pattern manipulates the basic yarn over/decrease unit is a great confidence builder.

Knitted lace is a fabric made with yarn overs and decreases, but you can use other ways to get lace-type fabrics. Using a very large needle with a fine yarn makes an open and airy piece of knitting. Our favorite shawl pattern is a simple garter stitch triangle (with increases worked at either end of every row) made in a fingering- or sport-weight yarn and worked on size US 13 (8 mm) needles. For extra visual interest, use a self-patterning sock yarn. Try it!

Yarn-over increase and decrease symbols

Like other charts for knitted stitch patterns, charts for knitted lace "picture" the patterns they represent. As you may expect, the two symbols you find most often in lace charts are the one for a yarn-over increase (usually presented as an *O*) and some kind of slanted line to mimic the direction of a decrease. Take a look at Figure 12-1 for an example.

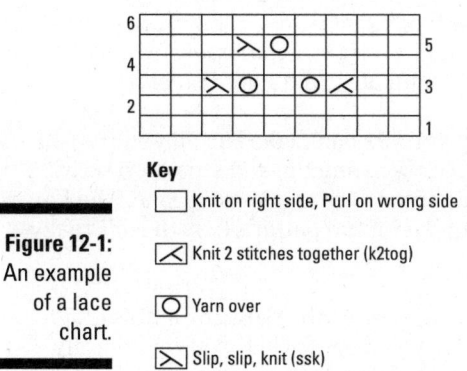

Key

| | Knit on right side, Purl on wrong side |

☑ Knit 2 stitches together (k2tog)

☑ Yarn over

☒ Slip, slip, knit (ssk)

Figure 12-1: An example of a lace chart.

Illustration by Wiley, Composition Services Graphics

Notice that each decrease symbol (k2tog or ssk) appears in only one square, even though a decrease involves 2 stitches. Charting the decrease this way allows the yarn-over symbol to occupy the square for the decreased stitch. Sometimes the yarn over shows up adjacent to the decrease, as it does in this pattern. Other times, the yarn over isn't placed directly before or after the decrease but rather somewhere else entirely in the pattern row. In either case, in most patterns the number of decrease symbols is the same as the number of yarn-over symbols because every increase has a corresponding decrease.

A k2tog (knit 2 stitches together) decrease slants to the right. A ssk (slip, slip, knit) decrease slants to the left. For instructions on these techniques, refer to Chapter 6.

No-stitch symbol

A lace chart sometimes has to show a changing number of stitches from one row to the next. To keep the stitches lined up on the chart the way they are in the fabric, the chart indicates that a stitch has been eliminated temporarily from the pattern by using the no-stitch symbol in the square that represents the decreased stitch. This symbol repeats in a vertical row until an increase is made and the stitch is back in play, as shown in Figure 12-2.

The chart in Figure 12-2 shows a pattern in which one stitch is decreased and left out for 10 rows and then created again and left in for the next 10 rows. The take-out/put-back-in pattern repeats every 20 rows. The black squares in the chart hold the place of the disappearing and reappearing stitch. Using the no-stitch symbol allows the grid to remain uniformly square. Otherwise, the edges of the grid would have to go in and out to match the number of stitches in each row.

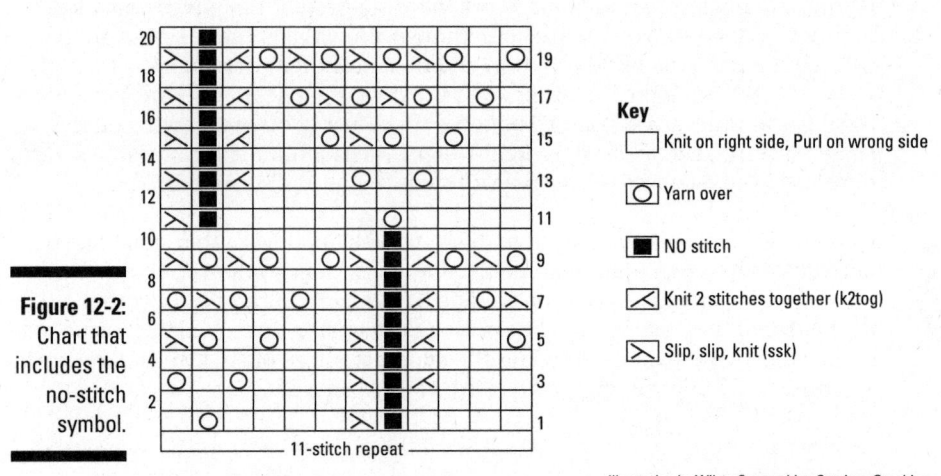

Figure 12-2: Chart that includes the no-stitch symbol.

Key

☐ Knit on right side, Purl on wrong side

◯ Yarn over

■ NO stitch

╱ Knit 2 stitches together (k2tog)

╲ Slip, slip, knit (ssk)

Illustration by Wiley, Composition Services Graphics

When you're working from a chart that uses the no-stitch symbol, skip the symbol when you get to it and work the next stitch on your needle from the chart square just after the no-stitch symbol.

When you suspect that your stitch count is changing, it probably is! If the stitch pattern doesn't say anything about the stitch count changing on different rows and you suspect that it does, you can sort it out by checking the instructions. Add up the number of yarn overs and decreases in each row of a written or charted pattern to see if they're the same (don't forget that double decreases take out 2 stitches).

Knitting Different Kinds of Lace

Knitted lace is varied enough that different categories have been created to describe (loosely) the different types, such as *eyelet lace, open lace,* and *faggot lace.*

The divisions between one kind of lace and another are porous. Better to think of lace patterns as belonging on a continuum — the more solid fabrics with scattered openings (eyelet) at one end, the lacy and open fabrics (allover and faggot patterns) at the other. The lace patterns in this section provide a good introduction to lacework for both beginning and intermediate knitters.

If you're really interested in lacework, here's a project that gives you a lot of practice and lets you create something useful: Make a series of swatches with all the patterns in this section and then sew them together — or simply work one pattern after the other — to create a great scarf. Use the same yarn throughout unless you want to observe the effect of different yarns on the same pattern. Lace worked on light-weight yarns intended for lace looks very different from lace worked with a worsted-weight or chunky yarn.

If you have lace squares knitted in different weights of yarn that don't line up perfectly to be sewn together side by side, turn them so the upper right corners of the squares are pointing up, and overlap each upper right corner to the center of the next square. Stitch along the upside-down V shape, using one of the same yarns you used to knit the squares. These offset lace squares form an appealingly uneven edge for a retro, vintage look.

No matter how many stitches and rows it takes to make a repeat, the marriage of increase and decrease is easy to see in simpler lace patterns and a little harder to track in more complicated ones. With practice, though, you'll quickly see how they work together, and you'll be able to work any lace pattern you fancy with confidence.

For your first forays into lace knitting, choose easier patterns. Specifically look for

- **Patterns that tell you right at the beginning to purl all the wrong-side rows:** In general, the simplest lace patterns call for yarn-over/decrease maneuvers on right-side rows only. More-advanced patterns have you make openings on every row.

- **Patterns made from vertical panels:** You can fairly easily tell if a pattern is organized as a series of vertical repeats because you'll see "lines" running up and down the fabric. You can place a marker after each repeat and keep track of one repeat at a time.

- **Patterns that maintain the same number of stitches on every row:** To maintain the number, every yarn-over increase has an equivalent decrease on the same row. Other patterns call for a yarn-over increase on one row and the corresponding decrease on another. In these latter patterns, the stitch count changes from row to row. Often, the pattern alerts you to these changes and tells you which rows you have to look out for, but even at that, this type of lace is still a bit more challenging.

When you knit lace, always work the edge stitch (or two) in plain stockinette stitch to stabilize the sides of your pieces and make it easier to sew them together. The same is true for cast-on and bound-off edges. If you use stockinette stitch at the edges, be sure to include these selvedge stitches in the number of stitches you cast on. (*Selvedge stitches* are extra stitches at the edge of your knitted fabric that serve to create an even, stable border.) For example, if the lace pattern calls for a multiple of 6 stitches plus 1 more and you want to include 2 stockinette stitches on either end, you add 4 selvedge stitches to the total cast-on count.

Designing your own lace

If you can work eyelet patterns, don't hesitate to try designing your own lace. On a sheet of graph paper, plot yarn overs with adjacent decreases in any arrangement you think is attractive. Keep the following in mind:

- Horizontal eyelets should be spaced 1 stitch apart.

- Vertical rows should be spaced 4 rows apart.

- Diagonal eyelets can be spaced every other row.

Eyelet patterns

Eyelet patterns generally have fewer openings than out-and-out lace patterns and are characterized by small openwork motifs distributed over a solid stockinette (or other closed-stitch pattern) fabric. The increase/decrease structure is usually easy to see in eyelet patterns, making them a good place to begin your lace exploration.

Ridged ribbon eyelet

You can thread a ribbon through these eyelets or use them in a colored stripe pattern. Figure 12-3 shows both a chart and a sample of this pattern.

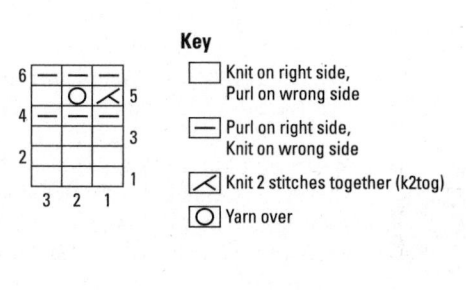

Figure 12-3:
Ridged ribbon eyelet and chart.

Key

☐ Knit on right side,
Purl on wrong side

— Purl on right side,
Knit on wrong side

⟋ Knit 2 stitches together (k2tog)

◯ Yarn over

Photograph and Illustration by Wiley, Composition Services Graphics

You work this pattern as follows:

Cast on an odd number of sts.

Rows 1 and 3 (RS): Knit.

Row 2: Purl.

Rows 4 and 6: Knit.

Row 5: * K2tog, yo; rep from * to last st, k1.

Cloverleaf eyelet

Figure 12-4 shows a three-eyelet cloverleaf arranged over a stockinette background.

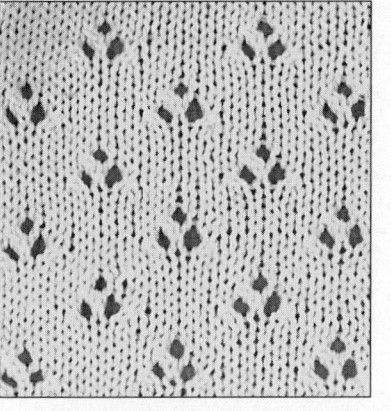

Photograph by Wiley, Composition Services Graphics

Figure 12-4:
Cloverleaf
eyelet
pattern.

This cloverleaf pattern requires a multiple of 8 stitches, plus 7 more. You work a double decrease between the two bottom eyelets. To knit this pattern, follow these steps:

Cast on a multiple of 8 sts, plus 7 sts.

Row 1 (RS): Knit.

Row 2 and all WS rows: Purl.

Row 3: K2, yo, sl 1, k2tog, psso, yo, * k5, yo, sl 1, k2tog, psso, yo; rep from * to last 2 sts, k2.

Row 5: K3, yo, ssk, * k6, yo, ssk; rep from * to last 2 sts, k2.

Row 7: K1, * k5, yo, sl 1, k2tog, psso, yo; rep from * to last 6 sts, k6.

Row 9: K7, * yo, ssk, k6; rep from * to end of row.

Row 10: Purl.

Rep Rows 3–10.

Open lace patterns

Out-and-out lace patterns have more openings than solid spaces in their composition. They're frequently used in shawls or any project that cries out for a more traditional lace look.

The patterns in this section are more *open* — meaning that they have more holes — than the eyelet patterns earlier. Try them in fine yarns on fine needles (think elegant cashmere scarves) or in chunky yarn on big needles for a nontraditional look.

Arrowhead lace

Arrowhead lace (see Figure 12-5) requires a multiple of 6 stitches, plus 1. Row 4 of this pattern uses the double decrease psso, meaning "pass slipped stitch over." "P2sso" means "pass 2 slipped stitches over." (Flip to Chapter 6 for a refresher on how to make this decrease.) Visit www.dummies.com/go/ knittingfd to see a video that demonstrates just how easy arrowhead lace — and other lace patterns — are to knit.

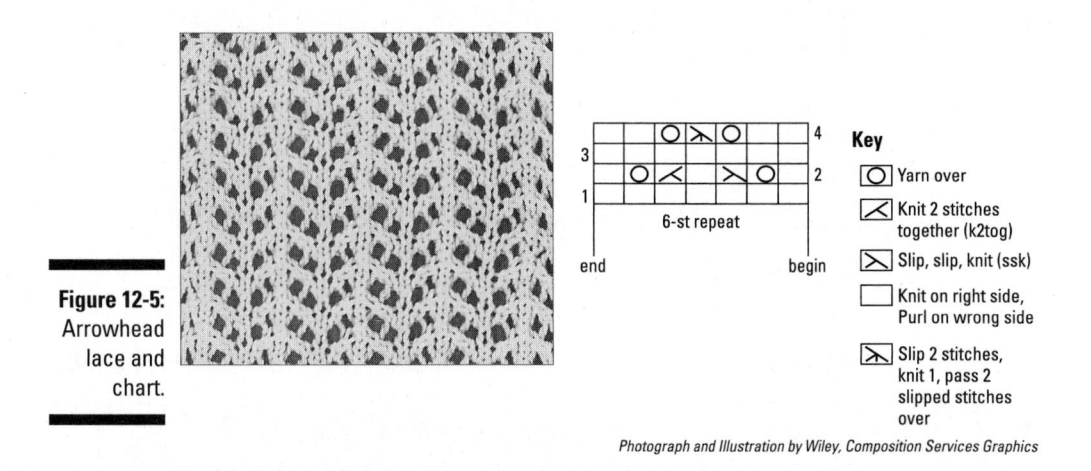

Figure 12-5: Arrowhead lace and chart.

Photograph and Illustration by Wiley, Composition Services Graphics

Knit this pattern as follows:

Cast on a multiple of 6 sts, plus 1 st.

Rows 1 and 3 (WS): Purl.

Row 2: K1, * yo, ssk, k1, k2tog, yo, k1; rep from * to end of row.

Row 4: K2, * yo, sl 2 kwise, k1, p2sso, yo, k3; rep from * to last 5 sts, yo, sl 2 kwise, k1, p2sso, yo, k2.

Rep Rows 1–4.

Miniature leaf pattern

Figure 12-6 shows a simple miniature leaf pattern in which each little "leaf" is surrounded by lace openings.

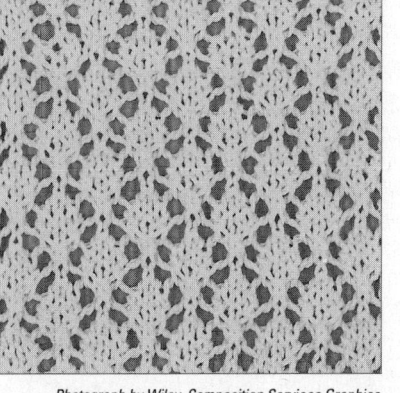

Figure 12-6:
Miniature
leaf open
lace pattern.

Photograph by Wiley, Composition Services Graphics

Knit this pattern as follows (if you prefer charts over written instructions, see the chart in Figure 12-7):

Cast on a multiple of 6 sts, plus 1 st.

Row 1 and all WS rows: Purl.

Row 2: K1, * k2tog, yo, k1, yo, ssk, k1; rep from * to end of row.

Row 4: K2tog, * yo, k3, yo, sl 2 kwise, k1, p2sso; rep from * to last 5 sts, yo, k3, yo, ssk.

Row 6: K1, * yo, ssk, k1, k2tog, yo, k1; rep from * to end of row.

Row 8: K2, * yo, sl 2 kwise, k1, p2sso, yo, k3; rep from * to last 5 sts, yo, sl 2 kwise, k1, p2sso, yo, k2.

Rep Rows 1–8.

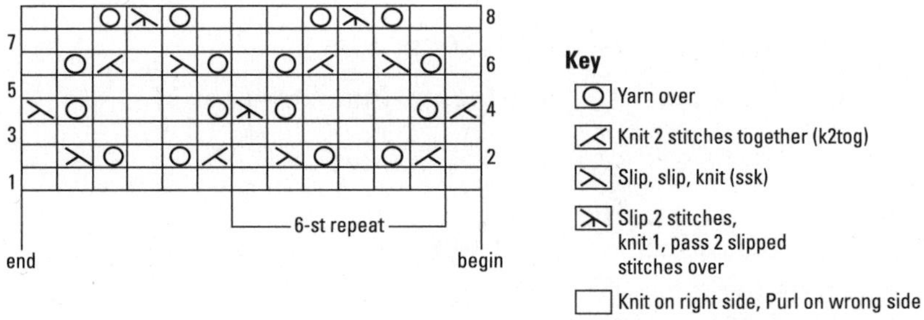

Figure 12-7:
Chart for the
miniature
leaf pattern.

end

begin

6-st repeat

Key

⊙ Yarn over

╱ Knit 2 stitches together (k2tog)

╲ Slip, slip, knit (ssk)

⋊ Slip 2 stitches,
knit 1, pass 2 slipped
stitches over

☐ Knit on right side, Purl on wrong side

Illustration by Wiley, Composition Services Graphics

Faggot lace

Faggot patterns (basic lace) are really a category unto themselves. They're composed of nothing but the simplest lace-making unit: a yarn over followed (or preceded) by a decrease. You can work a faggot unit over and over for a very open mesh-like fabric, as shown in Figure 12-8a. Or try working a faggot grouping as a vertical panel in an otherwise solid fabric or as a vertical panel alternating with other lace or cable panels, as shown in Figure 12-8b.

Figure 12-8: Faggot lace by itself (a) and combined with another lace pattern (b).

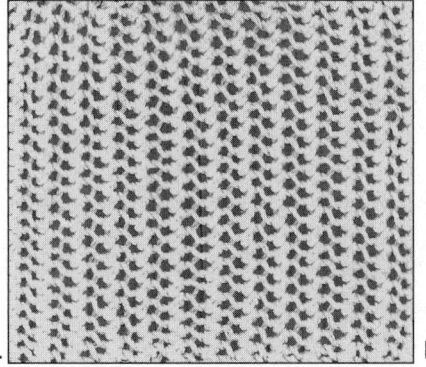 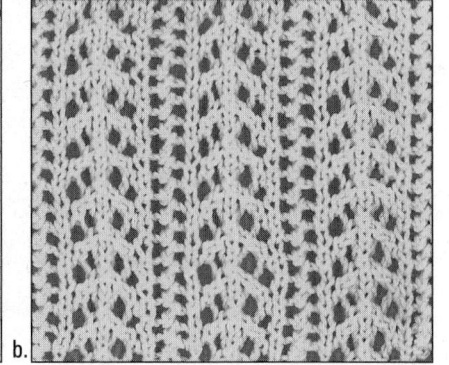

a.   b.

Photographs by Wiley, Composition Services Graphics

You can work faggot patterns with a knitted decrease (ssk or k2tog) or a purled decrease. The appearance of the lace changes very subtly depending on the decrease you use.

Basic faggot is made by alternating a yarn over and a p2tog decrease. We find this variation (called *purse stitch*) faster and easier to work than others. Follow these instructions (or see the chart in Figure 12-9):

Cast on an even number of sts.

Every row: K1; * yo, p2tog; rep from * to last st, k1.

Figure 12-9: Chart for faggot lace.

2-st repeat

end   begin

Key

☐ Knit on right side and wrong side

☑ Yarn over

◺ Purl 2 tog

Illustration by Wiley, Composition Services Graphics

To use the faggot repeat as a vertical panel in a garment (whether it's a sweater front or the middle of a scarf), work one repeat between as many stockinette stitches as you like.

Incorporating Lace into Other Pieces

If you want to incorporate knitted lace into a sweater and can't find a pattern that appeals to you, you can work in a lace pattern without a specific set of pattern instructions.

Numerous stitch dictionaries offer a variety of lace patterns to draw from. Our favorites are Barbara Walker's *Treasury of Knitting Patterns* books.

Lace insertions

The simplest way to incorporate lace into a knitted project is to work a vertical lace panel or eyelet motif (otherwise known as a lace *insertion*) into a plain stockinette or simple stitch sweater. Place the panel or motif anywhere in your sweater body, far enough away from a shaped edge so that the panel won't be involved in any increases or decreases. This way, you can concentrate on the lace stitches and avoid having to work any garment shaping around the yarn overs and decreases of your lace stitch.

If you insert an open lace stitch as a vertical panel, you may want to cast on a few stitches less than the pattern calls for because lace spreads out more than stockinette. Of course, if you want to be exact, you can work out the gauge of your lace insertion and the gauge of the stitch pattern in the sweater body and adjust the numbers accordingly.

You also can add lace as a horizontal insertion. Figure 12-10 shows arrowhead lace, but this time several row repeats have been inserted across a piece of stockinette stitch fabric.

Some stitch pattern books separate lace insertions from allover lace patterns, but if you find a pattern with a vertical orientation (arrowhead, for example), you can isolate a repeat and work it by itself as an insertion.

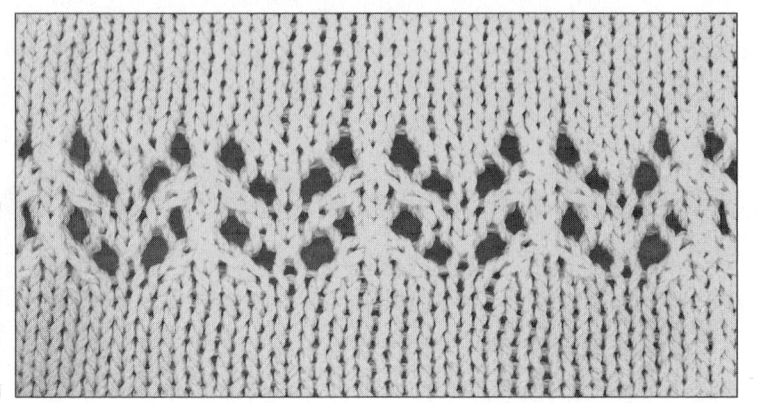

Photograph by Wiley, Composition Services Graphics

Figure 12-10:
Arrowhead lace used as a horizontal insertion.

Lace edgings

Dress up any sweater by adding a lace edge at the bottom of the sweater body or sleeve. Knitted lace edgings are borders designed with a scalloped or pointed edge. Frequently, they're made in garter stitch to give body to the edging and to ensure that it lies flat. Some edgings, such as hems and cuffs, are worked horizontally; you cast on the number of stitches required for the width of your piece, work the edging, and then continue in stockinette or whatever stitch your garment pattern calls for.

Other edgings are worked vertically and then sewn on later. In this case, you simply cast on the number of stitches required for the depth of the lace edging (from 7 to 20 sts, depending on the pattern) and work the edging until its length matches the width of the piece to which you plan to attach it. Then you bind off, turn the edging on its side, and sew it onto the edge of your project. Or, better yet, you can pick up stitches along the border of the edging itself and knit the rest of the piece from there. (See Chapter 18 for details on how to pick up stitches.)

Avoiding and Correcting Mistakes When Working Lace Patterns

The best way to avoid mistakes in lace-making is to envision how the yarn overs and decreases combine to create the pattern. Take, for example, the cloverleaf eyelet pattern (refer to Figure 12-1 earlier in the chapter to see its chart). This pattern creates the lace shown in Figure 12-11.

Looking at the end product closely, you can see how the increases and decreases work. The eyelets (the holes) are made with yarn-over increases, and the compensating decreases are worked right next to the yarn overs. The decreases look like slanted stitches and come before and after the two eyelets on the bottom of the cloverleaf and after the eyelet on the top. Simply by knowing what's happening with the increases and decreases, you can anticipate what stitch comes next and, in so doing, better avoid missing a yarn over or decrease.

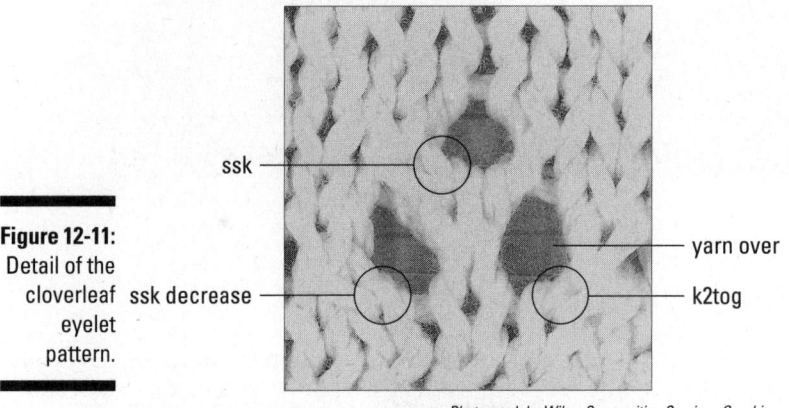

Figure 12-11:
Detail of the cloverleaf eyelet pattern.

Photograph by Wiley, Composition Services Graphics

Finding the error

Sometimes mistakes happen despite your best efforts. In knitting lace, you may "feel" the mistake before you see it. That is, your count will be off, or you'll get to the last stitches in a row and not have enough (or have too many) to knit them according to the pattern, or you'll realize that the hole you're creating is in the wrong place. When this happens, the first thing you need to do is find the error.

The way to do that is to look at the stitches on your needle and check each repeat for the right number of stitches. This point is where it really helps to be able to recognize yarn overs and decreases. Figure 12-12 illustrates a yarn over, an ssk decrease, and a k2tog decrease.

If you're working a pattern in which the stitch count is consistent on every row, tracking an extra or lost stitch is easy. If you're short a stitch, you've probably neglected to make a yarn over. If you find yourself with an extra stitch, you've probably forgotten to make a decrease.

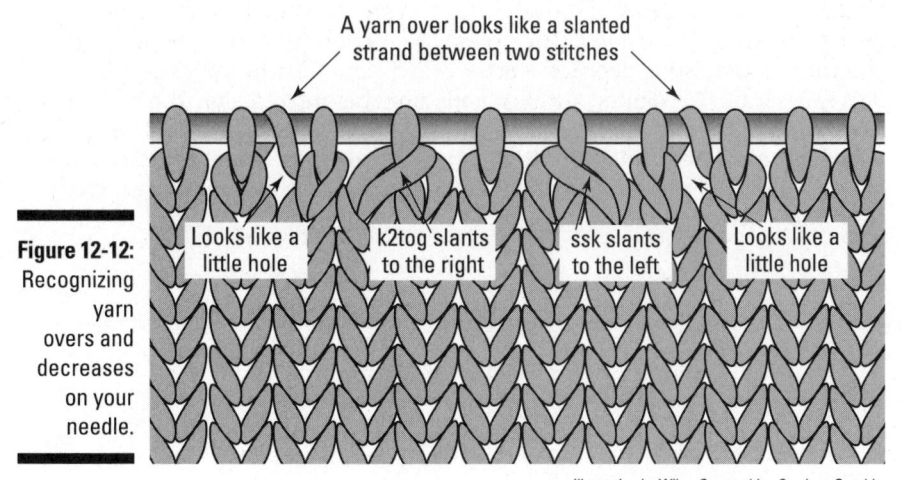

A yarn over looks like a slanted strand between two stitches

Figure 12-12: Recognizing yarn overs and decreases on your needle.

Looks like a little hole

k2tog slants to the right

ssk slants to the left

Looks like a little hole

Illustration by Wiley, Composition Services Graphics

Ripping out lace

If you make a mistake in a lace pattern and have to rip out stitches, take your time when picking up the recovered stitches. Yarn overs and decreases can be tricky to catch. (See Chapter 7 for information about ripping out and picking up recovered stitches.)

When you've ripped out as far back as you need to in order to fix the mistake, slowly take out one more row, pulling the yarn gently from each stitch one at a time and inserting the empty needle into the freed stitch before it has a chance to disappear. This method helps you catch all the yarn overs and decreases. Also, if your pattern is purled on all wrong-side rows, try to make the purl row the one you pick up from.

As you go, check that stitches end up in the ready-to-work position. Before starting work on your pattern again, read the last pattern row and compare it with the stitches on your needle to make sure that they're all there and that all yarn overs and decreases are in the right place.

Lifelines are truly a lifesaver when ripping out lace, especially if you've caught a mistake that's more than a few rows down. Using a slick, smooth strand that won't rub colored fibers onto your knitting (we like to use embroidery floss or cotton yarn), use a needle to thread the lifeline through the last row of stitches below your mistake. If you accidentally tear out more than you intended, you can put stitches back onto your needle from the lifeline. Some extra-cautious lace knitters make a habit of threading a lifeline into their knitting every 5 to 10 rows (depending on the complexity of the pattern) just in case something goes wrong! If this practice gives you peace of mind, go for it.

Blocking Lace

Lace fabrics need to be blocked for their patterns to show up well. The best way to block a lace piece is to wet-block it: Get it wet and spread it out in its final shape to dry. (See Chapter 17 for additional tips to block like a pro.)

Whether you wet-block or steam your piece, spread out the fabric in both directions, using blocking wires if you have them. If the bottom edges are scalloped or pointed, pin these shapes out to define them before blocking.

Practice Lace Projects

Accessories are natural projects for practicing lace patterns: You don't have any shaping to consider, and the flat panels really showcase the lace patterns. Try making the scarf, shawl, and market bag in this section; not only will you improve your lace-making techniques, but you'll also have terrific accessories!

Scarf with Faggot Lace

This scarf is simple to make. Work it up in a soft, cozy yarn, and you'll never want to be without it — except perhaps in the heat of summer.

Materials and vital statistics

- ✔ **Measurements:** 9 inches x 60 inches; can be shortened or lengthened as desired

- ✔ **Yarn:** Kollage Yarns "Creamy Flame" (80% milk/20% cotton; CYC #2, 200 yards, 1.8 ounces [50 grams]): Spearmint, 3 skeins

- ✔ **Needles:** One pair of size US 5 (3¾ mm) needles or size needed to obtain gauge

- ✔ **Other materials:** 2 stitch markers

- ✔ **Gauge:** 24 stitches per 4 inches in faggot lace scarf pattern

Directions

Cast on 52 sts.

Row 1 (RS): K5, place marker, * yo, p2tog, k4; rep from * to last 5 sts, place marker, k5.

Row 2: K2, p3, slip marker, * yo, p2tog, p4; rep from * to marker, slip marker, p3, k2.

Row 3 (RS): K5, slip marker, *yo, p2tog, k4; rep from * to marker, slip marker, k5.

Rep Rows 2 and 3 until the scarf reaches the desired length.

Variations

To make a different scarf on the same theme, try one of the following variations:

- ✔ Make the scarf in a different yarn. Use a heavier yarn for an entirely different fabric and feel. Remember to do a gauge swatch to determine whether you may also need to change the number of cast-on stitches to get the correct size scarf. This pattern has a stitch repeat of 6 stitches plus 10 stitches, so as long as you cast on a multiple of 6 plus 10, the scarf will be perfect.

- ✔ Add tassels or fringe to the ends of the scarf.

- ✔ Instead of using stockinette stitch between the faggot panels, work garter or moss stitch. (See Chapter 5 for garter stitch and Appendix A for moss stitch.)

- ✔ Instead of including the k4 panel in the pattern, work a cable panel between the faggot patterns. For an entire selection of cable patterns, head to Chapter 11.

Lace Leaf Shawl

You make this shawl as a basic rectangle with a built-in garter stitch border so that it's very easy to knit. When knitting lace, thinking about how the lace stitches will look in the fiber and the color you choose is important. A smooth wool or wool blend in a solid or semi-solid color will make the stitches visible and crisp on your shawl.

The last thing you want to do is put all that work into a project that doesn't show off the beautiful stitches. Here's where your gauge swatch is vital in choosing the right yarn. Make sure you wash and block your gauge swatch to see whether you like the finished fabric. If you do, then you're good to go! For this project, we chose a 100-percent yak yarn that blocks out lace stitches brilliantly.

Materials and vital statistics

- ✔ **Measurements:** Approximately 25 inches x 72 inches

- ✔ **Yarn:** Bijou Basin Ranch "Sport Weight" (100% yak; CYC #3, 328 yards, 3.5 ounces [100 grams]): Gray, 2 skeins

✔ **Needles:** One pair of size US 6 (4 mm) needles or size needed to obtain gauge

✔ **Gauge:** 24 stitches and 32 rows per 4 inches in miniature leaf pattern in a blocked gauge. Because this shawl isn't a fitted piece, checking gauge isn't vital, but if your gauge varies, you may not get the desired look.

Directions

Cast on 151 sts.

Preparation rows: Purl 6 rows for a garter stitch border.

Row 1 and all WS rows: Purl.

Row 2: Purl 6, place marker, k1, * k2tog, yo, k1, yo, ssk, k1; rep from * to last 6 sts, place marker, purl to end of row.

Row 4: Purl to marker, slip marker, k2tog, * yo, k3, yo, sl 2 kwise, k1, p2sso; rep from * to last 5 sts before marker, yo, k3, yo, ssk, slip marker, purl to end of row.

Row 6: Purl to marker, slip marker, k1, * yo, ssk, k1, k2tog, yo, k1; rep from * to marker, slip marker, purl to end of row.

Row 8: Purl to marker, slip marker, k2, * yo, sl 2 kwise, k1, p2sso, yo, k3; rep from * to last 5 sts before marker, yo, sl 2 kwise, k1, p2sso, yo, k2, slip marker, purl to end of row.

Rep Rows 1–8 until piece measures approximately 68 inches from the beginning. End with 6 rows of garter stitch. Bind off loosely.

Finishing: Weave in any loose ends; then wash and block your shawl to the finished measurements.

Simple Eyelet Lace Market Bag

Who needs the plastic or paper bags at the grocery store or farmers' market when you can knit your own market bag? Going green has never been as easy as with this basic lace bag with a stockinette stitch base for structure.

Speaking of structure, yarn choice is important when you're making a bag that has the potential of carrying a heavy load. We like to use plant fibers, such as cotton, for their strength. Even better, using a yarn from recycled blue jeans is a wonderful way to truly make this bag a green project.

Materials and vital statistics

- ✔ **Measurements:** 9 inches x 60 inches; can be shortened or lengthened as desired

- ✔ **Yarn:** Kollage Yarns "Riveting Marled Sport" (100% recycled cotton from recycled blue jeans; CYC #3, 350 yards, 3.5 ounces [100 grams]): Desert Denim, 3 skeins

- ✔ **Needles:** One 16-inch size US 5 (3¾ mm) circular needle and four or five size US 5 (3¾ mm) dpns or size needed to obtain gauge

- ✔ **Other materials:** 2 stitch markers

- ✔ **Gauge:** 24 stitches per 4 inches in lace pattern

Directions

Body

Using a size US 5 16-inch circular needle, cast on 112 sts and join round, being careful not to twist the stitches. Place marker to denote end of round.

Preparation rows: Knit for 1 inch, and then begin lace pattern.

Round 1 (RS): * K2tog, yo; rep from * to end of round.

Rounds 2 and 3: Knit.

Rep Rounds 1–3 until piece measures 14 inches. End with a Round 3.

Base

Round 1 (decrease round): K2tog, * k24, k2tog, place marker, ssk; rep from * to last 2 sts, ssk — 8 sts decreased. (The new marker placed here is in addition to the marker placed earlier in the body of the bag. The two markers should look different so that you can tell the difference between them.)

Round 2 and all even rounds: Knit.

Round 3 (decrease round): K2tog, * k to 2 sts before marker, k2tog, slip marker, ssk; rep from * to last 2 sts, ssk — 8 sts decreased.

Rep Rounds 2 and 3 until 40 sts remain. Bind off all sts or divide stitches evenly on two double pointed needles.

Finishing: Do a three-needle bind-off (see Chapter 17) to close the bottom of bag. Weave in all ends.

Straps

Make two long I-cords (see Chapter 9 for instructions) and weave them through the eyelets for a drawstring and tie each into a circle. When the drawstring is pulled closed, they'll be useable as straps.

Variations

You can change up your market bag in a variety of ways. Following are some suggestions:

- ✔ Use a 100-percent wool yarn and knit the body of the bag for 20 inches before starting the lace pattern. Then full it, following the instructions in Chapter 14. The openness of the lace pattern will be less pronounced after fulling, but the bag will be more durable and insulating thanks to the wool.

- ✔ Experiment with unusual straps to make your bag stand out. Options include multiple strands of knitted I-cord that you braid together or even a braided fabric tube strap. Search thrift stores or the back of your closet for interesting old belts, which make great straps — and very sturdy ones to boot. Or opt for nylon webbing, sold in sewing stores.

- ✔ Make your bag from stripes of various leftover yarns. Better still, swap leftover yarn with your knitting friends; even if you all knit the same pattern, your bags will look quite different.

Chapter 13

Fair Isle and Intarsia Techniques

. . . .

In This Chapter

▶ Trying your hand at Fair Isle knitting

▶ Creating pictures with intarsia knitting

▶ Weaving in ends

▶ Playing around with some practice projects

. . . .

Almost anyone asked to imagine a sweater with color patterns can't help picturing a classic Fair Isle sweater from the Shetland Islands off the coast of Scotland. The traditional patterns, with their subtly changing color designs, have become so synonymous with color knitting that the basic technique of knitting repeating color patterns is referred to as *Fair Isle knitting* and any repeating color pattern is a *Fair Isle pattern*. Other kinds of color work — namely bold picture designs with large color areas — are worked by using a different technique called *intarsia*.

If you can knit and purl (see Chapter 4), follow a chart (Chapter 3), and drum up a little patience (you have to get that on your own), you can work wonderful color patterns in either technique. You need only a few simple techniques for handling the differently colored yarns. Practice these, and you're on your way to painting with yarn.

Knitting Fair Isle

When you work color patterns using more than one color in a row, you can work with two strands of yarn, carrying them along the back of your work and picking up and dropping them as you need them. This is Fair Isle knitting, or *stranding*, and it's the technique you use for working small repeating color patterns. (For designs involving large areas of color or picture-knitting with several colors, it's best to use a different strand of yarn for each color group — a technique called *intarsia*. Read about intarsia knitting in the later section "Painting with Yarn: Getting into Intarsia.")

In traditional Fair Isle knitting (sometimes referred to as *jacquard*), you work with two colors of yarn per row, knitting or purling with one color for a few stitches and then working with the other color for the next few stitches, according to your pattern. The strand of yarn not in use crosses the stitches on the wrong side of the fabric until it's knitted in again.

Fair Isle patterns follow two fairly consistent rules:

- ✔ No more than two colors per row
- ✔ No more than 5 to 7 stitches in any one stretch of color

Within these constraints, you can make extraordinarily complex color designs.

The number and variety of traditional Fair Isle patterns provide a lifetime's worth of exploration. You can work them up in the traditional manner or play with color, arrangement, and scale to make them more contemporary or more your own. Or you can start from scratch, using graph paper and colored pencils or markers to design your own motifs.

Charting the Fair Isles

Fair Isle charts read like stitch pattern charts. Each square represents a stitch, and the symbol or color given in each square represents the color in which to work the stitch. The pattern chart includes a key listing the symbols used and the colors they represent (for information on reading charts, refer to Chapter 3). Beyond these basic rules, here are some points specific to Fair Isle charts:

- ✔ The first row of the chart shows the first right-side row of your knitting and is worked from right to left. The second row of the chart shows the second and wrong-side row of your knitting and is worked from left to right.

- ✔ For repeating patterns, the chart shows only one or two repeats and indicates where you're to begin and end the chart for the piece you're working on.

- ✔ Most color patterns are worked in stockinette stitch. Unless your pattern tells you to do otherwise, knit the pattern on right-side rows and purl it on wrong-side rows.

The famous and sought-by-collectors Bohus Stickning sweaters from Sweden are knit very much like traditional Fair Isle sweaters, except they often incorporate purling on the right side of the color work, which adds texture and visual interest. Many photos of original and updated Bohus pieces are available at `www.solsilke.se/Nyheter.htm`.

✔ If the design uses a stitch pattern other than stockinette, the symbol will represent the color used *and* the type of stitch to make. For example, an X may tell you to purl with red on right-side rows and knit with red on wrong-side rows; the symbol Y may tell you to knit with red on right-side rows and purl with red on wrong-side rows.

✔ If you're knitting in the round, all rounds are right-side rounds. You work the chart from right to left on every round. See Chapter 8 for more on knitting in the round, or *circular knitting*.

For a black-and-white chart with symbols indicating colors, you may want to make a photocopy of it (enlarged if you like) and color it in so that you don't have to keep referring to the key to decipher tiny symbols.

Figure 13-1 shows a chart for a repeating triangle pattern 6 stitches wide and 4 rows high. This chart doesn't need a key; just pick two yarn colors and plug them in for the different symbols in the chart. (***Note:*** If only two colors are used in a pattern, generally the background is called MC, for *main color,* and the other color is called CC, for *contrast color.* When a pattern includes several colors, they're usually designated by letters — A, B, C, and so on.)

You can watch a video demonstration of Fair Isle knitting at `www.dummies.com/go/knittingfd`.

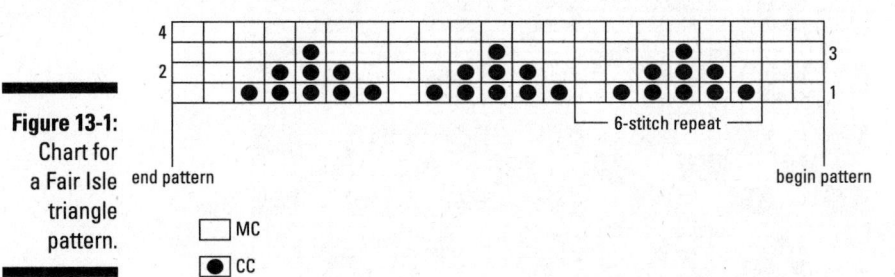

Figure 13-1:
Chart for a Fair Isle triangle pattern.

Illustration by Wiley, Composition Services Graphics

Figure 13-2 shows some Fair Isle patterns in chart form. Use them in the Everywhere Bag or the hats presented in Chapter 9.

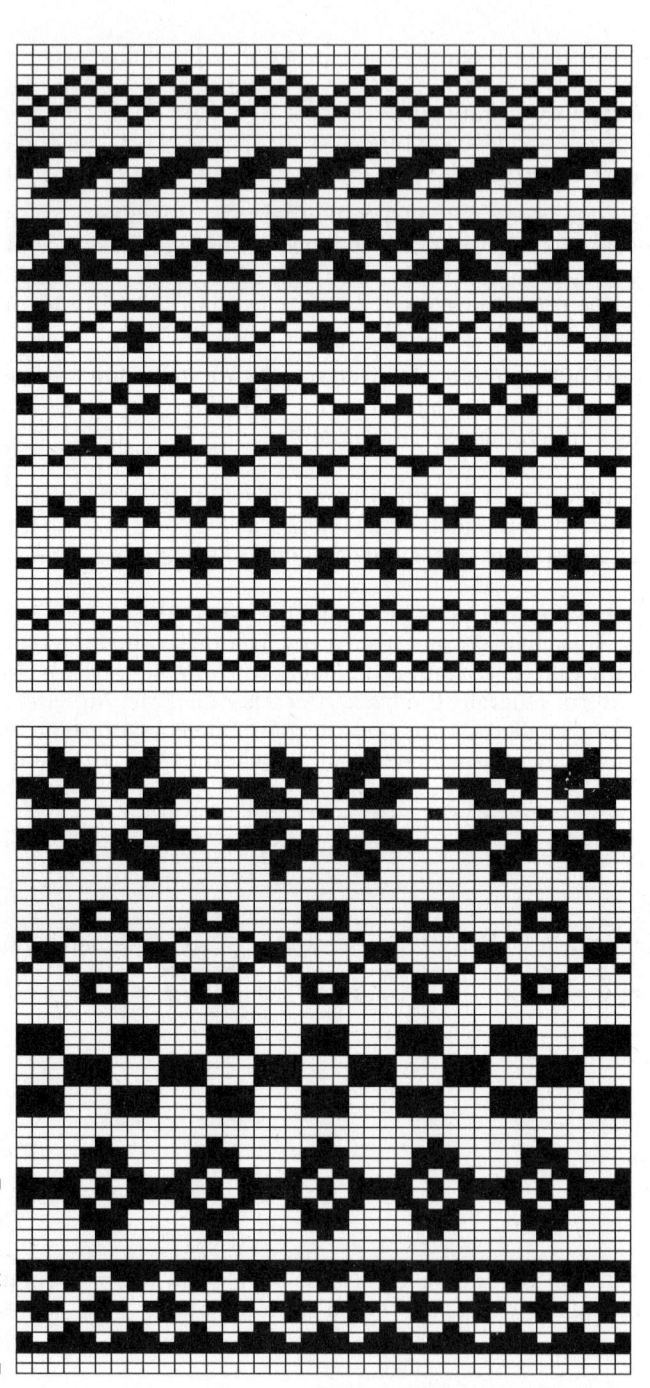

Figure 13-2:
Fair Isle
chart
pattern
possibilities.

Experimenting with color designs

If you want to experiment with a different color combination from the one in the pattern, make several copies of your pattern and color them in with different *colorways* (knitterese for "color combinations") until you find one you like. Knit a little of the pattern in your color choice to see whether it looks as good in yarn as it does on paper. If you're convinced that it does, you're ready to cast on.

If you want to chart your own color designs on graph paper, remember that knitted stitches aren't square. If you use square graph paper, your knitted picture will be a somewhat squashed version of your drawing. You can buy special knitter's graph paper with 1-inch segments of 5 x 7 squares to mimic knitted fabric (see Chapter 2). Or if you're comfortable using a computer, you can get software that prints out graph paper in any combination of rows and stitches you'd like. Some designers use Microsoft Excel for this — you need to make the cells approximately one-and-a-half times as wide as they are tall.

General rules for successful Fair Isle knitting

To knit Fair Isle, you begin with the square in the bottom right corner of the chart. This square represents the first stitch on your needle. Then you read and work the chart from right to left, knitting in whatever color the chart tells you to and working as many stitches in the first color as the chart shows. Then you switch to the next color and work the number of squares given in that color. What you do at the end of that row or round depends on whether you're knitting flat or in the round:

- ✔ **If you're knitting flat:** When you reach the end of your row, turn the work and continue, reading the chart from left to right.
- ✔ **If you're knitting in the round:** At the end of the first round, proceed to the next row in the chart and work it from right to left, just as you did the first row.

Beyond knowing whether (and when) to work the chart from right to left or left to right, you need to know how to change colors. As with stripes, when you start a new color at the end of a row, you can simply work the first stitch with the old and new yarn held together or tie the ends in a temporary bow until you weave in the ends. Refer to Chapter 10 for details on this yarn-joining technique.

The real key to successful color knitting is maintaining an even and elastic tension over your stitches. If you don't allow enough slack on the new yarn when you change colors in a row, your knitting will gather in and pucker. Too much slack, and the stitches at each end of the strand will become loose and sloppy. Spreading out the stitches between colors and gently extending the new yarn over them before you work the next first stitch are usually all you need to do to ensure a flexible and even fabric.

Fortunately, loose stitches are easy to fix. If you find loose or sloppy stitches at the beginning and end of color areas, give a little pull on the strand that connects them on the wrong side (called a *float*) to tighten the stitches. There's no easy fix for fabric that's knitted too tightly, however. If your floats are too taut and cause the knitted fabric to pucker, the only solution is rip it out and start again.

As you practice Fair Isle knitting, work with a medium-weight wool yarn if possible. Wool is forgiving, and the fuzzy fibers will work themselves together, covering any little holes where color changes don't quite meet up. A shot of steam from your iron further evens out any minor imperfections in your finished fabric.

One-handed or two? Ways to work Fair Isle

You can work Fair Isle with one hand or with two. When you work Fair Isle with one hand, you knit and purl as you normally do, dropping and picking up the different yarns as you need them. This method is a bit slower than the two-handed method, but it's one you probably know how to do, which means you don't have to learn anything else before you start knitting Fair Isle patterns.

If you plan to do a lot of color knitting, you should learn how to knit with two hands. You carry one yarn in the right hand and the other yarn in the left hand. The benefit is that you never have to drop one color to pick up and work the other color — you have both colors in your hands at all times! When you knit with two hands, you really cruise along.

Knitting with two hands is nothing more than being able to knit in both Continental and English style. Presumably, you've already mastered (or nearly mastered) one. Now you just need to learn the other. Pick a quick pattern, like a hat or scarf, and work it up using the technique you're not familiar with (see Chapter 4 for instructions for both techniques). When you've completed the project and you're proficient (if not perfect) at knitting with the other hand, you're ready to try two-handed Fair Isle knitting.

The next sections give you an opportunity to practice knitting Fair Isle patterns using just one or both hands.

Practicing one-handed Fair Isle knitting

To practice one-handed Fair Isle knitting, choose two colors of yarn: MC and CC (main color and contrast color). With the MC, cast on 21 stitches and use the charted design in Figure 13-1. You can repeat the two colors throughout, or you can reverse or change them after every 4 rows. It's worth trying out the chart both ways to see how a simple color sequence change can completely alter the effect of an easy two-color pattern.

On the knit side

Start your row with the MC and knit the number of stitches called for. (If you're following the chart in Figure 13-1, you'll knit 2 stitches in the MC.) When it's time to switch to the CC, drop the MC, insert your RH needle in the next stitch, and then wrap and finish the stitch with the CC. (You don't need to tie on the new yarn. You'll come back and weave in the end later.) Work the number of stitches your chart tells you to in the CC (5 stitches in Figure 13-1).

When your chart tells you to switch back to the MC, drop the CC. Spread out the stitches just worked in the CC, find the strand of MC, bring it *over* the strand of CC that's hanging down, and knit the next set of stitches in the MC (see Figure 13-3).

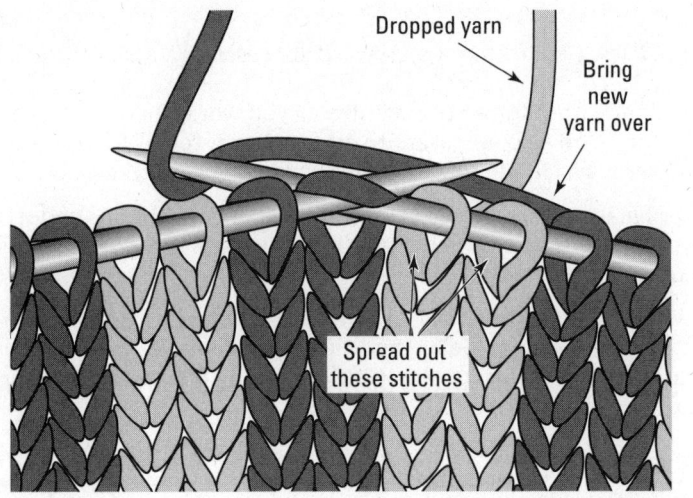

Figure 13-3:
Spread out the stitches and bring the new yarn over.

Dropped yarn

Bring new yarn over

Spread out these stitches

Illustration by Wiley, Composition Services Graphics

So far, so good. One more move and you're home free.

When the chart tells you to switch back to the CC, drop the MC. Spread out the stitches you just worked in the MC, find the strand of the CC, bring it *under* the strand of the MC left hanging, and then knit the next stitch in the CC (see Figure 13-4).

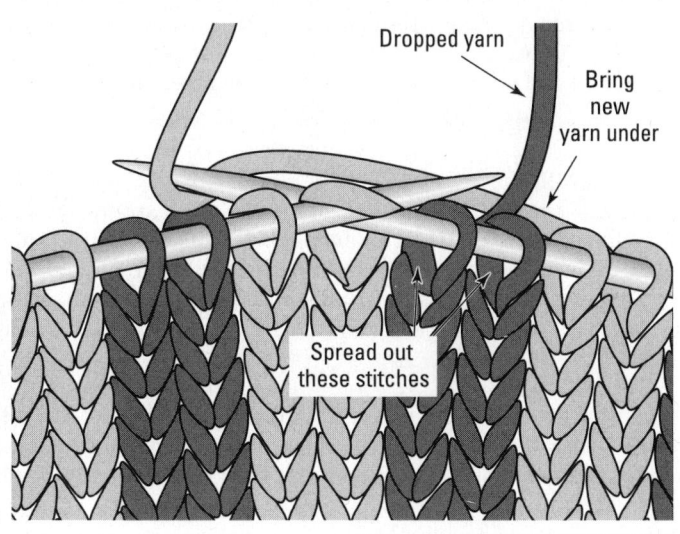

Dropped yarn

Bring new yarn under

Spread out these stitches

Figure 13-4: Spread out the stitches and bring the new yarn under.

Illustration by Wiley, Composition Services Graphics

Here are a few tips to steer you toward successful Fair Isle knitting:

- ✔ You may want to recite a mantra as you work, such as "green over, red under." You also may want to add "green 1, red 5" to your mantra if your pattern is a simple repeat — just to keep you on track.

- ✔ Designating one yarn as an "over" yarn and one as an "under" will keep your yarns from becoming tangled. It also will give you a very tidy-looking wrong side.

- ✔ When you've worked back to the first stitch you made in the second color, the loop will be big and sloppy because you didn't secure the loose end of the first color. Give a little tug on the end hanging down, and it will jump right into line.

On the purl side

Purl in the MC to the first color change, and drop the MC (don't forget to spread out the stitches!). Pick up the CC, bring it *over* the MC, and work the next set of stitches in the CC. When it's time to change colors again, bring the MC *under* the CC. Figure 13-5 shows this process in action.

Figure 13-5:
Change colors on the purl side by bringing the yarn over (a) or under (b).

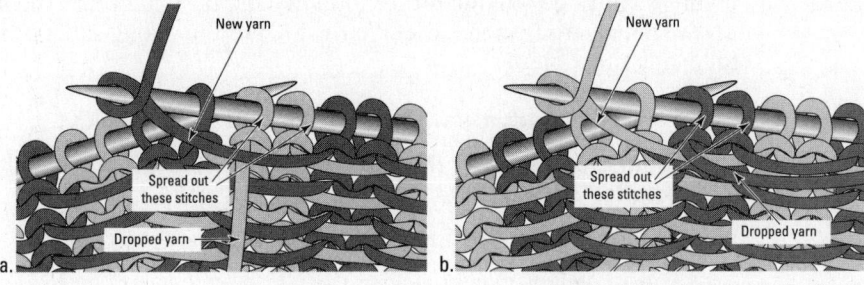

Illustration by Wiley, Composition Services Graphics

If, at the first change from the MC to the CC, the strand of the CC is several stitches left of your position, be sure to allow some slack between the last stitch of the CC in the previous row and the first stitch of the CC in the new row. Spread out the just-worked stitches on the RH needle before starting the next color, and keep up an under/over rhythm to minimize tangles.

Practicing two-handed Fair Isle knitting

When you use both hands to knit Fair Isle, you carry one yarn in your right hand and the other yarn in your left hand, alternating between them as the color pattern dictates.

Carry the dominant color in your dominant hand. If you normally knit English style, for example, carry the main color (MC) in your right hand and the contrasting color (CC) in your left hand. You always use English style to knit the yarn off your right hand, and you use Continental style to knit the yarn off your left hand.

No matter which method you use, make sure your floats — the strands along the back of your knitting — aren't too tight. If you're consistent in your knitting (always carrying the MC in your dominant hand), two-handed Fair Isle eliminates most of the over/under worries when stranding.

Managing the back: Catching floats

The strands of yarn carried on along the back of your knitting are called *floats*. If your pattern has too many stitches between one color change and the next, your floats will be long and sloppy and easily catch on rings and fingers when you take your sweater on and off. You can carry yarn for stretches longer than 5 or 7 stitches, but pushing the traditional limits requires another step: catching the float.

If you're knitting with one rather than two hands, you secure the float in the nonworking yarn (assume that it's the MC) to the wrong side of the fabric by following these steps:

1. **Work a few stitches with the CC and then drop the CC.**

2. **Bring the float color (MC) to the left _over_ the CC and hold it loosely in your left hand so that it doesn't fall.**

3. **Pick up the CC again and knit a few more stitches.**

   The MC will be caught against the fabric by the working strand of the CC.

4. **Repeat Steps 1 through 3 if necessary every 5 stitches or so until you begin working with the MC again.**

   Be sure that the nonworking strand remains relaxed across the back of the fabric and doesn't pull up.

Work the same way to catch the float when you're purling. Figure 13-6 shows how to catch the yarn on a knit row and on a purl row.

Figure 13-6:
Catching a float on knit (a) and purl (b) rows.

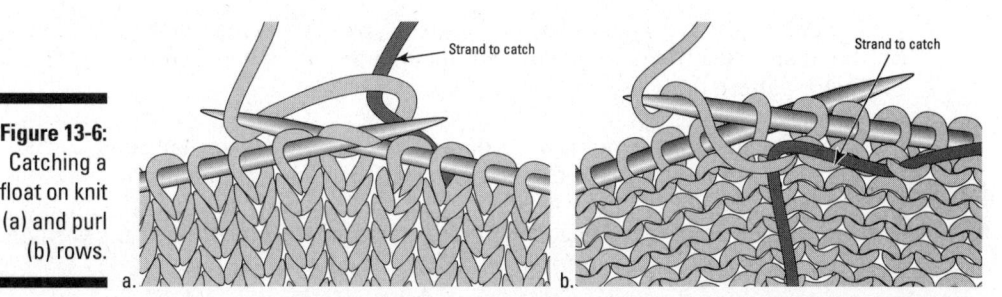

Strand to catch

Strand to catch

a.   b.

Illustration by Wiley, Composition Services Graphics

If you're knitting with two hands, picking up floats is even easier because you're always holding both the working and nonworking yarns, which means you don't have to keep dropping and picking up yarns. To catch the nonworking yarn (assume it's the one in your left hand), you simply put it into position to be caught with a slight movement of the finger holding it. After you catch it, another slight movement of your finger will hold it out of the way until you want to catch it again.

Although you can catch a float routinely every other stitch, you don't need to catch floats that frequently for most projects unless you're deliberately making a very dense and inelastic fabric. Catching the float strand too frequently can distort the stitches, and even with the utmost care, the woven yarn color will peek though on the right side. Catch the yarn only every 5 stitches or so when you're traveling a long distance with your carried yarn.

Embroidering with the duplicate stitch

Duplicate stitch is a simple way of adding a third (or fourth, or fifth) color to your knitting without actually knitting with it. Instead, you embroider the additional color(s) on the fabric, mimicking the stitch it covers.

Thread a tapestry needle with yarn that's the same or a similar weight to the one you've used to knit your piece. Take a good look at your fabric and find the stitches you want to color. Bring your needle up through the center of the V below the one you want to cover. Follow the V up around the base of the stitch above and bring the needle back through the same stitch where you came out.

Duplicate stitch is best used in small areas. Don't try to avoid two-color knitting by using duplicate stitch for a large motif because you'll stiffen the fabric and the background color will show through. Instead, use this embroidery for tiny motifs and color accents. For example, color the center few stitches of a diamond with it, or use it to paint detail in a knitted leaf or flower.

If your design has a lot of long floats and large color areas, you're better off working your colors by using the intarsia method, explained in the next section.

As we mention in Chapter 8, *steeks* are a way to open a knitted tube by cutting the fabric. Fair Isle sweaters often referred to as Nordic-style sweaters are often knit in a tube and then steeked to open the cardigan front. Working in the round when doing a Fair Isle pattern is considered easier because there's no purling.

Painting with Yarn: Getting into Intarsia

Intarsia is a color technique that lets you paint with yarn. You use this method when you're knitting a bold geometric pattern or an isolated flower or snowflake design, for example.

Intarsia is color knitting without floats. Instead of carrying different colors of yarn across the wrong side of your work so they're both always at the ready, you give each color area its own strand of yarn, waiting on a bobbin or wound into a small butterfly. When two colors meet, you intertwine the yarns in a way that prevents a gap where one color ends and the next one begins, and then you start working in the next color. Intarsia fabrics stay relaxed and stretchy because no strands are running across the back to stiffen and draw in the fabric.

Charting intarsia

Charts for intarsia patterns generally don't show patterns in repeats. The entire design, whether it's a single rose or a city skyline, is charted. A large intarsia pattern may take a page or more to display.

Follow an intarsia chart just like any other (see Chapter 3). Start at the bottom right corner and work to the left on the first row, changing yarns as the pattern indicates. Work the next (WS) row from left to right. Use a magnetic board and strip to help you keep your place (see Chapter 2 for information about these tools). Or grab a willing friend to sit with you and read the chart aloud — "3 red, 12 blue, 7 green . . ." — as you knit.

If you want to create your own design on graph paper, find some tips in the earlier sidebar "Experimenting with color designs."

Knitting intarsia

When working intarsia patterns, you want to keep your yarns separate and tangle-free — a task that's definitely easier said than done. The more colors you use, the more difficult it is. Knitters have come up with all sorts of solutions: Some use small balls of yarn, some use bobbins or thread cards similar to those used for organizing embroidery floss, some simply tie the yarn into butterflies (see Chapter 2). Which method you use is a personal choice — try a variety to see which one you prefer!

To practice knitting intarsia, gather yarns in a main color and a contrast color, MC and CC. Cast on 10 stitches in the MC. Then, with the CC, make a slip knot, slide it on the needle, and cast on 10 more stitches — for a total of 20 stitches. When you're ready to knit, the stitches in the CC will be the first ones to work on your needle.

To practice intarsia, follow the chart in Figure 13-7.

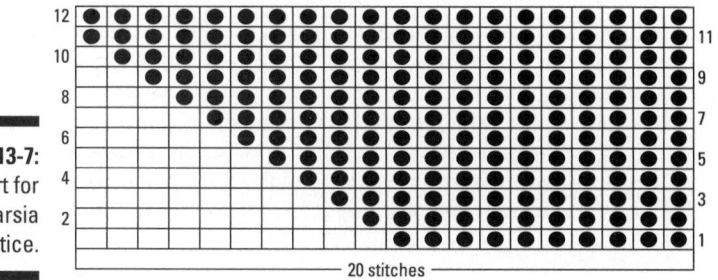

Figure 13-7: Chart for intarsia practice.

Illustration by Wiley, Composition Services Graphics

On the knit side

Work in the CC to the first stitch in the MC. Insert your RH needle into the first MC stitch, give a little tug on the CC, and bring the CC strand to the left *over* the MC strand. Keep a little tension on the CC while you pick up the MC from *under* the CC. Give a slight tug on the MC and knit the next stitch. You've just caught the strand you've finished using with the one you're about to use. Figure 13-8 shows how to switch from the MC to the CC. Continue knitting in the CC.

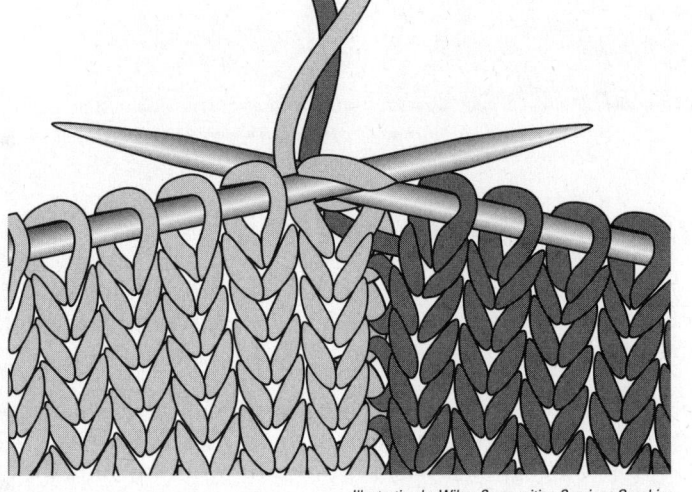

Figure 13-8: Switching colors on the knit side using intarsia.

Illustration by Wiley, Composition Services Graphics

On the purl side

Purl the number of stitches given on the chart for the MC. To work the first stitch in the CC, insert the RH needle into the first CC stitch, give a slight tug on the MC, and bring it to the left *over* the CC strand. Keeping a little tension on the MC, give a slight tug on the CC and bring it up from *under* MC to purl the next stitch (see Figure 13-9). You've caught the MC with the CC to prevent a hole where they meet. Over time, particularly if you're working with wool, the knit fabric will rub against itself and seal the hole permanently as small fibers from each strand of yarn tangle with their neighbors. Continue purling in the CC to the end of the row. Continue to work the chart through Row 12.

Intarsia doesn't work in circular knitting. After the first round, you'll find that all the ends you need to knit in the second round are on the opposite side of the motifs you're working. (Don't be tempted to pull them back across — the floats would be far too large!)

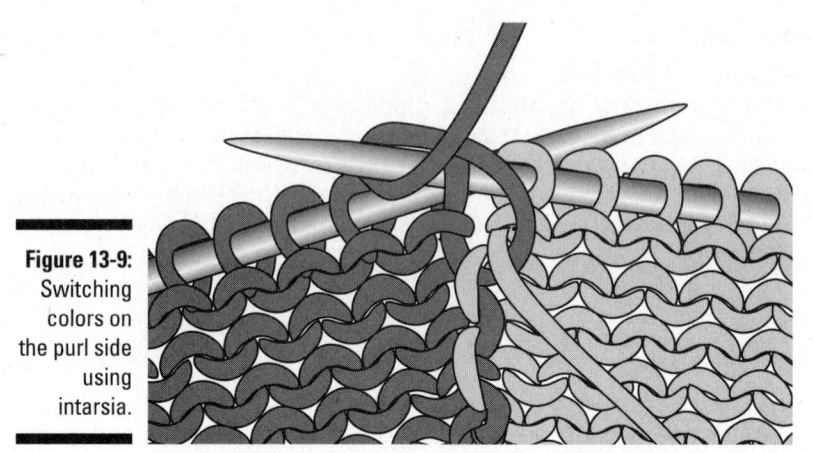

Figure 13-9:
Switching
colors on
the purl side
using
intarsia.

Illustration by Wiley, Composition Services Graphics

Using intarsia in motifs

Intarsia is very straightforward and easy when you're working with blocks of color having straight or diagonal edges or when you're making color changes within a few stitches of each other.

If you're knitting a more detailed design in which you need to make a color change that will bring the new color more than 7 stitches *to the right* in order to begin knitting, don't try to make the reach with your yarn; the first stitch will pull. Instead, break the yarn and start the color with a fresh end. Yes, you'll have another end to sew in, but your fabric will be smoother. Resolve to be patient.

Ending the Ends

Whether you're working a Fair Isle pattern or an intarsia design, color knitting involves yarn ends that have to be secured one way or another. Ends are a nuisance any way you look at it. You can use the quick method and work them into the fabric as you go. This gives less-than-perfect results, but sometimes it pays to throw perfection to the wind and do something reasonably well — instead of perfectly — in order to get on to the next project. The slow method can take hours but yields perfect results. You decide which way to go.

Weaving as you go: The quick method

It's possible to work in ends as you go by using the technique for weaving in floats described in the earlier section "Managing the back: Catching floats." Doing so saves you an enormous amount of time if you have many ends to finish off. However, this method has its drawbacks. Too frequently, the color you've ended shows through the stitches in the new color field and looks sloppy. And the two ends lying together along the wrong side can be bulky and sometimes throw off the tension. But if your design uses many colors, these little glitches are hardly noticeable from a few feet away — and how many people really get within a few feet of you in a typical day? The intricacy of the design will distract from any imperfections.

To weave in the ends where you change colors, drop the old color and work 2 stitches in the new color, leaving the ends at least 3 inches long. After the second stitch, hold both ends together and weave them on the wrong side for several stitches (refer to Figure 13-6 to see how to catch floats). Later, you can snip the ends ½ inch or so from the sweater.

Weaving in later: The slow method

If you decide to weave in the ends with a tapestry needle after you've finished knitting your piece, you have the chance to tweak any misshapen stitches at the color changes. Gently pull and prod the yarn ends and neighboring V legs until the stitches are neat and even. Then you can weave the ends in along the color boundaries in *opposite* directions — yarn on the left weaves to the right, yarn on the right weaves to the left — to better distribute their bulk. You also can direct the colors where they won't peek through. Head to Chapter 17 for the ins and outs of weaving in your yarn ends.

Practice Projects

Simple shapes make for easy color knitting. The Hit the Slopes Headband allows you to try different patterns and experiment with color combinations while knitting a simple rectangle, and you can continue to practice your Fair Isle skills by knitting up a cute pair of leg warmers. The Intarsia Tooth Fairy Pillow lets you experiment with knitting a motif using the intarsia technique.

Hit the Slopes Headband

For this simple headband, work in the round following the snowflake motif chart and changing colors as indicated.

Materials and vital statistics

- ✔ **Measurements:** 21 inches x 3 inches
- ✔ **Yarn:** Cascade Yarns "Cascade 220 Sport" (100% Peruvian highland wool; CYC #3, 164 yards, 1.76 ounces [50 grams])
    - **Color A:** Light Gray, 1 ball
    - **Color B:** Light Pink, 1 ball
    - **Color C:** White, 1 ball
- ✔ **Needles:** One 16-inch size US 5 (3½ mm) circular needle or dpns to work in the round or size needed to obtain gauge
- ✔ **Other materials:** Stitch marker, yarn needle to weave in ends
- ✔ **Gauge:** 24 stitches per 4 inches in stockinette stitch (6 stitches per 1 inch)

Directions

Using Color A, cast on 112 sts. Place a stitch marker to indicate the beginning of the round, and then join to work in the round.

Start with 4 rounds of garter stitch to give the headband a nice border edge. Remember, garter stitch in the round is a combination of 1 purl (or knit) row followed by 1 knit (or purl) row.

For the body of the headband, work in stockinette stitch. Knit 2 rounds even and follow the chart in Figure 13-10 for the snowflake motif. Keep the background stitches in Color A throughout, but work the motif stitches as follows:

Rounds 1–4: Color B

Rounds 5–9: Color C

Rounds 10–13: Color B

Knit 2 rounds even in Color A.

Work 3 rounds in garter stitch and bind off.

Finishing: Weave in loose ends and block gently with steam.

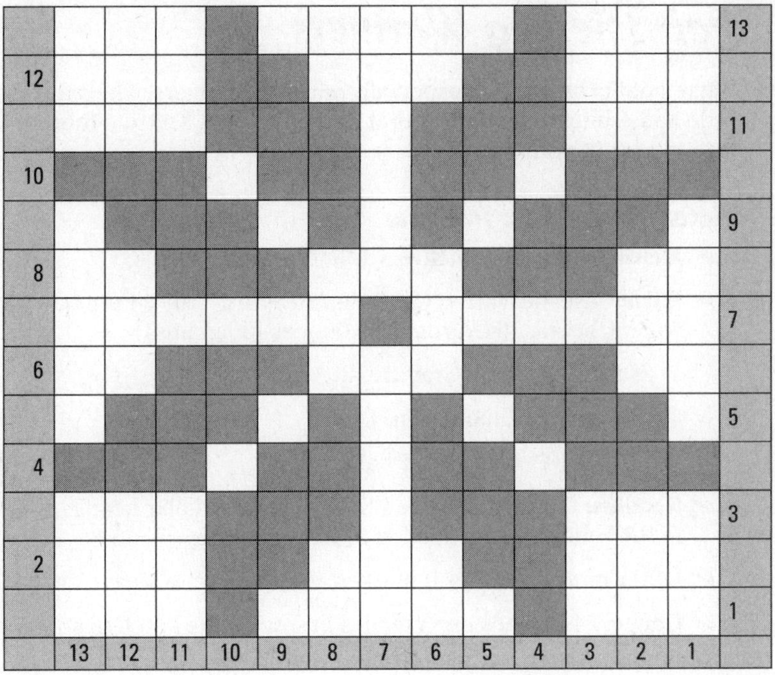

Figure 13-10:
Snowflake
Fair Isle
chart for Hit
the Slopes
Headband.

Illustration by Wiley, Composition Services Graphics

Variations

Here are a couple of ways to vary this headband:

- Change the color of the motifs to match your winter coat.

- Turn the headband into a slouchy hat by working another 5 inches in stockinette after the motif is complete. This will require more Color A yarn.

  When you're ready for the crown of the hat, begin with a decrease round: *knit 12, k2tog; rep from * to the end of the round — 8 stitches decreased. Knit 1 round even then repeat the decrease round. ***Note:*** The number of stitches between the k2togs will decrease by 1 with each decrease round. Do this until you have 8 sts remaining. Then cut the yarn, leaving a long tail. Using a yarn needle, thread the tail through the live stitches on the needle and then pull tight like a drawstring. Tuck the tail to the inside and weave in the ends. Voilà!

Fair Isle Leg Warmers

What's old is new again, especially with leg warmers. They add that perfect little something to any outfit that bares the legs. Knitting these is also a great way to try out your new Fair Isle skills.

Materials and vital statistics

- **Measurements:** 14 inches x 14 inches
- **Yarn:** Cascade Yarns "Cascade 220 Sport" (100% Peruvian highland wool; CYC #3, 164 yards, 1.75 ounces [50 grams])

  - **Color A:** Dark Gray, 1 ball
  - **Color B:** Lime Green, 1 ball
  - **Color C:** Magenta, 1 ball

- **Needles:** One 16-inch size US 5 (3½ mm) circular needle or dpns to work in the round or size needed to obtain gauge
- **Other materials:** Stitch marker, yarn needle to weave in ends
- **Gauge:** 24 stitches per 4 inches in stockinette stitch (6 stitches per 1 inch)

Directions

Using Color A, cast on 84 sts. Place a stitch marker to indicate the beginning of the round and then join to work in the round.

Start with a 2 x 2 ribbing for approximately 2 inches to give the leg warmers a nice border edge.

When you work ribbing in the round, having an even number of stitches in the rib is important. That way, the last 2 stitches will be opposite the first 2 stitches. If you begin with 2 knits and end with 2 purls, the ribbing looks seamless!

For the body of the leg warmer, work in stockinette stitch, following the charts for the diamond motif (see Figure 13-11) and the snowflake motif (see Figure 13-10). Keep the background stitches in Color A throughout, but for the motif stitches, work the diamonds in Color B and the snowflakes in Color C.

You'll have a total of 12 diamond motifs around the leg warmer and 6 snowflake motifs. For the height of the leg warmer, work 1 diamond motif, 1 snowflake motif, 1 diamond motif, 1 snowflake motif, and 1 diamond motif.

To balance the leg warmer, finish with 3 inches of 2 x 2 ribbing, and then bind off in pattern.

Finishing: Weave in loose ends and block gently with steam.

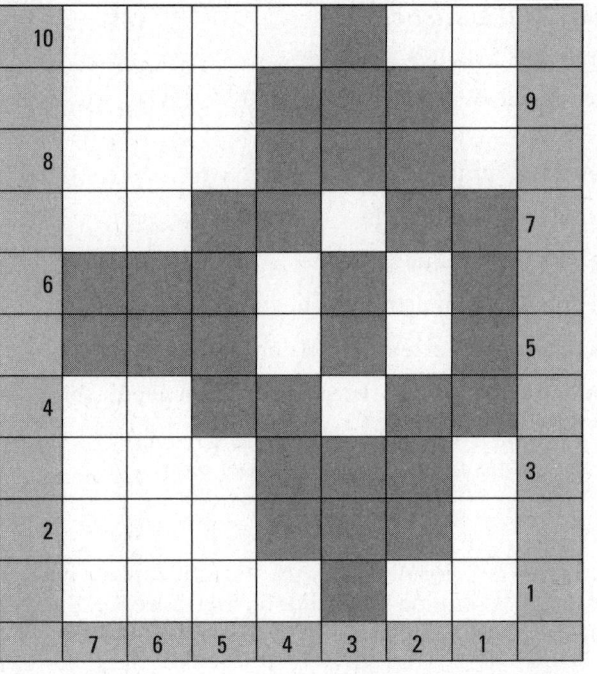

Figure 13-11: Diamond Fair Isle chart for Leg Warmers.

Illustration by Wiley, Composition Services Graphics

Variations

Try these leg-warmer variations:

- ✔ Change the color of the motifs to match your winter coat!
- ✔ Turn the leg warmers into a wine cozy simply by adding some eyelets in the 2 x 2 ribbing using yarn overs. Remember that you'll need to couple every yarn over you make with a decease so you don't end up with too many stitches. Make an I-cord and thread it through the eyelets to use as a drawstring.

Intarsia Tooth Fairy Pillow

This pillow uses a simple intarsia tooth motif for the front of the pillow and cute 2-row stripes on the back. It's perfect for the little tyke in your life.

Materials and vital statistics

- ✔ **Measurements:** 6 inches x 5 inches
- ✔ **Yarn:** Red Heart "With Love" Solids (100% acrylic; 370 yards, 7 ounces [200 grams])
  - **Color A:** Tan; 1 skein
  - **Color B:** White; 1 skein
  - **Color C:** Light Blue; 1 skein

  You can substitute similar yarns in your favorite colors.
- ✔ **Needles:** One pair of size US 9 (5½ mm) needles
- ✔ **Other materials:** Stitch marker, fiberfill, yarn needle, black embroidery thread for eyes and mouth
- ✔ **Gauge:** 16 stitches per 4 inches (4 sts per inch)

Directions

Pillow front: With the Color A, cast on 26 sts. Knit 7, place marker, knit 12, place marker, knit 7. Continue in St st for 5 rows more. On the next row (RS), begin working the chart in Figure 13-12 between the markers.

Work to marker, slip marker, and then following the first row of the chart, knit 2 sts in the Color A, 3 sts in Color B; with another ball of Color A, knit 2 sts; with another ball of Color B, knit 3 sts; with another ball of Color A, knit 2 sts. Slip marker and continue in St st and work the remaining sts of the row with Color A.

Continue to work the established patterns, changing colors as necessary when indicated by the chart.

When doing intarsia, you don't want to have the yarn float across stitches as in Fair Isle. When a new color is necessary, it's important that you start a new ball of that color; do not pull the color needed across stitches to use it again.

When the chart is complete between the markers, continue to work in St st using only Color A for 6 rows. Bind off.

Pillow back: With Color A cast on 26 sts. Work in St st and 2-row stripes, alternating Color A with Color C, until the piece measures the same as the front of the pillow.

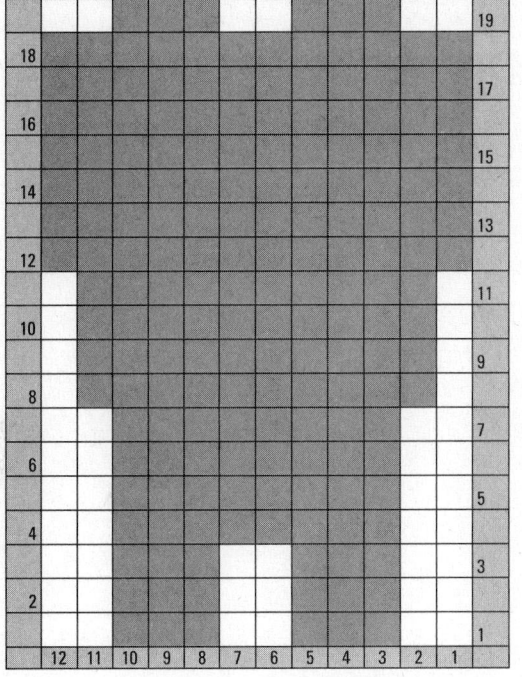

Figure 13-12:
Chart for
the Intarsia
Tooth Fairy
Pillow.

Pocket: With Color C cast on 8 sts. Work in St st for 8 rows. On the next row (RS) purl, then bind off.

Finishing: Weave in loose ends and block the pieces gently. Sew the pocket to the back of the pillow at the corner.

Sew the front of the pillow to the back. With WS together, close the seam along the bottom edges using the grafting technique. Sew up the sides using the mattress stitch, leaving a small space to insert the fiberfill, and then sew the opening closed after the pillow is filled. (See Chapter 17 for information about blocking and seaming techniques.)

Embroider the eyes and mouth of the tooth on the front for a touch of whimsy.

Chapter 14

Fulling Fun: Making Your Project's Presence Felt

*F*ulling is a funky, fun, and easy technique that transforms a knitted piece into something totally different. With some hot water, a little soap, and a lot of agitation, you can make a fabric that's denser, stronger, and warmer!

If you've ever accidentally thrown a 100-percent wool sweater in the washer only to discover your extra-large garment reduced to the size of a doll sweater and the thickness of a hot pad, then you've already fulled a garment (albeit unintentionally).

This chapter explains what fulling is (including how it differs from the more commonly heard *felting*) and how to do it by hand or by machine. We also offer a few practice projects to help you explore this finishing technique.

Are you nervous about letting your knitting take a Whirlpool plunge? Practice the process with a sweater you recycle from your local thrift store. That way, you have no personal attachment to the project, and if it goes wrong, you're not out days of knitting time. Then turn to Chapter 20 for a few project ideas to turn your felted thrift store sweater into something new!

Distinguishing between Fulling and Felting

Many times, you hear knitters say they're going to *felt* a bag they knit. True, the end result will be a fabric that's felt-like, but because they're beginning with a knitted fabric and not raw fleece, the knitters are actually *fulling* a bag. These terms seem to be interchangeable in many knitters' vernacular, but the two are different. Here's how:

- ✔ **Fulling:** Fulling is the process of adding heat, moisture, and tremendous agitation to a knitted, woven, or crocheted fabric made of wool in order to make it shrink. The fabric becomes much stronger, fluffier, and warmer yet is still very pliable.

- ✔ **Felting:** Felting is the process of adding heat, moisture, and agitation to raw fleece in order to create a fabric that's strong, warm, and typically a lot stiffer than a fulled fabric.

The major difference between the two is that felting uses raw fleece that has no initial structure to get the same result as fulling, which uses a knitted fabric.

Creating the Right Conditions to Full Knitted Fabric

Fulling may be the intentional and controlled felting of a fabric, but it isn't an exact science. Too many variables can affect the result. Knowing these variables and maintaining their balance is the best way to ensure a good fulling experience.

Finding a fulling-friendly project

Even though a sweater is made out of 100-percent wool and has the *ability* to be fulled, that doesn't mean it should be fulled. When a project is fulled, it shrinks as the stitches become meshed together. So if your pattern wasn't written with this in mind, fulling may make your size large sweater fit an 18-inch doll with the proportions of the sweater all wrong.

Most knitting patterns that are for a fulled project are in stockinette stitch or garter stitch, because they full pretty evenly. What about textured stitches? You can full a project that has cables or ribbing, but making sure the fabric doesn't get overfulled and become mush takes a bit more vigilance. Look at the Fulled Cabled Bag In-the-Round in the practice projects at the end of the chapter. This project combines stockinette stitch, garter stitch, and cables. During the fulling process, we made sure that the cables weren't getting overworked before the other stitches had a chance to do their thing. To make sure the fulling was consistent over the whole bag, we checked the bag frequently and took it out of the washing machine at just the right moment — that point when the stitches were visible yet hazy and interlocked to create a solid fabric.

You can spice up any simple fulled project by adding colorwork to the pattern (see Chapter 10 for stripes or Chapter 13 for Fair Isle and intarsia). Sometimes even different colors in the same yarn brand and fiber don't full the same, so make sure you knit and full the gauge swatch with the colors you plan to combine in your project. Fulling the gauge swatch also allows you to see whether the colors will bleed on one another.

Choosing your fiber

Fulling works only with 100-percent wool that hasn't been chemically treated to be a super wash; it doesn't work on any synthetic. However, not all wool fiber fulls or felts well. Some animal fibers work better than others, and sometimes the dye used to color the wool makes the fiber not want to cooperate.

Some common fiber choices for fulling include the following:

- ✔ Sheep
- ✔ Angora
- ✔ Alpaca
- ✔ Llama
- ✔ Mohair
- ✔ Yak

Most fulled projects use a bulky or super bulky yarn, but some double a worsted-weight yarn to achieve the bulky weight. Fulled projects also use a larger gauge (see the next section), which requires more yarn. If you're pulling yarn from your stash to complete a fulled project, make sure you have enough yarn.

To make sure your wool will give you the results you want, full the entire gauge swatch. Fulling the gauge swatch shows you how much the fabric fluffs up (also known as *bloom*), how pliable it will be, and how much it will shrink. Knowing that 4 sts per inch and 6 rows before fulling will become 3 sts per inch and 4 rows after fulling is important if you plan on fulling something that needs to fit, like a hat or gloves.

Getting the right fabric gauge

When you plan to full a knitted fabric, you need to knit it in a loose gauge. Usually, that means knitting about 2 mm larger in size than you normally would for the yarn you're using. (***Note:*** If you're using a pattern for a fulled project, the pattern gives you the exact size of needle you need, so adjusting to an even larger needle isn't necessary.) You want the stitches to be big enough so that the scales of the wool have room to expand and mesh with one another. If the fabric weave is too tight to begin with, the wool doesn't have space to move; the resulting fulled fabric will have textured stitch definition, and the end product can tear and break because it no longer has the stretch of knit.

When the fulling process is complete, not only is the project significantly smaller, but the stitches that began as larger knits look hazier, like firm remnants of what they once were (see Figure 14-1) — or the stitches may not be visible at all. The visibility of the stitches depends on the amount of time you full the fabric.

Figure 14-1:
Knitted
fabric
unfulled (a)
and fulled (b).

a

b

Photograph by Wiley, Composition Services Graphics

Some of our friends love to full because it can hide mistakes. Because the knitted fabric is going to be fulled, a little oopsie while you knit will never show up. So don't fret too much if you accidentally put a purl where you shouldn't have; in the fulled project, you won't see the mistake!

Controlling water temperature, soap, agitation, and time

Whether you're using a washing machine or you're hand fulling, the fulling process relies heavily on four factors: water temperature, soap, agitation, and time. The more you can control these factors, the better your results.

- ✔ **Water temperature:** Adding water encourages the scales of the wool to open up so they can adhere to each other. Hot water works best for opening the scales, but the fiber may begin to adhere too quickly in some places and not so much in others, making the fulling process hard to manage. For a more consistent finish, we recommend using water that's about as warm as a hot bath if you're new to fulling. As you become more familiar with the process, feel free to start using hot water. In any case, always rinse with cold water.

- ✔ **Soap:** A little laundry detergent will work to full a knitted fabric, but because laundry detergent is made to be gentle on fabrics and not disturb scales, the fulling process may not be as solid as it would be if you used a true soap product. The pH balance in soap (like Ivory) is what helps the fibers open enough to adhere to one another. A little bit will go a long way. We like to use liquid form and only about a teaspoon — just enough to make the scales on the wool open up.

- ✔ **Agitation:** We're not talking about the anxiety you may feel when you think about purposefully shrinking something you just spent weeks knitting. *Agitation* is what you need to do to the fibers so that they'll mesh together. In a washing machine, the agitator often does the job for you. If you're hand fulling, you use your hands to knead the fiber and generate friction. Many hand fullers also use an old-fashioned washing board or a toilet plunger (new, not used) to help the process. Needless to say, hand fulling takes a bit more elbow grease and consequently time, but it's easier to control.

- ✔ **Time:** The amount of time needed to full something properly depends on the fiber used, the size of the piece, the temperature of the water, and the fulling method.

You know the fulling is complete when the project appears to be just about where you want it. Even if it's *almost* right, go ahead and take it out to air-dry. Later, you can full a little more if need be, but you can't reverse the fulling process.

The Fulling Experience: How to Full

You can full a knitted fabric by hand or by machine. The two methods result in the same end product. Machine fulling is less work and is definitely faster than hand fulling, but hand fulling offers the most control.

To see which method of fulling you prefer, make two gauge swatches and try both methods. One way may work better for your project than another. It's best to find that out with the gauge swatches rather than the actual project.

Hand fulling

Hand fulling is a great way to jump into the fulling process. With hand fulling, you can stop and check the fabric at every stage and as often as you like. You can also adjust the fulling amount per stitch pattern in any given project simply by agitating select stitches more or less.

To hand full a project, follow these steps:

1. **Fill a basin that's large enough to fit the project with warm to hot water.**

2. **Dissolve the soap in the water.**

   Not a lot of soap is needed — just enough to generate some suds on the fabric.

3. **Immerse the project in the water.**

   If the water is too hot, use rubber gloves to help you tolerate the temperature. If the water cools before the fulling process is compete, add more hot water.

4. **Start to knead the fabric.**

   Use your hands to generate friction so that the scales of the wool will open up and fuse to each other. For more agitation, you can use a plunger on the fabric or even scrub the fabric on a washboard.

   Refrain from overstretching the fabric or pulling on it too much, and do not rub the knitting together. If you rub the front of a bag to the back of the bag, for example, the two will adhere and the bag won't open.

5. **Remove the project from the water frequently to check on the process.**

   If the stitches pull apart easily, then the process isn't complete. Remember, you want the stitches to become a solid fabric but not total mush.

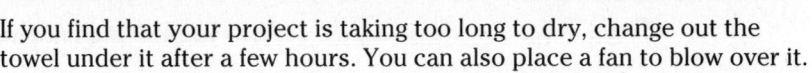

6. **When the fulling is complete, rinse out the soap in cold water. Squeeze out any excess water.**

7. **Roll the project in a towel to soak up any remaining moisture.**

8. **Lay the project out flat on a dry towel, away from sunlight, to air-dry.**

   If you find that your project is taking too long to dry, change out the towel under it after a few hours. You can also place a fan to blow over it.

Machine fulling

You can full a project in a top-loading washing machine or a front-loading machine, as long as the machine lets you open the door to check on the project.

To machine full a project, follow these steps:

1. **Set the washer on a hot water/cold rinse cycle, no spin, and minimum size load.**

   Folds caused by the spin cycle are hard to remove.

2. **Dissolve soap in the water.**

   You don't need a lot of soap — just enough to generate some suds on the fabric.

3. **Place the project in a pillowcase or pillow cover and either zip it shut or close it with a heavy-duty elastic.**

   This cover catches fibers that come off in the washing process so they don't clog your machine.

4. **Place the pillowcase in the washer and wash.**

5. **Check the fulling process every 1 to 5 minutes.**

   The length of time required to full your project depends on your machine, soap, and local water conditions. Check frequently. As you do more fulling, you'll get used to the amount of time your machine takes to do the work, and you can adjust that time as needed, but be vigilant. Don't get distracted and stray away from the washing machine, or you could come back to a ruined project.

   The fulling process is irreversible. You can always full a little more, but you can't unfull! Remove the project before it's too late. If the project starts to full unevenly, you can always finish the fulling process by hand.

If the stitches pull apart easily, then the process isn't complete. If you find that the fibers of your project aren't meshing together well, add a couple of tennis balls, old jeans, or shoes to the basin of the washing machine. These items act as additional agitators and help the fibers interlock.

6. **When the fulling is complete, rinse out the soap in cold water. Do not use the spin cycle.**

7. **Roll the project in a towel to soak up any remaining moisture.**

8. **Lay the project out flat on a dry towel, away from sunlight, to air-dry.**

Taking a stab at needle felting

Needle felting is the art of using special needles to attach wool yarn or fleece to a flat piece of wool fabric, creating a drawing or sculpture. Adding needle felting to a finished project is a form of appliqué felting. You can also use needle felting for sculptural felting or three-dimensional felting.

Needle felting does not require soap and water. Instead, sharp barbs on a needle actually grab at the scales on the wool and make them mesh with the wool fabric. To get started, you need the following tools:

✔ A thick piece of foam or a felting brush that allows the felting needles to go through the fiber and beyond without damaging the needles or surface below

✔ A needle-felting tool with either a single barbed needle or many needles

✔ Wool yarn or roving in a variety of colors

✔ A fulled or felted project to use as the fabric

Note: New to the market are needle-felting machines. Similar to a sewing machine, these machines use barbed needles to work wool into fabric.

With these supplies, needle felting is as easy as "painting" with the fiber. First think about

your design. You can create an easy pattern like stripes or polka dots, or you can create a flower. Better yet, be creative and freeform random shapes.

When you have an idea of what you want to do, place the foam or felting brush under the fabric you want to needle felt. Then tear off bits of wool yarn or fleece. Lay the fiber on the fabric and begin to punch the needles through the fiber and the fabric repeatedly. Be sure to move the needles around so that the fiber attaches itself to the fabric.

As the fiber begins to attach itself, you can add more fiber in the same color or new colors or go in a totally different direction. With the fabric as your canvas and the fiber as your paint, the options are endless.

Not everybody can create freeform shapes, so here's a little tip: Use a cookie cutter as a guide for your needle felting. Place the cookie cutter on the fabric and fill it with fiber. Then punch the needle through both fiber and fabric, filling in the entire space of the cookie cutter. To get dimension, repeat the process with many layers of fiber, and the shape will really pop. Now you have some great shapes with little work!

Practice Fulling Projects

You can full any project that uses 100-percent wool, but not all projects are meant to be put through that process. Here are a couple of projects that we specifically wrote for fulling.

Fulled Cabled Bag In-the-Round

Everyone will be asking where you got this bag, and when you tell them you made it, they're sure to ask you how! This roomy felted tote with a basic cable pattern carries all your stuff in style. To achieve the bulky yarn effect needed for ideal fulling, you knit this bag holding two strands of yarn together throughout the pattern.

Materials and vital statistics

- **Measurements:** 15 inches wide x 18 inches tall after felting

- **Yarn:** Cascade Yarn "Cascade 220" (100% wool; CYC #4, 220 yards, 3.5 ounces [100 grams]): Vermeer Blue, 6 skeins

- **Needles:** One 32-inch size US 11 (8 mm) circular needle, set of 5 dpns size US 11 (8 mm) or size needed to obtain gauge

- **Other materials:** Stitch marker, cable needle, stitch holder or scrap yarn, tapestry needle

- **Gauge:** 12 stitches and 16 rows per 4 inches in stockinette stitch pattern with the yarn double-stranded (4 stitches per inch). Stitches and rows aren't visible after fulling, so measure before fulling your gauge swatch.

Directions

Base

Holding 2 strands of yarn together and using a circular needle, cast on 50 sts. The base is made flat (in rows). Work in garter stitch (knit every row) until base measures 3 inches. On the last row, do not turn.

Body of bag

Place a marker on the needle, * rotate the base 90 degrees, working along short edge pick up and knit 15 sts, place marker, rotate the base 90 degrees, ** working along long edge pick up and knit 50 sts, place marker; rep from * to ** once more, k50 sts to beginning marker — 130 sts. Do not join; turn the work.

Set-up row (RS): Working along the long side of the bag, * (p2, k6, p2) repeat to first marker, slip marker, working along the short side of the bag, knit to next marker; repeat from * once more — each long side has five k6 sections and the short sides are knit.

Place a marker of a different color on the needles to signify the beginning of the round and then join to work in the round. From this point forward, you work the bag in the round.

Next round (RS): * (P2, k6, p2) repeat to first marker, slip marker, knit to next marker; rep from * to beginning marker.

Round 1 (cable round): * (P2, C3F, p2) repeat to first marker, slip marker, knit to next marker; rep from * to beginning marker — five C3Fs on each long side.

(See Chapter 11 for a refresher on cables.)

Rounds 2, 3, 4, 5, 6 (RS): * (P2, k6, p2) repeat to first marker, slip marker, knit to next marker; rep from * to beginning marker.

Repeat Rounds 1–6 for established pattern until piece measures about 18 inches from the picked up edge.

Edging
Create a garter stitch edge around the top of the bag by alternating a purl round and a knit round.

Round 1: Purl around all stitches.

Round 2: Knit around all stitches.

Repeat Rounds 1 and 2 ten times; then repeat Round 1 once.

Next round: Working along the long side, * bind off all stitches to first marker, remove marker, k to marker, remove marker and then place stitches just knit on holder. Repeat from * once more.

Straps
Place 15 stitches from the holder onto a dpn. With the RS facing you and working in rows, continue to work in the established garter stitch pattern. (Remember that garter stitch knit flat is just a combination of knit rows.)

Knit in garter stitch until strap measures 25 inches, ending on a WS row. Set the strap aside to prepare the other side of the bag.

Place the 15 stitches from the holder on the opposite edge of the bag on another dpn. With RS facing each other, join the strap to the edge of the bag with a three-needle bind off (see Chapter 17).

Finishing

Using a tapestry needle, weave in all the tails to the inside of the bag.

Fulling

Refer to the section "The Fulling Experience: How to Full" earlier in this chapter and follow the instructions for hand fulling or machine fulling. Either one will work for this project.

Variations

To make a different bag on the same theme, try one of the following variations:

✔ Use a cable pattern along the side of the bag instead of keeping the side in stockinette stitch. Instead of making the strap in garter stitch, let the cable pattern along the side of the bag extend to the strap.

✔ Make the bag in stockinette stitch instead of cables. Create a separate panel with cables on it and sew it to the outside of the bag as a pocket.

✔ Forget the cables altogether and create a bag that has a lot of pizzazz by holding a strand of nonfeltable fiber like an elf eyelash or glitzy eyelash to the strands of wool when you knit. This will give the bag a fuzzy look as the wool felts around the other fiber.

Fulled Scarf in Horseshoe Lace

This scarf is made from a lite version of Icelandic Lopi. A quick spin in the warm cycle of your washing machine will give it a light fulling, making it soft and fluffy. You make the scarf in two identical sections rather than in one long piece in order to achieve a pointed edge on either end.

Materials and vital statistics

✔ **Measurements:** 9 inches x 50 inches; size may vary depending on needle size and how much the fabric contracts in the felting process

✔ **Materials:** Lite Lopi (100% wool; 109 yards, 1.76 ounces [50 grams]); 4 skeins

✔ **Needles:** One pair of size US 10 (6 mm) needles

Directions

Cast on 43 sts.

Preparation rows: Knit 2 rows for a garter stitch border.

Row 1 (RS): K2, * yo, k3, sl 1, k2tog, psso, k3, yo, k1; rep from * to last st, k1.

Row 2: K2, p39, k2 (43 sts).

Row 3: K2, * k1, yo, k2, sl 1, k2tog, psso, k2, yo, k1, p1; rep from * to last rep, end last rep with k3 instead of k1, p1.

Rows 4, 6, and 8: K2, * p9, k1; rep from * to last rep, end last rep with k2 instead of k1.

Row 5: K2, * k2, yo, k1, sl 1, k2tog, psso, k1, yo, k2, p1; rep from * to last rep, end last rep with k2 instead of p1.

Row 7: K2, * k3, yo, sl 1, k2tog, psso, yo, k3, p1; rep from * to last rep, end last rep with k2 instead of p1.

Rep Rows 1–8 until piece measures approximately 26 inches from the beginning. End by making Row 8 the last row.

With a tapestry needle, thread a piece of scrap yarn through the stitches on the needle.

Work a second scarf piece in the same manner as the first one.

Finishing

When you have two identical scarf halves, you can either sew them together or graft the pieces at the center back for a more knitterly finish (see Chapter 17 for details on grafting). Finally, to ensure maximum control of the fulling process, hand full the piece following the instructions in the earlier section "Hand fulling."

Part IV
Making Knitted Garments

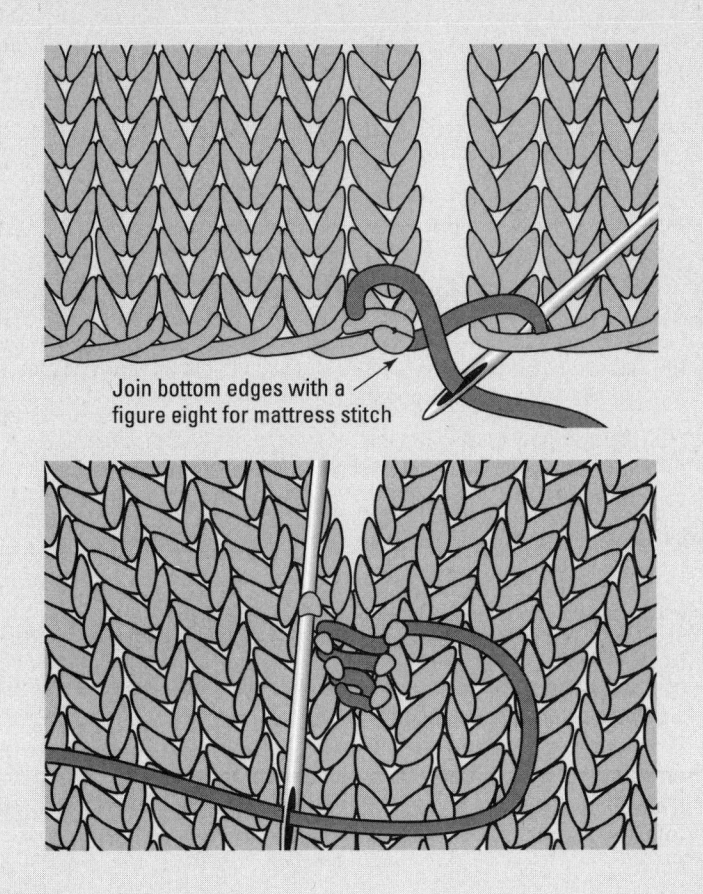

Join bottom edges with a figure eight for mattress stitch

You may be hesitant to knit a garment such as a sweater for yourself because you're afraid it won't fit right and will look handmade. It's all about the fit, baby! At www.dummies.com/extras/knitting, you can find advice on finding the right garment fit for you and then transferring that perfect fit to the design of your knitted garments.

In this part . . .

- ✔ Advance beyond scarves, hats, and bags to put all your skills to use and knit your own sweater.

- ✔ Discover how to read the instructions for a sweater pattern. Pick up some tips and tricks to make the whole sweater-making process easier.

- ✔ Assemble all the parts of your garment into one final piece with easy step-by-step instructions.

- ✔ Fool your friends into thinking your handmade sweater is actually store-bought thanks to perfect finishing techniques.

- ✔ Tackle the perfect starter garment projects with easy-to-follow patterns and schematics.

Chapter 15

Anatomy of a Sweater Pattern

In This Chapter

▶ Perusing a photo for important details

▶ Making your way through a knitting pattern

Sweater patterns tell you how to make the individual pieces of a sweater and how to put them together. Whether from a book, magazine, leaflet, or website, sweater patterns are set up in a predictable way. You find information about sizes, materials needed, gauge, and any special pattern stitches or abbreviations listed before the actual piece-by-piece instructions. This chapter runs you through the kinds of information you find in a typical sweater pattern.

You don't have to go deep into a sweater pattern before you see things like "sl 1, k1, psso," "yb," and "ssk" — common abbreviations to knitters. If they look indecipherable to you, skip to Chapter 3 where these and other terms are conveniently listed and explained.

Picture This: Studying the Garment Photo

When you sit down with a new sweater pattern — or better yet, when you're choosing one — begin by paying close attention to the picture of the sweater you want to knit. This step may seem obvious, but studying the photograph or drawing and noting the details will clarify parts of the instructions that may otherwise be confusing. Study the picture of your sweater and answer these questions:

✔ Is it a pullover or a cardigan?

✔ How is it constructed? Can you tell from the picture whether the sweater is designed with a drop shoulder or a set-in sleeve, two common sleeve styles?

✔ Does the shoulder slope, or is it worked straight across? (If you can't tell from the photo, check the schematic. The shoulder design will be clear in the line drawing that often comes with the instructions.)

✔ Is the body of the sweater shaped in any way, or is it a simple rectangle?

✔ Is the sweater worked primarily in stockinette stitch? If other pattern stitches are used, can you identify them? Are they knit-and-purl patterns, cables, or something else?

✔ Is there a color pattern? If so, is it an allover pattern, or is it placed along the hem or across the yoke? Does it look like a repeating pattern to knit by using the Fair Isle technique, or is it a pattern with larger color areas to knit in the intarsia method? (See Chapter 13 for details on these methods.)

✔ Is there ribbing at the bottom edges, or does the sweater begin some other way?

✔ Does it have a round neckline or a V-neck? Is it finished with a ribbed neckband? A collar? A crocheted edge?

✔ If the sweater is pictured on a model, how's the fit? Does the collar lie properly around the neck? Does the sleeve cap pull? If the sweater doesn't fit the model well, chances are that it won't look good on you. (Then again, it just might.)

The point of all these questions? Know thy sweater.

Assessing the Pattern at a Glance

Looking at a picture of the knitted garment can tell you only so much about how the sweater is constructed. For the nitty-gritty details, you need to read the pattern — preferably before you begin.

Knowing as much as you can about your sweater upfront helps you anticipate the steps in the instructions and forestall many a mistake. If you find that something in the instructions is confusing in the first read-through, don't be alarmed; it may make sense by the time you get to that point in the instructions with needles and yarn in hand.

The following sections walk you through the various bits of info a typical sweater pattern contains.

It's a good idea to photocopy the pattern so you have a working copy that you can highlight, take notes on, or make changes to without messing up the original pattern.

How hard is "easy"? Level of difficulty

Many patterns tell you right away the level of difficulty the pattern writer has assigned to it. Here are the categories:

- ✔ A *beginner* sweater uses basic stitches (knits and purls) and involves minimal shaping and simple finishing.
- ✔ An *intermediate* project uses more-challenging stitch patterns and/or shaping and finishing.
- ✔ An *experienced* or *expert* pattern may require all your powers of concentration. It frequently features tricky pattern or color work, and it may involve complicated shaping or construction details. Work on it only when you can give it all your attention.

Having more than one project going at a time is always a good idea. We recommend that you have something portable and rather brainless to give you a feeling of accomplishment and to keep your hands going while you watch TV or wait for a website to load and another more challenging project to work on when you have the time and quiet to concentrate on it.

How big is "big"? Knitted measurements

Most patterns begin by listing the sizes given in the instructions. Older patterns may list them in numbered chest sizes — for example, 38 (40, 42, 44, 46). Most current patterns give sizes in the designations small (medium, large) or in some combination of the two systems. Be sure you know your measurements before choosing the size to knit!

The size section is the first place you see parentheses in a knitting pattern, and it pays to notice where the size you want to make is located in the pattern: before or inside the parentheses. Every time a number or measurement is given in the pattern, the one for your size will be in the same place in relation to the parentheses. For example, if the pattern is written for small, medium, and large sizes — presented "small (medium, large)" — and you're making a small, the numbers for your size will always be written first outside the parentheses. If you're making a large, your numbers will always be last in the parentheses.

Before you start knitting, take the time to circle all the instructions in your size throughout the entire pattern (this is when your photocopy comes in handy). If you use a pencil, you can then erase the circles when finished so you can knit the pattern again later in a different size without confusion.

Sweater patterns generally tell you what the finished garment should measure when laid out on a flat surface. Sometimes only the chest/bust width is given. Other times, you also find measurements for overall length, sleeve length, and/or upper arm circumference. Use this info to help you determine which size to knit. For more information about choosing which size to make, see Chapter 16.

Materials

The pattern tells you what materials and equipment you need to make your sweater. In the "Materials" section of the pattern, you can find the following:

- ✔ **The brand and specific name of the yarn used:** It gives the fiber content of the yarn, the weight and often the number of yards per skein, the color number and name of the yarn, and the number of skeins or balls required for the sweater. If the sweater hasn't been designed for a specific yarn company and isn't a vehicle for selling a particular brand, the pattern may simply call for yarn in a specific weight — for example, worsted-weight (see Chapter 2 for more on different yarn weights).

- ✔ **The size and type of needles you need:** Often, needles in two sizes are listed — the smaller for cuffs and bottom borders and the larger for the body of the sweater. If the pattern uses double-pointed needles or a circular needle (say for a neckband or collar), or if the entire sweater is worked in the round, the pattern tells you which size needle(s) to use and in what length.

  Following the particular needles specified, you always see the phrase "or size to obtain gauge." This phrase often appears in full capitalization or in italics. Why? Because gauge matters. Head to Chapter 3 for everything you need to know about gauge and why it's so important.

- ✔ **Any special equipment or gadgets required:** Constructing some sweaters requires special tools — for example, a cable needle, stitch markers, stitch holders, and so on. These tools are listed after the needles.

- ✔ **Buttons or other finishing materials:** If the sweater is a cardigan, the number and size of the buttons called for are listed. If pompoms, embroidery, or other embellishments are in order, the materials needed to make them are listed here.

Check the materials list and make sure that you have what you need when you're purchasing yarn and needles for a project. You don't want to find yourself unable to continue working on your project after the stores have closed because you don't have a particular tool in your supply box.

Gauge

In the "Gauge" section of the pattern, you find a formula that reads something like this:

14 sts and 21 rows to 4" (10 cm) over St st, using larger needles.

This notation is the gauge formula. It tells you how many stitches and rows are in a 4-inch square of the sweater fabric (in this case, stockinette stitch). If you want to make a sweater that corresponds to the measurements given, you must duplicate this gauge. We can't say it enough! You can find more information on gauge in Chapter 3.

Gauge isn't a standard, and you should make a gauge swatch for everything you plan to knit — especially if you want the finished project to fit when you're done.

Special pattern stitches

If your sweater has any special pattern stitches or instructions, they may be listed and explained separately and not given again in the body of the instructions. For example, you may see the following:

Seed Stitch

Row 1 (RS): * K1, p1; rep from * to end of row.

Row 2: K the purl sts and p the knit sts.

Rep Row 2 for pattern.

Then, in the instructions proper, when you read "work seed stitch for 8 rows," come back to this section to find out how to work seed stitch.

You also may find that a special abbreviation is explained. For example, you may see the following:

C3R (cross 3 right): Sl 1 st to cn and hold to back, k2, p1 from cn.

When you come across C3R in your instructions, you don't have to scratch your head and wonder, "What the heck?" You can look in the opening information for an explanation. (And if the instruction used in this example is making you wonder, "What the heck?" refer to the abbreviations in Chapter 3.)

Schematics and charts

The *schematic* is a small outline drawing of each sweater piece in the pattern. The pattern usually includes one schematic showing the body front and back with the neckline sketched in and another schematic of one sleeve. Cardigans usually show a single front, a back, and a sleeve.

Listed along the edges of the drawing are the dimensions of the piece in each size — for example, the width and length of the sweater, the distance from the bottom of the sweater to the armhole, the depth of the armhole, and the depth and width of the neck. Figure 15-1 shows a schematic for a toggle jacket.

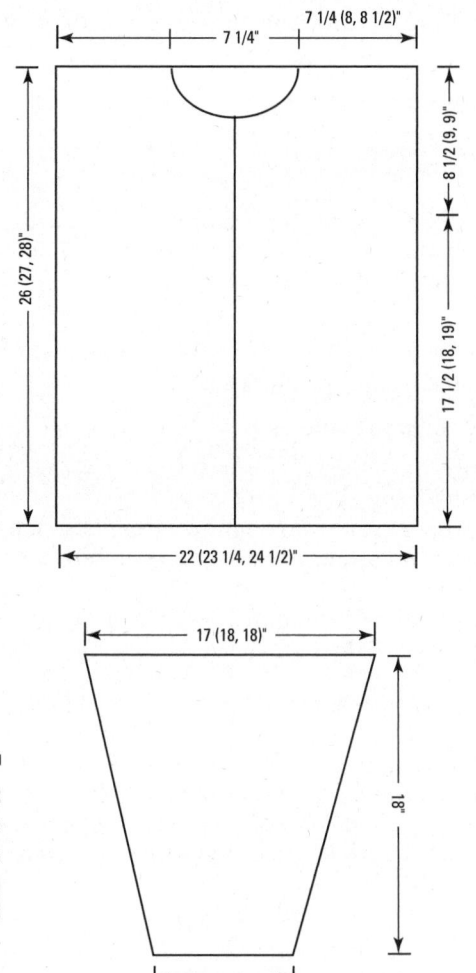

Figure 15-1: A sample schematic showing shape and measurements.

Schematics are a big help because they show you the structure of the sweater at a glance: whether the armhole is straight or shaped and whether the sleeve cap is tall and narrow or short and wide. As you become more familiar with the way actual measurements fit you, you'll be able to tell quickly from the schematic whether you want to knit the pattern as-is or make changes.

Depending on the design of the sweater and the way the pattern's written, a sweater pattern may include a chart to show a stitch, cable, or color pattern. Or it may include a chart to show an unusual feature of the garment, such as a shawl collar. Figure 15-2 shows a chart for a repeating color motif and indicates how you should use it.

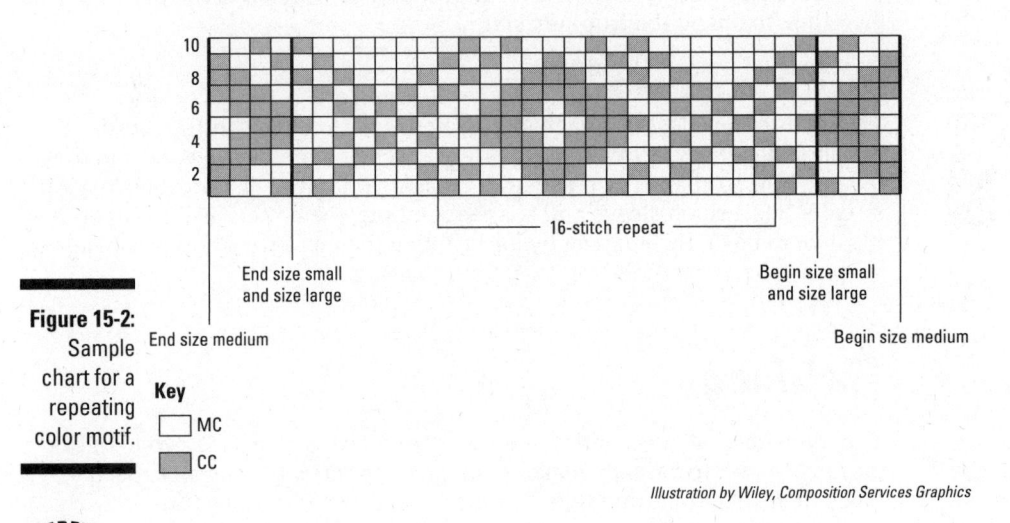

Figure 15-2:
Sample chart for a repeating color motif.

End size medium ... Begin size medium

End size small and size large ... Begin size small and size large

16-stitch repeat

Key
☐ MC
▨ CC

Illustration by Wiley, Composition Services Graphics

On right-side rows, work the chart from right to left. On wrong-side rows, work the chart from left to right. Refer to Chapter 3 for more on how to read charts.

If you collect vintage knitting patterns, you'll seldom see a chart or schematic. Instead, all the moves are painstakingly written out. Some people who learned to knit under the row-by-written-row system regret its demise. Others welcome the picture over the written instructions. The good news is that if you understand better when things are described with words, you can write out charts in word form — and vice versa. If you have a pattern with interminable and obscure directions, read them carefully with graph paper and pencil in hand and make yourself a chart to better understand the text.

Knitting instructions

After all the introductory information, the instructions for knitting your sweater begin. In general, most patterns for cardigans and pullovers begin with the back piece. Here the pattern tells you how many stitches to cast on and what to do with them.

The instructions are usually sequenced like this:

✔ Instructions for the back

✔ Instructions for the front (or fronts if you're knitting a cardigan); generally, the instructions for the front mirror those of the back until it's time to shape the front neckline

✔ Instructions for the sleeves

The instructions describe each step as you work from the bottom border to the shoulder. They tell you what pattern stitches or colors to work, and they tell you how to shape (increase or decrease) your piece. If, for example, your sweater has a set-in sleeve and shaped armhole, the pattern will alert you that it's time to begin the shaping by interrupting the text with a boldface heading such as **"Shape armhole"** or **"Armhole shaping."**

Finishing

The "Finishing" section of the pattern tells you what to do with your knitted pieces in order to actually make them into a sweater. It gives any special blocking instructions and tells you the order in which to sew the pieces together. You also find instructions for additional sweater details, such as how to make the neckband, cardigan bands, collar, crochet edge, and so on.

Chapter 16

How to Knit a Sweater, Step by Step

In This Chapter

▶ Getting your supplies together

▶ Determining size and checking gauge

▶ Casting on and knitting the parts of the sweater

▶ Keeping track of your progress with a diagram

*B*eing able to knit and purl, manipulate stitches (increasing, decreasing, and so on), and create special effects such as cables and stripes is fun in and of itself, no matter what you create. You can happily knit for years, using these techniques to make hats, scarves, afghans, bags, and other pieces that require just a little simple shaping or assembly. At some point, though, you may want to try your hand at something more challenging: knitting sweaters.

Before you cast on your first stitch, take a little time for a few simple preparatory steps: deciding on the perfect size, determining your gauge, and drawing a quick diagram of your sweater pieces. Of course, you can forget these steps and jump right in, just as you can toss your map in the backseat and drive from Maine to California by following the sun. But your trip is more likely to go smoothly if, before leaving, you check your oil and tires, study your map, and highlight the route to follow. This approach may be less spontaneous, but after you're on the road, you won't hit any dead ends that halt your progress.

This chapter runs you through the sweater-making process, from getting ready to knit to making the back, front, and sleeves. After you complete your back, front, and sleeves, you're ready to finish your sweater. Turn to Chapters 17 and 18 for information on those tasks.

Gathering Your Materials

To knit your first sweater, you need three things: a good pattern, good yarn, and needles. If possible, look for your materials in a knitting shop rather than a big-box or craft store. People who work in a yarn shop are generally very knowledgeable and can steer you to good pattern choices and quality yarn. If you run into any problems with the pattern or find that something confuses you, they'll be delighted to help you figure it out.

The following sections offer some tips to give you a good start in gathering your materials.

A good pattern

For your first sweater, choose a simple style with minimal shaping. A dropped-shoulder pullover is a good choice, or try the Easy Top-Down Raglan sweater pattern in Chapter 19, which is knit in the round. Save a cardigan with buttonholes for your next project.

Also look for a pattern that calls for size US 7, 8, or 9 needles (that's 4½ mm, 5 mm, and 5½ mm, respectively). On needles this size, your project will knit up relatively quickly. You'll also be able to see, count, and manipulate individual stitches without straining your eyes — or patience. Plus, if a pattern calls for US 7, 8, or 9 needles, the yarn will be medium weight, one of the easier weights to work with. (Refer to Chapter 2 for details on yarn weights.)

 A child's sweater that knits up quickly is a good practice sweater. You get to work through all the steps of sweater making in miniature — and little kids look great in anything, whether the sleeves are an exact match or not. Plus, if you make it too big, the child will grow into it; if you make it too small, you have a ready-made gift or a doll's outfit.

 Make a photocopy of your pattern so that you can write on it freely as you knit. Keep the copy in a protective plastic sleeve to carry around with your knitting. The same goes for any charts that come with the pattern.

Chapter 15 guides you through the parts of a typical sweater pattern. We recommend that you review it before starting a sweater project.

Yarn

Choosing materials for your first sweater may be daunting if your local knitting store is a yarn and color wonderland. This section gives you some suggestions to help you narrow down the choices.

Wool is the best choice for a first sweater because it knits up easily, blocks beautifully, and looks great. Choose a color on the lighter side so that it's easy to see individual stitches, and make sure that the yarn is a pretty color you'll enjoy knitting. When selecting yarn, look for a *superwash* wool. With superwash, you can launder the sweater in the washing machine and tumble dry, whereas regular wool has a tendency to felt under those conditions.

If you're averse to wool for some reason, look into a blend of other natural fibers before turning to synthetics. Avoid all-cotton yarn for your first sweater unless you've worked up a lot of the smaller projects in this book and feel that you've had plenty of practice making stitches. Cotton yarn doesn't have much give and can be frustrating to work if your hands are new to needles and yarn.

If you must use a 100-percent synthetic yarn, choose a good-quality one (check with the salesperson at your local yarn shop for a recommendation) and resolve to be very careful in the blocking process. (You may want to take a quick look through Chapter 2 before you head to the yarn shop to choose materials for your first sweater.)

Knitting needles

If you're using straight needles, they should be at least 12 to 14 inches long. If you have trouble with stitches slipping off your needles, choose wooden or plastic needles for your first sweater.

Depending on the size of the sweater, you may choose to use a longer circular needle instead. When you have many stitches on a short, straight needle, getting the stitches spread out comfortably can be difficult, which can affect the finished gauge. Using a 24-inch or longer circular needle as a straight needle (meaning that you don't connect the ends to knit in the round) eliminates this problem.

Other supplies to have handy

Before you leave the knitting store, double-check the materials list in the pattern to see whether you need to have any other supplies at the ready, such as stitch holders, markers, a pompom maker, or a tapestry needle for sewing up seams or adding buttons.

Keep the following supplies together in a zippered bag with your knitting projects, and you won't have to get up and hunt around for them when you'd rather be knitting. See Chapter 2 for more information on some of these tools.

✔ Calculator

✔ Crochet hook

✔ Pencil and paper

✔ Ring stitch markers

✔ Safety pins

✔ Scissors

✔ Scrap yarn (preferably smooth, white cotton)

✔ Spare double-pointed needle

✔ Tape measure and a small ruler

✔ Tapestry needle

Including an emery board for taming a renegade nail that keeps snagging on your yarn isn't a bad idea, either.

Before You Cast On

Before you put yarn to needles, you have a couple of small tasks to accomplish: determine the best size sweater to make and check your gauge thoroughly.

Step 1: Pick a size

Sit down with your materials and take your pattern in hand. Go past the section that says "Sizes" and look for "Knitted Measurements." Don't be tempted to choose a size arbitrarily; one designer's medium is another designer's small. Instead, choose the size in the pattern that most closely matches the size you want your garment to measure. Choose according to the bust or chest measurement, or measure a sweater you love that fits you well and then find the closest match.

Most patterns are written for more than one size. Generally, instructions for the smallest size are listed first, followed by those for the larger sizes. So a pattern that includes instructions for small, medium, large, and extra-large sizes would present info in this form: S (M, L, XL). If the instructions say, "Cast on 100 (112, 120, 128) stitches," you cast on 100 stitches for a size small, 112 stitches for a size medium, 120 for a size large, and 128 for a size extra-large. Similarly, if the instructions say, "Repeat last 2 rows 8 (9, 11, 12) times" you know to knit these last 2 rows 8 times for a small sweater, 9 times for a medium sweater, and so on. *Note:* Many patterns give a size measurement *in addition to* an actual measurement: for example, "chest 32 (34, 36), actual size 36 (38, 40)."

Finding the perfect size

If you're wondering whether 21 inches across the chest would fit better than 23 inches, there's an easy way to find out. We're guessing you've probably never measured your favorite sweater. Did you know that it measures 24 inches in width (48 inches in circumference) and 26 inches in length? Probably not. But now's the time to unfold it from the shelf (or dig it out of the pile on the chair), find your tape measure, and see what measurements feel good to you.

Obviously, if your most comfortable sweater is oversized and baggy and the sweater you're planning to knit is short and fitted, you shouldn't use your favorite sweater as a starting point. Look through your closet for something that fits the way you envision your future sweater will fit, measure it, and compare the measurements to those given in the pattern. Or pocket your tape measure along with your knitting notebook and a pen and head to your favorite clothing store. Fill your fitting room with sweaters, try them on, measure the ones that fit well, note the numbers in your knitting notebook, neatly refold the sweaters, and return them with a gracious

smile to the salesperson. You'll know what sizes fit you best based on accurate measurements and styles.

What if you're knitting for someone else and you don't have that person's favorite sweater on hand to measure? Unless you're making a present for this person, call and ask. If it's a gift and the person is of average height and build, you're probably safe knitting a medium. Or if it's for your favorite guy, you can't go wrong with a large (or extra-large if he's tall).

One wonderful thing about knitted fabric is that it's forgiving. It stretches. In desperation, you can even block it out or block it in — to a point. (See Chapter 17 for information about blocking.) Width is really the only measurement you need to be concerned with when you start your sweater. Length can be adjusted fairly easily after you're underway. It's worth a little (or a lot of) investigation time upfront to ensure that, at the long-awaited moment when the sweater pieces have been knit and blocked and sewn together, you have a masterpiece that fits.

When you've determined which set of measurements to follow, get out a yellow highlighter or a pencil and carefully mark every number that refers to your size. If you've made a copy of your pattern as we recommend earlier, you won't have to mark on the original.

Step 2: Find your gauge

Go to the section in your pattern that gives the required — that's *required* — gauge for the pattern. How is the gauge in your pattern measured? What size needles do you use, and which pattern stitch do you work? To brush up on the process of measuring gauge, refer to Chapter 3.

Always work your gauge swatch on the exact same needles and with the very same yarn you'll use for your project, not just needles of the same size and/ or the same yarn in a different color. Needles of the same size but made out of different material, such as wood or Teflon-coated steel, can make a difference in the size of the stitch you make.

To find your gauge, follow these steps:

1. **Work a swatch to a length and width of 5 inches or more and then thread a piece of scrap yarn through the stitches on the needle.**

2. **Block your swatch, ideally in the same manner you'll block your sweater and let it rest.**

   See Chapter 17 for blocking instructions.

3. **After the swatch has rested, measure it to determine your gauge.**

4. **Re-knit the swatch as necessary to get the exact gauge you need.**

   • If you have more stitches per inch than the pattern calls for, go up one needle size.

   • If you have fewer stitches per inch than the pattern calls for, go down one needle size.

Tinker with your needle size until you come as close as you can to the *stitch gauge* required by the pattern. Stitch gauge determines how wide a sweater is, so if you're off on stitch gauge, your sweater will be off widthwise. After you cast on and start knitting the actual sweater, you can't do much to make your sweater wider or narrower.

Row gauge *will* affect your sleeve shaping and raglan shaping, and the placement of a cable or other distinctive vertical pattern may be interrupted in an awkward place if your row gauge is off. But you can work around a not-so-perfect row gauge with a little diagramming and planning, as we explain in the later section "Graphing sleeves (it's worth it)".

Knitting . . . at Last!

After you've read through the instructions and established your gauge, it's time to cast on and launch your sweater. Most sweater patterns proceed in a predictable way, usually beginning with the back, followed by the front and then the sleeves.

If you're knitting in the round, you'll proceed a bit differently, depending on the type of sweater:

✔ **Top-down sweaters:** When you knit a *top-down sweater,* you begin at the neck and knit your way down to just under the arms, knitting the tops of the sleeves as you go. (It may sound confusing, but these garments are some of the easiest and fastest sweaters to knit; you can find instructions for just such a sweater, the Easy Top-Down Raglan, in Chapter 19.) After you finish the body, you return to the sleeves and finish them separately.

✔ **Bottom-up sweaters:** For these sweaters, you knit the bottom portion of the sweater first, all the way to the underarms. Then you join the sleeves, which have been knit separately, and decrease the sweater yoke all the way to the neck opening.

Knitting the back

Most sweater patterns instruct you to begin with the back. They tell you which needles to use to get started, how many stitches to cast on, and which stitches to begin with. This section offers helpful advice on getting off to a good start.

Get into the habit of keeping track of how many rows you've knit as you work the sweater back (and front). Why? Because if the back and front match row for row, you can sew them together using the mattress stitch (explained in Chapter 17). Using safety pins, pin the first stitch from which you want to count. Then, as you knit, stop every once in a while, count 20 rows, and pin the next stitch. If you pin a stitch every 20 rows, it's easy to keep track of the row number, and you won't have to count from the very beginning each time.

Casting on

For the two-strand cast-on method (refer to Chapter 4), you have to know how much yarn to allow for the number of stitches you'll be casting on. Allow 1 to 1½ inches for each stitch to be cast on.

Leave enough of a tail to use later to seam up the side of the sweater. For this tail, add 12 inches to the amount you need for the cast-on stitches. If this extra-long end gets in your way as you knit, make a butterfly with it as described in Chapter 2. Or use a plastic bread clip as a bobbin for the extra-long tail.

Strengthening the cast-on edge

Cast-on edges take a lot of wear, and a well-worn and loved sweater can begin to fray or even break along the bottom edge. You can discourage this wear by casting on with a double strand of yarn (simply cast on with two balls of yarn) and then continuing with a single strand. After the cast-on row, simply drop the second strand and cut it off, leaving an end long enough to weave in later.

Selecting the right side

After you've worked a few rows, take a look at the cast-on edge. You'll see that it looks different from each side: One side shows small neat bumps, and the other shows overlapping diagonal stitches. It's up to you to decide which side you prefer for the right side of your sweater. If you use the two-strand cast-on method and make the first row a right-side row, the little bumps will show on the right side. If you'd rather use the other side of the cast-on row as the right side, make the first row of your knitting a wrong-side row.

When you move on to the front and the sleeves, be sure to use the same side as the right side. Otherwise, the edges of your piece won't be the same.

Switching needles when it's time

Many sweaters use smaller needles for cuffs, hems, and necks and use larger needles for the body. The instructions tell you when to change to the larger or smaller needles. At the change row, simply knit the next row with one of the smaller (or larger needles). Here's an example from a pattern:

> With smaller needles and the MC, cast on 101 (107, 117) sts.
>
> Work k1, p1 rib for 3½ inches.
>
> Change to larger needles and work in St st until piece measures 12½ (13, 13) inches from beg.

To switch needles in this example, you work to the end of the change row and knit the next row by using one of the larger needles. Essentially, you're knitting from the smaller needle to the larger one. At the end of this row, the stitches are now on the larger needle, and the smaller needle is empty. Put aside the smaller needles and continue on in the stitch pattern(s) given in your pattern with the larger needles.

Measuring your piece

As accurate as your gauge swatch may be, knitting a piece so much larger than a swatch can throw off your careful measurements. For peace of mind, take a gauge reading after you work a good 4 inches or so. Work to the halfway point in your row so that you can spread out the stitches along both needles to the width of the fabric. Lay out your piece on a flat surface and measure it. If it's supposed to measure 22 inches across, check to see that it does.

When it's time to measure the length of your piece, work to the center of the row, lay the piece flat, and measure it from the very bottom — the first row — to the knitting needle. Take your measurement somewhere in the middle, not on the edge; your edges will be more stretched and wobbly and not as stable as the center knitting.

Shaping an armhole

If your sweater has a shaped armhole, the instructions tell you when to begin the armhole shaping, where and how to decrease, and how many stitches you should have left after you complete the shaping. It may say something like this:

Armhole shaping

Bind off 3 sts at beg of next 2 rows. Dec 1 st each side every other row 1 (3, 5) times — 56 (60, 62) sts. Work even until armhole measures 5 (5½, 6) inches.

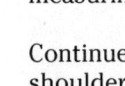

Before starting any decreasing, put a safety pin into one of the stitches on the LH needle to mark the beginning of the armhole. You'll measure from that mark when you're determining the depth of the armhole. Be sure to lay the measuring tape flat; do not follow the curved edge of the armhole.

Continue to work the back until you've worked the number of inches to the shoulder given in your pattern.

Shaping the shoulder and neck

If the shoulder is shaped, you work the shoulder and neck shaping right after you work the armhole shaping. You're likely to see instructions like this:

Shoulder and neck shaping

Bind off 6 sts at beg of next 4 (2, 2) rows, 7 sts at beg of next 2 (4, 4) rows. Bind off rem 18 (20, 22) sts for back neck.

Some patterns with straight shoulders tell you to bind off all the stitches on the last row of the back piece and don't distinguish shoulder stitches from back-neck stitches. If the instructions don't give specific numbers for shoulder stitches, look at the final line in the instructions for the front. There, you should be able to find the number of stitches remaining for each shoulder after you've worked the neckline shaping.

Sometimes the shoulder and neck shaping are separated, with the shoulder shaping coming first and the neck shaping later. Simply follow the instructions as they're given, and you'll be fine.

Sloping the shoulders

If your pattern is designed with a straight shoulder and you want it to angle up slightly from shoulder edge to neck, changing your pattern is easy. Instead of binding off all the shoulder stitches at once, bind off several groups of stitches over several rows in stair-step fashion.

For an average gauge of 4 to 6 stitches an inch, three steps make a good slope. Divide the number of stitches for one shoulder by 3 to determine how many stitches to bind off for each shoulder step. If the number of stitches in the shoulder isn't evenly divisible by 3, make the first two steps the same number of stitches and the third step at the neckline the odd one.

On a piece of graph paper, mark off enough squares in a horizontal line to represent the right shoulder and fill in the steps. (If you have enough room on your graph paper, map out enough squares to represent the back neck and both shoulders, too.) See the following figure.

When you reach the shoulder and are ready to bind off, with the right side facing, bind off the number of stitches for the first "step" at the beginning of the next 2 rows. Then bind off the number of stitches for the second step at the beginning of the next 2 rows. Then bind off the remaining shoulder stitches at the beginning of the next 2 rows. Finally, bind off the back neck stitches.

Original shoulder bind-off

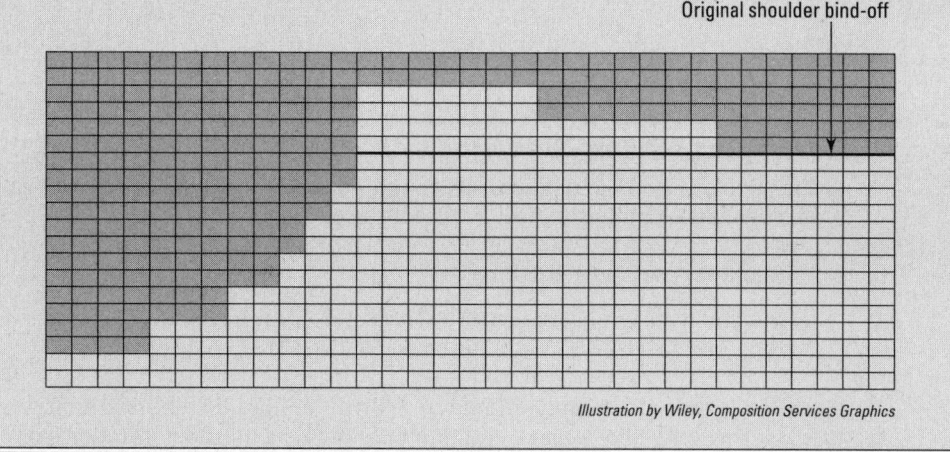

Illustration by Wiley, Composition Services Graphics

At this point, you've completed your sweater back. You're a quarter of the way to a finished sweater, and you have a useful tool: a very accurate gauge swatch. Block the back (see Chapter 17) and have it at the ready in case you need to measure the gauge one more time.

Knitting the front

The front of a sweater is generally worked in the same way as the back as far as the neckline. Your pattern tells you to work the front until it measures a certain length and to "end with a WS (wrong-side) row." You begin the neckline on the next RS (right-side) row.

Shaping the front neck

To shape a neckline, you begin by binding off a group of stitches at the center of your sweater piece. Your pattern tells you "join a second ball of yarn" before you begin to bind the stitches off. You need two balls of yarn to work the remainder of the neckline, one for each side.

To join the second ball of yarn, simply start knitting and binding off with the strand from the second ball. When you return to shape the left side of your neckline, pick up and use the yarn from the first ball.

Shaping the shoulders

Often the shoulder shaping begins while the neckline is still being worked (your pattern says "at the same time" if this is the case). At this point, get out the graph paper. It's helpful to chart the neckline shaping stitch by stitch, especially if the shoulders are shaped as well, because the chart clearly shows what you should be doing and when.

Here's a set of example instructions for front neck and shoulder shaping:

> Next row (RS): Work 27 sts, join second ball of yarn and bind off center 15 sts, work to end. Working both sides at once, bind off from each neck edge 3 sts once, 2 sts twice, then dec 1 st every other row twice. AT SAME TIME when piece measures same length as back to shoulder, shape shoulder as for back.

Because the back shoulder shaping instructions were "Bind off 9 sts at beg of next 6 rows," you do the same for the front shoulder shaping. Figure 16-1 shows this pattern charted.

Note: When you begin shoulder shaping while still working the neckline, you shape the right and left sides of your piece on different rows. Your shaping is symmetrical but off by one row. You can see this difference by checking the bind-offs at either side of the center front neck edge.

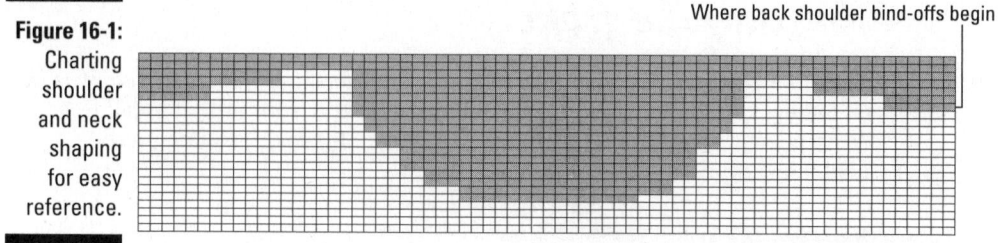

Figure 16-1:
Charting
shoulder
and neck
shaping
for easy
reference.

Putting the front and back together

If you take the time to count rows as you knit up the back (which we recommend in the earlier section "Knitting the back") and you make the front the exact same number of rows, you can use the nearly invisible and fun-to-do mattress stitch to seam them together. If, on the other hand, you rely on measuring your pieces to check their sameness, you don't necessarily have the *exact* same number of rows in both front and back pieces, and you have to seam up your sweater by using the less-than-wonderful backstitch. Head to Chapter 17 for a variety of ways to assemble sweater pieces.

Knitting sleeves

When you've worked your way to the sleeves, you're almost home free. Sleeves are smaller than body parts and therefore go quickly. And shaping makes them interesting to knit.

In general, sleeves begin at the cuff, are worked in the same stitch patterns as the back and front, and are shaped by regular increases along the sides. Your pattern tells you how many stitches to cast on, what stitch to work, when to change needles to a larger size if required, when to begin increasing, and how often to increase. In general, patterns instruct you to increase at regular row intervals, although sometimes they tell you to increase at intervals measured in inches.

Advice for making sleeves easy

Here are some tips for knitting sleeves:

✔ If you work the increases 2 stitches in from the edges, seaming your sleeve is a breeze because you have a straight line of undistorted stitches to work with. To do so without throwing off your pattern, add 2 *selvedge stitches* (border stitches that add stability) on both sides of the piece. Then knit these 2 stitches at the beginning and end of the rows, working the increases and pattern stitches between them.

✔ Using two balls of yarn and one (circular) needle, cast on for two sleeves and work them both at the same time. Doing so ensures that you end up with identical pieces. Just cast on the number of stitches required for one sleeve. Then use the second ball of yarn as you cast on the same number of stitches on the same needle. Work each sleeve with its own ball of yarn. (This strategy is also helpful when working two fronts of a cardigan.)

✔ If you're working a sweater with a dropped shoulder, you can pick up stitches along the armhole edge of the body and knit from the armhole down to the cuff, saving yourself from having to sew the sleeve to the body. (Find out about picking up stitches in Chapter 18.) Check to see how many stitches your sleeve is supposed to have when you've worked all the increases; that's the number to pick up. Work 1 inch before you begin decreasing.

Graphing sleeves (it's worth it)

Once in a while, you may run into a glitch in sleeve-making if the pattern tells you to increase every so many rows and your row gauge is different from the designer's. Your sleeve may measure the correct length before you've worked all the necessary increases, but you end up with a sleeve that's the right length but the wrong width at the armhole.

If you're working an angled or shaped-sleeve cap, the top of your sleeve needs to fit *exactly* into the carved-out shape in the sweater body. To ensure that your sleeve is the correct length *and* width when you reach the armhole, graph it. (You can buy large sheets of graph paper at an artist's supply store or simply tape two pieces together lengthwise.) If you're working a cable or lace pattern that requires a certain number of stitches, graphing your sleeve offers the further advantage of helping you see when you've increased enough stitches to begin working the pattern over them.

To graph a sleeve, follow these steps:

1. **Draw a line at the bottom of your graph paper to represent the first row after the bottom rib or border of the cuff; mark the center.**

2. **Go to the sweater back you've finished and blocked and take a new and improved gauge reading.**

   Subtract the cuff measurement from the length that your sleeve should measure to the armhole. Multiply the row gauge per inch by the length that your sleeve should measure from the end of the rib or border to the underarm.

3. **Count this number of rows from your bottom line and mark the top row to represent the underarm.**

4. **At the underarm mark, count out a horizontal line of squares to represent the width your sleeve should be at this point.**

Make sure that the centers of top and bottom rows are aligned.

5. **Mark a row about 1 inch below the underarm; check your pattern for the first increase row and mark it.**

   The rows of squares between the marked rows represent the number of rows you have in which to make your increases.

6. **Draw in the rest of the increases.**

   If you get them all in *before* reaching the top line, you're all set. If not, reconfigure the increases so that they're closer together, and you can be sure of ending up with the correct number of stitches when your sleeve measures the right length.

Figure 16-2 shows a chart of a sleeve with increases.

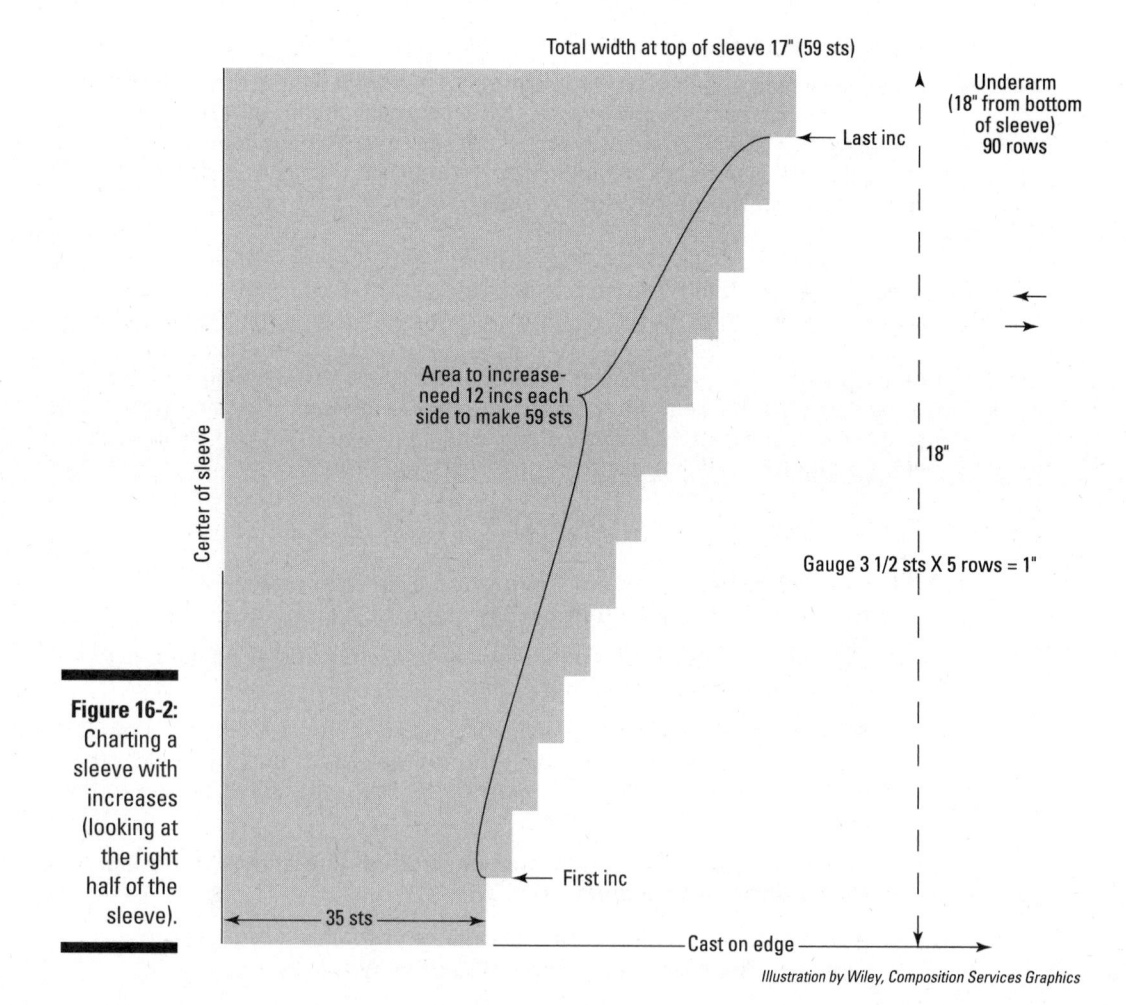

Figure 16-2: Charting a sleeve with increases (looking at the right half of the sleeve).

Total width at top of sleeve 17" (59 sts)

Underarm (18" from bottom of sleeve) 90 rows

Last inc

Area to increase- need 12 incs each side to make 59 sts

18"

Gauge 3 1/2 sts X 5 rows = 1"

Center of sleeve

First inc

35 sts

Cast on edge

The Big Picture: Keeping Track of Where You Are

You don't knit a sweater in one sitting. No matter how much you love to knit, eventually you have to put it down. For this reason, we highly recommend that you develop a system to remind yourself of where you are at the moment you put down your knitting and where you're going when you pick it up again later.

Our favorite method for tracking a sweater in progress involves making a diagram. We're indebted to Gertrude Taylor's *America's Knitting Book* (Simon & Schuster Trade) for the idea for this system. What follows is our version of her system.

A *diagram* is a quick outline drawing you make of your sweater piece. On it, you can show all the knitting information embedded in the text of your pattern. If your sweater pattern is a map of your entire sweater, the diagram you make is a map of the piece you're working on at the moment. It gives you an instant visual picture of where you are, where you're headed, and the steps you have to take to get there. Figure 16-3 shows a diagram of a sweater back.

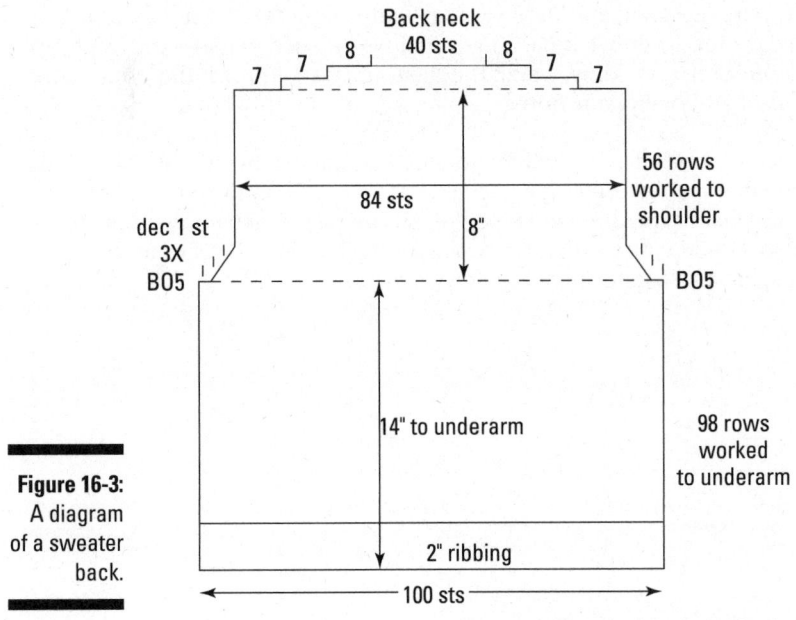

Figure 16-3: A diagram of a sweater back.

Back neck
40 sts
7 7 8   8 7 7

84 sts
8"

56 rows worked to shoulder

dec 1 st
3X
BO5   BO5

14" to underarm

98 rows worked to underarm

2" ribbing

100 sts

Illustration by Wiley, Composition Services Graphics

We usually work from a general diagram on plain white paper; then we move to graph paper when we get to the shaping area so we can chart out every stitch. Because most sweater patterns have you begin with the back, draw a diagram for that piece first and enter the information that will remind you of the steps en route to the finished piece, such as the following:

- ✔ How many stitches to cast on
- ✔ How many inches to work in the border stitch
- ✔ Where to begin binding off the armhole
- ✔ How many stitches to bind off
- ✔ How many stitches to decrease

As you work through the sweater, you can mark off your route as you go (doing so is helpful if you put your work down for a few days) and make notes on things you want to remember. If we're working on a sweater with armhole shaping, for example, we note on the diagram the number of rows we've worked to the first shaping row. This way, when we're working on the front, we know exactly how many rows to work for the piece to be the same as the back.

As we work through shaping, we can mark off our progress by checking off the decreases as we make them. When we reach the shoulder, we count the rows between the beginning of the armhole shaping and the shoulder and note it on the diagram, and then we finish any shoulder and neck shaping the pattern calls for. Then we have a map that we can use to make the front, up to the point of the neckline. Using the diagram, we can work the front as we did the back, following our notes.

If you'd rather keep track of where you are in a pattern in an easier way, look for removable highlighting tape available at teacher's supply stores. It looks like regular clear tape but can be peeled off the page when you're done with it. It's also a good way to keep track of a particular set of directions you're knitting again and again, such as a stitch pattern.

Chapter 17

Getting It Together: Blocking and Assembling Your Pieces

*W*hen you finish making the various pieces of your project, whether they're the back and front panels of a pillow or the sleeves and body of a sweater, you've reached the Cinderella moment: It's time to turn those crumpled, curling, lumpy knitted pieces sprouting the odd end of yarn into smooth, flat, even pieces waiting to be joined into a beautifully crafted item. No matter what's gone before, the finishing is what makes or breaks the final product.

For people who love to knit, weaving in ends, blocking, and seaming aren't exciting because they aren't knitting. However, when you know how to finish your pieces neatly, you have the expertise necessary to make the finishing process at least a manageable interval between the end of knitting one project and the beginning of a new one (if not exactly a pleasure). And the pleasure that comes from seeing your Fairy Godmother powers at work will inspire kinder feelings toward this part of the process.

The purpose of this chapter is to introduce you to the techniques you need to complete the three basic finishing tasks:

✔ **Weaving in** the loose ends of yarn that you left hanging when you changed colors or when you had to start a new ball of yarn

✔ **Blocking** your knitting to smooth out your stitches and to set the shapes of your pieces

✔ **Joining** your knitted pieces together if you're making anything more complicated than a scarf or a potholder

Tying Up Loose Ends

The first step in the finishing process is taking care of all the loose ends hanging about. If you've managed to make all the yarn changes at the side edges, that's where you'll find most of the ends. Otherwise, you'll have loose ends scattered here and there that require different techniques for successfully making them disappear.

Although various techniques exist for weaving in ends (and weave you must; there's no getting around it because knots will show on the right side of the work and may unravel over time), keep in mind that your goal is a nice, smooth fabric without glitches or an unattractive ridge in the middle of your knitting. You can hide your loose ends by doing any of the following:

- ✔ Weaving them vertically up the side edges
- ✔ Weaving them in sideways on the wrong side of the fabric
- ✔ Weaving them in along a bound-off edge

Use whichever method safely tucks in your ends *and* results in a smooth, unblemished right side. Every situation (thickness of yarn, location of join) is different. Try the techniques in this section, and if you discover something that works better in a given circumstance, use it.

Weaving in the entire length of a 6-inch yarn end is unnecessary; you need to weave the end over only a few stitches. With wool yarn, running a yarn end in over 3 or 4 stitches is enough to secure it. The fuzzy nature of the fibers helps the woven ends "stick" to the rest of the fabric. With slick yarns, such as rayon and polished cotton, you need to weave the ends in over 5 or 6 stitches to prevent them from working their way out. Then cut away the excess, leaving about ¼ inch free.

If for some reason you left an end that's too short to comfortably thread through a needle, run your needle through the appropriate nearby loops as if it were threaded. With the eye of the needle at the short yarn end, finagle the yarn end through the eye of the tapestry needle and pull the needle through the loops. The end will be woven in and secured.

Weaving ends up the sides

If you joined yarns at the side edges by temporarily tying the two ends together in a bow, follow these steps to weave in the ends:

1. **Untie the bow.**

   Don't worry. Your knitting won't unravel.

2. **Thread one end through the tapestry needle and weave it *down* the side loops at the edge of your knitting.**

3. **Thread the other end through the tapestry needle and weave it *up* the side loops at the edge of your knitting (see Figure 17-1.)**

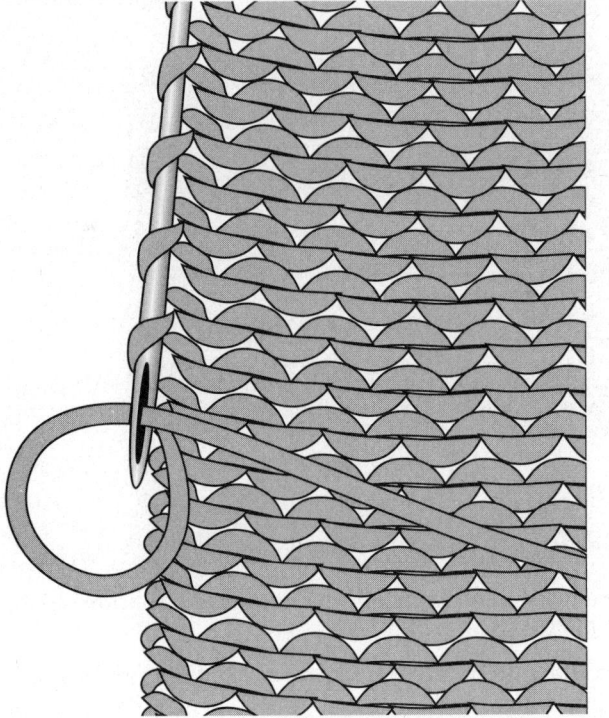

Illustration by Wiley, Composition Services Graphics

Figure 17-1:
Weave the
yarn end
through the
side loops.

If you joined the ends by working the two strands together for the edge stitch (instead of tying your two ends together), use a tapestry needle to pick out one of the ends and then weave it up the side as outlined in the preceding steps. Weave the other end in the opposite direction. If the two strands are thin and won't add much bulk to the edge stitch, don't bother to pick out one of the ends. Just weave each end into the sides in opposite directions.

Weaving the ends horizontally

If you switched yarns in the middle of a row and have loose ends dangling there, you need to weave the ends in horizontally. Untie the knot or pick out one of the stitches if you worked a stitch with a double strand of yarn.

Take a careful look at the purl bumps on the back side of your fabric. You'll notice that the tops of the purl stitches look like "over" bumps, and the running threads between the stitches look like "under" bumps (see Figure 17-2).

Figure 17-2:
Identify the over and under parts of the stitches on the purl side.

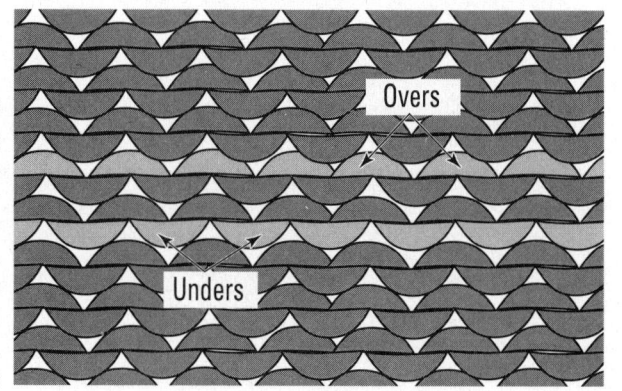

Illustration by Wiley, Composition Services Graphics

Using a tapestry needle, weave the ends in as follows:

1. **Weave the end on the right in and out of the *under* bump; then continue working to the left.**

2. **Weave the end on the left in and out of the *over* bump; then continue working to the right.**

   The ends cross each other, filling in the gap between the old yarn and the new, as shown in Figure 17-3.

Work fairly loosely so as not to pull the fabric in any way. Check the right side of the fabric to make sure that it looks smooth.

If your yarn is particularly slippery, weave in the end by following the path of the neighboring stitches around the under and over bumps, as shown in Figure 17-4. This method creates a little extra bulk, but it completely secures the strand.

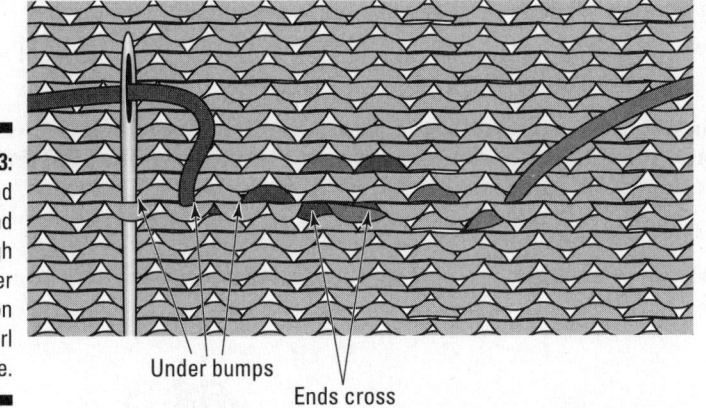

Figure 17-3:
Thread the strand through the under bumps on the purl side.

Under bumps

Ends cross

Illustration by Wiley, Composition Services Graphics

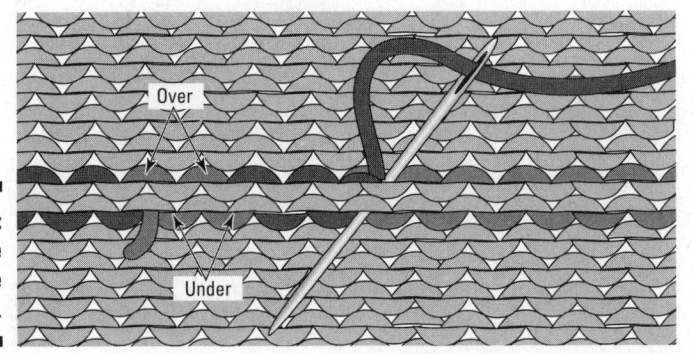

Over

Figure 17-4:
Follow the path of the stitch.

Under

Illustration by Wiley, Composition Services Graphics

After you work your ends into the fabric, snip them about ½ inch from the surface and gently stretch and release the fabric to pull the tails into the fabric.

Weaving ends into a bound-off edge

When you're weaving in an end at a bound-off edge that forms a curve, you can weave in the end in a way that creates an uninterrupted line of bound-off stitches. You can use this technique, for example, where you've joined a second ball of yarn at the start of neckline shaping or on the final bound-off stitch of a neckband worked on a circular needle. Here's how:

1. **Thread a tapestry needle with the yarn end.**

2. **Find the chain of interconnected V's that form the bound-off edge (shown in Figure 17-5).**

3. **Insert the needle under the legs of the first of the interconnected V's, and then take it back through the initial stitch, mimicking the path of a bound-off stitch (see Figure 17-5).**

   Remember to start at the V next to the loose end.

4. **Finish weaving in the end by running the needle under the series of V-legs along one side of the bound-off edge.**

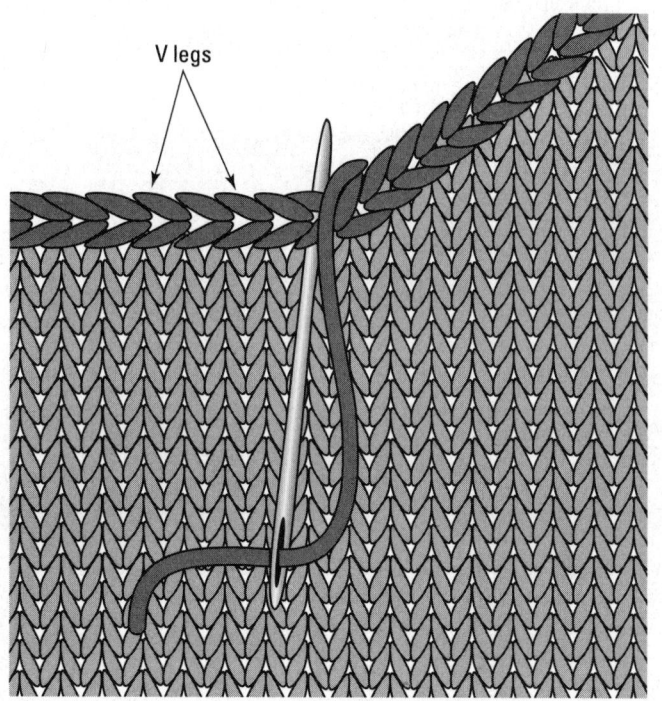

V legs

Figure 17-5:
Weave in an
end along
a bound-off
edge.

Illustration by Wiley, Composition Services Graphics

Tweaking V's

As you're weaving in ends, keep an eye out for loose or misshapen stitches on the right (front) side of your fabric. While you're holding the tapestry needle, you can tweak them back into line by using the tip of your needle to adjust the legs of the stitch, as shown in the following figure.

Remember that a row of stitches is connected. If you have a loose or sloppy stitch, you can pull on the legs of the neighboring V's in either direction for as many stitches as you need to in order to redistribute the extra yarn. If one side of the V is distorted or larger than the other, pull slightly on the other side or tweak the stitch in whatever way is necessary to even it out.

You don't need to get too fussy about the appearance of every single stitch. Blocking straightens any general and minor unevenness, but sometimes, especially in color work, the stitches around the color changes can use a little extra help.

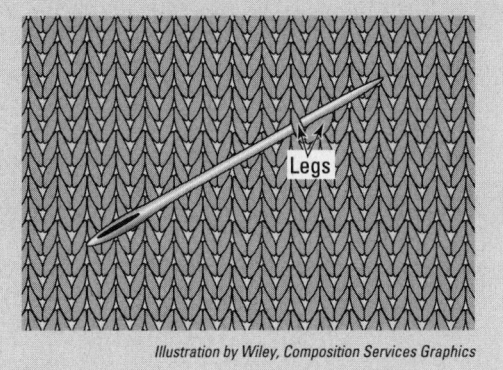

Illustration by Wiley, Composition Services Graphics

Better Blocking

When you *block* a piece of knitting, you wet it down or steam it to coax it into its final shape, letting the moisture and/or heat smooth out all the uneven stitches and straighten out wavy, rolling edges. Blocking is crucial to the final look of your work. All those long hours of careful stitch creation deserve your best efforts now.

 Don't try to seam up your sweater before you block the pieces. Curling edges make it hard to see what you're doing. If you're ready to block something you've knit in the round, move on to the section "Three-dimensional blocking" later in this chapter to find out what to do next.

 Before you block your piece, check for any stitches left "open" to be sewn or grafted together later. If you put them on a pin-type stitch holder, use a tapestry needle to rethread them onto a colorfast piece of scrap yarn long enough that you can tie the ends together without bunching up the stitches. When you're blocking, you want your pieces to lie nice and flat.

Getting your blocking equipment together

You can block any knitted fabric as long as you have a tape measure and a large, flat surface on which to spread out your pieces, such as a bed or a spot on the floor that pets or children won't disturb. But you'll find the job more pleasant — and get better results — if you invest in some blocking equipment. See Chapter 2 for more information on any of the specialized equipment presented in this section. You need the following whether you wet block or steam your pieces:

- **A large, flat, preferably padded surface for laying out your pieces:** It should be at least a little larger than the knitted piece itself. Many knitting stores sell boards specifically for blocking, but you also can find directions online that show you how to make your own. Just type "knitting blocking board" or something similar into your favorite search engine.

- **Blocking wires:** You can block your pieces without these, but you'll have much nicer results if you invest in a set.

- **Pins (preferably T-pins):** They hold your knitted fabric to the blocking board. Don't use pins with colorful plastic heads because the steam will melt them.

- **A tape measure:** After all the trouble you went to knitting to gauge and specific measurements, you want to block your pieces to the correct size, don't you? (We hope the answer is yes!)

- **A steam iron or spray bottle for water:** This gets your knitted piece wet.

- **A large towel if you're wet blocking:** Loosely rolling your knitted piece in a towel removes some of the water.

- **Schematic drawings of your pieces:** These help you determine the exact shape you need.

Steam, dunk, or spray? Deciding which blocking method to use

The best blocking method for your project depends on the fiber of your yarn, the amount of time you have, and the stitch pattern you've used. You can wet block just about anything that's colorfast with superb results. Steam blocking is faster than wet blocking and is fine for sweaters in stockinette stitch and that were worked in a yarn not susceptible to steam damage. But don't use it on acrylics or for stitch patterns with texture you want to highlight, especially cables.

Read the following list to identify your blocking options for different kinds of yarn, and then go on to the appropriate sections later in this chapter to find out exactly how to steam or wet block.

- **Noncolorfast yarns:** You can wet or spray block just about anything with superior results — *except* yarn that you suspect may be less than colorfast. Before blocking a striped or color-patterned sweater, wet a 20-inch sample of each color and wrap the strands around a paper towel. Let them dry. If any of the colors bleed onto the paper, forget wet blocking. Steam the pieces and send the completed sweater to the dry cleaner when it needs a wash.

- **Mohair and other fuzzy yarns:** Wet block fuzzy yarns such as mohair. Steam will flatten them. When the pieces dry, you can gently run a special mohair brush, or your own hairbrush, over them to fluff up the fibers again; just be sure to use a light touch.

- **Wool, cotton, and blended yarns:** You can steam block wool, cotton, and many blends with great success. Steaming is quicker than wet blocking because the drying time is significantly less, but it requires care and attention because you have a hot iron up-close-and-personal to knitted fabric.

- **Synthetic yarns:** *Don't* steam a synthetic yarn. It will die before your eyes. Too much steam-heat destroys a synthetic yarn's resilience. Wet or spray block this yarn instead.

No matter the fiber, cabled and/or richly textured sweaters are best wet blocked with the right side facing up. While the sweater pieces are damp, you can mold and sculpt the 3-D patterns. Steaming will flatten them somewhat.

If you have any doubts about the fiber of your yarn and how it will respond to heat, experiment on your gauge swatch before working on your actual piece. You'll quickly find out whether steam enhances or ruins your yarn.

Wet blocking

Wet blocking offers a chance for the yarn to relax, get clean, and settle into place so it looks its best.

When you *wet block* a knitted piece, you get it completely wet in a sink or basin of water. Take this opportunity to add a little gentle soap or wool wash to the water and swish out whatever dirt and grime your piece may have picked up while you worked on it. (Wool washes sold at yarn stores not only clean the fiber but may also include lanolin and other fiber conditioners.)

Just be sure to give the piece several good rinses, unless you use a no-rinse formula. Have a large towel at the ready and follow these steps:

1. **Get as much water out of your piece as you can *without* stretching or wringing it out.**

   Some ideas:

   - Press the piece against the empty sink basin to eliminate some of the water.

   - Press the piece between your palms to squeeze a little more water out of it, but don't wring it out.

   When you lift the piece out of the sink, lift it out in both hands, making sure not to let any part of it stretch down.

2. **Without stretching the piece, spread it out on the towel and fold the ends of the towel over it; then gently and loosely roll up the towel to absorb more water.**

   Roll loosely, because you don't want to get the piece too dry. It should be more wet than damp — just not dripping wet — when you lay it out to block. Plus if you roll too tightly, you'll have creases in your knitted piece.

3. **If you're using blocking wires, unroll the piece and weave in the wires along the edges.**

   Blocking wires come with instructions on how best to do this.

4. **Gently lay your piece out on the blocking board.**

   For a stockinette piece, lay it face down on the blocking board; for a textured or cabled sweater, lay it right side up. If your board has a cover with a grid, line up the centerlines of your pieces with the grid.

5. **Spread your piece out to the correct dimensions without distorting the direction of the stitches.**

   Using your schematic for reference and the grid as a guide, start at the center. If you're blocking a sweater, check that your piece is the right width and the correct length from the bottom edge to the beginning of the armhole (see Figure 17-6) and from the beginning of the armhole to the shoulder.

6. **Pin and smooth all pieces.**

   You need to pin in only a few places to keep the piece flat. Run your palms lightly over the piece to help keep everything smooth and even.

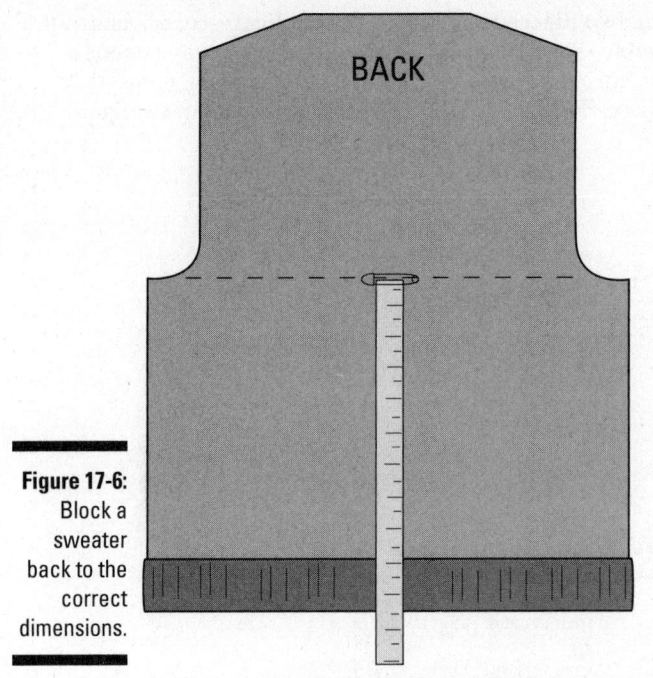

Figure 17-6:
Block a
sweater
back to the
correct
dimensions.

Illustration by Wiley, Composition Services Graphics

7. **Sculpt your piece while it's wet.**

   - **If your design has a ribbed border:** Decide how much you want the rib to hug you. If you want it to pull in as much as possible, keep the rib compressed. If you want it to pull in only slightly or to hang fairly straight, pin it out completely to the width of the piece.

   - **If you're blocking a cabled or highly textured piece:** Pinch and mold the contours of the cable crossings to highlight their three-dimensional qualities.

   - **If your piece is lace:** Spread out the fabric so that the openings are really open.

   - **If the bottom edge of your piece is scalloped or pointed:** Pin out the waves or points.

8. **Go away and start another knitting project while this one dries.**

   Drying may take a day or so.

If you're in a hurry, you can get your piece to dry in a matter of hours by placing a fan in front of it. The bigger the fan, the more quickly the piece dries. A window fan does the trick in no time.

When you're blocking two pieces that should be identical — cardigan fronts and sleeves, for example — lay them out side by side if you have enough space, and either measure back and forth or line them up on symmetrical gridlines for comparison. Figure 17-7 shows you how to line up cardigan fronts.

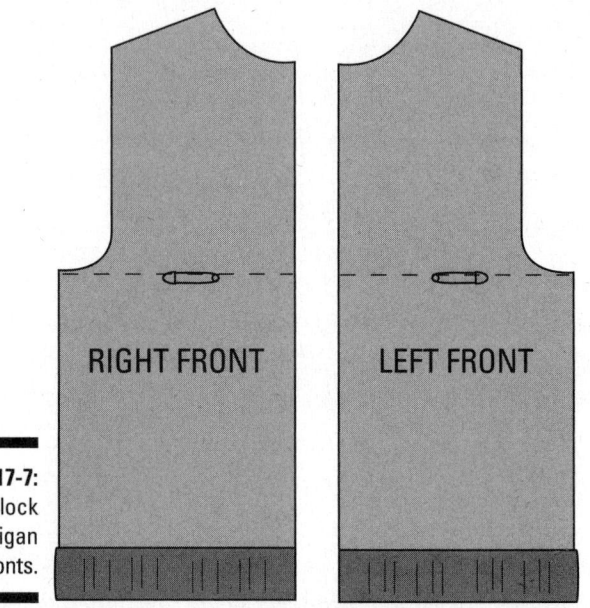

RIGHT FRONT   LEFT FRONT

Figure 17-7: Block cardigan fronts.

Illustration by Wiley, Composition Services Graphics

If you're short on blocking space, you can lay out fronts and sleeves one at a time on top of each other to ensure that they'll be identical when dry. When they're still damp but not dry, move the top piece off and lay it down gently to the side for the last stages of drying.

If you decide to block one piece at a time, you can still ensure that your pieces have identical dimensions. Block the first piece according to the dimensions on your diagram. When it's dry, before taking it off the board, stick straight pins into the blocking board to mark the outline of the piece you're removing. Put them in at the bottom right and left corners and at the top right and left corners to show the corners of the outline. Then lay down the next piece within the parameter of the pins.

Spray blocking

Spray blocking is much like wet blocking. Just do the following:

1. **If you're using blocking wires, thread them along the side edges.**

2. **Spread out your knitted piece(s) on your blocking board, wrong side up for stockinette stitch or right side up for texture and cables.**

3. **Align and measure until you have everything straight and matching your schematic.**

4. **Pin the edges every few inches (if you're not using blocking wires) or closer together if you see that the edge is rolling severely between pins.**

5. **With a clean spray bottle filled with room-temperature water, spray your piece until it's saturated.**

6. **Press gently with your hands to even out the fabric, pinching and molding any three-dimensional details.**

7. **Let the sweater dry.**

   This usually takes a day or two, depending on the thickness of the project, general humidity, and so on.

8. **When your piece is dry, remove it from the blocking board.**

Steam blocking

Follow these steps to steam block a piece:

1. **Lay out your knitted piece as described in the "Wet blocking" section.**

2. **Hold a steam iron over the piece about ½ inch away from the surface.**

   You want the steam to penetrate the piece without the weight of the iron pressing down on it. If your knitting is cotton, you can let the iron touch the fabric very lightly, but keep it moving and don't let the full weight of the iron lay on the surface.

   If you're worried about hurting the fabric, lay a damp towel over the piece and steam through the towel to the fabric. This extra layer isn't necessary; it's just another way to protect the time and money you spent on the almost-finished project.

3. **After steaming, let your piece rest and dry for at least 30 minutes.**

Handheld steamers are perfect for all your steam blocking needs. Steam the piece as it lies flat so it doesn't get any unwanted stretch from hanging on a hanger.

Three-dimensional blocking

Not all knitting is flat. However, all knitting needs to be blocked.

For sweaters worked in the round, you can use wet blocking, spray blocking, or steam blocking. Lay out the completed sweater, arranging it according to the dimensions of your schematic. If you plan to make most of your sweaters in the round, consider investing in a *wooly board,* an adjustable wooden frame with arms that you can dress in your wet sweater. After the sweater dries, take it off the frame and — voilà! — your sweater is flat, smooth, and even.

You can steam block hats while they lie flat, one side at a time. Or find a mixing bowl that's the right size, wet your hat, and drape it over the upside-down bowl to dry. Styrofoam heads designed to hold wigs are also great for blocking hats. If you've made a tam or beret, you can block it over a dinner plate. Be creative!

If you plan to knit a lot of socks and mittens, add blockers to your next Christmas or birthday list. *Blockers* are wooden sock and mitten-shaped templates with biscuit-type holes cut out to aid air circulation. They come in various sizes for your different projects. Simply wet down your socks or mittens, pull them on over the forms, and let them dry to smooth perfection.

Basic Techniques for Joining Pieces

After you block your sweater or project pieces, it's time to put them together. You can choose between traditional sewing methods and techniques that mimic and work with knitted stitches.

- ✔ If you choose the more knitterly techniques, the ones you use will be determined by how the stitches are coming together: head to head, side to side, or head to side, all of which are shown in Figure 17-8.

- ✔ If you opt for the sewing method, the later section "Sewing seams with backstitch" explains the backstitch and how to use it to sew sweater pieces together.

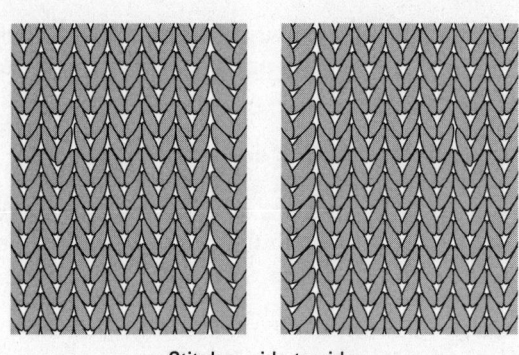

Stitches side to side

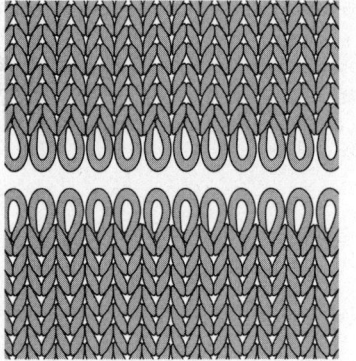
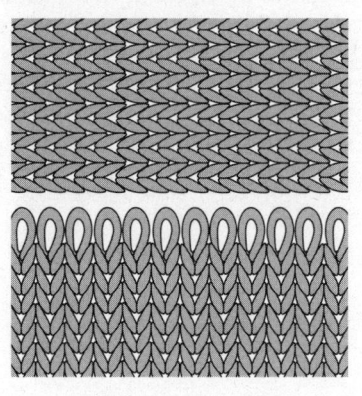

Figure 17-8:
Assess how
stitches are
lined up for
assembly.

Stitches head to head   Stitches head to side

Illustration by Wiley, Composition Services Graphics

The techniques in the following sections help you join your pieces together
in ways becoming to knitting. These techniques work with the structure of
the stitches, creating seams that are smooth and flexible.

When you've finished seaming your sweater pieces together, no matter
which method you use, steam all the seams and press down on them with
your fingertips to encourage them to lie flat.

Three-needle bind-off (head to head)

Use the three-needle bind-off when you're joining stitches head to head (refer
to Figure 17-8). The technique is the quickest and easiest joining method and

creates a stable — and visible — seam. With a three-needle bind-off, you get to do two things at once: bind off and join two pieces together — perfect for joining shoulder seams.

For the three-needle bind-off, you need three needles: one each to hold the shoulder stitches and one for working the actual bind-off. If you don't have three needles of the same size, use a smaller one for holding the stitches of one or both of the pieces to be bound off, and use a regular-size needle for binding off.

To work the three-needle bind-off, thread the open stitches of your pieces onto a needle — one for each piece. If you've left a long tail end (about four times the width of the stitches to be joined), you can use it to work the bind-off. Thread your first needle through the stitches on the first piece so the point comes out where the tail is. When you're threading the second needle through the second piece, make sure your needle tips will point in the same direction when your pieces are arranged with right sides together (see Figure 17-9). If you haven't left a tail end for this maneuver, you can start working with a fresh strand and weave in the end later.

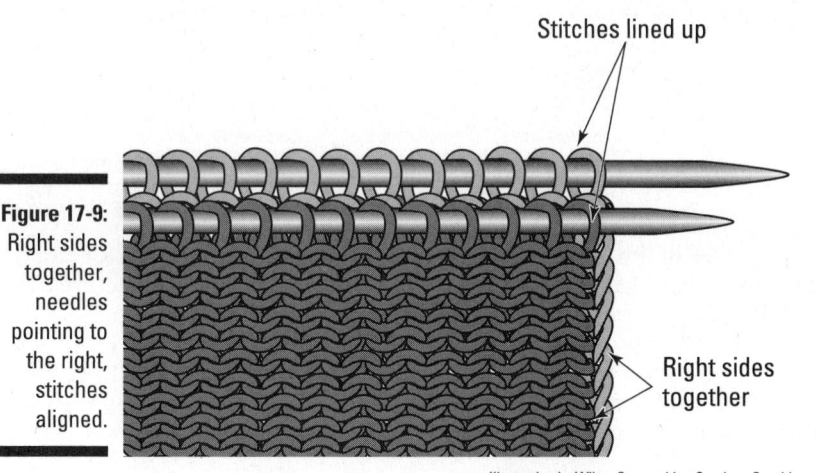

Stitches lined up

Figure 17-9:
Right sides together, needles pointing to the right, stitches aligned.

Right sides together

Illustration by Wiley, Composition Services Graphics

For this method, you knit and bind off the usual way, but you work stitches from two LH needles at the same time. Follow these steps:

1. **Insert the third needle knitwise (as if you were knitting) into the first stitch on *both* needles, as Figure 17-10 shows.**

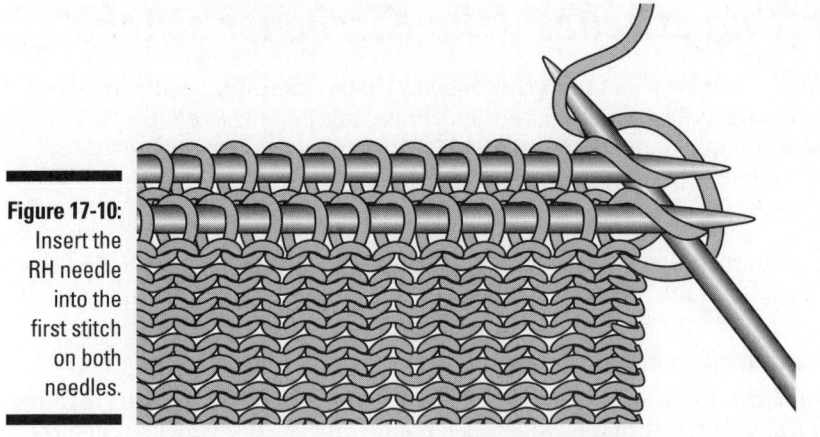

Figure 17-10:
Insert the RH needle into the first stitch on both needles.

Illustration by Wiley, Composition Services Graphics

2. **Wrap the yarn around the RH needle as if to knit, and draw the loop through both stitches.**

3. **Knit the next pair of stitches together in the same way.**

4. **Using the tip of either LH needle, go into the first stitch knitted on the RH needle and lift it over the second stitch and off the needle, as shown in Figure 17-11.**

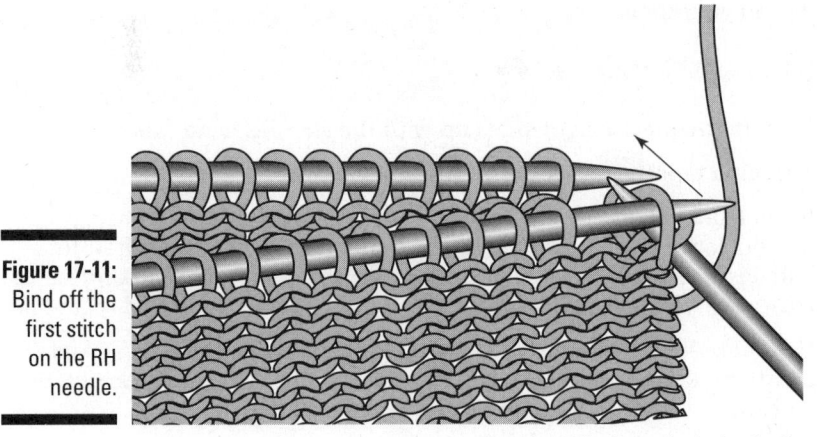

Figure 17-11:
Bind off the first stitch on the RH needle.

Illustration by Wiley, Composition Services Graphics

5. **Continue to knit 2 stitches together from the LH needles and bind off 1 stitch until you bind off the last stitch and pull the yarn tail through the last loop.**

Grafting stitches (the Kitchener stitch)

Grafting (also known as the *Kitchener stitch*) uses a tapestry needle to mock knit, creating a very stretchy and almost invisible join between pieces. It's a good technique to use when you want to give the illusion of uninterrupted fabric, such as when joining the center back seam of a scarf you've worked in two pieces.

You can graft stitches together when you want to join pieces head to head or head to side, as the following sections explain.

Grafting head to head

The smoothest join — and also the stretchiest — is made by grafting together *live stitches* (stitches that haven't been bound off yet). But you also can graft two bound-off edges if you want more stability. Just work the same steps for grafting live stitches, working in and out of the stitches just below the bound-off row.

If you plan to graft live stitches, don't bind off the final row. Instead, leave a yarn tail about four times the width of the piece, and with a tapestry needle, run a piece of scrap yarn through the live stitches to secure them while you block your pieces. Blocking sets the stitches, enabling you to pull out the scrap yarn without fear of the stitches unraveling. If you're working with a slippery yarn and the stitches want to pull out of their loops even after blocking, leave the scrap yarn in the loops and pull it out 1 or 2 stitches at a time as you graft them.

Here's how to graft your pieces:

1. **Line up the pieces right sides up with the stitches head to head.**

2. **Thread a tapestry needle with the working yarn.**

   If you left a tail on the side that you want to begin grafting from, use it. If not, start a fresh strand and weave in the end later. You graft the stitches from right to left, but if you're more comfortable working left to right, or if your yarn tail is at the other end, you can reverse direction.

   Use a tapestry needle with a blunt tip for any kind of seaming on knits. Sharp points can pierce the yarn too easily. Always aim to go in and out and around stitches when you sew pieces together.

3. **Starting in the bottom piece, insert the needle up through the first loop on the right and pull the yarn through.**

4. **Insert the needle up through the first right loop on the upper piece and pull the yarn through.**

You can see Steps 3 and 4 in Figure 17-12.

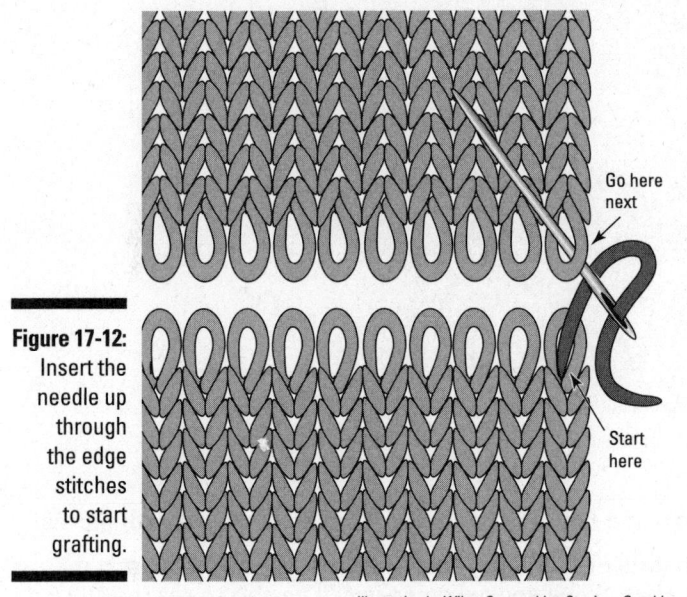

Figure 17-12: Insert the needle up through the edge stitches to start grafting.

Go here next

Start here

Illustration by Wiley, Composition Services Graphics

5. **Insert the needle down into the first loop on the bottom piece (the same loop you began in) and come up through the loop next to it; pull the yarn through.**

6. **Insert the needle down into the first loop on the upper piece (the same one you came up through in Step 4) and up through the stitch next to it; pull the yarn through.**

You can see Steps 5 and 6 in Figure 17-13.

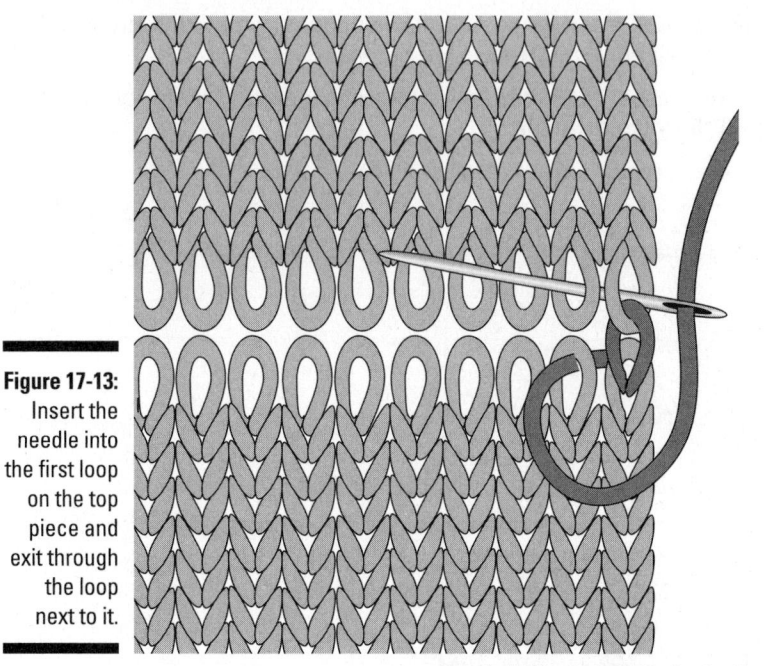

Figure 17-13:
Insert the needle into the first loop on the top piece and exit through the loop next to it.

Illustration by Wiley, Composition Services Graphics

7. **Repeat Steps 5 and 6 until you come to the last stitch on both pieces.**

Follow the rhythm down and up, down and up, as you move from one piece to the other. When you get going, you'll be able to see the mock stitches you're making, as in Figure 17-14.

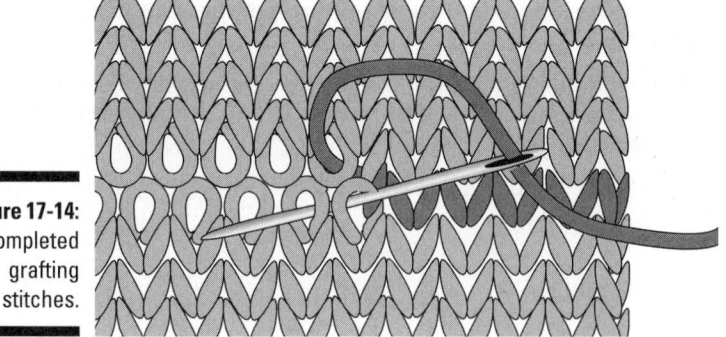

Figure 17-14:
Completed grafting stitches.

Illustration by Wiley, Composition Services Graphics

8. **When you come to the last stitch, insert the needle down into the last stitch on the bottom piece and then down into the last stitch on the top piece; run the end along the side loops and snip.**

With the exception of the first grafting stitch (Steps 3 and 4) and the last one (Step 8), you go through 2 stitches on each piece — the stitch you've already come up through and the new stitch right next to it — before changing to the other piece. Work with even tension, trying to match the size of the stitches you're marrying. If, after you finish, you find any grafted stitches that look out of kilter, you can go back with the tip of your needle and tweak them, working out any unevenness.

Grafting head to side

Grafting head to side makes a smooth and weightless seam. As in head-to-head grafting, you make a mock knit stitch, but instead of going in and out of stitches lined up head to head, you graft the heads of stitches on one piece to the *sides* of stitches on the other piece. (Actually, as in the mattress stitch, you pick up running threads when you're joining to the sides of the stitches; the next section covers the mattress stitch.) Grafting head to side is a great method for joining a sleeve top to a sweater body on a dropped shoulder sweater, which has no shaped armhole or sleeve cap.

Before working this graft, make sure that you can recognize the running thread between the 2 side stitches. (See the following section for help identifying running threads.) Then line up your pieces, heads on the bottom and sides above, as shown in Figure 17-15.

Keep in mind that 1 square inch of stockinette fabric has more vertical rows of stitches than stitches across. For every 1 inch of heads, you need to pick up 1 inch of sides (running threads). This task is actually quite easy. For example, if your gauge is 5 stitches and 7 rows to the inch, you should pick up five running threads out of every seven as follows: Pick up one running thread, then two running threads together, then one running thread, then two together, then one running thread. Then start over. If you look closely at Figure 17-15, you can see that two running threads have been picked up every few stitches to compensate for the difference in vertical and horizontal stitches per inch.

Follow these steps to graft heads of stitches to sides of stitches:

1. **With a tapestry needle and yarn, come up through the first head stitch on the right or left end of your work.**

    Figure 17-15 shows how to work from right to left, but you can work in either direction.

2. **Go around the running thread between the first 2 side stitches (see Figure 17-15).**

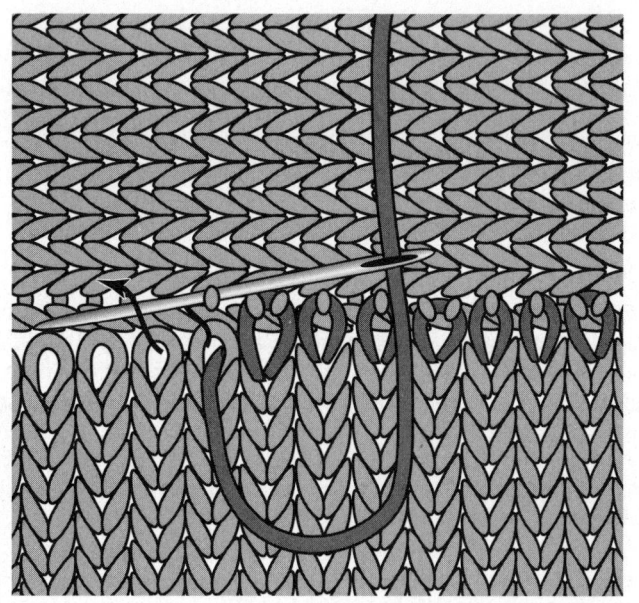

Illustration by Wiley, Composition Services Graphics

Figure 17-15:
Graft heads
of stitches
to sides of
stitches.

3. **Go back down into the same head stitch you came out of and up through the next head stitch — the stitch to the right if you're traveling in that direction or to the left if you're going that way.**

4. **Repeat Steps 2 and 3.**

The best version of this seam is made by grafting live stitches to the armhole edge, but you can use it with a bound-off edge as well. Just go into the stitches (heads) directly below the bound-off edge.

Mattress stitch

Mattress stitch makes a practically invisible and nicely flexible seam for joining pieces side to side. You can't use it successfully, however, on pieces that have a difference of more than 2 rows. It's worth keeping track of your rows when working backs and fronts to be able to join them at the sides with this wonderful technique.

To join knitted pieces with the mattress stitch, lay out your pieces next to each other, right sides facing up, bottom edges toward you. You seam from the bottom edge up. If you've left a tail of yarn at the cast-on edge, you can use it to get started.

To work mattress stitch, you need to be able to recognize the running threads between the first 2 edge stitches. If you gently pull these stitches apart, you'll see the series of little horizontal — running — threads connecting them (see Figure 17-16).

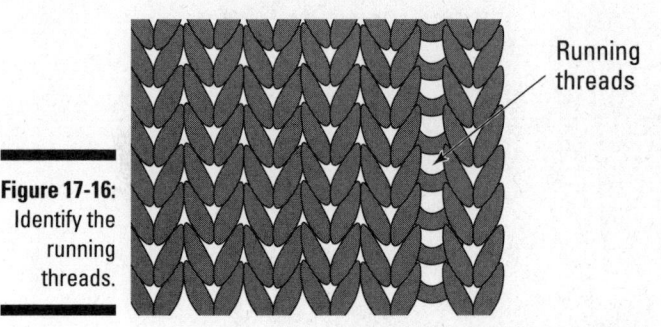

Running
threads

Figure 17-16:
Identify the
running
threads.

Illustration by Wiley, Composition Services Graphics

Thread the tail of yarn or a fresh piece on a tapestry needle. Working through the two threads on the cast-on row, join the bottom edges of the pieces by using a figure 8, as shown in Figure 17-17. The direction you work the figure 8 depends on whether you begin on the right or left side. If you begin from the right piece, you work your figure 8 to the left; if you begin from the left piece, you work to the right.

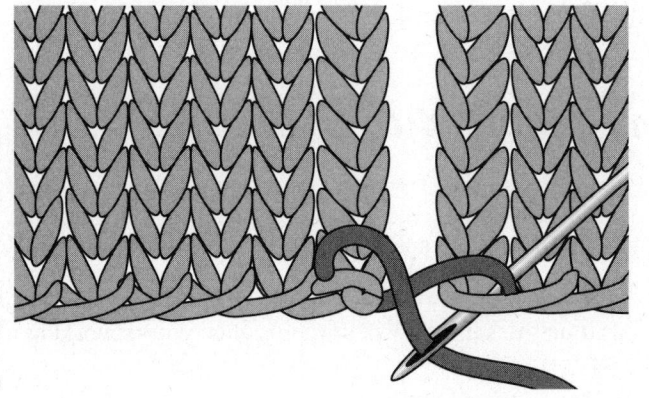

Figure 17-17:
Join the
bottom
edges with
a figure 8
for mattress
stitch.

Illustration by Wiley, Composition Services Graphics

To work the mattress stitch, follow these steps:

1. **Locate the running thread between the first and second stitches on the bottom row of one piece (refer to Figure 17-16).**

2. **Bring your needle under the thread to pick it up; then pick up the running thread between the first and second stitches on the opposing piece, as in Figure 17-18.**

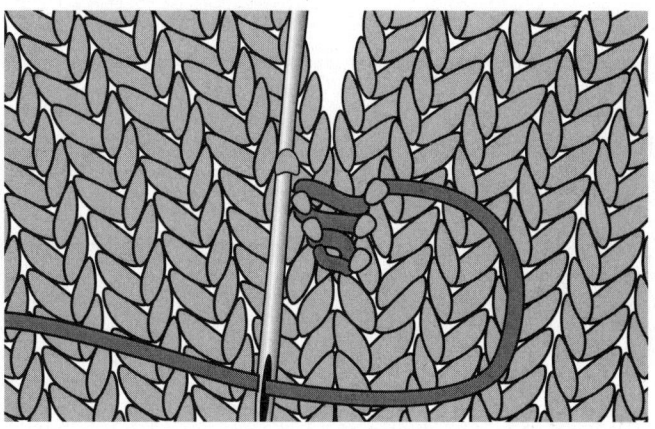

Figure 17-18:
Pick up the
running
thread in
mattress
stitch.

Illustration by Wiley, Composition Services Graphics

3. **Work back and forth from running thread to running thread to running thread, keeping the tension easy but firm.**

   Check the tension by pulling laterally on the seam from time to time. The amount of give should be the same as between 2 stitches.

When you've finished your seam, take a moment to admire it.

Sewing seams with backstitch

When you join knitted pieces by using backstitch, you sew them together in the conventional manner: *right* sides together with your tapestry needle moving in and out along the seam line. Try to maintain a knitterly frame of mind and, when possible, work the stitches consistently — either in the trough of running threads between the first 2 stitches when you're working vertically or along the same row of stitches when you're working with a horizontal edge.

Mattress stitch on other stitches

As long as you can find the running threads between the first 2 edge stitches, you can use the mattress stitch invisibly on a variety of knitted fabrics.

✔ **Reverse stockinette:** If you look closely at the back of stockinette fabric, you see that the purl (or "over") bumps are separated by "under" bumps. The under bumps are the running threads between stitches. For the mattress stitch, locate the under bump between the 2 edge purl bumps and alternate picking them up on each piece.

✔ **Garter stitch:** For garter stitch, you need to pick up only one running thread every other row — the one that's easy to see. The rows in garter stitch are so condensed that the fabric will actually stretch along the seam if you try to pick up the running stitch on every row. So give yourself a break.

✔ **Ribbed borders:** Working the mattress stitch on a ribbed border is no different from working it on stockinette or reverse stockinette. Study the stitches until you can recognize the column of running threads between the first 2 stitches (knit or purl). Then pick up one running thread at a time as you go back and forth between pieces.

Always take the time to figure out how your ribs will come together where they meet so that your rib pattern will circle around unbroken. If you're working a knit 2, purl 2 rib, begin and end each piece with 2 knit stitches. When you seam them by using the mattress stitch, you'll have a single 2-stitch rib. For a knit 1, purl 1 rib, as long as you begin with a knit stitch and end with a purl stitch, you'll have an unbroken sequence when seamed.

To help you keep your needle going in and out of the right slot between stitches, run a few strands of sewing thread in a bright color along the seam line — in and out of running threads or in and out of a row of stitches. Pull it out after you complete your seam.

Here's what you do to complete the backstitch:

1. **Pin the pieces right sides together.**

   If you haven't counted rows and one piece is slightly longer or wider than the other, you have to ease in the extra fabric so the pieces begin and end in the same place. If you blocked the front and back to the same dimensions, they should line up fairly well even if one piece has more rows than the other.

2. **With a tapestry needle and yarn, bring the needle from the bottom up through both layers 1 stitch in from the edge. Go around the edge, come out in the same spot to secure the end of the yarn, and bring the bottom edges of the pieces together.**

3. **Go around again and come out 1 stitch farther up from the initial stitch, as shown in Figure 17-19a.**

4. **Insert the needle back through the initial stitch and bring the tip out through both layers again, a few stitches from where it last came out, as shown in Figure 17-19b.**

Keep needle going in and out along running stitches (under bumps) between first two stitches

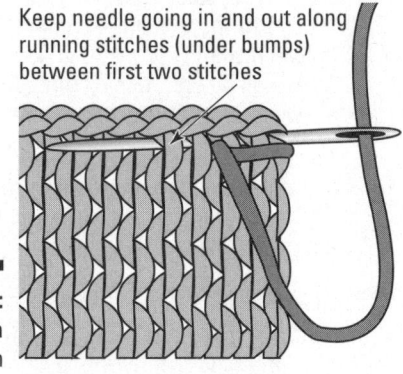
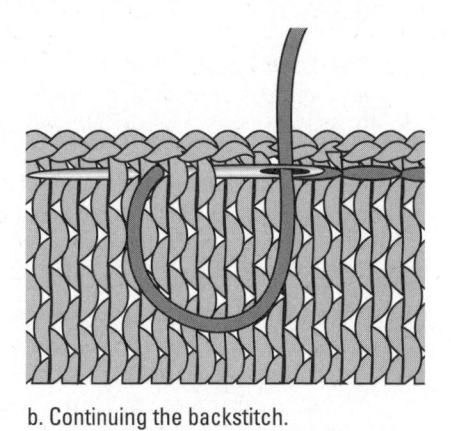

Figure 17-19:
Work a backstitch seam.

a. Beginning a backstitch seam.

b. Continuing the backstitch.

Illustration by Wiley, Composition Services Graphics

5. **Continue in this manner — going forward, coming back — and keep an even tension.**

Bring your needle in and out in the spaces between stitches and avoid splitting the working yarn as well. Also give your knitting a gentle stretch as you work to keep it flexible.

Determining the Order of Sweater Assembly

As you assemble sweaters, you usually follow a fairly predictable order of assembly that goes something like this:

1. **Tack down any pockets and work pocket trims or embroidery details on sweater pieces before seaming them together.**

2. **Sew the shoulder seams.**

Sew both shoulders for a cardigan or a pullover with a neckband picked up and worked on a circular needle. Sew only one shoulder if you want to work the neckband on straight needles, and then seam the second shoulder and neckband together.

3. **Work the neckband and front bands on cardigans.**

4. **Sew the tops of sleeves to the sweater front and back.**

5. **Sew the side seams.**

6. **Sew the sleeve seams.**

7. **Sew on buttons on cardigans.**

If you've worked your sweater in a medium or lightweight plied yarn, you can use the same yarn for seaming the parts. If the yarn is heavy or a single ply that shreds, use a finer yarn *in the same fiber* in a similar color.

Joining back to front at the shoulder

The first pieces to join after blocking are the front and back at the shoulder (stitches head to head). You have three choices for this seam:

- ✔ Use the three-needle bind-off, which makes it possible to bind off the edges of two pieces and seam them together at the same time.
- ✔ Graft the shoulder stitches together.
- ✔ Use the backstitch to seam the pieces together.

Because most knitters would rather knit than sew, the first option is a good one to learn as you develop your finishing repertoire. Refer to the earlier section "Basic Techniques for Joining Pieces" for instructions on how to work any of these joins.

After you join your front and back pieces at the shoulder, work the neckband of the collar before adding the sleeves or seaming the sides so that you have less bulk to contend with. Chapter 18 covers neckline details.

Attaching a sleeve to a sweater body

How you attach the sleeves to your sweater body depends on the design of your sleeve cap and armhole. If you're making a dropped-shoulder sweater or one with an angled armhole and straight cap, you can use the head-to-side grafting technique explained in the earlier section "Grafting head to side." If you're making a sweater with a set-in sleeve, you need to use the backstitch for seaming; see the earlier section "Sewing seams with backstitch" for instructions.

To attach a set-in sleeve to a sweater body, follow these steps:

1. **Mark the center of the sleeve cap at the top edge and align it with the shoulder seam on the sweater body, as shown in Figure 17-20.**

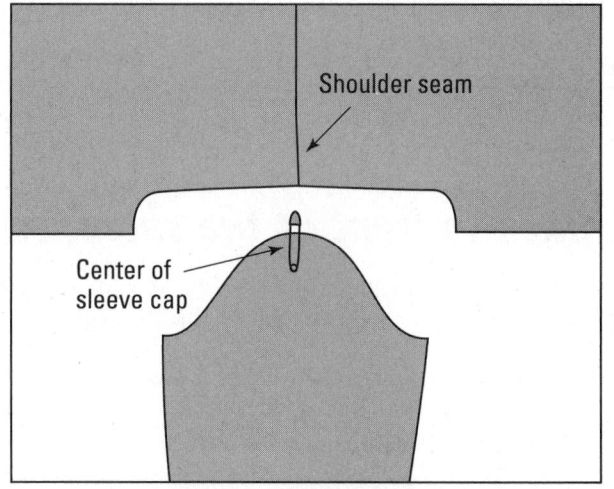

Shoulder seam

Center of sleeve cap

Figure 17-20:
Align the set-in sleeve and armhole.

Illustration by Wiley, Composition Services Graphics

2. **With the right sides together, pin the center top of the sleeve cap to the shoulder seam.**

3. **Working on only one side at a time, line up the bound-off stitches at the beginning of the armhole, shaping both the sleeve and sweater body, and pin the pieces together there.**

4. **Pin the sleeve cap edge to the armhole every inch or so between the bound-off stitches and the shoulder, as in Figure 17-21.**

5. **Use the backstitch to sew the pieces together along the edge from the bound-off stitches to the shoulder.**

    When you come to the vertical section of the armhole in the sweater body, keep your stitches in the trough between the first 2 stitches.

6. **When you reach the shoulder, pin the other half of the armhole and sleeve and sew from the shoulder to the bound-off stitches.**

7. **Steam your seam well, pressing down on it with your fingertips as the moisture penetrates.**

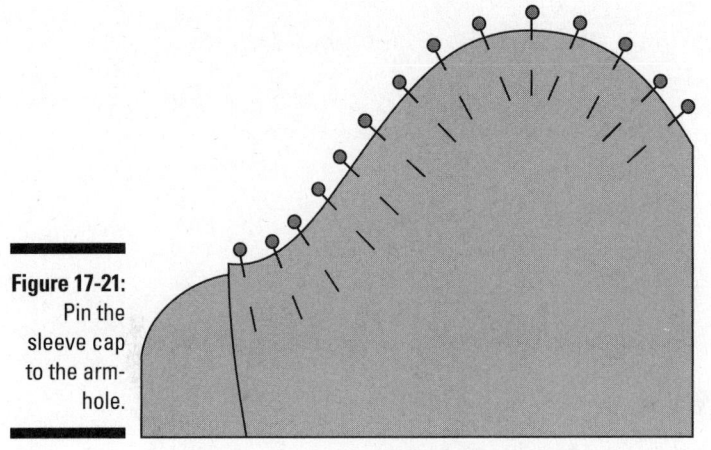

Figure 17-21:
Pin the sleeve cap to the arm-hole.

Illustration by Wiley, Composition Services Graphics

Making side and sleeve seams

After you complete the shoulder seams and neckband and attach the sleeves to your sweater body, the rest is all downhill. If you counted rows and you have the same number (almost) on the front and back pieces, you can use the mattress stitch to seam your pieces together — and you won't believe how good they look.

If your front(s) and back have a different number of rows (off by more than 2), use the backstitch technique to seam them together.

Sometimes you may be off by a couple of stitches as you seam two sides together. If you seam the sleeves from the cuff to the armhole, hide these extra stitches in the armpit area. You can do the same if you seam the front and back together starting at the hem and working toward the armhole.

Chapter 18

Finishing Touches: Neckbands, Edging, Buttonholes, and More

Most knitting patterns for sweaters give you the most basic, generic plan for making a sweater. After you work the pieces, block them, and seam the shoulders, you must bring your own expertise to the finishing details — neckbands, edgings, buttonholes, and cardigan bands. This chapter takes you on a beginner's tour of techniques for picking up stitches evenly, making cardigan bands, and installing buttonholes. By no means do the procedures shown here exhaust the possibilities for finishing your sweater, but they're a great place to start.

Picking Up Stitches to Knit

The cast-on edges of knitted garments are generally very presentable and need no finishing. Not true for the other edges of a knitted piece. Edges not encased in a seam, such as necklines, the center front edges of a cardigan, and the armholes on a vest, require some kind of finishing or edging. Usually, a neckline gets a neckband or collar, and cardigans feature knitted bands along the front edges for buttons and buttonholes.

Picking up stitches is a knitter's way to avoid sewing on these extra edgings. Instead of creating a collar or button band separately and sewing it onto a knitted garment, you can use needles and yarn to pull up new loops along a knitted edge and knit a border right then and there. Some knitters are so enamored of picking up stitches that they make sleeves for garments by picking up stitches around the armholes and knitting the sleeves upside down to the cuffs. (Knitters are very ingenious.) Follow the instructions in this section to pick up a row of completely new stitches and knit from there.

You can pick up stitches from three kinds of edges:

- ✔ Horizontal, such as the bound-off stitches along a back neck
- ✔ Vertical, such as the center front of a cardigan
- ✔ Diagonal or curved, such as the shaped section of a front neckline

To pick up stitches, you need the yarn for your project and one needle in the size you plan to use for your band or collar. Most patterns specify the needle size required for collars, cuffs, and other bands; if yours doesn't, one or two sizes smaller than the needles used for the main part of your knitting generally works well.

Be sure to block your sweater back and fronts before picking up stitches. (See Chapter 17 for details on blocking.) You won't have to cope with edges that want to curl in or out; your blocked edges to be picked up will lie nice and flat — and therefore be easy to work.

Picking up stitches along a horizontal edge

The easiest, most straightforward form of picking up stitches is along a horizontal edge because you pick up 1 stitch in each bound-off stitch. When you're done, you should barely see a transition between the stitches you picked up and the new set of stitches. You use this method when picking up stitches along a back neck edge and for the center front stitches that form the base of a round neckline. Follow these simple steps:

1. **With the RS facing, starting at the right end of the work, insert the needle into the first stitch (the V) from front to back just below the bound-off edge.**

   Make sure that your needle isn't just going under the threads of the bound-off stitches but into the entire stitch below (the one you can see clearly), as shown in Figure 18-1.

2. **Wrap the yarn around the needle just as if you were knitting and then pull a loop through.**

   You can secure the loose yarn end temporarily by tying it onto your knitting, or you can just keep picking up stitches and secure it later. After you pick up the first stitch, the yarn will be taut.

3. **Repeat Steps 1 and 2, pulling through one loop in each stitch across the row.**

4. **After you finish picking up all the stitches you need to for your finished edge, turn your work around (so that the WS is facing you) and work the first WS row in your stitch pattern.**

That's all there is to it!

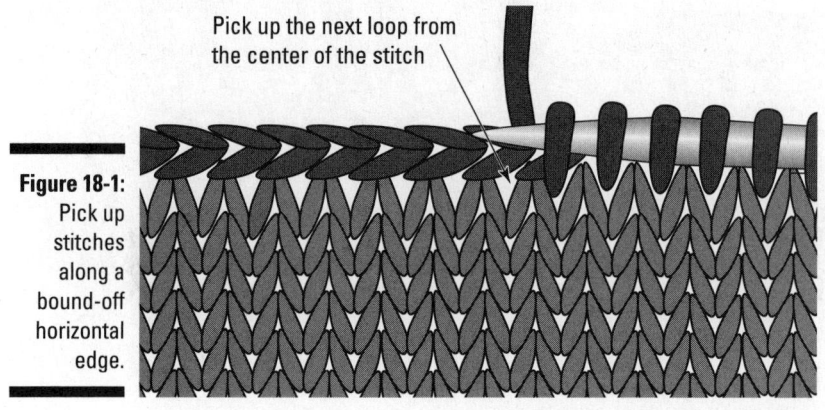

Pick up the next loop from the center of the stitch

Figure 18-1:
Pick up stitches along a bound-off horizontal edge.

Illustration by Wiley, Composition Services Graphics

Picking up stitches on a vertical edge

To pick up stitches along a vertical edge, such as a cardigan front, use the same pull-through-a-stitch procedure covered in the preceding section for a horizontal edge. This time, however, bring the loop up between the running threads connecting the first 2 stitches along the edge, as shown in Figure 18-2. Here's how to do it:

1. **With the RS facing and starting at the right end of the work, insert your needle between the running threads of the first 2 stitches from front to back.**

2. **Wrap the yarn as if to knit, and pull the new loop through.**

3. **Repeat Steps 1 and 2, pulling stitches up through the column of running threads until you've picked up the number of stitches you need for your finished edge.**

There are more vertical rows of stitches per inch than there are stitches across. When you pick up stitches along a vertical edge, you match stitches to rows. To keep the correct ratio of stitches to rows, you need to skip a running thread interval every few stitches. The rule of thumb is to pick up 3 stitches out of every 4 rows. You can see this technique in Figure 18-2 and find more information about it in the section "Bring on the Bands" later in this chapter.

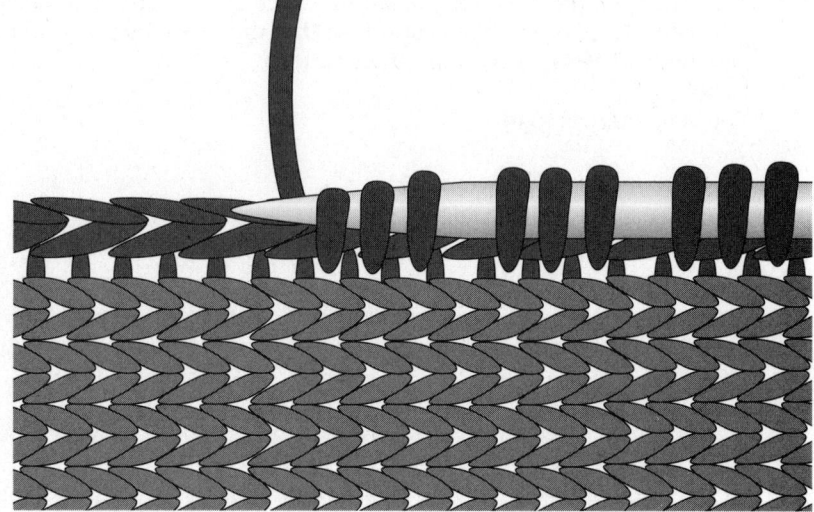

Figure 18-2:
Pick up
stitches
along a
bound-off
vertical
edge.

Picking up stitches on a diagonal or curved edge

Most curved edges are made by a series of stepped bind-offs followed by decreases that give a far-from-smooth curved line. Not to worry. The picked-up band saves the day with an attractive continuous curve.

When you pick up stitches along a curved edge, avoid working in the very edge stitch. Instead, work into a stitch or between stitches at least 1 full stitch in from the edge. Your aim is to make a nice-looking line for your border to begin on, not to see how close you can work to the uneven edge of your knitting.

Pick up stitches on the bound-off edge of the back neck and the center front bound-off section as shown in the earlier section "Picking up stitches along a horizontal edge." Along the side neck edges, pick up between running threads and then in the center of stitches as you follow the line of stitches marking the curve of the neck. In Figure 18-3, the darkened stitches show you where to insert your needle to pick up stitches along a curve.

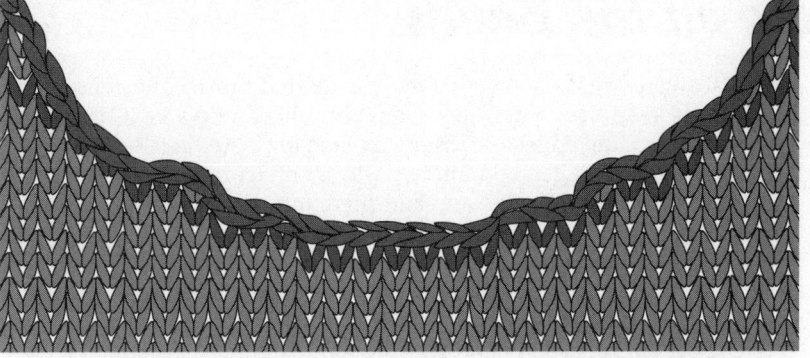

Figure 18-3:
Pick up stitches on a bound-off curved neckline.

When you have to pick stitches up along the neck edge for a collar that isn't rib, pick up with the WS facing. That way, when the collar is turned, the fabric faces the right way.

Picking up: A reality check

Picking up stitches is relatively simple when you get the hang of it. The rub comes when you painstakingly pick up a cardigan border or neckband according to your pattern instructions. You pick up the exact number of stitches called for, knit the correct number of rows given in the stitch pattern, and bind off the last stitch. Then, after all your effort, you find that your otherwise lovely cardigan has a stretched and droopy button band or that you can't squeeze your head through the neck of your pullover.

Your pattern tells you how many stitches to pick up around the neck, but it may or may not tell you how to distribute them: so many along the back neck and so many along the left and right front neck edges. It may be up to you to figure out how many stitches to pick up where. Also, if the gauge on your border pattern is different from the sweater designer's or if you alter the pattern in any way, your border may not fit as planned. Use your pattern as a guide, but keep a critical eye on your own work. At the first sign that your band is starting to gape or your neckband is shrinking the neck opening, be prepared to toss your sweater map in the backseat. Resolve to pick up stitches according to your knitted pieces, *not* according to your pattern. Just remember that if you're changing the number of stitches to pick up, you must come out with a number that works as a multiple of your stitch pattern.

Bring on the Bands

Cardigan sweaters usually have bands that border the center front. Cardigan bands keep the center edge from stretching, add a neat trim to an otherwise rough-looking edge, and create a place for fastenings — usually buttons. You can knit a cardigan band in two ways: knit from the bottom up, or pick up stitches along the edge and knit them out sideways.

- **Vertically knit bands:** These bands are knitted in the same direction as the sweater body, from bottom to top. You can knit them as part of the front (usually in a noncurling stitch such as rib, seed, or garter) or make them separately and sew them on later.

- **Horizontally knit bands:** These bands are usually made by picking up stitches along the center front edge and knitting at a right angle to the sweater body for an inch or so. Like vertical bands, you can knit them separately to be sewn on later if, unlike most knitters, you'd rather sew than knit.

It's a good idea to have some understanding of how these bands work — how to plan and make them. When you're familiar with both types, you just may decide to turn your perfectly fitting pullover pattern into a cardigan.

When you're making a vertical or horizontal band in a ribbed stitch (1 x 1 or 2 x 2), end your band on a knit rib and add an extra knit stitch at the outside edge. Edge stitches never look great and tend to curl and disappear. The extra knit stitch tucks itself in and becomes an unobtrusive facing. What you notice is a symmetrical band with a tidy edge. Try it!

Bottoms up! Vertical bands

On a vertical band, you work the stitches in the band in the same direction as the body of the sweater. A vertical band allows you to create a ribbed band that matches the bottom ribbed edge of your sweater.

Knitted-in vertical bands

Vertical cardigan bands knitted in at the same time as the sweater are convenient and easy. No need for further finishing — you just knit to the end of the row for your front panel and continue to knit the stitches for the band. Their drawback is their lack of stability. Worked on the same size needle as the sweater body, the bands don't always make a taut edge. If you find your band less than successful, try one of the following remedies:

> ✔ Work the band in a stitch pattern with a shorter row gauge, such as a garter stitch band on a stockinette stitch body.
>
> ✔ Work the band on separate double-pointed needles in a smaller size (slightly awkward but doable). Just work the band on the smaller short needle and then work the body on the larger needles. When you come back to the band, pick up the other double-pointed needle, work back and forth on the band, leave the smaller needle suspended in the band, and return to the larger needle.

Vertical bands knitted separately

You can work vertical bands as separate pieces and later join them to the front of the cardigan. You just cast on the number of stitches you need to achieve the width of your band and then knit it up — be prepared for a lot of turning! Generally, you make the band on a smaller needle than the sweater body to give it more stability. Sew the band to the sweater edge by using the mattress stitch, which you can find in Chapter 17.

Horizontal picked-up bands

The key to knitting attractive horizontal picked-up bands is to find the right number of stitches to pick up along the front edge of your sweater. Too many, and you have a droopy band that stretches the sweater front; too few, and the band draws up the sweater at the center front. Sweater patterns tell you how many stitches to pick up along a cardigan edge in one of two ways: They give you a pick-up rhythm, something like, "Pick up 3 out of every 4 rows," or they give you a total number of stitches to pick up.

When you pick up stitches along a vertical edge and knit the band from there, you're working at a right angle to your knitted piece — stitches to rows. One inch of rows on the vertical edge has to match 1 inch of stitches on the band you're knitting. Most of the time, this means picking up a few stitches and then skipping 1 stitch at regular intervals — a pick-up rhythm.

The rhythm method

Be grateful when instructions give you the pick-up rhythm. You don't have to worry about getting a particular number of stitches into a band. Instead, you're concerned with a ratio of rows to stitches.

Rhythm instructions are easy to test. Along the cardigan edge (or along your gauge swatch), pick up 32 stitches and work in the rhythm your pattern gives you. Work the stitches for 1 inch (see Figure 18-4), and then check the edge you've made. Be honest. If the band is nice and flat and doesn't pucker, stretch, or distort the front edge in any way, you're on. Rip out those test stitches and pick up the stitches in the same way all along the edge.

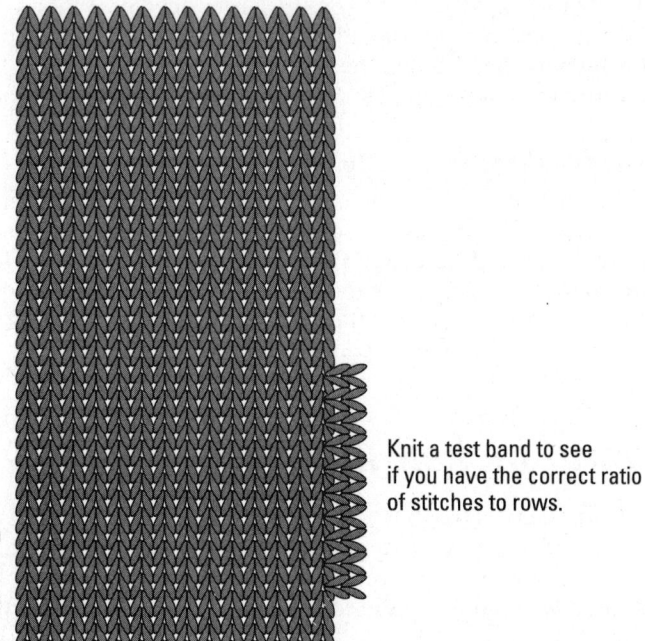

Knit a test band to see if you have the correct ratio of stitches to rows.

Figure 18-4: Knit a test band.

Illustration by Wiley, Composition Services Graphics

If the test band puckers and draws in, you're skipping too many stitches. Instead of 3 out of 4 rows, try 4 out of 5 or 5 out of 6. And if the band stretches the edge of your sweater, you aren't skipping enough stitches. Try picking up 2 out of 3. Keep experimenting until you get the right ratio; then rip out the test band and proceed with your plan.

The section method

If your pattern gives you a total number of stitches to pick up, you have to ration the total out in equal sections along the front edge and pick up stitches evenly along the edge. The following steps tell you how to do this:

1. **Divide the front edge into equal sections about 2 inches long.**

   You can measure out sections with a ruler, but it's better to count rows. Use safety pins to mark them.

2. **Count the number of sections you've marked.**

3. **Divide the number of stitches the pattern says to pick up by the number of sections, and pick up that number of stitches between pins.**

   For example, if the pattern tells you to pick up 120 stitches and you've made 12 sections, pick up 10 stitches in each section.

You may want to test your band by picking up stitches in a few sections (about 6 inches or so total) and knitting a band from them to ensure that the band doesn't distort the edge.

Hole in One: Buttonholes

Unless you plan to tie it, snap it, or leave it hanging open, you need to add buttons and buttonholes to a cardigan. Knitted buttonholes are rarely gorgeous, but with a little thought and planning, you can make buttonholes that don't sacrifice good looks to workaday function.

The appearance of a buttonhole has a lot to do with how it fits into the background stitch on which it's worked. A buttonhole that looks great on stockinette fabric may look clumsy on a ribbed band, for example. Take the time to practice a buttonhole in the stitch pattern you're using. Aim to make the buttonhole and stitch pattern work together. If you plan ahead and buy your buttons before working your buttonholes, you can test your buttons in your practice buttonholes to guarantee a good fit.

Horizontal and *vertical* describe how a buttonhole is worked — between rows or between stitches, respectively — and/or how it looks in a finished band. Keep in mind that a vertical buttonhole is horizontal on a picked-up cardigan band.

All-purpose horizontal buttonhole

Most knitting patterns give instructions for a generic cast-off/cast-on 2-row buttonhole that read like this: "Bind off 3 stitches, cast on 3 stitches over bound-off stitches on next row." Although this method works, it makes a loose and unattractive buttonhole. The technique for a horizontal buttonhole creates a more durable buttonhole — and it looks better, too (see Figure 18-5).

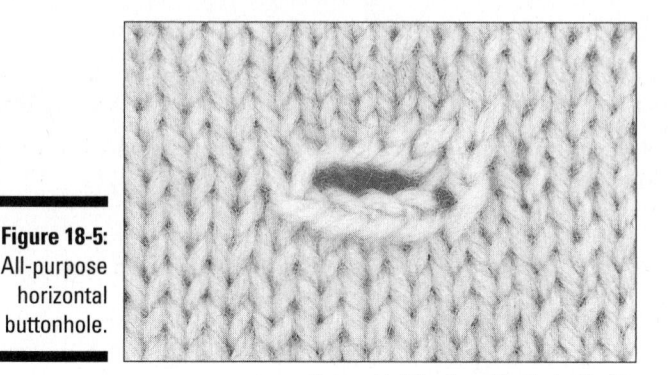

Photograph by Wiley, Composition Services Graphics

Figure 18-5:
All-purpose
horizontal
buttonhole.

These instructions are for a 4-stitch buttonhole, which takes 2 rows to complete. To make it, you need to know how to cast on by using the thumb or cable method (refer to Chapter 4).

1. Work Row 1 (RS).

   1. Work to the position of the buttonhole.

   2. Bind off 4 stitches.

   3. Knit the next stitch tightly (hold the yarn taut).

   4. Continue working in the pattern to the end of the row.

      If you count your stitches, you should have 4 fewer stitches on your needle for each buttonhole you've worked on the row.

2. Work Row 2.

   1. Work to the bound-off stitches of the buttonhole.

   2. Using the thumb or cable cast-on method, tightly cast on 4 stitches.

   3. With the tip of the LH needle, pick up the outer edge of the loop from the first bound-off stitch (see Figure 18-6) and purl it together with the next stitch.

      Turn your fabric around to easily see the loop you need to pick up.

   4. Continue to purl or work in the pattern to the end of the row.

      All done!

Fitting in

When you practice a horizontal buttonhole, keep in mind that it must work with your button choice *and* with the stitch pattern of your fabric. Whether you make your buttonhole over an odd or even number of stitches helps determine how it fits into its background. If possible, use the following pointers to ensure that your buttonholes blend neatly into their setting:

✔ In a 1 x 1 rib, seed stitch, or moss stitch pattern, make the buttonhole over an odd number of stitches so that you can center it between two knit ribs.

✔ In a 2 x 2 rib pattern or double seed stitch pattern, make the buttonhole over an even number of stitches so that you can plant it symmetrically between knit stitches.

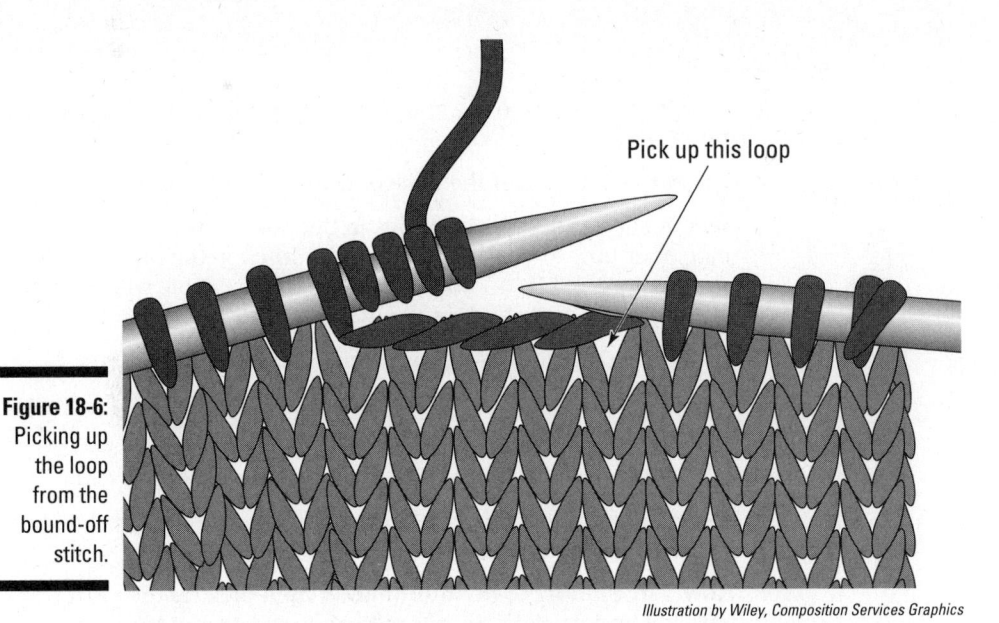

Figure 18-6: Picking up the loop from the bound-off stitch.

Pick up this loop

Illustration by Wiley, Composition Services Graphics

Simple vertical buttonhole

A vertical buttonhole (see Figure 18-7) is stretchier than a cast-off horizontal buttonhole. You work each side of the buttonhole with a separate ball of yarn. Test it with your buttons to know how many rows to work to achieve the right size hole. The instructions that follow are for working this buttonhole in 1 x 1 ribbing, where you can place the buttonhole in the purl trough to camouflage it.

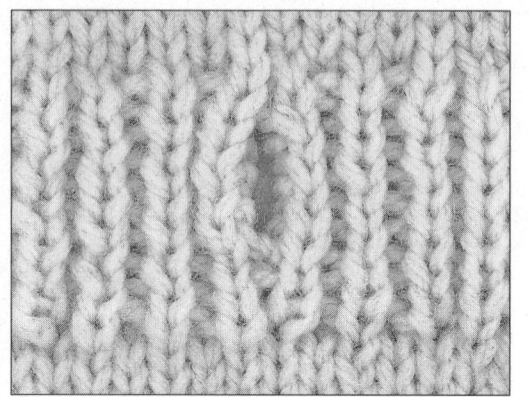

Photograph by Wiley, Composition Services Graphics

1. **Work Row 1 (RS).**

    1. Work in rib pattern to the spot for the buttonhole, ending with a knit stitch.

    2. Purl into the front and the back of the next (purl) stitch.

       See the bar increase instructions in Chapter 6 if you don't remember how to do this. Increasing 1 stitch in the purl trough allows for symmetry — both sides of the buttonhole will be bordered by a purl stitch on the RS.

    3. Continue in the rib pattern to the end of the row.

2. **Work Row 2.**

    1. Work in the rib pattern to the increased stitch (look for a stray stitch between a knit and a purl) and knit the increased stitch.

    2. Drop the yarn and, with another ball of yarn and beginning with k1, work in the rib pattern to the end of the row.

3. **Work Row 3 by ribbing to the buttonhole; then pick up the yarn from the other side and work in the rib pattern to the end of the row.**

4. **Repeat Rows 2 and 3 as many times as needed for the right size buttonhole.**

5. **Close the buttonhole.**

    • On a RS row, purl the 2 stitches at the top of the hole together.

    • On a WS row, knit the 2 stitches at the top of the hole together.

6. **To finish, cut the separate strand and weave in the ends.**

    Weaving the ends in along the edges of the buttonhole helps keep it from stretching.

To work a vertical buttonhole in a 2 x 2 rib (k2, p2, k2, p2), work the slit between 2 purl stitches.

Round (eyelet) buttonhole

The eyelet buttonhole (see Figure 18-8) may not appeal to you if you're a seamstress because it doesn't look like a sewn buttonhole — it's round, not slit-like. But we love this buttonhole. It's easy to remember, simple to execute, and adjusts to fit whatever button is appropriate for the yarn and needle size you're using.

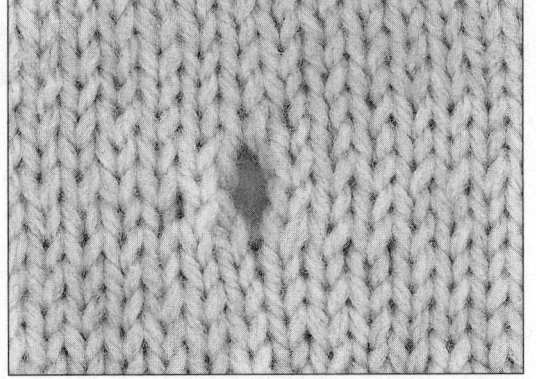

Figure 18-8:
Eyelet but-
tonhole.

Photograph by Wiley, Composition Services Graphics

We give instructions for working this buttonhole in stockinette fabric, but it also sits discreetly in the purl troughs of ribbing and is all but invisible in garter stitch, which is more than can be said for a lot of knitted slitlike buttonholes. You work this eyelet buttonhole over 1 stitch, and it takes 3 rows to complete. You may want to review how to make the different kinds of yarn overs in Chapter 6 before you get started.

Always pair a decrease with the yarn over when you work an eyelet buttonhole.

To work the buttonhole in stockinette stitch, follow these steps:

1. **Work Row 1 (RS).**

    1. Knit to 2 stitches before the buttonhole stitch.

    2. Make a double yarn over by bringing the yarn through the needles to the front, over the RH needle to the back, and then to the front between the needles again.

You can make a slightly smaller buttonhole by making a *single* yarn over rather than a double one. Just wrap the yarn once rather than twice.

    3. Knit the next 2 stitches together.

    4. Knit to the end of the row.

2. Work Row 2.

    1. Purl to the yarn over.

    2. Purl into the yarn over, letting the second wrap drop from the left needle.

    3. Purl to the end of the row.

3. Work Row 3.

    1. Knit to the stitch above the buttonhole.

    2. Knit into the hole (not the stitch above) and carry on.

If you're using the eyelet buttonhole in place of a horizontal buttonhole, work it in what would be the second bound-off stitch of a horizontal buttonhole. Use graph paper if needed to figure out where to place the eyelet.

Button Up!

Never underestimate the power of a button to make or break a sweater. The perfect button can enhance the theme of a sweater, such as a shimmery pearl button on a dressy sweater or a rustic bone button on an outdoorsy sweater. On the other hand, the contrast of a rugged button on a dressy sweater or a shell button on a bulky sweater may make an otherwise ho-hum garment really sing with originality. You can even design an entire sweater around a single spectacular button or sew on several buttons that share a theme but don't necessarily match. Be brave and experiment.

Plotting button placement

Knit up the front panel of your sweater (if you're planning a knit-in band) or the band that will carry the buttons before you work the piece with the buttonholes. This way, you can use safety pins or ties of contrasting yarn to mark where the buttons should go and plan where to make the corresponding buttonholes.

For a woman's sweater, buttons generally go on the left front panel. For a man's sweater, they go on the right. For both, make sure to use enough buttons to prevent gaps.

Begin by positioning the top and bottom buttons on your band. Use your eyes to determine the best distance from the edge for these two buttons. The top button generally should start ½ inch to 1 inch from the top of the sweater. (For a delicate or medium-weight sweater, place the top button closer to the neck.) The bottom button on a standard cardigan should be ½ inch to 1 inch from the bottom edge. If you're working a jacket-type cardigan, you may want to place the bottom button higher up for freedom of movement.

After you place the top and bottom buttons, count the rows (or stitches for a picked-up band) between these buttons to determine where to place the others evenly between them. Don't rely on measuring with a ruler. For greater accuracy, chart your button placement on graph paper.

So happy together: Keeping your buttons buttoned

Cardigan instructions simply tell you to sew on your buttons opposite the buttonholes. But a couple of refinements will help your buttons stay snuggly in their holes and keep your bands lined up neatly.

- ✔ **To place a button for a vertical buttonhole:** Center both the button and the buttonhole along the center lines of the front bands. Then plot your button/buttonhole pair so that the center of the button lines up with the top corner of the buttonhole. This placement will discourage the button from sneaking free.

- ✔ **To place a button for a horizontal buttonhole:** Don't center both the buttons and buttonholes in their respective bands. When you button your sweater, the button won't stay centered in the hole; instead, the bands will pull apart until the button catches in the corner of the buttonhole. Avoid this sliding problem by positioning the button away from the center, toward the outer edge of the band. When you button up, your bands will remain aligned, one on top of the other.

Sewing on buttons

If you used a plied yarn for your sweater or project, you can unply a single strand and use it to sew on your buttons. You also can use embroidery thread.

As you sew your buttons on, don't be afraid to go into the yarn strands of the sweater. If you try to secure a button by going around the strands and only in and out of the holes between stitches, your button will be unstable and will pull the stitch out of shape.

Most knitted fabric is dense enough to require a button with a *shank* — a small metal or plastic loop on the back of the button to sew through. If you want to use a button with holes in it instead, you can make a thread shank to allow room for the depth of the band fabric. The following steps tell you how:

1. **Lay a toothpick or skinny double-pointed needle between the holes on the top of the button, and sew the button onto the sweater by stitching around the toothpick or needle, as in Figure 18-9.**

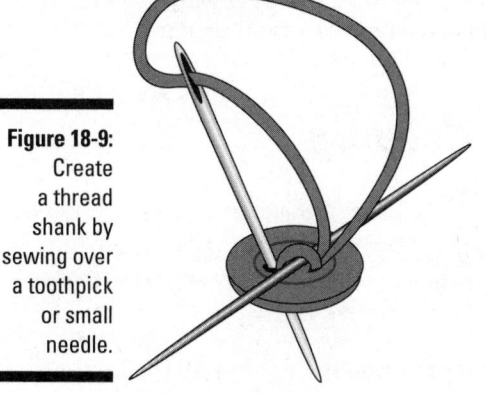

Figure 18-9:
Create a thread shank by sewing over a toothpick or small needle.

Illustration by Wiley, Composition Services Graphics

2. **Before knotting off, slide out the toothpick or needle, lift the button to take up the slack, and wind the thread several times around the "shank" on the underside of the button.**

3. **Bring the thread to the wrong side of the sweater, knot off, and weave in the end.**

Voilà! A button that won't retract into the buttonhole.

Chapter 19

Starter Garments

. . . .

In This Chapter

▶ Putting your knitting skills into practice

▶ Knitting a sweater, a baby's layette, and a vest with a hood or collar

. . . .

Making accessories is a great way to develop your knitting skills and explore creative possibilities, but making a soft, attractive garment to wrap yourself in is another kind of satisfaction entirely.

The projects in this chapter use simple shapes and garment construction to introduce you to sweater-making and enable you to apply the techniques and skills you've picked up in this part of the book.

The projects are basic with detailed instructions. You can knit up all three quickly on relatively big needles. Make them as they are, use them as a springboard for trying ideas from earlier chapters, or work up one of the variations listed at the end of each pattern.

In the "Materials and vital statistics" sections, we list the specific yarns used in our samples, but feel free to substitute any other yarn that meets the gauge. Or you can take what you know about gauge and dimensions and apply it to these patterns, writing in your own numbers to achieve the fit you want.

Women's Easy Top-Down Raglan

This Easy Top-Down Raglan sweater pattern couldn't be any more basic. In fact, it's probably one of the easiest sweater patterns you'll ever follow. Figure 19-1 shows the schematic for this top-down sweater.

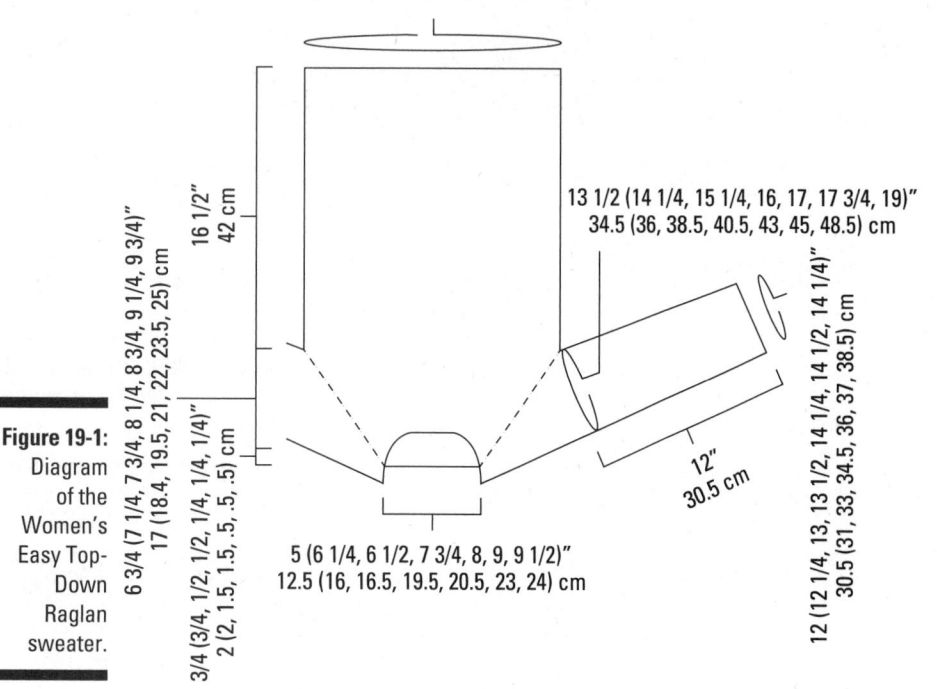

34 1/4 (37 3/4, 41 1/2, 45, 48 3/4, 52 1/4, 56)"
87 (96, 105.5, 114.5, 124, 132.5, 142) cm

13 1/2 (14 1/4, 15 1/4, 16, 17, 17 3/4, 19)"
34.5 (36, 38.5, 40.5, 43, 45, 48.5) cm

16 1/2"
42 cm

6 3/4 (7 1/4, 7 3/4, 8 1/4, 8 3/4, 9 1/4, 9 3/4)"
17 (18.4, 19.5, 21, 22, 23.5, 25) cm

3/4 (3/4, 1/2, 1/4, 1/4, 1/4, 1/4)"
2 (2, 1.5, 1.5, .5, .5, .5) cm

12 (12 1/4, 13, 13 1/2, 14 1/4, 14 1/2, 14 1/4)"
30.5 (31, 33, 34.5, 36, 37, 38.5) cm

12"
30.5 cm

5 (6 1/4, 6 1/2, 7 3/4, 8, 9, 9 1/2)"
12.5 (16, 16.5, 19.5, 20.5, 23, 24) cm

Figure 19-1:
Diagram of the Women's Easy Top-Down Raglan sweater.

Illustration by Wiley, Composition Services Graphics

Materials and vital statistics

- **Measurements:** 34¼ (37¾, 41½, 45, 48¾, 52¼, 56) inches. We provide instructions for the smallest size, with larger numbers in parentheses. When only one number is given, it applies to all sizes. The sweater is shown in size 37¾ inches.

  Measure yourself around the chest under your arms (armpit level); this number is your chest measurement. Because most sweater patterns give a finished measurement, measuring a favorite sweater that fits well is also a good idea. That way, you know exactly what finished measurement you prefer in a sweater.

- **Yarn:** Lion Brand "Superwash Merino" (100% superwash merino; CYC #3, 306 yards, 3.5 ounces [100 grams]): Dijon #486-170, 4 (4, 5, 5, 5, 6, 6) balls

- **Needles:** 16-inch and 32-inch sizes US 5 (3¾ mm) and US 6 (4 mm) circular needles, sizes US 5 and 6 dpns or sizes needed to obtain gauge

- ✔ **Other materials:** Stitch markers, stitch holders or waste yarn, five small buttons, thread, sewing needle, and a tapestry needle to weave in ends

- ✔ **Gauge:** 22 stitches and 30 rows/rounds per 4 inches in stockinette stitch with larger needle. Take time to save time: Check your gauge.

Directions

Yoke

With a 16-inch size US 6 circular needle, cast on 48 (58, 56, 64, 62, 72, 70) sts. Don't join; work back and forth in rows.

Pm for raglan (RS): K2 (4, 4, 5, 5, 7, 7) sts for front, place marker, k8 (8, 6, 6, 4, 4, 2) sts for sleeve, place marker, k28 (34, 36, 42, 44, 50, 52) sts for back, place marker, k8 (8, 6, 6, 4, 4, 2) sts for sleeve, place marker, k2 (4, 4, 5, 5, 7, 7) sts for front.

Raglan and neck shaping:

Inc Row (WS): * P to 1 st before marker, p1f/b, sl marker, p1f/b; rep from * 3 more times, p to end — 8 sts increased.

Inc Row (RS): K1, m1, * k to 1 st before marker, k1f/b, sl marker, k1f/b; rep from * 3 more times, k to last st, m1, k1 — 10 sts increased

Rep the last 2 rows 4 (4, 5, 6, 7, 7, 8) more times — 138 (148, 164, 190, 206, 216, 232) sts total; 17 (19, 22, 26, 29, 31, 34) sts each front, 28 (28, 30, 34, 36, 36, 38) sts each sleeve, 48 (54, 60, 70, 76, 82, 88) sts for back.

Purl 1 WS row even.

Inc Row (RS): K1, m1, * k to 1 st before marker, k1f/b, sl marker, k1f/b; rep from * 3 more times, k to last st, m1, k1 — 10 sts increased.

Rep the last 2 rows once more. Do not turn after the last RS row — 158 (168, 184, 210, 226, 236, 252) sts total; 21 (23, 26, 30, 33, 35, 38) sts each front, 32 (32, 34, 38, 40, 40, 42) sts each sleeve, 52 (58, 64, 74, 80, 86, 92) sts for back.

To shape the neck, place marker for beg of round, then use the cable method to CO 10 (12, 12, 14, 14, 16, 16) sts for front neck, join to work in the round and knit to end of round — 168 (180, 196, 224, 240, 252, 268) sts total; 52 (58, 64, 74, 80, 86, 92) sts each front and back; 32 (32, 34, 38, 40, 40, 42) sts each sleeve.

Raglan shaping:

Inc Round: * K to 1 st before marker, k1f/b, sl marker, k1f/b; rep from * 3 more times, knit to end — 8 sts increased.

Knit 1 round even.

When you have too many stitches on the 16-inch circular, change to the longer circular needle by holding the new needle in your right hand and knitting the stitches from the old needle onto the new needle.

Rep the last 2 rounds 17 (19, 20, 20, 21, 23, 24) more times — 312 (340, 364, 392, 416, 444, 468) sts total; 88 (98, 106, 116, 124, 134, 142) sts each front and back, 68 (72, 76, 80, 84, 88, 92) sts each sleeve.

Dividing body and sleeves:

Remove beg of round marker and knit to the next raglan marker (left front), remove marker, place the next 68 (72, 76, 80, 84, 88, 92) sleeve sts onto stitch holder or waste yarn, remove marker, use the cable method to CO 3 (3, 4, 4, 5, 5, 6) sts, place marker for new beg of round, CO 3 (3, 4, 4, 5, 5, 6) more sts, knit across back sts to next raglan marker (right back), remove marker, place the next 68 (72, 76, 80, 84, 88, 92) sleeve sts onto stitch holder or waste yarn, remove marker, use the cable method to CO 6 (6, 8, 8, 10, 10, 12) sts, knit to end of round — 188 (208, 228, 248, 268, 288, 308) sts.

Body

Continue working in stockinette st in the round until piece measures 16 inches from underarm.

Change to smaller needle and work in garter st for 6 rounds, ending after a knit round. Bind off all sts purlwise.

Sleeve

Return 68 (72, 76, 80, 84, 88, 92) held sts from one sleeve onto larger dpns. Beg at center of underarm CO sts, pick up and knit 3 (3, 4, 4, 5, 5, 6) sts, knit across held sts, then pick up and knit another 3 (3, 4, 4, 5, 5, 6) sts along rem underarm CO sts — 74 (78, 84, 88, 94, 98, 104) sts. Place marker for beg of round.

Work in stockinette st in the round until piece measures 1 inch from underarm.

Sleeve shaping:

Dec Round: K1, k2tog, knit to last 3 sts, ssk, k1 — 2 sts decreased.

Knit 17 (13, 11, 9, 8, 7, 6) rounds even.

Rep the last 18 (14, 12, 10, 9, 8, 7) rounds 3 (4, 5, 6, 7, 8, 9) more times — 66 (68, 72, 74, 78, 80, 84) sts remain.

Continue to work in stockinette st in the round until piece measures 11½ inches from underarm.

Change to smaller dpns and work in garter st for 6 rounds, ending after a knit round. Bind off all sts purlwise.

Rep for second sleeve.

Finishing

Block piece to measurements.

Neck trim: With smaller circular needle or dpns, beg at center of back, pick up and knit 14 (17, 18, 21, 22, 25, 26) sts along first half of back, 8 (8, 6, 6, 4, 4, 2) sts along sleeve, 12 (14, 15, 17, 18, 20, 21) sts along front neck to CO sts, 10 (12, 12, 14, 14, 16, 16) sts along CO sts, 12 (14, 15, 17, 18, 20, 21) sts along front neck to sleeve, 8 (8, 6, 6, 4, 4, 2) sts along sleeve, then 14 (17, 18, 21, 22, 25, 26) sts along rem half of back — 78 (90, 90, 102, 102, 114, 114) sts. Place marker for beg of round work in garter st for 6 rounds, ending after a knit round. Bind off all sts purlwise.

Sew decorative buttons along raglan lines at one shoulder.

Baby's Layette: Cardigan, Booties, Hat, and Blanket

Layettes make for great starter projects because they knit up quickly and use the same pattern for multiple pieces. This layette consists of a cardigan, booties, a hat, and a blanket that any new parent will love.

Cardigan

This cardigan is quite possibly the simplest construction imaginable — garter stitch with a few seams. It knits fast and looks great on any baby. (Then again, what *doesn't* look great on a baby?) Figure 19-2 shows the schematic for the layette cardigan.

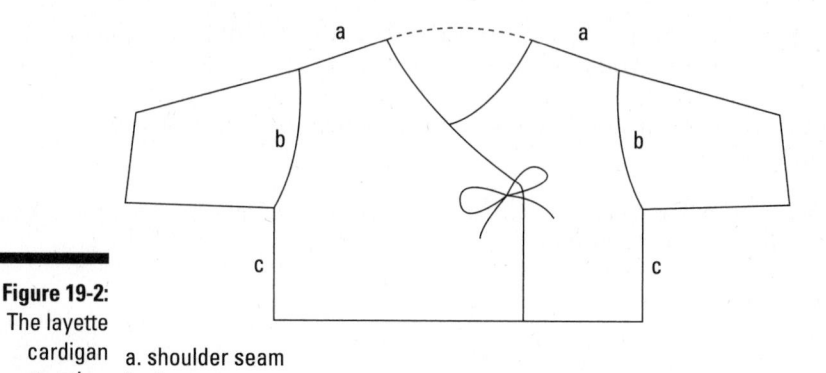

Figure 19-2:
The layette
cardigan
construction.

a. shoulder seam
b. sleeve seam
c. side seam

Materials and vital statistics

- ✔ **Size:** Newborn to 3 months

  - **Finished chest circumference:** 17 inches

  - **Finished sleeve length:** 6 inches

  - **Finished length:** 10 inches

- ✔ **Yarn:** Berroco "Comfort DK" (50% superfine nylon/50% superfine acrylic; CYC #3, 178 yards, 1.76 ounces [50 grams]): Color 2740, 2 skeins

- ✔ **Needles:** One pair each of size US 6 (4 mm) and US 4 (3¼ mm) needles or size needed to obtain gauge

- ✔ **Gauge:** 22 stitches and 24 rows per 4 inches

Directions

The following sections break down the instructions for creating this cardigan piece by piece.

Back

Using size US 6 needles, cast on 50 sts and work in garter st for 9 inches.

Neck and shoulder shaping:

To shape the neck, you bind off stitches in the middle of the row. Doing so creates the shoulders, which you then work separately:

Row 1: K35, turn.

Row 2: Bind off 20 sts, k to end of row. (The bound-off stitches form the neck. After these stitches are bound off, you've effectively divided the shoulders; you'll proceed to work first one, then the other.)

Row 3: Knit.

Row 4: Bind off 5 sts, k to end of row — 10 sts remain.

Work this shoulder in garter st until back measures 10 inches. Bind off shoulder sts.

Pick up remaining sts and repeat shaping from Row 3 for the second shoulder.

Front
Make 2 (both the same).

With size US 6 needles, cast on 34 sts and work in garter st for 5 inches.

Neck shaping:

To create the neck, you decrease stitches along what will become the neck edge.

Row 1: Ssk, k to end of row.

Row 2: Knit.

Rep Rows 1 and 2 until 10 sts remain, then knit until same length as back. Bind off.

Sleeve
Make 2 (both the same).

With size US 6 needles, cast on 35 sts and work 10 rows in garter st.

Inc at each end every 4th row until you have 55 sts. Work straight until sleeve measures 6 inches. Bind off loosely.

Finishing
Block the pieces to size.

Sew the shoulder seams and then set the sleeves into the body.

Sew the side seams and sleeves together.

Make a fastener by adding ribbon, a button and buttonhole, or three sets of I-cord ties evenly down the front. (For the I-cord, work six 5-inch ties of 5 sts each on size US 4 needles.)

Booties

Booties look complex, but these are anything but. The ribbon trim pulls together the edges to create the top and close across the foot — just right for teeny tiny baby feet! (We list 1 skein of yarn needed in the materials here, but you won't use it all on one pair of booties; use the rest in the other layette pieces.)

Materials and vital statistics

- **Size:** Newborn to 3 months
- **Yarn:** Berroco "Comfort DK" (50% superfine nylon/50% superfine acrylic; CYC #3, 178 yards, 1.76 ounces [50 grams]): Color 2740, 1 skein
- **Needles:** One pair of size US 6 (4 mm) needles or size needed to obtain gauge
- **Gauge:** 5½ stitches and 6 rows per 1 inch

Directions

With size US 6 needles, cast on 38 sts.

Rows 1–6: Work in garter st.

Row 7: K2, m1 in next 2 sts, k10, m1 in next 4 sts, k2, m1 in next 4 sts, k10, m1 in next 2 sts, k2 (50 sts).

Row 8: Knit.

Row 9: K17, m1 in next 4 sts, k8, m1 in next 4 sts, k17.

Rows 10–13: Work in garter st.

Row 14: K17, (k2tog, k2) twice, k2tog, k4, (k2tog, k2) twice, k2tog, k17.

Row 15: Knit.

Row 16: K17, (k2tog, k1) twice, k1, (k2tog, k1) twice, k2tog, k17 — 46 sts.

Row 17: Knit.

Row 18: K17, k2tog 6 times, k17.

Row 19: Bind off.

Finishing: Starting at cast-on seam, sew along seam and up side of work to form the bootie. Thread ribbon or I-cord through the final row for decoration if desired.

Hat

Knit flat and seamed, this adorable hat will keep sun and chill off baby's head. It also knits up super-quick. Make more than one in different colors for the ultimate accessory. (We list 1 skein of yarn in the materials, but you won't use it all on one hat; use the rest in the other layette pieces.)

Materials and vital statistics

- ✔ **Size:** Newborn to 3 months
- ✔ **Yarn:** Berroco "Comfort DK" (50% superfine nylon/50% superfine acrylic; CYC #3, 178 yards, 1.76 ounces [50 grams]): Color 2740, 1 skein
- ✔ **Needles:** One pair of size US 6 (4 mm) needles or size needed to obtain gauge
- ✔ **Gauge:** 5½ stitches and 6 rows per 1 inch

Directions

Using size US 6 needles, cast on 74 sts and work in garter st for 3 inches.

Begin decreases:

Row 1: K3, k2tog tbl, (k10, k2tog tbl) 5 times, k to end of row.

Row 2: Knit.

Row 3: K3, k2tog tbl, (k9, k2tog tbl) 5 times, k to end of row.

Row 4: Knit.

Continue in this manner, decreasing k9, k8, k7, and so on, until 14 sts remain.

Last row: (K2tog tbl) 7 times.

Finishing: Cut yarn about 18 inches from work. Draw yarn through remaining 7 sts and pull tightly. Use the remaining yarn to sew down the side seam.

Blanket

This blanket isn't square or rectangular . . . it's actually kite-shaped, with lengthy edges perfect for wrapping baby tight or (some time from now) dragging behind a toddler's cautious steps. In other words, it's not just a blanket, it's a capital-B Blankie, knit in the same sturdy, washable yarn used throughout the layette.

Materials and vital statistics

- ✔ **Size:** Approximately 30 inches x 30 inches, slightly stretched
- ✔ **Yarn:** Berroco "Comfort DK" (50% superfine nylon/50% superfine acrylic; CYC #3, 178 yards, 1.76 ounces [50 grams]): Color 2740, 6 skeins
- ✔ **Needles:** 36-inch size US 11 (7½ mm) circular needle or size needed to obtain gauge
- ✔ **Gauge:** 3½ stitches and 4 rows per 1 inch in garter stitch

Directions

Use double strands throughout:

Using a size US 11 circular needle, cast on 3 sts.

Row 1: M1, k to end (4 sts).

Row 2: M1, k to end (5 sts).

Rep Row 2, increasing 1 st each row until you have 16 sts total.

Begin stockinette insert:

Row 14: M1, k6, p1, k to end of row (17 sts).

Row 15: M1, k to end of row (18 sts).

Row 16: M1, k6, p3, k to end of row (19 sts).

Row 17: M1, k to end of row (20 sts).

Continue working the odd and even rows as established, increasing the number of purl sts by 2 on each even row until you have 130 sts total.

Dec Row 1: K2tog, work in pattern as established to end of row.

Work the decreases as established, decreasing the number of purl sts by 2 on each odd row, until the stockinette insert is finished; then continue in garter st until 3 sts remain.

"Work in pattern as established" simply means that after you work the edge stitches (whether decreases or increases), you continue to knit or purl every row between those edge stitches.

Finishing: Bind off and weave in ends very securely.

Chunky Cabled Vest with Hood or Collar

This vest is a great way to venture into a pieced garment with easy cables. The pattern is written in seven sizes, so there's something for everybody. You can add a hood that gives a dramatic look to a fairly simple piece. However, the vest is just as eye-catching without it.

Work this simple vest from the bottom up in three pieces and then join and pick up stitches for either a hood or a ribbed collar. You can see the schematic for the vest construction in Figure 19-3. This project is great for combining your new knitting skills.

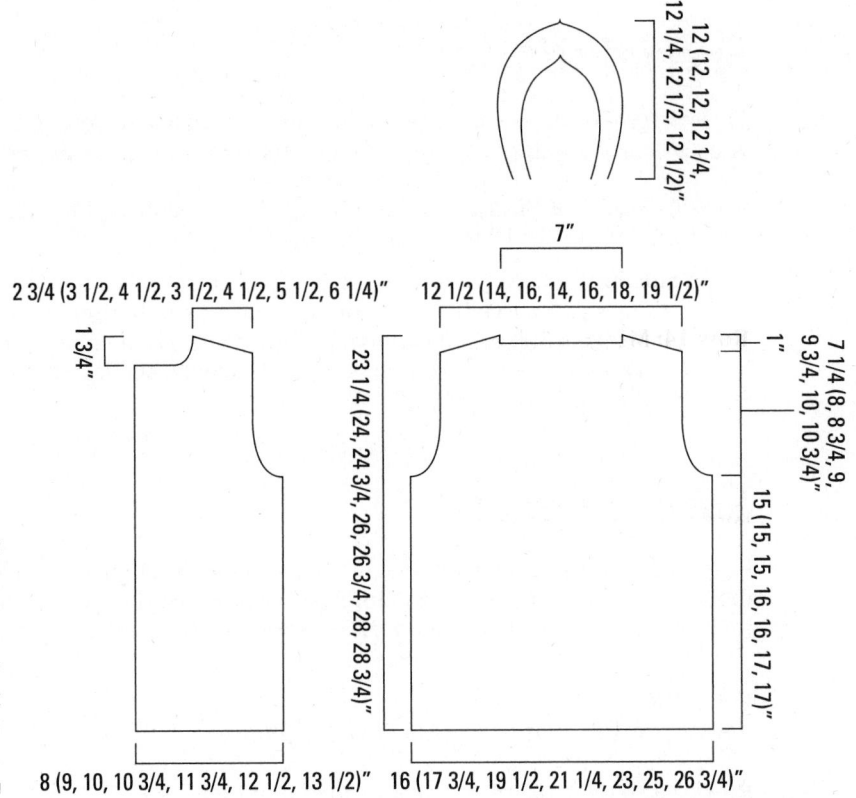

Figure 19-3:
Schematic of the Chunky Cabled Vest with Hood or Collar.

Illustration by Wiley, Composition Services Graphics

Materials and vital statistics

- ✔ **Size:** XS (S, M, L, XL, 2X, 3X). Directions are given for the first size, with other sizes following in parentheses. Wherever only one number is given, it applies to all sizes.

    - **Finished chest circumference:** 33½ (37¼, 41, 44¼, 48, 51¾, 55½) inches

    - **Finished length:** 33½ (37¼, 41, 44¼, 48, 51¾, 55½) inches

- ✔ **Yarn:** Schachenmayr SMC "Extra Merino Big" (100% merino wool); CYC #5, 90 yards per 1.76 ounces [50 grams]); Color: 05597 anthracite marl, 9 (10, 12, 13, 15, 17, 18) balls

- ✔ **Needles:** 24-inch size US 9 (5½ mm) circular needle, to help hold the full width of the back piece as well as pick up stitches around the neck, or size needed to obtain gauge

- ✔ **Other materials:** Stitch holders, stitch markers, cable needle, tapestry needle, eight toggle-style buttons

- ✔ **Gauge:** 18 stitches and 24 rows per 4 inches

Special stitches

This pattern includes some special stitches to familiarize yourself with before you get started. Refer to these explanations as you work the pattern:

- ✔ **C6B (Cable 6 Back):** Slip 3 stitches to cable needle and hold in back, k3 from LH needle, k3 from cable needle.

- ✔ **1-row buttonhole (requires 3 sts):** Slip next 2 stitches to RH needle, pass first stitch over second stitch, slip next stitch from LH needle to RH needle, pass first stitch over second stitch, slip remaining stitch back to LH needle, cast on 3 stitches onto RH needle, slip last stitch from RH needle to LH needle, k2tog.

Stitch patterns

In addition to the special stitches in the preceding section, this pattern includes stitch patterns — yes, that's patterns within the pattern. Review these stitch patterns and refer to them as you knit the vest:

2 x 2 rib

Worked over a multiple of 4 sts plus 2 as follows:

Row 1 (RS): K2, * p2, k2; rep from * to end of row.

Row 2: P2, * k2, p2; rep from * to end of row.

Rep Rows 1 and 2 for 2 x 2 rib.

Cabled pattern

Worked over a multiple of 8 sts plus 2 as follows:

Row 1 (RS): P2, * k6, p2; rep from * to end of row.

Row 2: K2, * p6, k2; rep from * to end of row.

Row 3: Rep Row 1.

Row 4: Rep Row 2.

Row 5: P2, * C6B, p2; rep from * to end of row.

Row 6: Rep Row 2.

Row 7: Rep Row 1.

Row 8: Rep Row 2.

Rep Rows 1–8 for cabled pat.

You can see the cabled pattern chart in Figure 19-4.

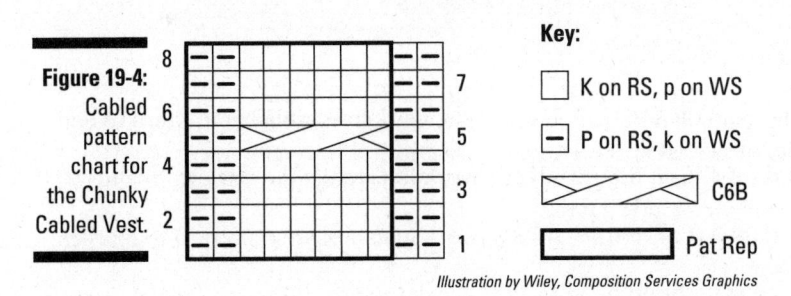

Figure 19-4: Cabled pattern chart for the Chunky Cabled Vest.

Key:

☐ K on RS, p on WS

⊟ P on RS, k on WS

⬦ C6B

☐ Pat Rep

Illustration by Wiley, Composition Services Graphics

Directions

The following sections break down the instructions for creating this vest piece by piece.

Back

Cast on 74 (82, 90, 98, 106, 114, 122) sts, and work in 2 x 2 rib for 3 inches, ending after a WS row.

Because the ribbing instructions are written in measurement rather than rows, we suggest that you make a note of how many rows you work to get the full 3 inches. That will make knitting the front pieces to the exact same measurements easier.

Work in cabled pattern for 72 (72, 72, 78, 78, 84, 84) rows.

Armhole shaping:

Working in established cabled pattern, bind off 3 (3, 3, 5, 5, 5, 5) sts at beg of next 4 rows and then dec 1 st at each edge every RS row 2 (2, 2, 6, 6, 6, 6) times — 58 (66, 74, 66, 74, 82, 90) sts remain.

Work 38 (42, 46, 40, 44, 46, 50) more rows evenly in pattern.

Shoulder and neck shaping:

Place a marker on either side of center 30 sts.

Next 3 rows:

Row 1 (WS): Bind off 4 (6, 7, 6, 7, 8, 10) sts, work in established pattern to end.

Row 2: Bind off 4 (6, 7, 6, 7, 8, 10) sts, work in established pattern to end.

Row 3: Bind off 5 (6, 7, 6, 7, 9, 10) sts, work in established pattern to marker.

Note: If you want a hood on your vest, work the next 30 sts and place them on a holder; then work to end. If you want a collar rather than a hood, bind off the next 30 sts and then work to end.

Note: At this point in the pattern, you work each shoulder separately.

Right shoulder only:

Working in established pattern, bind off 5 (6, 7, 6, 7, 9, 10) sts at beg of next RS row. Work the WS row even, then bind off rem 5 (6, 8, 6, 8, 9, 10) sts on next RS row.

Left shoulder only:

With RS facing, join new yarn at neck edge to left shoulder sts still on the needle and work in established pattern to end.

Bind off rem 5 (6, 8, 6, 8, 9, 10) sts on next WS row.

Left front

Using size US 9 needles, cast on 38 (42, 46, 50, 54, 58, 62), and work in 2 x 2 rib for 3 inches, ending after a WS row.

Next 2 rows:

Row 1 (RS): P2 (0, 2, 0, 2, 0, 2), work in cabled pattern to last 2 (0, 2, 0, 2, 0, 2) sts, p2 (0, 2, 0, 2, 0, 2).

Row 2: K2 (0, 2, 0, 2, 0, 2), work in established cabled pattern to last 2 (0, 2, 0, 2, 0, 2) sts, k2 (0, 2, 0, 2, 0, 2).

Work in established pattern, keeping 2 (0, 2, 0, 2, 0, 2) sts at each edge purled on RS, for 70 (70, 70, 78, 78, 84, 84) more rows.

The length of the left front piece will be the same length as the back hem to armhole.

Armhole shaping:

Working in established cabled pattern, bind off 4 (3, 4, 5, 6, 5, 6) sts at beg of next 2 RS rows and then dec 1 st at armhole edge every RS row 2 (2, 2, 6, 6, 6, 6) times — 28 (34, 36, 34, 36, 42, 44) sts remain.

Work 32 (36, 40, 34, 38, 40, 44) more rows evenly in pattern.

Neck shaping:

Next row (WS): If you want the hood, work the first 10 (12, 10, 12, 10, 12, 10) sts and place them on a holder; then work to end.

If you want the collar, bind off the first 10 (12, 10, 12, 10, 12, 10) sts and then work to end.

Dec 1 st at neck edge every row for the next 4 rows and then work 2 rows evenly in pattern.

Shoulder shaping:

Bind off 4 (6, 7, 6, 7, 8, 10) sts at beg of next RS row, 5 (6, 7, 6, 7, 9, 10) sts at beg of next RS row, and then rem 5 (6, 8, 6, 8, 9, 10) sts on next RS row.

Counting your rows in the Chunky Cabled Vest

When you're counting rows on the Chunky Cabled Vest with Hood or Collar, you can easily identify the cables. Keeping track of how many total cables you've completed isn't hard, but knowing how many rows you've completed between one cable and the next may be tricky. To better keep track, we like to use removable stitch markers on the seam edge on each row that we work a cable. That way, we can easily count the number of rows after the marker to know when the next cable row should take place.

Don't remove these markers, because they can be handy in the finishing, too. When you're finished knitting all the pieces and ready to seam the fronts to the back, you can match up the makers and know that your vest will be lined up perfectly!

Right Front

Cast on 38 (42, 46, 50, 54, 58, 62) and work in 2 x 2 rib for 3 inches, ending after a WS row.

Next 2 rows:

Row 1 (RS): P2 (0, 2, 0, 2, 0, 2), work in cabled pattern to last 2 (0, 2, 0, 2, 0, 2) sts, p2 (0, 2, 0, 2, 0, 2).

Row 2: K2 (0, 2, 0, 2, 0, 2), work in established cabled pattern to last 2 (0, 2, 0, 2, 0, 2) sts, k2 (0, 2, 0, 2, 0, 2).

Work in established pattern, keeping 2 (0, 2, 0, 2, 0, 2) sts at each edge purled on RS, for 71 (71, 71, 79, 79, 85, 85) more rows.

Armhole shaping:

Working in established cabled pattern, bind off 4 (3, 4, 5, 6, 5, 6) sts at beg of next 2 WS rows and then dec 1 st at armhole edge every RS row 2 (2, 2, 6, 6, 6, 6) times — 28 (34, 36, 34, 36, 42, 44) sts remain.

Work 33 (37, 41, 35, 39, 41, 45) more rows evenly in pattern.

Neck shaping:

Next row (RS): If you want the hood, work the first 10 (12, 10, 12, 10, 12, 10) sts and place them on a holder. Then work to end.

If you want the collar, bind off the first 10 (12, 10, 12, 10, 12, 10) sts and then work to end.

Dec 1 st at neck edge every row for the next 4 rows.

Shoulder shaping:

Bind off 4 (6, 7, 6, 7, 8, 10) sts at beg of next WS row, 5 (6, 7, 6, 7, 9, 10) sts at beg of next WS row, and then rem 5 (6, 8, 6, 8, 9, 10) sts on next WS row.

Finishing

Block pieces to measurements on schematic shown in Figure 19-3.

Sew shoulder seams.

Armhole edging:

With RS facing, pick up and knit 78 (82, 86, 94, 102, 106, 110) sts along armhole edge and work in 2 x 2 rib for 1 inch.

Bind off all sts in pattern.

Work other armhole the same.

Sew side seams.

Option: Hood

Follow the instructions in this section to add a hood and button band to your vest.

Hood

Sl 10 (12, 10, 12, 10, 12, 10) sts from right front neck holder back onto the needle. With RS facing and new yarn, pick up and knit 10 sts up right shoulder edge, work across 30 sts from back neck holder, pick up and knit 10 sts down left shoulder edge, and work across 10 (12, 10, 12, 10, 12, 10) sts from left front neck holder — 78 (82, 78, 82, 78, 82, 78) sts.

Next row (WS): K4 (2, 4, 2, 4, 2, 4), * p8, k2; rep from * to last 2 (0, 2, 0, 2, 0, 2) sts, k2 (0, 2, 0, 2, 0, 2).

Work in cabled pattern for 12 (12, 12, 12¼, 12¼, 12½, 12½) inches, working cables on the newly picked up panels on the same rows as the already established panels.

Bind off all sts. Fold hood in half and sew top seam.

Button band

With RS facing, pick up and knit 94 (94, 98, 106, 110, 114, 118) sts up inner right front edge to neck, 110 (110, 110, 110, 110, 114, 114) sts around hood edge, and 94 (94, 98, 106, 110, 114, 118) sts down inner left front edge — 314 (314, 318, 326, 330, 342, 346) sts.

Work 3 (3, 3, 3, 3, 5, 5) sts in 2 x 2 rib, beg with a WS row.

Next row (RS): Work 4 (4, 6, 10, 4, 6, 8) sts in established rib, work 1-row buttonhole, * work 9 (9, 9, 9, 11, 11, 11) sts in established rib, work 1-row buttonhole; rep from * 7 more times, work in established rib to end.

Work 4 (4, 4, 4, 4, 6, 6) more rows evenly in established rib. Bind off all sts in pattern.

Sew on buttons opposite buttonholes. Weave in all loose ends with tapestry needle.

Option: Ribbed Collar

Follow the instructions in this section to add a ribbed collar and button band to your vest.

Buttonhole band

With RS facing, pick up and knit 94 (94, 98, 106, 110, 114, 118) sts up inner right front edge to neck, and work 3 (3, 3, 3, 3, 5, 5) sts in 2 x 2 rib, beg with a WS row.

Next row (RS): Work 4 (4, 6, 10, 4, 6, 8) sts in established rib, work 1-row buttonhole, * work 9 (9, 9, 9, 11, 11, 11) sts in established rib, work 1-row buttonhole; rep from * 7 more times, work in established rib to end.

Work 4 (4, 4, 4, 4, 6, 6) more rows evenly in established rib. Bind off all sts in pattern.

Button band

With RS facing, pick up and knit 94 (94, 98, 106, 110, 114, 118) sts down inner left front edge, and work 8 (8, 8, 8, 8, 10, 10) in 2 x 2 rib, beg with a WS row.

Bind off all sts in pattern.

Sew on buttons opposite buttonholes. Weave in all loose ends with tapestry needle.

Getting to know Elizabeth Zimmerman

You can find many ways to knit a sweater (or a hat, or a mitten, or a sock). Knitting legend Elizabeth Zimmerman, in her words, "unvented" many a technique for knitting garments. Her innovative use of circular knitting, her common-sense approach to knitting garments and accessories, and her incomparable wit have earned her a strong following. Look to her books for knitting ideas and basic patterns that allow ample room for your own creative variations:

- ✔ *Knitter's Almanac* (Dover)

- ✔ *Knitting Without Tears* (Fireside Books)

- ✔ *Knitting Workshop* (Schoolhouse Press)

Collar

With RS facing, pick up and knit 8 (8, 8, 8, 8, 10, 10) sts across top edge of buttonhole band, 78 (82, 78, 82, 78, 82, 78) sts around neck edge, and 8 (8, 8, 8, 8, 10, 10) sts across top of button band — 94 (98, 94, 98, 94, 102, 98) sts.

Work in 2 x 2 rib for 1 inch and then bind off all sts in pattern.

Variations

Try some of the following variations to redesign the Chunky Cabled Vest into a garment all your own:

- ✔ Use different buttons — a matching set or a variety of eclectic buttons.

- ✔ Make the vest shorter for a cropped version or longer for a coat.

- ✔ Work the vest with pockets at the side seams or add patch pockets rather than hidden ones. For patch pockets, complete the sweater and then knit two squares the size you want your pockets to be. Sew them onto the fronts unobtrusively with the mattress stitch, or use a decorative blanket stitch in a contrasting color.

- ✔ Make patch pockets and the collar in a different color.

- ✔ Work a little embroidery on the pockets and collar.

Part V
The Part of Tens

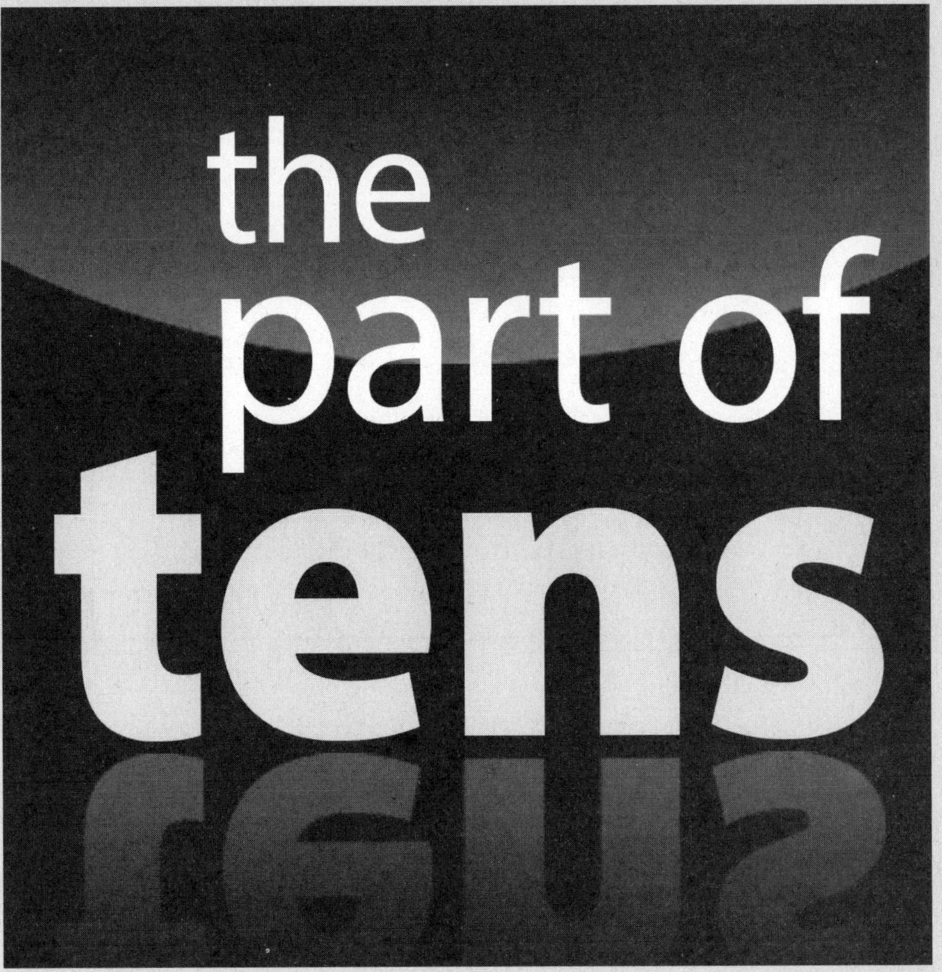

the

part of

tens

In this part . . .

- ✔ Impress friends and family with handmade gifts — or just keep yourself busy — thanks to ten easy knitting projects that you can work up in a flash.

- ✔ Take a break and try out ten exercises to relax your knitting muscles and ease tension so you can get back to your project with renewed energy.

Chapter 20

Ten Quick Knitting Projects and Gifts

In This Chapter

▶ Crafting wearable gifts

▶ Getting the most out of leftover yarn

▶ Giving new life to existing knitted pieces

More often than not, the hunt for an appropriate gift happens at the last minute. No more running to the mall on a crowded Saturday afternoon for you! As a knitter, you can make special, one-of-a-kind gifts that wow the recipients much more than any mass-produced item. These patterns and projects are very simple and in many cases help you put swatches or other bits of previously knitted items to use.

Large-Gauge Wrist Warmers

For a fast hand-knit project, grab the bulkiest yarn you have and cast on for wrist warmers. Instead of knitting in the round on short circular needles or dpns, knit flat and seam later. You'll be done in no time.

Materials

✔ **Yarn:** Bulky-weight yarn; 50–60 yards

✔ **Needles:** One pair of size US 10 (6 mm) or US 11 (7½ mm) needles; yarn or tapestry needle to weave in ends

Directions

Cast on 10 to 15 sts, depending on how long you want the finished wrist warmers to be.

Knit every row (garter st) until piece is long enough to wrap around your wrist or the recipient's.

Bind off and seam together.

Repeat for second wrist warmer.

For extra fun and embellishment, sew on a big, bold button, a knitted flower (see the later section "Knitted Flower Pin"), or knitted I-cord in a wavy pattern.

Log Cabin Swatch Potholder

Who doesn't need potholders? Wool's natural ability to insulate makes it a great choice for this gift; avoid acrylic or other fiber blends that may melt. The potholder is fast and easy to make — you can even make it from existing swatches. The charming edges in the style of a log cabin quilt pattern tie the whole thing together.

Materials

- ✔ **Yarn:** 100% wool; enough yarn to knit two pattern swatches from elsewhere in the book (cables and other dense patterns are best — no lace, please!), or two existing swatches and 50–60 yards extra yarn for finishing edge
- ✔ **Needles:** Needles in size used for swatches or one size smaller, plus two similarly sized dpns for I-cord; yarn needle for weaving in ends

Directions

Knit two swatches of the same size (preferably 4 x 4 inches or larger). If you already have two such swatches in your knitting basket, grab those. Then follow these instructions to finish the potholder:

1. **Place the swatches back to back, with the right sides facing out and cast-on edges aligned.**

2. **Place your LH needle through the first stitch on the first swatch and then through the first stitch on the second swatch.**

3. **Insert your RH needle and knit this stitch.**

4. **Repeat Steps 2 and 3 until you've picked up all the stitches on the first edge, joining the two swatches together at one side.**

   This technique is almost like a cross between picking up stitches and the three-needle bind-off, but without the binding off!

5. **Knit 1 inch and bind off.**

6. **Turn the swatch on its side and repeat Steps 2 through 5 on the second edge.**

   If you like bold colors, change your yarn color with each new picked-up edge of the potholder.

7. **Repeat Step 6 on the third and fourth edges.**

8. **When all edges are covered, use dpns to knit 3 inches of I-cord and stitch it to one corner as a loop to hang up the potholder.**

Swatch Scarf

The Swatch Scarf is a great way to use up the swatches (including lace) you made in testing stitch patterns throughout the book! For simple assembly, just seam the swatches together end to end. But what if your swatches are all different sizes? Use the log cabin technique from the potholder in the preceding section to add length or width to the sides of each swatch until they're all the same size. Then seam them together!

Materials

- **Yarn:** 1 skein (or multiple leftover balls) of yarn for edges
- **Needles:** One pair of size US 8 (5 mm) or US 10 (6 mm) needles; yarn needle for seaming
- **Other materials:** Knitted swatches in the same size or various sizes

Directions

To create this scarf, your swatches need to be the same size. Measure your largest swatch and then follow these steps to increase the size of the remaining swatches as needed and assemble the scarf:

1. **Place your LH needle through the first stitch on the first swatch.**

2. **Insert your RH needle and knit this stitch.**

3. Repeat Steps 1 and 2 until you've picked up all the stitches on that first edge.

4. Knit until the size of the piece matches your largest swatch and then bind off.

5. Turn the swatch on its side and repeat Steps 1 through 4 on the second edge.

6. Repeat Step 5 on the third and fourth edges.

7. Repeat this process until all your swatches are the same size.

8. Seam the swatches, right sides together, into the desired scarf width and length. (Use one of the finishing techniques in Chapter 17.)

Braided Novelty Yarn Scarf

Do you have lots of leftover novelty yarn from various projects? Need a quickie scarf? If so, this project is for you.

Materials

- **Yarn:** Novelty yarn (at least 3 to 5 different kinds look best); smooth yarn (we like Cascade 220), neutral color (white, black, gray, or beige), 1 skein.

- **Other materials:** Masking tape; scissors; table or ironing board (or any surface approximately 5–6 feet long)

Directions

1. With a small piece of masking tape, tape the beginning of one strand of yarn to the table.

2. Wrap the yarn around the table several times or until it runs out.

3. Before cutting the strand, secure it with another piece of masking tape near the beginning.

4. Repeat Steps 1 through 3 with all your yarn, including the neutral color.

5. Tie two pieces of yarn in a tight bow around the wrapped yarn at either end of the table. Do this for each type of yarn.

6. Remove the yarn from the table and trim both ends using scissors until all lengths of yarn are even.

7. Gather all the strands together, and make a loose knot at one end.

8. **Divide the bunch into three parts, and braid — very loosely — until you reach the end.**

9. **Tie another loose knot at the end of the braid, and trim the yarn ends if desired.**

Knit Journal

Every knitter needs a way to keep track of patterns, ball bands, swatches, notes, and all the other project-related things that accumulate at the bottom of the knitting basket. A knit journal is the solution. Sure, you could buy one ready-made, but making one is so much more fun!

Materials

- One three-ring binder or a notebook with a cardboard or hard cover
- Swatches, knitted fabric, an old sweater, or other knitted piece sufficient in size to cover your notebook front and back (*Note:* For this project, don't use pieces that are longer or wider than the final dimensions. Shortening knitted fabric, though possible, is more difficult than lengthening it.)
- Scissors or a rotary cutter and mat
- Buttons, yarn for yarn embroidery, or other embellishments (optional)
- Hot glue gun and popsicle stick or sewing machine with coordinating thread (see the Directions for options)

Directions

1. **Lay out your swatches or other knitted fabric and make them the exact size of your notebook's cover.**

   For a 1-inch thick, 8½ x 11-inch three-ring binder, for example, your piece should be 18 x 11 inches (2 times 8½ + the 1-inch thickness on the side by 11 inches tall).

   If you're using swatches, you may need to stitch them together, and if they're not quite big enough, you can always add a little length or width using the log cabin technique from the earlier Log Cabin Swatch Potholder project.

2. **Add any embellishments you want to the knitted fabric.**

3. **Secure the knitted cover to the back of the notebook.**

For notebooks with soft covers (such as thin plastic three-ring binders, thin cardboard sketchbook covers, and so on), you can use a sewing machine to stitch the knitted cover down around the top, side, and bottom edges of both the front and back covers.

For notebooks or binders with hard covers, apply a very thin layer of hot glue to the back cover (use a popsicle stick to spread the glue as soon as it's out of the gun) and position your knitted piece. Then pull the knitted piece around to the front, apply another thin layer of glue on the front side, and press the knitted fabric into place.

A little glue goes a very long way. Use too much, and it will soak through the front of the fabric, which isn't very attractive.

Recycled Sweater Mittens

Recycling is good for both the environment and your wallet. This project and the next two all use yarn and old sweater pieces to make speedy one-of-a-kind gifts. So raid your closet or the thrift store and get started!

Materials

- One sweater or other knitted piece, at least 50% wool (preferably 100% wool), not felted
- Chalk or marker for tracing
- Paper for creating pattern (optional)
- Scissors or a rotary cutter and mat
- Yarn and yarn needle for embroidered embellishment (optional)
- Sewing machine or needle and thread

Directions

1. **Use chalk or a marker to trace your hand in mitten position (fingers together, thumb pointing out) on the knitted material. Add a little extra width to the cuff area to make the mittens easier to put on after shrinking.**

2. **Cut two of the mitten shapes from your knitted material, flip the pattern over, and trace and cut two more shapes.**

3. **Embroider a design on the mittens, if desired.**

Thread a sharp yarn needle with wool yarn in the color of your choice and stitch anything you like — monograms, daisies, straight lines, you name it!

4. **With right sides out (and therefore wrong sides together), stitch the mittens together around all edges except the bottom opening.**

   Don't worry about the bottom edge unraveling; the next step is to felt (or full) the fabric, and felted material is permanently locked together.

5. **Run the mittens through the hot wash/cold rinse cycle of your washing machine to felt the fabric.**

6. **Remove the mittens from the washing machine and try them on. Make adjustments as necessary for a better fit.**

   If the size is perfect, you're done. If they need to be a little smaller, put them through another wash cycle or directly into the clothes dryer on medium or high heat. To stretch the mittens out a bit, pull on them with your hands and then allow them to air dry.

Thrift Store Sweater Bag

Bags are universally popular as gifts because they're useful in all sorts of situations. And handmade bags from knitted fabric are great because you don't have to worry about sizing. This recycled sweater bag is both easy and fun to make.

Materials

- ✔ One sweater with wool content of 50% or greater, not felted
- ✔ Scissors or rotary cutter and mat
- ✔ Sewing machine or needle and thread
- ✔ Coordinating yarn for I-cord handle, or purchased handles
- ✔ One pair of size US 8 (5 mm) dpns for I-cord handle (optional)
- ✔ Buttons, yarn for yarn embroidery, or other embellishments (optional)

Note: You also can stitch together swatches for this bag if you have lots of them sitting around, or you can use pieces from old sweaters.

Directions

1. **Cut straight across the sweater just below the armpits so that you have a tube.**

If you're using swatches or other pieces to make the bag, sew them together into a tube shape that's the desired size of the bag.

2. **Turn the tube inside out and sew across the cut edge.**

   If you don't use a sewing machine, be sure to sew tight stitches by hand. The bottom of the sweater (which is usually ribbing) is now the top of your bag.

3. **If you're using purchased bag handles, skip to Step 4. If you want a braided I-cord handle, knit three 5-inch I-cords. Braid the cords and sew across the top and bottom edges on your sewing machine or with needle and thread.**

4. **Run both the bag and the I-cord handle (if you have one) through the hot wash/cold rinse cycle of your washing machine to felt them.**

5. **Allow the pieces to air dry, and stitch the handle into place or attach the purchased handle.**

6. **Add yarn embroidery, buttons, other embellishments, or even a sewn-in lining if you like.**

Drink Cozy

This quick gift keeps hot stuff hot or cold stuff cold anytime. (Don't forget that wool is an excellent natural insulator!) The knitted cozy is also great for water bottles if you're tired of condensation dripping everywhere.

Materials

- Old sweater or other knitted piece with 50% wool content
- Aluminum beverage can to use as template
- Chalk or marker for tracing can
- Scissors or rotary cutter and mat
- Sewing needle and thread
- Yarn and yarn needle for embroidered embellishment (optional)

Directions

A beverage cozy is much like a short wrist warmer. To knit one, simply follow the pattern in the earlier Large-Gauge Wrist Warmers project. But for a thick, deluxe cozy with its own built-in coaster, follow these steps:

1. **Felt your knitted piece in a hot wash/cold rinse cycle of your washing machine.**

2. **Trace the bottom of the can onto the felted fabric using chalk or a marker. Cut out the circular shape.**

3. **Lay the can on top of the felted fabric and cut a piece long and tall enough to wrap around the can, adding ½ inch for seaming.**

4. **Embellish your fabric as desired.**

   You can yarn embroider a monogram or design.

5. **With right sides together, stitch up the seam of the cozy using a needle and thread.**

   Depending on the thickness of your felt, you may want to iron the seam to flatten it. Use lots of steam and the hot (or "cotton") setting.

6. **Turn the cozy right side out and position the circle from Step 2 on the bottom of the can, right side out. Sew the coaster to the bottom edge of the cozy.**

There are many, many variations to this basic drink-cozy concept. Make a taller wine bottle cozy for a hostess gift, or make several cozies in sizes to fit around old glass jars and use them as decorative vases (group them in uneven numbers for maximum effect). Whatever you make, have fun!

Felted Checkbook Cover

Writing checks isn't fun, but you can make the dreaded task more pleasant with a gorgeous felted checkbook cover. It's as easy as 1-2-3:

1. **Cut a piece of felted knitted fabric to the outer dimensions of the boring plastic checkbook cover your bank gave you.**

2. **Remove your checks (in case of a glue disaster) and then lightly coat the outside of the cover with hot glue.**

3. **Apply the knitted piece to the cover and trim to size if needed.**

Knitted Flower Pin

Flower pins are hot embellishments, useful for everything from bags to jackets to hats. You can knit one — or two, or an entire garden's worth — lickety-split with this simple pattern.

Materials

- ✔ **Yarn:** Worsted-weight yarn for flower, 50 yards, any color; worsted-weight yarn for leaf, 25 yards, contrasting color
- ✔ **Needles:** One pair of size US 8 (5 mm) needles (or size appropriate for yarn); sharp yarn needle for assembly
- ✔ **Other materials:** Pin back (available from craft stores, or cannibalize your jewelry drawer); straight pins to hold piece during assembly

Directions

Cast on 40 sts.

Row 1 (and all odd-numbered rows): Knit.

Row 2 (and all even-numbered rows): * K1, inc 1; repeat from * to end of the row. (*Note:* You're making a ruffle by increasing into every other stitch on every other row.)

Rep Rows 1 and 2 until piece measures 1½ inches from beg.

Bind off.

To mold the knitted piece into a flower shape, follow these steps:

1. **Starting at the short edge, roll the piece until it resembles a rose or a peony.**
2. **Stick straight pins into the flower from the sides to hold it while you stitch the bottom.**
3. **Using a sharp yarn needle threaded with the same color yarn as your petals, grasp the top edge of the flower and sew around the bottom edge, placing your needle all the way through from one side to the other as you go to hold the layers together.**

   Don't be afraid to pull your stitches tight. It looks more flowerlike if the bottom edge is smaller than the top.

To make a leaf, knit a small square with your contrasting yarn and seam the right and bottom sides together to make a cuplike leaf shape. Sew the leaf to the back side of the flower, and then sew on the pin back.

Chapter 21

Ten Unkinking Exercises for Knitters

. . . .

In This Chapter

▶ Soothing sore shoulders and arms

▶ Letting go of tension in your hands and wrists

. . . .

Sitting in one position and concentrating on your knitting for long (or even short) periods of time can make you stiff in your shoulders and neck. Not to mention that holding needles and making small movements with your hands can cramp fingers and wrists. The exercises in this chapter will keep your body's knitting parts loose, limber, and fatigue-free if you take a break and do them every 20 minutes or so while you're working.

If you find your wrists are sore after knitting with straight needles for long stretches of time, you may want to try knitting with circular needles instead. The slight difference in wrist position when using circulars can make a big difference, particularly if you have carpal tunnel syndrome or a similar condition.

Five Ways to Slough Stress from Your Shoulders and Arms

At the first signs of tightness in your shoulders or arms, take a few minutes to do these exercises (preferably in this order, but you can always focus on one more than the others to reduce a particular nagging pain):

✔ Bring your shoulders up to your ears and hold for 3 to 5 seconds. Then relax your shoulders down into their natural position.

✔ Interlace your fingers and stretch your arms out in front of you, with your palms facing away from your body. Hold this pose for 10 seconds.

- Keeping your fingers interlaced and your palms facing out, reach your arms over your head. Stretch up, up, and up until you can feel the stretch as far down as your upper rib cage. Hold for 10 to 15 seconds and breathe deeply.

- Standing or sitting up straight, interlace your fingers and cup the back of your head. Bring your elbows back and pull your shoulder blades together. Hold for 5 seconds, and then relax.

- Place your right hand on your left shoulder. With your left hand, grab your right arm just above the elbow and look over your right shoulder. While looking over your shoulder, use your left hand to gently pull your right arm to the left until you feel your muscle stretch. Hold for 10 to 15 seconds. Change sides and stretch the other shoulder and arm.

Five Ways to Relax Your Hands and Wrists

Need to uncramp tightened fingers and wrists? Practice the following stretches, and be sure to keep breathing as you do them:

- Spread and stretch your fingers as widely as you can. Hold for 10 seconds. Then ball your fingers into fists and hold for another 10 seconds.

- With your arms extended straight out in front of you, bend your wrists back, bringing your fingers straight up. Hold for 10 seconds. Then bend your wrists down and point your fingers to the floor, holding for another 10 seconds.

- While keeping your elbows bent and close together, interlock your fingers and rotate your hands and wrists clockwise ten times. Reverse direction and rotate your hands and wrists in the other direction ten times. (This move feels a little awkward at first, but it works.)

- With your arms extended in front of you, slowly rotate your wrists so that the backs of your hands are together. Hold this position and enjoy the stretch.

- Arrange your hands palm to palm in front of you (think of a prayer position). Keeping your palms together, rotate your wrists away from your body, pointing your fingers downward until you feel a mild stretch. Hold for 5 to 8 seconds without letting your shoulders tense up or lift.

End your stretches by allowing your arms to hang loosely at your sides. Then shake your hands and wiggle your fingers.

Relaxing your neck muscles

Neck stretches are a great unkinking technique. Sit (or stand) with your arms hanging naturally at your sides. Keeping your shoulders relaxed and down, do the following moves (just don't forget to breathe!):

1. **Tilt your head forward gently to stretch the back of your neck and hold for 5 seconds.**

2. **Turn your head to one side, look over your shoulder, and hold for 5 seconds.**

3. **Slowly turn and look over your other shoulder, holding for 5 seconds.**

4. **Tilt your head to one shoulder and (you guessed it) hold for 5 seconds.**

5. **Tilt your head to your other shoulder, holding for 5 seconds.**

Part VI
Appendixes

the

appendixes

Check out some quick-reference essential knitting info at www.dummies.com/
extras/knitting, including pattern abbreviations, common techniques, and
measurement conversions.

In this part . . .

- ✔ Expand your knitting repertoire with more stitch patterns that you can incorporate into any number and variety of projects.

- ✔ Find inspiration — and more knitting supplies — by exploring some of our favorite knitting resources, including websites, magazines, podcasts, and stores.

Appendix A

More Stitches and Cool Effects

Knitting is really nothing more than pulling a series of loops through loops. How you pull the loops — the direction of the needle, the order in which you work the stitches, the colors you incorporate, and so on — contributes to the wide variety of fabrics that you can create. Earlier chapters introduce you to patterns that are part of the standard repertoire of most knitters. The patterns included here broaden your range.

Moss Stitch

Moss stitch, shown in Figure A-1, is an elongated version of seed stitch (see Chapter 5). Instead of alternating the pattern every other row, however, you work 2 rows of the same sequence of knits and purls before you alternate them.

Figure A-1:
Moss stitch.

Photograph by Wiley, Composition Services Graphics

Cast on an uneven number of sts. (An uneven number makes this pattern symmetrical — either side can be the right side.)

Rows 1 and 4: K1, * p1, k1; rep from * to end of row.

Rows 2 and 3: P1,* k1, p1; rep from * to end of row.

Rep Rows 1–4 for pattern.

Double Seed Stitch

In this variation of seed stitch, you double seed stitch horizontally and vertically — alternate 2 knits with 2 purls for 2 rows and then reverse the sequence. Figure A-2 shows double seed stitch.

Figure A-2:
Double seed
stitch.

Photograph by Wiley, Composition Services Graphics

Cast on a multiple of 4 sts, plus 2 sts. (Either side can be the right side.)

Rows 1 and 4: K2, * p2, k2; rep from * to end of row.

Rows 2 and 3: P2, * k2, p2; rep from * to end of row.

Rep Rows 1–4 for pattern.

Basketweave Stitch

Like many stitches, basketweave stitch looks complicated but is actually very easy to create. The following pattern is for the 3 x 5 basketweave in Figure A-3.

TIP

You can use any number of stitches for each block — 4 x 4, 5 x 5, 3 x 7, and so on — for variations on the basic basketweave.

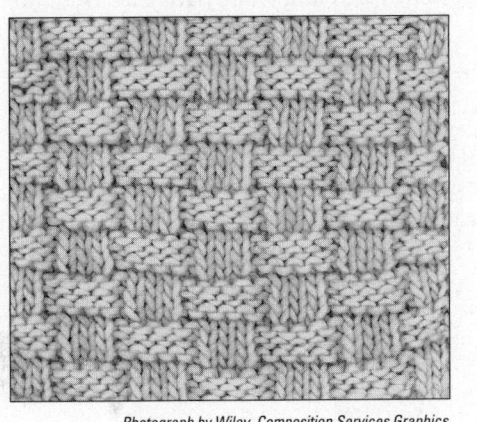

Figure A-3:
Basketweave
pattern.

Photograph by Wiley, Composition Services Graphics

Cast on a multiple of 8 sts, plus 5 sts.

Rows 1 and 5 (RS): Knit.

Rows 2 and 4: K5, * p3, k5; rep from * to end of row.

Row 3: P5, * k3, p5; rep from * to end of row.

Rows 6 and 8: K1, p3, * k5, p3; rep from * to last st, k1.

Row 7: P1, k3, * p5, k3; rep from * to last st, k1.

Rep Rows 1–8 for pattern.

Double Basket Pattern

Double basket pattern combines ribs and ridge patterns, as Figure A-4 shows.

Figure A-4:
Double basket pattern.

Photograph by Wiley, Composition Services Graphics

Cast on a multiple of 18 sts, plus 10 sts.

Row 1 (RS): * K11, p2, k2, p2, k1; rep from * to last 10 sts, k10.

Row 2: P1, k8, p1, * p1, (k2, p2) twice, k8, p1; rep from * to end of row.

Row 3: * K1, p8, (k2, p2) twice, k1; rep from * to last 10 sts, k1, p8, k1.

Row 4: P10, * p1, k2, p2, k2, p11; rep from * to end of row.

Rows 5–8: Rep Rows 1–4.

Row 9: Knit.

Row 10: (P2, k2) twice, p2, * p10, (k2, p2) twice; rep from * to end of row.

Row 11: * (K2, p2) twice, k2, p8; rep from * to last 10 stitches, (k2, p2) twice, k2.

Row 12: (P2, k2) twice, p2, * k8, (p2, k2) twice, p2; rep from * to end of row.

Row 13: * (K2, p2) twice, k10; rep from * to last 10 sts, (k2, p2) twice, k2.

Rows 14–17: Rep Rows 10–13.

Row 18: Purl.

Rep Rows 1–18 for pattern.

Twisted Rib and Garter Stitch Check

Twisted rib and garter stitch (see Figure A-5) consists of two stitch patterns that you're already familiar with if you read Chapter 5: 1 x 1 rib and garter stitch. The difference is that in the ribbed section presented here, you work the knit columns on the right and wrong sides of the fabric with twisted stitches for a sharp, crisp look.

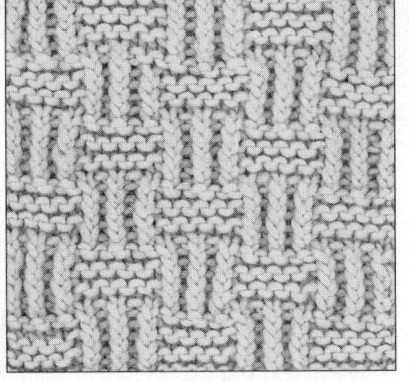

Figure A-5:
Twisted rib and garter stitch.

Photograph by Wiley, Composition Services Graphics

Cast on a multiple of 10 sts, plus 5 sts.

Rows 1, 3, and 5 (RS): K5, * (k1tbl, p1) twice, k1tbl, k5; rep from * to end of row.

Rows 2, 4, and 6: K5, * (p1tbl, k1) twice, p1tbl, k5; rep from * to end of row.

Rows 7, 9, and 11: (K1tbl, p1) twice, k1tbl, * k5, (k1tbl, p1) twice, k1tbl; rep from * to end of row.

Rows 8, 10, and 12: (P1tbl, k1) twice, p1tbl, * k5, (p1tbl, k1) twice, p1tbl; rep from * to end of row.

Rep Rows 1–12 for pattern.

Ripple Stitch

In ripple stitch (see Figure A-6), the purl stitches make wavy lines. You can change the contour of the waves (make them higher or lower) to your liking. Just plot this pattern on a piece of graph paper and chart your variation.

Figure A-6:
Ripple
stitch.

Photograph by Wiley, Composition Services Graphics

Cast on a multiple of 8 sts, plus 6 sts.

Row 1 (RS): K6, * p2, k6; rep from * to end of row.

Row 2: K1, * p4, k4; rep from * to last 5 sts, p4, k1.

Row 3: P2, * k2, p2; rep from * to end of row.

Row 4: P1, * k4, p4; rep from * to last 5 sts, k4, p1.

Row 5: K2, * p2, k6; rep from * to last 4 sts, p2, k2.

Row 6: P6, * k2, p6; rep from * to end of row.

Row 7: P1, * k4, p4; rep from * to last 5 sts, k4, p1.

Row 8: K2, * p2, k2; rep from * to end of row.

Row 9: K1, * p4, k4; rep from * to last 5 sts, p4, k1.

Row 10: P2, * k2, p6; rep from * to last 4 sts, k2, p2.

Rep Rows 1–10 for pattern.

Diamond Brocade

Knitted brocade is characterized by an allover pattern of slightly raised stitches. This diamond brocade, which you see in Figure A-7, is a good example of a true brocade appearance.

Figure A-7:
Diamond
brocade.

Photograph by Wiley, Composition Services Graphics

Cast on a multiple of 8 sts, plus 1 st.

Row 1 (RS): K4, * p1, k7; rep from * to last 5 sts, p1, k4.

Row 2: P3, * k1, p1, k1, p5; rep from * to last 6 sts, k1, p1, k1, p3.

Row 3: K2, * p1, k3; rep from * to last 3 sts, p1, k2.

Row 4: P1, * k1, p5, k1, p1; rep from * to end of row.

Row 5: * P1, k7; rep from * to last st, p1.

Row 6: Rep Row 4.

Row 7: Rep Row 3.

Row 8: Rep Row 2.

Rep Rows 1–8 for pattern.

Guernsey Knit-Purl Pattern

Figure A-8 shows a traditional combination knit-and-purl pattern from a Guernsey-style sweater. The chart appears in Figure A-9. (If you're not familiar with working from a charted pattern, turn to Chapter 3 for instructions.)

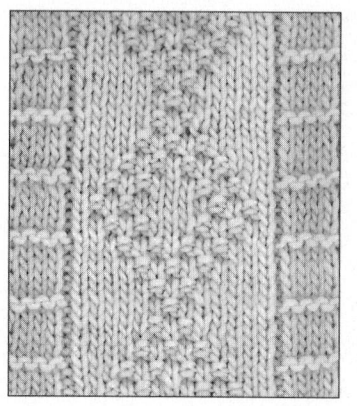

Figure A-8: Guernsey knit-purl pattern swatch.

Photograph by Wiley, Composition Services Graphics

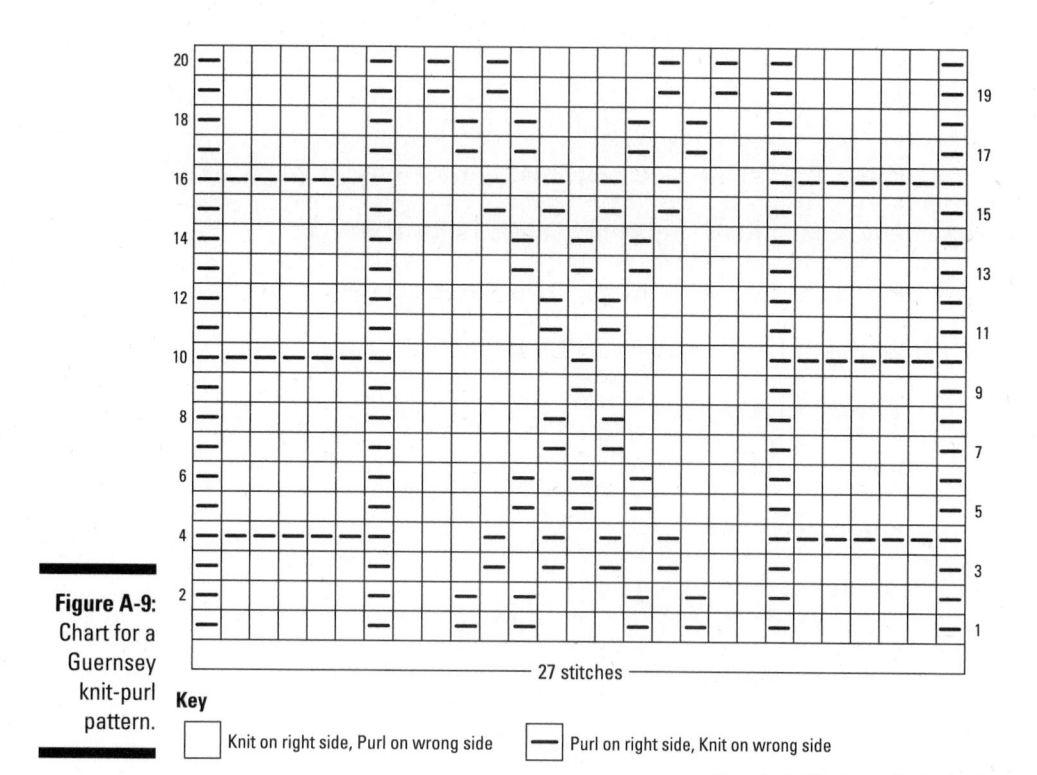

Figure A-9: Chart for a Guernsey knit-purl pattern.

27 stitches

Key

☐ Knit on right side, Purl on wrong side   — Purl on right side, Knit on wrong side

Illustration by Wiley, Composition Services Graphics

When working charts, keep track of the row you're on by using a sticky note or magnetic strip. (See Chapter 2 for details on handy knitting tools.) You work a chart from the bottom up, so mark your row by covering the row *above* the one you're working on. Keeping the row you've just worked exposed on your chart allows you to check that the stitch you're working on lines up with the stitch below it.

Bobbles

You make bobbles (see Figure A-10) by increasing several stitches in a single stitch and then knitting back and forth on them before binding off, creating a knob on the surface of the fabric. The more stitches you increase in a single stitch and the more rows you work on them, the larger the bobble.

Figure A-10:
Bobbles.

Photograph by Wiley, Composition Services Graphics

Abbreviation:

MB = Make bobble: Knit into the front of the stitch, then the back, then the front, then the back, and then the front one last time, and slide the old stitch off — 5 sts in 1. Turn your work so that the WS is facing you (the stitches are on the LH needle). Purl the 5 sts. Turn the work around again and knit the 5 sts again. With the tip of the LH needle, pull the second stitch over the first and off the RH needle. Repeat with the third, fourth, and fifth sts.

Cast on a multiple of 6 sts, plus 5 sts.

Rows 1 and 3 (RS): Knit.

Rows 2, 4, and 6: Purl.

Row 5: K5, * MB, k5; rep from * to end of row.

By knitting on the RS and WS of the bobble, you make a textured garter stitch bobble. For a smooth bobble, purl the 5 stitches when the WS of the bobble is facing you.

 If things start to feel tight as you work into the front and back of the stitch, insert just the tip of the LH needle into the stitch. After you wrap, however, be sure to bring your needle far enough through the wrap that the new stitch forms on the thickest part of the needle.

Chevron

When you stack increases on top of increases and decreases on top of decreases, the stitches slant away from the column of increases and toward the column of decreases, creating chevron patterns (see Figure A-11). The bottom edge of this pattern forms points or scalloped borders, depending on whether the decreases and increases are worked in a single stitch or spread over several stitches. Although this pattern looks tricky to execute, it's relatively simple.

Abbreviations:

dbl dec = Double decrease: sl next 2 sts as if to knit, k1, pass 2 sl sts over.

dbl inc = Double increase: (k1, yo, k1) into next st.

Cast on a multiple of 12 sts, plus 3 sts (includes 1 extra st on each side for a selvedge stitch).

Row 1 (RS): K1, k2tog, * k4, dbl inc, k4, dbl dec; rep from * to last 3 sts, ssk, k1.

Row 2: Purl.

Rep Rows 1 and 2 for pattern.

Figure A-11:
Chevron
pattern.

Photograph by Wiley, Composition Services Graphics

Fancy Ribs

Standard rib patterns, which we explain in Chapter 5, create vertical stripes by alternating a given number of knit stitches with a given number of purl stitches. But who says all ribs have to be the same? The patterns in this section put a spin on the traditional rib technique to create fun and interesting designs.

Mistake stitch ribbing

Mistake stitch ribbing, which you see in Figure A-12, is a 2 x 2 rib worked over 1 fewer stitch than required to make it even.

Figure A-12:
Mistake
stitch
ribbing.

Photograph by Wiley, Composition Services Graphics

Cast on a multiple of 4 sts, plus 3 sts.

Work every row: * K2, p2; rep from * to last 3 sts, k2, p1.

Rep for pattern.

Interrupted rib

Interrupted rib pattern looks different from each side, but both sides are handsome, making this a nice pattern for projects in which both the front and back are visible, like scarves and afghans. Figure A-13 gives you an idea of what the pattern looks like.

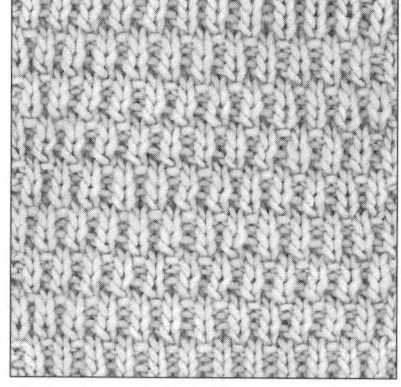

Figure A-13:
Interrupted
rib.

Photograph by Wiley, Composition Services Graphics

Cast on an even number of sts.

Rows 1–3: * K1, p1; rep from * to end of row.

Row 4 and 8: Purl.

Row 5–7: * P1, k1; rep from * to end of row.

Rep Rows 1–8 for pattern.

Diagonal ribbing

With diagonal ribbing, the ribs in the fabric slant in one direction when viewed from one side and slant in the other direction when viewed from the reverse side. Figure A-14 shows the finished pattern.

Figure A-14: Diagonal ribbing.

Photograph by Wiley, Composition Services Graphics

Cast on a multiple of 8 sts, plus 6 sts.

Row 1: K1, p4, * k4, p4; rep from * to last st, k1.

Row 2: K4, * p4, k4; rep from * to last 2 sts, p2.

Row 3: K3, * p4, k4; rep from * to last 3 sts, p3.

Row 4: K2, p4, * k4, p4; rep from * to end of row.

Row 5: P1, * k4, p4; rep from * to last 5 sts, k4, p1.

Row 6: P4, * k4, p4; rep from * to last 2 sts, k2.

Row 7: P3, * k4, p4; rep from * to last 3 sts, k3.

Row 8: P2, * k4, p4; rep from * to last 4 sts, k4.

Rep Rows 1–8 for pattern.

Fisherman's rib

Fisherman's rib pattern (see Figure A-15) makes a fabric with a ribbed appearance but with more depth and softness than a standard rib.

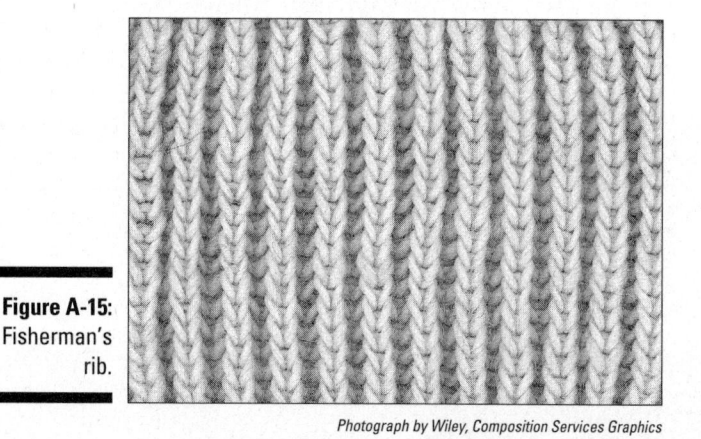

Figure A-15:
Fisherman's rib.

Photograph by Wiley, Composition Services Graphics

Cast on an even number of sts.

Row 1: Purl.

Row 2: * P1, knit next st in the row below, allowing old stitch to drop from needle; rep from * to last 2 sts, p2.

Rep Row 2 only for pattern.

Appendix B

Knitting Resources

• •

All sorts of resources — books, magazines, websites, and so on — are available to inspire and assist knitters. Those presented here, which represent just the tip of the knitting-resources iceberg, are ones that knitters of all levels will find useful.

Online Resources

As knitting has become more popular, the number of computer- and Internet-based resources for knitters has grown exponentially. And because most sites link you to other sites, you can spend days visiting yarn country via cyberspace.

The following knitting websites provide not only quality patterns and articles but also online forums to discuss knitting, tools to organize your needles, projects in progress, yarns, and much more:

- ✔ www.craftsy.com: An online community dedicated to educating makers about all things crafty; includes online knitting classes, yarn sales, and a huge database of patterns
- ✔ www.knitty.com: A web magazine about knitting, complete with free patterns
- ✔ http://knittersreview.com: An e-newsletter and knitting forum site
- ✔ www.ravelry.com: An online community with many knitting tools
- ✔ www.knittingdaily.com: An online knitting guild with free patterns and lots more
- ✔ http://community.knitpicks.com: An online community that offers tutorials, photo management, and a forum

The next sections highlight additional online resources.

Beginner websites

If you're a beginner looking for more information on the basics, try the following sites:

- ✔ www.learntoknit.com (sponsored by the Craft Yarn Council of America)
- ✔ www.knitting.about.com
- ✔ www.tkga.com (official site of the Knitting Guild Association)

Yarn, supplies, patterns, and more

For yarn, supplies, patterns, and other equipment, check out these sites:

- ✔ **Yarn Market:** www.yarnmarket.com
- ✔ **Knit Picks:** www.knitpicks.com
- ✔ **Halcyon Yarn:** www.halcyonyarn.com
- ✔ **Patternworks:** www.patternworks.com
- ✔ **Schoolhouse Press:** www.schoolhousepress.com
- ✔ **WEBS:** www.yarn.com
- ✔ **Loopy Ewe (specializes in socks and other small projects):** www.theloopyewe.com
- ✔ **Yarn Barn of Kansas:** www.yarnbarn-ks.com
- ✔ **Jimmy Beans Wool:** www.jimmybeanswool.com

Online audiobooks and technique demonstrations

Tired of reading? Need something to listen to while you knit? You're in luck; a wealth of knitting-related audiobooks and podcasts are out there for you to enjoy. Here are some of our favorites:

- ✔ www.marlybird.com/podcast
- ✔ www.blogtalkradio.com/fiberhooligan
- ✔ www.knitpicks.libsyn.com

> ✔ `www.yarn.com/podcasts`
>
> ✔ `www.knittingnewscast.com`
>
> ✔ `www.knitmoregirlspodcast.com`

You can even find many knitting techniques demonstrated for you live on sites such as `www.youtube.com`! And don't forget this book's companion video content available for viewing anytime on `www.dummies.com/go/knittingfd`.

Software

Depending on your needs, you can find knitting-related software just for you. Some are available for free online, and others range in price up to several hundred dollars. Check out some of these options:

> ✔ To print your own knitter's graph paper to the exact gauge of your chosen yarn, use the form at `www.tata-tatao.to/knit/matrix/e-index.html`. This graph paper is great for making your own charts.
>
> ✔ To design your own knitting charts, use software such as Knit Visualizer (`www.knitfoundry.com`), Intwined Pattern Studio (`www.intwinedstudio.com`), EnvisioKnit Design Studio (`www.envisioknit.com`), or Cochenille (`www.cochenille.com`).

Magazines

Knitting magazines are a great source of technical information, patterns, inspiration, suppliers, knitting news, new products, and happenings. Be sure to subscribe to at least one and check out the others at your favorite magazine rack. Most knitting magazines have their own websites. Try exploring these sites to start:

> ✔ *Creative Knitting:* `www.creativeknittingmagazine.com`
>
> ✔ *Interweave Knits:* `www.interweaveknits.com`
>
> ✔ *Knitter's:* `www.knittinguniverse.com`
>
> ✔ *Vogue Knitting:* `www.vogueknitting.com`
>
> ✔ *Love of Knitting:* `www.loveofknitting.com`

Index

About the Authors

Pam Allen has been designing sweaters for more than 20 years, and her patterns have appeared in such publications as *Family Circle* and *Woman's Day*. In addition to *Knitting For Dummies,* she's the author of *Scarf Style* and co-author of *Wrap Style, Lace Style, Bag Style,* and *Color Style* (all published by Interweave Press). She lives in Portland, Maine.

Shannon Okey is the author of nearly a dozen books on knitting and other fiber arts, a columnist for knitting publications, and a knitting blogger. She hosts a call-in podcast about knitting and has appeared on many television shows, including *Knitty Gritty, Uncommon Threads,* and *Crafters Coast to Coast.* You can find her online at www.knitgrrl.com.

Tracy L. Barr is a professional writer and editor. She learned to knit when she was 10 and in the three-plus decades since has continued to be an avid knitter.

Marlaina "Marly" Bird fled the world of financial services to launch her very popular Yarn Thing podcast and hasn't looked back since. To Marly, a bi-craftsy girl who both knits and crochets, the yarn is the star, not how you work with it. She's creative director for Bijou Basin Ranch Yarns and the co-author of *Curvy Crochet* (Leisure Arts, 2011). Her designs have appeared in *Knitter's Magazine, Knit Simple, Interweave Crochet, Interweave Knits, Knitscene, Creative Knitting, Love of Knitting, Love of Crochet, Crochet Today, Knitting Today,* and *Petite Purls* and in the books *Knitter's Book of Socks, Unexpected Afghans, Simply Crochet, Perfectly Plus,* and *Knitting Plus.* Marly teaches classes around the country at a variety of wool festivals and STITCHES Expos as well as online at www.craftsy.com. In her spare time, she's a wife to a very understanding husband and raises three kids in suburban Denver. Enter the world of Marly at www.marlybird.com.

Dedication

To my Grandma Topping, who started me on this adventure by handing me a hook and some yarn.

—Marly

Author's Acknowledgments

Marly would like to thank her Wiley editor Elizabeth Rea, whose patience, edits, and knowledge of knitting made for a better book; Jolene Vetterling, who helped manage the schedule and projects better than any other assistant/best friend could; Shiri Mor and Kristen TenDyke for their stellar technical editing skills; Tara Barbier, Josiah Bird, Isabella Castaneda, Alyssa Killian, and Michelle Corbett Schmitt for "letting their pretty kick in"; Noriko Ho, Tina Jackson, Julie Leibold, Amy Machael, Chaitanya Muralidhara, Candace Musmeci, Kristina Palmer, and Terri Randolph for their blazing knitting needle skills; Starry Heinze for introducing Marley to this wonderful craft with the first edition of this very book; Mike and Darlene Corbett for their constant encouragement and unwavering faithfulness; and last but certainly not least, John and the kids — your love makes life worth living!

Publisher's Acknowledgments

Associate Editor: David Lutton

Project Editor: Elizabeth Rea

Senior Copy Editor: Danielle Voirol

Copy Editor: Megan Knoll

Technical Editor: Penny Little

Art Coordinator: Alicia B. South

Project Coordinator: Patrick Redmond

Project Manager and Producer: Paul Chen

Photographers: Matt Bowen, Marly Bird

Cover Image: © Marly Bird